PRACTITIONER'S GUIDE TO HOUSING DEVELOPMENT PERMITS IN CALIFORNIA

After AB 130 (2025)

Clay E. Toombs

Disclaimer: This book is not legal advice. The Author is not an attorney and does not provide legal services. Interpretations of laws contained in this book are from the perspective of an experienced practitioner, but other interpretations may prevail in practice or in a court of law. Always follow the advice of your own attorney who understands the particulars of your project and your situation.

The Author welcomes comments and suggestions from the real estate development, land use, and legal community to improve this book. Should the Reader have questions or suggestions, please email book@marginaldevelopment.com.

ABOUT THE AUTHOR

Clay E. Toombs is an expert in the strategic application of California's complex and constantly changing land use and development regulations. He has been entitling projects throughout California for over 18 years, including over 10 years in private practice. A fierce advocate for housing, he is tenacious in using state laws to reduce risk, time, and cost, because only **projects that *pencil* produce housing.**

Clay holds a Master of Real Estate Development, a Master of Business Administration, and a B.S. in Aeronautical Management Technology, all from Arizona State University. Before his career in real estate development, he was a professional pilot and has over 10,000 hours of flight time.

Contact:

book@marginaldevelopment.com

Website:

https://marginaldevelopment.com/

NO AI Content or Training

No generative or other artificial intelligence (AI) technologies produced any part of the contents of this book.

Library of Congress Control Number: 2026904382

International Standard Book Number:

- 979-8-9948944-0-8 (Paperback)
- 979-8-9948944-1-5 (PDF)

Recommended bibliographical listing:

Toombs, Clay E. *Practitioner's Guide to Housing Development Permits in California — After AB 130 (2025)*, 2026.

PREFACE

This book distills the Author's research and experience working as a land use consultant and development manager in jurisdictions from Petaluma to San Diego. It is the guide he wished he'd had when struggling to understand and apply the constantly evolving laws that apply to housing development permits.

The book thoroughly covers the state laws that prescribe how jurisdictions are required to process housing development permit applications in California; and is a reference guide for **practitioners** — for the people on both sides of the planning counter whose job it is to get projects ***approved***.

Recent History of Housing Legislation

Prior to 2017, California's state housing and development laws had been relatively stable, but home production had failed to keep up with population growth for decades. California's housing shortage had grown to 2 million units by 2016, and only about 100,000 units were being built each year. Then-Governor Jerry Brown and his predecessors had been loath to enact reforms to environmental laws. State efforts to reverse the declining rate of home-building had relied on carrots, like the Density Bonus Law first enacted in 1979, rather than sticks that would force local governments to approve more housing projects that could actually "pencil" and be built.

In 2016, Governor Brown proposed a state law that would require "by-right" (i.e., ministerial) approval of housing projects that were consistent with zoning standards. That law would have made such projects exempt from the California Environmental Quality Act (CEQA) and from local government's ability to *arbitrarily* disapprove them. Facing opposition from local governments that feared erosion of "local control" over zoning, and the loss of support from labor and environmental groups, Brown's plan failed to pass the legislature.[1]

Recognizing the acute and growing housing crisis, the California Legislature introduced over 130 bills intended to address the housing crisis during 2017.[2] Governor Brown and the legislature had not passed meaningful housing legislation since he returned to the Governor's mansion in 2012, but in September 2017 he signed a slate of 15 housing bills into law.[3]

Current Governor Gavin Newsom made housing the central issue of his 2017 campaign,[4] and while the state is nowhere near the 3.5 million housing units over 10 years that Newsom pledged,[5] he has largely delivered on his promise to change land-use law to make it easier to develop housing. Since 2017, the State of California has passed around 200 bills aimed at addressing the housing crisis, and over 40 housing bills were passed in 2025 alone.

Governor Brown's by-right housing proposal has not been fully realized — market-rate housing projects that comply with local zoning are much harder to disapprove, but not entirely ministerial or always exempt from CEQA. However, 2025 was a huge year for CEQA reform with the passage of AB 130 and SB 131. One of the most significant new laws is a CEQA exemption that is widely applicable to infill housing. In some ways the legislature and Newsom have gone further than Brown imagined.

[1] https://www.spur.org/publications/urbanist-article/2017-01-11/bye-bye-right-housing
[2] https://www.hklaw.com/files/Uploads/Documents/Articles/WhitePaper/CaliforniasNewHousingProductionLaws.pdf
[3] https://www.kqed.org/news/11713988/jerry-browns-two-legacies-on-housing
[4] https://medium.com/@GavinNewsom/the-california-dream-starts-at-home-9dbb38c51cae
[5] https://calmatters.org/housing/2022/10/newsom-california-housing-crisis/

One of the bills that did ***not*** pass in 2025 led the Author to finally write this book. AB 1294 would make the development permit review process much simpler and more consistent with a statewide application form and a statewide list of required information (LORI), and the full development permit application would be **deemed complete** upon submittal of all the items in the LORI. Alas, AB 1294 has not yet passed, and this book is about 40 pages longer than it could have been. A lot of the issues discussed in Chapter 5: Overall Development Permit Review Process & How AB 130 Changes It will be solved if AB 1294 passes in 2026.

What this Book Does / Does Not Cover

This book covers the entirety of the Housing Accountability Act plus provisions of the Permit Streamlining Act, California Environmental Quality Act, and various other state laws that pertain to the processing of housing development permits. It is current with information from 2025 legislation including AB 130, SB 131, SB 158, and AB 712.

It focuses on discretionary permits but generally applies to development permits processed ministerially. However, it does not cover the various special laws that provide for streamlined ministerial processing. It touches on the State Density Bonus Law but does not cover that law in any detail.

Text Styles in this Book

This book uses various text styles. The headings and subheadings organize the information, while text colors and fonts highlight information.

This color is used to highlight changes to state laws that passed in 2025.

> Quotations from various laws are in this color and font.

> Quotations from sources other than laws are in the same font, but black text.

In the PDF version, this underlined text style is a hyperlink to a source on the web. Links connect to helpful resources, to footnote references, or to the current version of a cited law. The main table of contents and each of the chapter tables of contents are also hyperlinked. Jump from the table of contents to any heading in the book; then use the internal links with this underlined text style to cross-reference sections with more detail and context.

Some PDF viewers have a **back button** that will return you to the location you were reading before clicking the internal hyperlink, or you may be able to ***add*** a back button. For example, in Adobe Reader, you can go to View> Show/Hide> Toolbar Items> Page Navigation and select the backward arrow to add it to your toolbar.

This book uses various combinations of *italics*, **bold**, and underlined text to ***emphasize*** or call **attention** to key words and phrases.

Within quotations, **unless** the quote is introduced with "emphasis in original," the **emphasis was *added* by the Author**.

How to Use this Book

Thank you for purchasing this book! It is available in two versions: a downloadable PDF, and a paperback. If you bought one version and would like to also have the other, your ***discounted paperback or PDF*** is waiting for you at: https://marginaldevelopment.com/. If you prefer to print the PDF, the author grants the original purchaser of this PDF the right to print one copy. After printing, the cover page, and final two pages of the PDF version can be inserted into the covers and spine of a three-ring view-binder.

Think of this book as both a guide and a reference manual. As a **reference** manual, the PDF is full of links to the cited laws, and to dozens of resources. You can jump from the main table of contents or any of the chapter tables of contents to headings throughout the book, then follow hyperlinks to other sections with more detail and context. As a **guide**, the paperback is great for perusing the information at your leisure, and as a handy desk reference; or you could put the PDF on your favorite e-reader.

If you are **new** to the material, you might want to read it from the beginning, skipping over sections that seem too complex or pedantic. Chapters 1, 2, and 3 are a great introduction for those who do not live and breathe land use law. If you are an **expert** in California housing law, you may want to skip to Chapter 4: CEQA Review for Housing Projects After AB 130 and SB 131, and also read Chapter 5: Overall Development Permit Review Process & How AB 130 Changes It, to see what is new for 2026.

If you work in policy, as a **housing advocate** or in the **Legislature**, Chapter 5: Overall Development Permit Review Process & How AB 130 Changes It is required reading! There is definitely a need for clean-up legislation after the big changes enacted in 2025, and AB 1294 (the Author's must-pass legislation for 2026) goes a long way toward solving the issues identified in that chapter.

Chapter 6: SB 330 Preliminary Application is great information for anyone involved in the planning permit process, including **architects**. The vesting rights provided by an SB 330 preliminary application are superior to those that would apply if no SB 330 preliminary application were submitted, as explained in Chapter 7: Vesting the Development Standards. Failure to submit an SB 330 preliminary application is a big mistake, friends!

Chapter 8: Completeness Review is a step-by-step guide to managing the process of obtaining a determination that the *application* is complete, and Chapter 9: Compliance Review covers the process of determining that the *project* is "consistent, compliant, and in conformity" with the *applicable* development standards. These two chapters will be especially helpful for **development managers**.

Chapter 10: Deadlines and Enforcement is important to all practitioners, but especially for **planning staff**. Most of the deadlines, and the consequences of missing them, fall on the jurisdiction, and thus jurisdictions should be especially careful to meet all deadlines. The penalties on the jurisdiction when **applicants** must enforce state housing laws have increased in recent years. With the passage of AB 712 in 2025, violations of *all* housing reform laws carry fines and requirements to pay the applicant's costs of suit, similar to the provisions of the Housing Accountability Act.

How to Provide Feedback

The Author recognizes that housing laws are ever changing and subject to interpretation. Not everything in this book will be correct in every situation, and this book is not intended as legal advice. The Author welcomes comments, suggestions, and constructive criticism and will incorporate improvements into future versions of this book. Send feedback via email to book@marginaldevelopment.com.

TABLE OF CONTENTS

TABLE OF TEXT BOXES

TABLE OF FIGURES

CHAPTER 1: LEGISLATIVE BILLS AND ORGANIZATION OF STATE LAWS

This overview introduces the key state laws that govern how local jurisdictions are required to review and approve permits for development projects in California. It explains the basics of legislative bills that create and amend California laws. It shows how state laws are organized and explains how to read law citations and cross-references. It defines the term "jurisdiction" as used in this book, and related terms for various state agencies. And it explains how to find and navigate the official sources of legislative bills and state laws as a primer for the Reader's own research.

Where to Find More Information

The California Budget & Policy Center has a simple guide to How California Policies are Made, with links to additional resources. The California State Senate has a useful Citizen's Guide to Participation[6] that covers topics like how to turn an idea for new legislation into a bill.[7] The law libraries of California universities all have useful resources; one of the best, with explainers and dozens of links, is the UC Berkeley Library California Government Information: Legislative and Laws webpage.

CHAPTER CONTENTS

[6] Online version: https://www.senate.ca.gov/citizens-guide, and printable PDF: https://www.senate.ca.gov/sites/senate.ca.gov/files/publications/legislative_process_guide.pdf.
[7] https://www.senate.ca.gov/citizens-guide/legislative-process.

The Term "Law"

This book uses the term "law" in the general sense to refer to laws of all kinds. Georgetown Law Library maintains a State Guide for California[8] that summarizes the various laws of the state, and provides many resources for further research.

The terms below are defined for the Government Claims Act, but are general enough to serve for this introduction. Each citation is to a section of the Government Code:

> 810.6. "Enactment" means a constitutional provision, statute, charter provision, ordinance or regulation.
>
> 811. "Law" includes not only enactments but also the decisional law applicable within this State as determined and declared from time to time by the courts of this State and of the United States.
>
> 811.6. "Regulation" means a rule, regulation, order or standard, having the force of law, adopted by an employee or agency of the United States pursuant to the federal Administrative Procedure Act (Chapter 5 (commencing with Section 500) of Title 5 of the United States Code) or as a regulation by an agency of the state pursuant to the Administrative Procedure Act (Chapter 3.5 (commencing with Section 11340) of Part 1 of Division 3 of Title 2).
>
> 811.8. "Statute" means an act adopted by the Legislature of this State or by the Congress of the United States, or a statewide initiative act.

Local laws are created by "ordinance" or "resolution" and codified in a "county code" or, for incorporated cities, a "municipal code." For purposes of the Powers and Duties of Legislative Bodies of counties or cities, the term "code" means:

> 50022.1. (a) "Code," as used in this article, means any statute, or any published compilation of rules, regulations or standards adopted by the federal government or the State of California, or by any agency of either of them. It shall include any codification or compilation of existing ordinances of the adopting local agency. It shall include any nationally recognized or approved published compilations of proposed rules, regulations or standards of any private organization or institution ...

Legislative Bills

State statutes start as bills introduced in each chamber of the California State Legislature. "SB" stands for Senate Bill, and "AB" for Assembly Bill. Each bill is numbered, and the numbers are reused each year, so bills are referred to by number and year. Bills are also referred to by number and the author of the bill, especially while the bill is making its way through the legislative process. Some important bills are given descriptive names.

For example, SB 330 (2019) or SB 330 (Skinner) refers to an important bill that passed in 2019 that was authored by then-State-Senator Nancy Skinner. SB 330 was named the Housing Crisis Act of 2019. Because submitting an "SB 330 preliminary application" is the first step in compelling a jurisdiction to follow the law and approve a housing project, the public often uses "SB" or "SB 330" as shorthand to refer to state housing laws in general, but SB 330 (2019) is just one of scores of housing bills passed since 2017.

Organization of State Laws

The bills passed by the California legislature and signed by the Governor are codified into 29 Codes.[9] While there is no "official version" of the California Codes,[10] the Legislative Counsel maintains the California Legislative

---

[8] Note that in the PDF version of this book, this underlined text style is a hyperlink to a source outside the book. If it is a hyperlink for a law citation, it will open a webpage for the current text of the cited law, usually directly to the Section containing the provision, but sometimes to the law in its context. In this case, the hyperlink is to a useful resource: Georgetown Law Library's State Guide for California. For more information, see Text Styles in this Book.

[9] https://en.wikipedia.org/wiki/California_Codes.

[10] California Style Manual (4th ed. 2000), p. 47. https://sdap.org/wp-content/uploads/downloads/Style-Manual.pdf.

Information website with the current version of the Codes as well as information on legislative bills. Several of the 29 Codes contain laws relevant to housing. While it is not necessary to understand the full organization of the state laws, some examples will help to show how the Codes are organized:

- The Government Code (abbreviated "Gov. Code" in this Guide) prescribes laws that cities, counties, and other local agencies must follow in conducting their affairs.
  - Title 7 of the Government Code contains the state laws for Planning and Land Use.
    - Division 1 of Title 7 is titled **Planning and Zoning Law**.
      - Chapter 3 of Division 1 of Title 7 of the Government Code pertains to local planning, including general plans, specific plans, and other matters.
        - Article 10.6 of Chapter 3 of Division 1 of Title 7 is the **Housing Element Law** and contains Sections 65580 through 65589.11 of the Government Code.
          - Section 65589.5 of Article 10.6 of Chapter 3 of Division 1 of Title 7 of the Government Code is the **Housing Accountability Act**.
            - Section 65589.5 is a long code section and is divided into subdivisions (a) through (r). Within each subdivision, the code is further broken down, as explained under Organization Within Sections of Code.[11]
      - Chapters 5, 6, 7, 7.5, 8, and 9 of Division 1 of Title 7 of the Government Code are the **Mitigation Fee Act**. (See Gov. Code § 66000.5.)
      - Chapter 4.3 of Division 1 of Title 7 of the Government Code is the **Density Bonus Law**.
      - Chapter 4.5 of Division 1 of Title 7 of the Government Code is the **Permit Streamlining Act**.
        - Section 65941.1 of the Permit Streamlining Act was added by SB 330 (2019) (see Legislative Bills), creating the SB 330 preliminary application.
      - Chapter 12 of Division 1 of Title 7 of the Government Code is the **Housing Crisis Act of 2019**.
        - There are only three Sections in Chapter 12, and although it is **law** titled the Housing Crisis Act of 2019, most of the provisions of the **bill**, SB 330 (2019), called the Housing Crisis Act of 2019 are found in other sections of the Government Code. (See What Did SB 330 Actually Do?.)
    - Division 2 of Title 7 is the **Subdivision Map Act**, which regulates the division of land into legal parcels that can be sold and purchased.
- The Public Resources Code (abbreviated "PRC" in this Guide) covers a wide range of topics from geology to grease traps.
  - The Public Resources Code is not divided into Titles.
    - Division 13 of the Public Resources Code is the **California Environmental Quality Act** (CEQA).

There are many other state laws (named or not) that deal with aspects of housing, but when this Guide refers to a law by title, it refers to the **bold-faced** laws shown above.

Organization Within Sections of Code

Within the Sections of state statutes, the provisions are further organized into subdivisions, paragraphs, subparagraphs, clauses, and subclauses. For example, Gov. Code § 65589.5 is the entirety of the Housing Accountability Act. It is divided into subdivisions (a) through (r). Subdivision (h) provides definitions "for the purposes of this

[11] The dashed underline text style is a hyperlink to a heading in this book. For more information, see Text Styles in this Book.

section" meaning section 65589.5 of Article 10.6 of Chapter 3 of Division 1 of Title 7 of the Government Code, which is the Housing Accountability Act. Take a look at the definition of "housing development project" at paragraph (2) of subdivision (h):

> (h) The following definitions apply for the purposes of this section:
>
> ...
>
> (2) "Housing development project" means a use consisting of any of the following:
>
> (A) Residential units only.
>
> (B) Mixed-use developments consisting of residential and nonresidential uses that meet any of the following conditions:
>
> (i) A mixed-use development that meets both of the following:
>
> (I) At least two-thirds of the new or converted square footage is designated for residential use.
>
> (II) (ia) No portion of the project is designated for use as a hotel, motel, bed and breakfast inn, or other transient lodging.
>
> (ib) (Ia) Notwithstanding sub-subclause (ia), if a mixed-use project as defined in this paragraph includes a hotel, motel, bed and breakfast inn, or other transient lodging, the portion of the mixed-use project which does not include a hotel, motel, bed and breakfast inn, or other transient lodging shall be considered a housing development project.
>
> (Ib) The local agency may separately approve the portion of the project that includes a hotel, motel, bed and breakfast inn, or other transient lodging, which shall not be eligible for any benefits conferred on a housing development project by state law, including, but not limited to those available to a development under Section 65913.4.
>
> (ic) For purposes of this subclause, the term "other transient lodging" does not include either of the following:
>
> (Ia) A residential hotel, as defined in Section 50519 of the Health and Safety Code.
>
> (Ib) After the issuance of a certificate of occupancy, a resident's use or marketing of a unit as short-term lodging, as defined in Section 17568.8 of the Business and Professions Code, in a manner consistent with local law.
>
> (ii) At least 50 percent of the new or converted square footage is designated for residential use and the project meets both of the following:
>
> (I) The project includes at least 500 net new residential units.
>
> (II) No portion of the project is designated for use as a hotel, motel, bed and breakfast inn, or other transient lodging, except a portion of the project may be designated for use as a residential hotel, as defined in Section 50519 of the Health and Safety Code.
>
> (iii) At least 50 percent of the net new or converted square footage is designated for residential use and the project meets all of the following:
>
> (I) The project includes at least 500 net new residential units.
>
> (II) The project involves the demolition or conversion of at least 100,000 square feet of nonresidential use.
>
> (III) The project demolishes at least 50 percent of the existing nonresidential uses on the site.

> (IV) No portion of the project is designated for use as a hotel, motel, bed and breakfast inn, or other transient lodging, except a portion of the project may be designated for use as a residential hotel, as defined in Section 50519 of the Health and Safety Code.
>
> (C) Transitional housing or supportive housing.
>
> (D) Farmworker housing, as defined in subdivision (h) of Section 50199.7 of the Health and Safety Code.

The entirety of the Housing Accountability Act is Gov. Code § 65589.5 and it is not possible to link directly to a subdivision or deeper level of the organization of the statute. This book uses the format Gov. Code § 65589.5(h)(2)(B)(i)(II)(ib)(Ia) to refer to the deepest level of the organization that reads:

> (ib) (Ia) Notwithstanding sub-subclause (ia), if a mixed-use project as defined in this paragraph includes a hotel, motel, bed and breakfast inn, or other transient lodging, the portion of the mixed-use project which does not include a hotel, motel, bed and breakfast inn, or other transient lodging shall be considered a housing development project.

The statutes would refer to the above text as sub-sub-subclause (Ia) of sub-subclause (ib) of subclause (II) of clause (i) of subparagraph (B) of paragraph (2) of subdivision (h) of Section 65589.5 of the Government Code.

Cross-References Within and Between Codes

Cross-references between the 29 Codes are expressed in the form subclause () of clause () of subparagraph () of paragraph () of subdivision () of Section ## of Article ## of Chapter ## of Division ## of Title ## of the Name of Code. If there is no reference to the name of the Code, the reference is within the same Code. The words Section, Article, Chapter, Division, and Title are capitalized; subdivision, paragraph, subparagraph, clause, subclause, etc. are not capitalized.

The long form — "subclause (I) of clause (i) of subparagraph (C) of paragraph (3) of subdivision (h) of Section 65589.5" — is seldom used outside the statutes themselves.[12] A short format like Gov. Code § 65589.5(h)(3)(C)(i)(I) is more common. It is also common to refer to long portions of a Code with statements such as "subdivision (d) of the Housing Accountability Act" or "Division 13 of the Public Resources Code."

As an example showing cross-references within and between Codes, here is the beginning of subdivision (b) of Section 65915 of the Government Code, which is part of the State Density Bonus Law:

> (b) (1) A city, county, or city and county shall grant one density bonus, the amount of which shall be as specified in subdivision (f), and, if requested by the applicant and consistent with the applicable requirements of this section, incentives or concessions, as described in subdivision (d), waivers or reductions of development standards, as described in subdivision (e), and parking ratios, as described in subdivision (p), if an applicant for a housing development seeks and agrees to construct a housing development, excluding any units permitted by the density bonus awarded pursuant to this section, that will contain at least any one of the following:
>
> (A) Ten percent of the total units of a housing development, including a shared housing building development, for rental or sale to lower income households, as defined in Section 50079.5 of the Health and Safety Code.

The cross-references in paragraph (1) to subdivisions (f), (d), (e), and (p) are all in reference to the same Section 65915 of the Government Code, because neither the Code nor the Section are stated. The cross-reference in sub-paragraph (A) is to the definition of "lower income households" in Section 50079.5 of the Health and Safety Code.

---

[12] The California Style Manual of the California Supreme Court prescribes how codes should be cited in court documents. https://sdap.org/wp-content/uploads/downloads/Style-Manual.pdf.

The California Legislative Information Website

California bills and Codes can be searched at the California Legislative Information website: https://leginfo.legislature.ca.gov/faces/home.xhtml. On the **Home** tab, use the Quick Code Search function to go directly to a law section. Select the Code by its three-letter abbreviation in the drop down and enter the Code section, then click "Go" (see Figure 1). To see the California Codes and their three-letter abbreviations, look under the **California Law** tab.

To search for bills in the *current* two-year legislative session, on the **Home** tab, use the Quick Bill Search function. To search for a bill in either the current or a *previous* legislative session, select the **Bill Information** tab. The **Bill Information** tab has a dropdown menu for Session Year, because bill numbers are reused from one two-year legislative session to the next. For example, SB 330 (2019) can be found as shown in Figure 2. On the **Bill Information** tab, you can search by Keyword(s), Author, Code, or a specific Code section. Searching by Code section is useful to see all the bills that propose to amend that Code section. For example, if you want to know what new laws are proposed to amend the Housing Accountability Act, you would select the current Session Year, select GOV from the Code dropdown menu, and enter 65589.5 in the Code Section.

The California Code of Regulations

Many state laws empower state **agencies** to adopt regulations. These regulations have the force of administrative law. (Gov. Code § 811.66.) The Office of Administrative Law reviews proposed regulations and publishes them in the California Code of Regulations (abbreviated "CCR"). The CCR is **not** one of the 29 Codes that are published on the California Legislative Information website. The official source of the CCR is Thomson Reuters Westlaw, except that Title 24, the California Building Standards Code, is managed by the Department of General Services.

Chapter 3, of Division 6, of Title 14 of the California Code of Regulations is the **CEQA Guidelines**. See Chapter 3: California Environmental Quality Act (CEQA) Basics for an introduction to CEQA.

The United States Code

Some state laws contain cross-references to the United States Code, the official source for which is the Office of the Law Revision Counsel of the United States House of Representatives. Citation in this book to the United States Code will be to the Search and Browse the United States Code function the Office of the Law Revision Counsel's United States Code website.

Figure 1: How to use the California Legislative Information website's Quick Code Search.

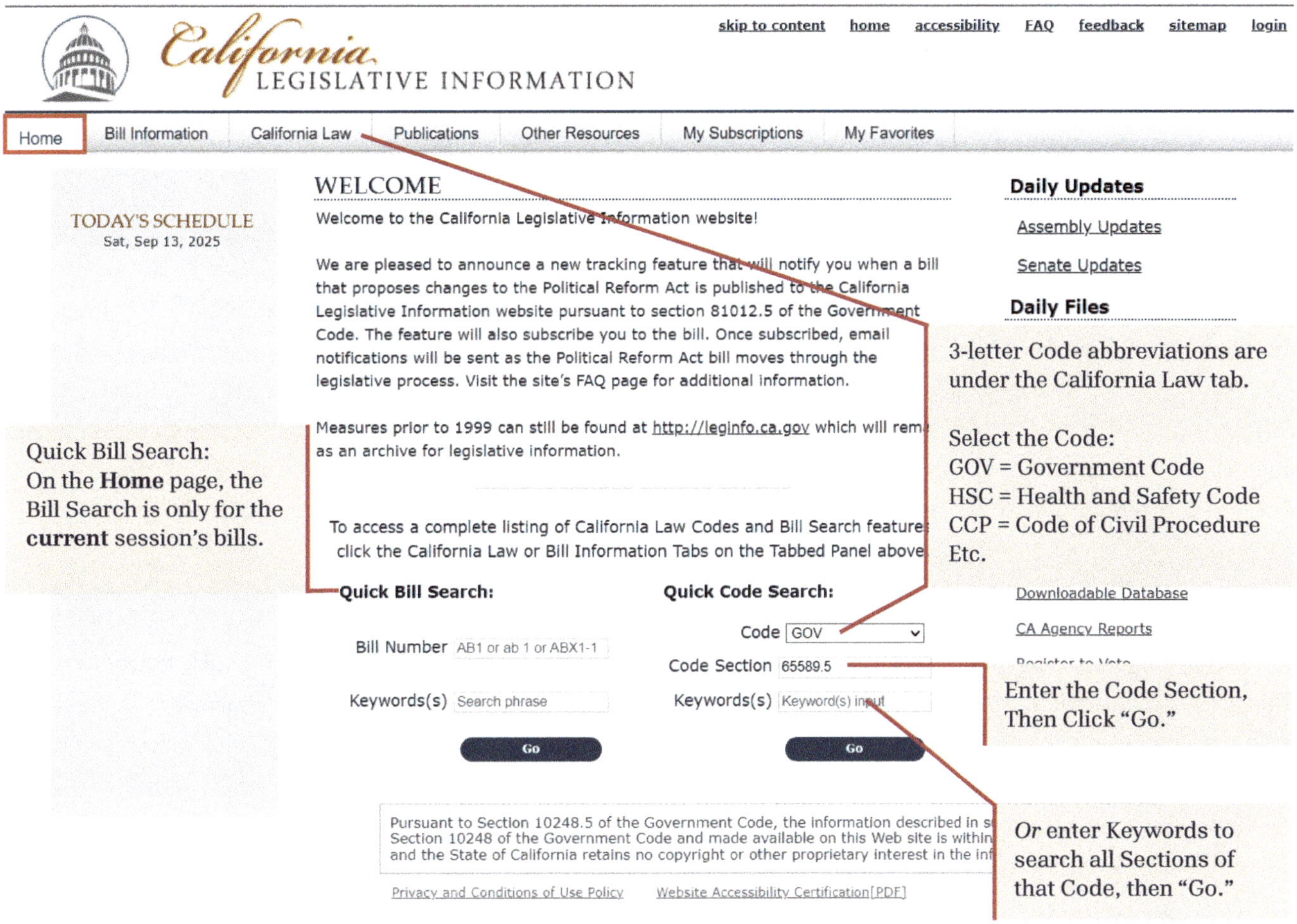

Figure 2: How to use the Bill Information tab to find California legislative bills passed in previous sessions.

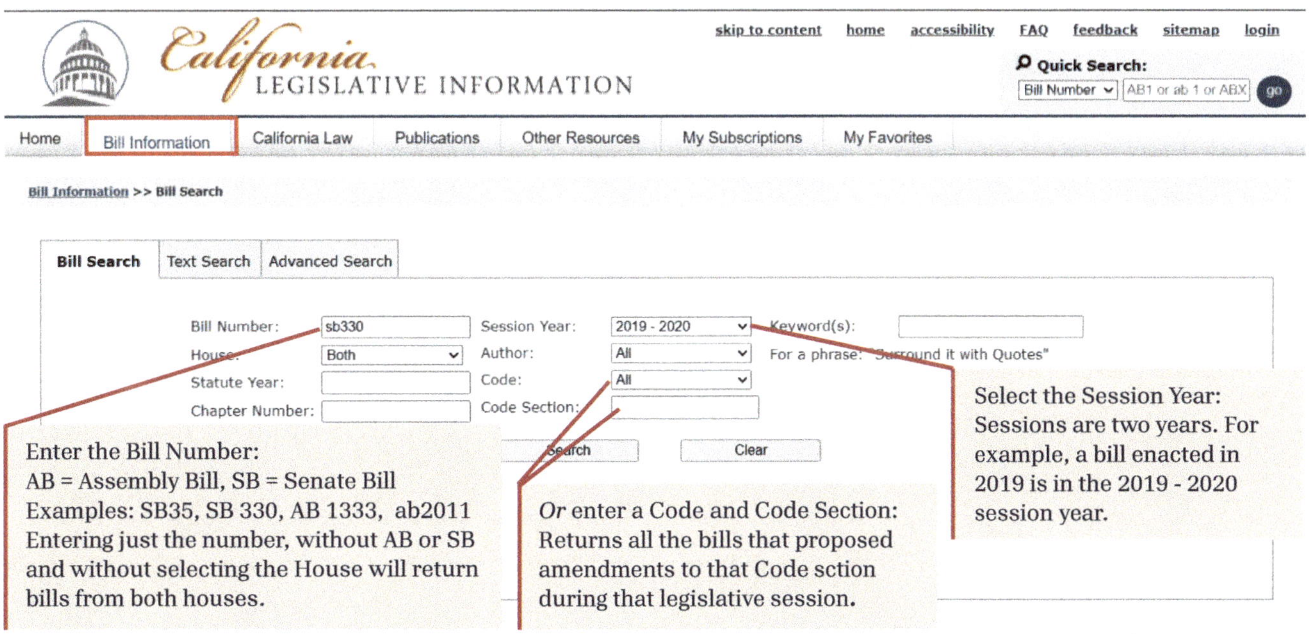

CHAPTER 2: KEY CONCEPTS FOR PROJECTS AND PERMITS

Chapter 1: Legislative Bills and Organization of State Laws briefly explained how the laws created and amended by legislative bills are codified and organized. Within the organization of the state laws, some portions are given names, and the three key "Acts" that regulate housing development permit applications are the **California Environmental Quality Act** (CEQA), **Permit Streamlining Act**, and **Housing Accountability Act**. This section introduces key terms and concepts in the context of those three Acts, including the definitions of **jurisdiction**, **discretionary**, **ministerial**, **project**, and **permit**.

Where to Find More Information

The Author highly recommends that practitioners (on both the applicant and jurisdiction side of the process) use the various resources published by the California-based Institute for Local Government. These resources range from short handouts on the basics of land use planning to comprehensive training for planning commissioners, including *The Planning Commissioner Handbook* (available as a series of webpages or a PDF Book) that is an excellent guide for **all** practitioners working in land-use entitlements. For a comprehensive overview that complements the material in this chapter see The Planning Framework chapter. The Housing Laws and Policies chapter covers many important topics not included in this book.

The term "jurisdiction" as used by the Author in this book means a city or county (or the City and County of San Francisco) and is synonymous with the term "local government." Georgetown Law Library maintains a helpful website with a good overview of local governments in California.

CHAPTER CONTENTS

The Term "Jurisdiction" and Other Public Entities and Agencies

The Author uses "jurisdiction" to refer to the **local government that will review the development permit application.** In most cases, the jurisdiction reviewing and approving the development application will be a county or a city. However, there may be additional Public Entities involved in reviewing and approving the application.

Jurisdiction Means City or County

State laws do not often use the term "jurisdiction." They use terms like "local public entity," "local agency," and "city or county."

The Government Code prescribes how the functions of government, including the processing of development permits, must be conducted. Division 1 of Title 7 of the Government Code is the Planning and Zoning Law in which most of the state housing laws are found (see Organization of State Laws). Chapter 3 of Division 1 of Title 7 regulates Local Planning, including the preparation of the general plan and its "elements." Article 10.6 of Chapter 3 is the **Housing Element Law**, within which is the Housing Accountability Act (Section 65589.5).

The term **"jurisdiction" is defined** for purposes of the **Housing Element Law** at Gov. Code § 65582(d):

> 65582. As used in this article, the following definitions apply unless specified otherwise:
>
> ...
>
> (d) "Community," "locality," "local government," or "**jurisdiction**" means a city, city and county, or county.
>
> ...

The term "jurisdiction" (at least for the Housing Element Law) is defined as a city, county, or city and county,[13] and is synonymous with "local government."

Public Entities

Counties and cities are types of public entities. Be aware that throughout the Government Code, **terms may be defined differently for different Sections**. Some general definitions in the Government Code for distinct types of public entities are:

> 811.2. "Public entity" includes the state, the Regents of the University of California, the Trustees of the California State University and the California State University, a county, city, district, public authority, public agency, and any other political subdivision or public corporation in the State.
>
> 900.4. "Local public entity" includes a county, city, district, public authority, public agency, and any other political subdivision or public corporation in the State, but does not include the State.
>
> 900.6. "State" means the State and any office, officer, department, division, bureau, board, commission or agency of the State claims against which are paid by warrants drawn by the Controller.
>
> 18. "State" means the State of California, unless applied to the different parts of the United States. In the latter case, it includes the District of Columbia and the territories.
>
> 20. "City" includes "city and county" and "incorporated town,"[14] but does not include "unincorporated town" or "village."
>
> 21. "Town" includes "unincorporated town" and "village."

---

[13] The terms "city or county" and "city, county, or city and county" are synonymous, since the term "city" includes "city and county." (Gov. Code § 20) The City and County of San Francisco is the only "city and county" in the state.

[14] When a "town" incorporates (i.e., becomes a "municipal corporation" separate from the county) it becomes a "city" for purposes of state law. Many incorporated towns continue to refer to themselves as "Town of ...," for example the Town of Los Gatos is an incorporated town, which is a "city" per the definition at Gov. Code § 20.

The Term "Agency" for CEQA and Permit Streamlining Act Purposes

Counties and cities are types of public agencies. Within Division 1 of Title 7 of the Government Code is the Permit Streamlining Act, which is Chapter 4.5. The Permit Streamlining Act was created to regulate the processing of permits required to develop projects as defined by CEQA (see The California Environmental Quality Act (CEQA) Applies to Discretionary Projects and The Permit Streamlining Act Applies to All Housing Development Permits). For purposes of the **Permit Streamlining Act**, there are several types of agencies defined:

ARTICLE 2. Definitions [65925 - 65934]

> 65925. Unless the context otherwise requires, the definitions in this article govern the construction of this chapter.
>
> ...
>
> 65929. "Lead agency" means the public agency which has the principal responsibility for carrying out or approving a project.
>
> 65930. "Local agency" means any public agency other than a state agency. For purposes of this chapter, a redevelopment agency is a local agency and is not a state agency.
>
> 65931. "Project" means any activity involving the issuance to a person of a lease, permit, license, certificate, or other entitlement for use by one or more public agencies.
>
> 65932. "Public agency" means any state agency, any county, city and county, city, regional agency, public district, redevelopment agency, or other political subdivision.
>
> 65933. "Responsible agency" means a public agency, other than the lead agency, which has responsibility for carrying out or approving a project.
>
> 65934. "State agency" means any agency, board, or commission of state government. For all purposes of this chapter, the term "state agency" shall include an air pollution control district.

In accordance with the CEQA Guidelines, The Jurisdiction is Usually the "Lead Agency" that makes the CEQA determination for a project.

The Government of Cities and Counties

Title 3 of the Government Code provides the rules for the Government of Counties, and Title 4 provides the rules for the Government of Cities.

Regarding counties:

> 23000. A county is the largest political division of the State having corporate powers.
>
> 23003. A county is a body corporate and politic, has the powers specified in [Title 3 of the Government Code] and such others necessarily implied from those expressed.
>
> 23700. Counties may enact charters or revise existing charters according to the provisions of this chapter.
>
> 25000. (a) Each county shall have a board of supervisors ...

A county is a public entity (i.e., a public corporation "having corporate powers"). **The governing body of a county is its board of supervisors**. The board of supervisors is also the **legislative body** of the county. A county must have at least five supervisors, but a *charter* county may have a greater number of supervisors as specified in the county charter.

Regarding cities:

> 34000. As used in [Title 4 of the Government Code], "legislative body" means board of trustees, city council, or other governing body of a city.

> 34101. Cities organized under a charter shall be "chartered cities."
>
> 34102. Cities organized under the general law shall be "general law cities."

Cities are areas that have been "incorporated" as a municipal corporation to create Public Entities separate from the county in which they are located. General law cities follow the rules in Title 4 of the Government Code, while for *charter* cities, the city charter acts like a local constitution for the government of the city, so long as it is consistent with state law.

The governing body or legislative body of a city depends on its charter, or for general law cities, the choice of "alternative forms of government" allowed by Chapter 4 of Division 2 of Title 4. **This book refers to the legislative body of a city as a "city council,"** which is the most commonly used term.

Planning Agency of the Jurisdiction

The Planning and Zoning Law, Title 7 of the Government Code, provides that **there is a "planning agency" in each city and county** and prescribes the planning agency's functions. Per Gov. Code § 65100:

> 65100. There is in each city and county a planning agency with the powers necessary to carry out the purposes of this title. The legislative body of each city and county shall by ordinance assign the functions of the planning agency to a planning department, one or more planning commissions, administrative bodies or hearing officers, the legislative body itself, or any combination thereof, as it deems appropriate and necessary. In the absence of an assignment, the legislative body shall carry out all the functions of the planning agency.

The legislative body of a city or county shall either "carry out all the functions of the planning agency" or "assign the functions of the planning agency ... as it deems appropriate and necessary."

Decisionmakers and Decisionmaking Bodies

In most jurisdictions, the functions of the planning agency are assigned to some combination of:

1. A planning department headed by a planning director.
2. A planning commission appointed by, and reporting to, the legislative body (city council or county board of supervisors), usually with each member of the legislative body appointing one member of the planning commission.
3. Hearing officers, who typically include the planning director and/or zoning administrator(s), with authority to review and approve certain types of development permit applications.
4. Advisory bodies such as design review and historic preservation commissions/committees that do not approve projects but rather review them and make recommendations to the hearing officer, planning commission, or legislative body.

The legislative body and planning commission are typically the "**decisionmaking bodies**" of the jurisdiction, and the city councilmembers, county supervisors, planning commissioners, planning director, and zoning administrator(s) are "**decisionmakers.**" Advisory bodies do not make decisions, only recommendations. The jurisdiction's local code specifies the functions and authority of each decisionmaker and decisionmaking body, including which types of development permits they may approve.

An approval or disapproval of a development permit by a "**lesser decisionmaker**" than the legislative body can be appealed in accordance with the jurisdiction's code. Approval or disapproval by the legislative body is final, unless a court intervenes.[15]

---

[15] Or, if the local code provides some mechanism for "reconsideration" of the decision.

Discretionary vs. Ministerial

The review and approval process for a housing development permit (also called a "land-use permit," "planning permit," "entitlement for use," or simply "entitlement") depends on whether approval of the permit (and therefore the project) is a **ministerial** or **discretionary** action. The distinction between discretionary and ministerial projects is important primarily for two reasons:

5. Ministerial actions **are not subject to** the California Environmental Quality Act. Development permits are only subject to environmental review if the jurisdiction has **discretion** to approve or disapprove the project.
6. Ministerial actions **are not subject to** public hearings or review by elected officials. They are "by right" and the jurisdiction does not have discretion to disapprove ministerial permits if they comply with applicable codes.

The review and approval of *development* permits is usually discretionary, meaning the jurisdiction has discretion to deny/disapprove the permit and therefore the project. However, state housing laws require ministerial review and approval of several types of housing development projects (e.g., ADUs).

This book is primarily about processing discretionary housing development permits. It is generally applicable to ministerial projects but does not explain any of the **special** state laws that provide for ministerial review and approval of projects.

Discretionary Does NOT Mean Subjective

The term "discretionary" does not mean "subjective." State law prohibits jurisdictions from applying subjective standards or personal judgement when reviewing and approving a housing project, whether that review is ministerial ***or*** discretionary. As defined in Gov. Code § 65589.5(h)(9):

> "Objective" means involving no personal or subjective judgment by a public official and being uniformly verifiable by reference to an external and uniform benchmark or criterion available and knowable by both the development applicant or proponent and the public official.

As explained under Which Compliance Comments Are Actually Applicable?, regardless of whether a jurisdiction considers a housing development permit application to be discretionary or ministerial, the project is only required to comply with **objective** development standards.

What is a Discretionary Project?

The contrast between a ministerial and a "discretionary action" is explained in the CEQA Guidelines § 15002(i):

> (i) Discretionary Action. CEQA applies in situations where a governmental agency can use its judgment in deciding whether and how to carry out or approve a project. A project subject to such judgmental controls is called a "discretionary project." See Section 15357.
>
> > (1) Where the law requires a governmental agency to act on a project in a set way without allowing the agency to use its own judgment, the project is called "ministerial," and CEQA does not apply. See Section 15369.
> >
> > (2) Whether an agency has discretionary or ministerial controls over a project depends on the authority granted by the law providing the controls over the activity. Similar projects may be subject to discretionary controls in one city or county and only ministerial controls in another. See Section 15268.

The term "discretionary project" is defined in Guidelines § 15357:

> "Discretionary project" means a project which requires the exercise of judgment or deliberation when the public agency or body decides to approve or disapprove a particular activity, as distinguished from situations where the public agency or body merely has to determine whether there has been conformity with applicable statutes, ordinances, regulations, or

> other fixed standards. The key question is whether the public agency can use its subjective judgment to decide whether and how to carry out or approve a project. ...

While approval of development permits for most projects is discretionary, For Housing Development Projects, State Laws Limit Discretion of jurisdictions to disapprove (or approve other than as proposed) permits for housing development projects.

What is a Ministerial Project?

The term "ministerial" is defined in Guidelines § 15369:

> "Ministerial" describes a governmental decision involving little or no personal judgment by the public official as to the wisdom or manner of carrying out the project. The public official merely applies the law to the facts as presented but uses no special discretion or judgment in reaching a decision. A ministerial decision involves only the use of fixed standards or objective measurements, and the public official cannot use personal, subjective judgment in deciding whether or how the project should be carried out. Common examples of ministerial permits include automobile registrations, dog licenses, and marriage licenses. A building permit is ministerial if the ordinance requiring the permit limits the public official to determining whether the zoning allows the structure to be built in the requested location, the structure would meet the strength requirements in the Uniform Building Code, and the applicant has paid his fee.

Guidelines § 15268 describes how to determine if a project is ministerial. Generally, the **jurisdiction** determines which types of projects and permits are ministerial and which are discretionary:

> (a) Ministerial projects are exempt from the requirements of CEQA. **The determination of what is "ministerial" can most appropriately be made by the particular public agency** involved based upon its analysis of its own laws, and each public agency should make such determination either as a part of its implementing regulations or on a case-by-case basis.
>
> (b) In the absence of any discretionary provision contained in the local ordinance or other law establishing the requirements for the permit, license, or other entitlement for use, the following actions shall be presumed to be ministerial:
>
> (1) Issuance of building permits.
>
> (2) Issuance of business licenses.
>
> (3) Approval of final subdivision maps.
>
> (4) Approval of individual utility service connections and disconnections.
>
> (c) Each public agency should, in its implementing regulations or ordinances, provide an **identification or itemization of its projects and actions which are deemed ministerial** under the applicable laws and ordinances.
>
> (d) Where a project involves an approval that contains elements of both a ministerial action and a discretionary action, the project will be deemed to be discretionary and will be subject to the requirements of CEQA.

In addition to the guidance above, Guidelines § 15022(a)(1)(B) explicitly requires that local agencies adopt "a list of projects or permits over which the public agency has only ministerial authority."

In practice, jurisdictions seldom treat any development project as ministerial unless state law explicitly requires that the project be approved ministerially. Again, there are many provisions of state law that require local jurisdictions to process housing development permits ministerially; this book makes mention of ministerial permits, projects, and processing where appropriate, but does not cover any of the special state laws that preempt local codes to make a housing project ministerial.

For Housing Development Projects, State Laws Limit Discretion

The discretion of a jurisdiction to disapprove (or require an applicant to make changes to) a **housing** project is ***very*** limited under state law. Only **objective** development standards can be applied to housing projects. Decision makers are prohibited from applying **subjective** standards or using their personal judgement in reviewing a housing development project. (Gov. Code § 65589.5(f)(1) and (9).)

Even for projects with no affordable housing, the Housing Accountability Act limits the discretion of jurisdictions to disapprove "... a proposed housing development project [that] complies with applicable, objective general plan, zoning, and subdivision standards and criteria, including design review standards...." (Gov. Code § 65589.5(j)(1).) Subdivision (d) of the Housing Accountability Act further limits the discretion of jurisdictions to disapprove projects that contain affordable housing units. The State Density Bonus Law requires jurisdictions to waive or reduce even objective development standards that would preclude construction of the proposed project. (Gov. Code § 65915(e).) These limits are covered in detail in Chapter 9: Compliance Review.

Limiting decision-makers' discretion does not make all housing projects ministerial, but it does limit the jurisdiction's ability to disapprove, impose conditions on, restrict the density of, or require the applicant to redesign a housing development project. The jurisdiction may exercise **only** the limited discretion allowed by state law (e.g., disapproving a project by making findings that the project would have an unmitigable impact on public health or welfare). (Gov. Code § 65589.5(j) and (d).)

The California Environmental Quality Act (CEQA) Applies to Discretionary *Projects*

An introduction to the California Environmental Quality Act (CEQA) is provided in Chapter 3: California Environmental Quality Act (CEQA) Basics, and the application of CEQA to housing development projects is covered in Chapter 4: CEQA Review for Housing Projects After AB 130 and SB 131, but the concept of what is a "project" is key to understanding how CEQA relates to other state laws governing the review and approval of projects.

As explained under CEQA and Housing, CEQA was enacted in 1970, and in 1972 the California Supreme Court ruled that CEQA applies not only to development undertaken by public agencies but also to **private** development. When a private entity proposes to undertake a project, one or more public agencies have jurisdiction over that project, and the private developer must apply for a permit to undertake the project.

Definition of "Project" in CEQA

An activity that may cause a change in the environment is a "project" as defined by CEQA at PRC § 21065:

> 21065. "Project" means an activity which may cause either a direct physical **change in the environment**, or a reasonably foreseeable indirect physical change in the environment, and which is any of the following:
>
> (a) An activity directly undertaken by any public agency.
>
> (b) An activity undertaken by a person which is supported, in whole or in part, through contracts, grants, subsidies, loans, or other forms of assista1nce from one or more public agencies.
>
> (c) An activity that involves the **issuance to a person of a lease, permit, license, certificate, or other entitlement for use** by one or more public agencies.

The general term for the CEQA approval to undertake a project is "entitlement for use." Before undertaking a project, a private entity must obtain an entitlement for use, unless that use is already allowed "by right" (i.e., the project site is already entitled to the use by the rules in that jurisdiction, or by operation of state law).

As will be explained under Chapter 3: California Environmental Quality Act (CEQA) Basics, when a jurisdiction has designated a land use as being "permitted by right" or a state law requires that the development permit be granted ministerially, the local jurisdiction does not have discretion to disapprove the development permit; the permit must be granted if the project is consistent with the requisite standards. **CEQA does not apply to *ministerial* permits or projects.**

The Permit Streamlining Act Applies to All Housing Development *Permits*

In 1977, the California Legislature enacted the Permit Streamlining Act in response to delays and inconsistencies in the processing of permit applications.[16] The purpose of the Permit Streamlining Act is to expedite decisions on development projects, per Gov. Code § 65921:

> 65921. The Legislature finds and declares that there is a statewide need to ensure clear understanding of the specific requirements which must be met in connection with the approval of development projects and to expedite decisions on such projects. Consequently, the provisions of this chapter shall be applicable to all public agencies, including charter cities.

The Permit Streamlining Act, therefore, was created to streamline the process of obtaining approval for "projects" as defined in CEQA.

Definition of "Development" in the Permit Streamlining Act

Just as CEQA defines "project" broadly to include any activity that may change the environment, the Permit Streamlining Act defines "development" to cover virtually anything that effects the land or water, per Gov. Code § 65927:

> 65927. "Development" means, on land, in or under water, the placement or erection of any solid material or structure; discharge or disposal of any dredged material or of any gaseous, liquid, solid, or thermal waste; grading, removing, dredging, mining, or extraction of any materials; change in the density or intensity of use of land, including, but not limited to, subdivision pursuant to the Subdivision Map Act (commencing with Section 66410 of the Government Code), and any other division of land except where the land division is brought about in connection with the purchase of such land by a public agency for public recreational use; change in the intensity of use of water, or of access thereto; construction, reconstruction, demolition, or alteration of the size of any structure, including any facility of any private, public, or municipal utility; and the removal or harvesting of major vegetation other than for agricultural purposes, kelp harvesting, and timber operations which are in accordance with a timber harvesting plan submitted pursuant to the provisions of the Z'berg-Nejedly Forest Practice Act of 1973 (commencing with Section 4511 of the Public Resources Code).
>
> As used in this section, "structure" includes, but is not limited to, any building, road, pipe, flume, conduit, siphon, aqueduct, telephone line, and electrical power transmission and distribution line.
>
> Nothing in this section shall be construed to subject the approval or disapproval of final subdivision maps to the provisions of this chapter.
>
> "Development" does not mean a "change of organization", as defined in Section 56021 or a "reorganization", as defined in Section 56073.

Virtually every physical activity or effect anywhere within the land and water of the State of California is "development" as defined in the Permit Streamlining Act.

[16] For historical background and a discussion of issues with the Permit Streamlining Act, see: Milene Minassians, *Saving the Permit Streamlining Act: The California Supreme Court Must Depart from Horn v. County of Ventura*, 30 Hastings Envt'l L.J. 105 (2024) https://repository.uclawsf.edu/hastings_environmental_law_journal/vol30/iss1/5/.

Definition of "Development Project" in the Permit Streamlining Act

The Permit Streamlining Act's definition of "development project" connects the term "project" defined in CEQA with the term "development" defined in the Permit Streamlining Act. Per Gov. Code § 65928 (text amended by SB 158 (2025) in **red**):

> 65928. (a) "Development project" means **any project undertaken for the purpose of development**. "Development project" includes a project involving the issuance of a permit for construction or reconstruction but not a permit to operate.
>
> (b) (1) (A) Except as otherwise provided in subparagraph (B), "development project" does not include any ministerial projects proposed to be carried out or approved by public agencies.
>
> (B) Notwithstanding subparagraph (A), "development project" **includes a housing development project, as that term is defined in paragraph (3) of subdivision (b) of Section 65905.5, that requires an entitlement from a local agency, regardless of whether the process for permitting that entitlement is discretionary or ministerial**.
>
> (2) "Development project" **does not include a postentitlement phase permit**, as that term is defined in Section 65913.3.

Originally, the Permit Streamlining Act did **not** apply to any ***ministerial*** **permits**, because CEQA does not apply to any ***ministerial*** **projects**. Over time, state housing laws, and local jurisdictions, have come to designate many types of housing projects as ministerial. To ensure that **all** housing development permits whether discretionary or ministerial are subject to requirements and protections of the Permit Streamlining Act, the Legislature has amended[17] the Permit Streamlining Act to apply to ***all*** housing ***development*** permits.[18] However, the Permit Streamlining Act does **not** apply to any postentitlement phase permits (see Definition of "Postentitlement Phase Permit).

The Housing Accountability Act Applies to *Housing* Development *Projects*

It is critical to understand that while the Permit Streamlining Act applies only to development **permits**, the Housing Accountability Act applies to housing development **projects**, including the entirety of the housing project from SB 330 preliminary application through certificate of occupancy. While the Permit Streamlining Act does not apply to postentitlement phase permits, **the Housing Accountability Act *does* apply to postentitlement phase permits.**

A key feature of the Housing Accountability Act is that its definition of "housing development project" is the ***use***, not just the permit for that use. The Housing Accountability Act holds jurisdictions accountable for approving the housing development project and any and all approvals related to that entitlement for use, including approvals that are required during the postentitlement phase. Gov. Code § 65589.5(h)(6) specifies a long list of actions and inactions by a jurisdiction that constitute a disapproval of a housing development project, including failure to comply with Gov. Code § 65913.3, which defines and relates to postentitlement phase permits.

---

[17] Although AB 130 significantly amended the wording of Gov. Code § 65928, the amendment was primarily a "clean-up" to simplify the Permit Streamlining Act by including **ministerial *housing*** development projects in the definition of "development project." Previous bills had made individual housing-related provisions of the Act apply to ministerial housing projects. Amending the definition makes the Permit Streamlining Act simpler and clearer, but it was earlier amendments in response to delay and obstruction by some local jurisdictions that made ministerial housing development permits subject to the Act. Postentitlement phase permits have never been subject to the Act.

[18] The Permit Streamlining Act is not exclusive to housing projects; it applies to permits to develop any type of project, as defined by CEQA. However, CEQA does not apply to ministerial projects, and the Permit Streamlining Act does not apply to ministerial projects **except** ministerial housing projects.

Definition of "Housing Development Project" Varies Between Housing Laws

All housing **development *permits*** are subject to the Permit Streamlining Act, whether the development permit is discretionary or ministerial. The Housing Accountability Act applies to housing **development *projects*** from SB 330 preliminary application to final certificate of occupancy. The definition of "housing development project" at Gov. Code § 65589.5(h)(2) (quoted below in Definition of "Housing Development Project" for the HAA — Amended by SB 838) applies for purposes of the Housing Accountability Act, but other sections of state laws have somewhat different definitions of a housing development project.

For example, the term "housing development project" in the Permit Streamlining Act is defined differently than in the Housing Accountability Act. In fact, the term is defined differently in different ***sections*** of the Permit Streamlining Act. Two examples:

1. For the requirement that jurisdictions compile a list of required items (LORI) for development permit applications, under Gov. Code § 65940(d) the term housing development project is defined by reference to Gov. Code § 65905.5(b)(3), which defines housing development project by reference to Gov. Code § 65589.5(h)(2) (i.e., the definition used in the Housing Accountability Act), **except** that for Gov. Code § 65905.5(b)(3) a housing development project includes a project consisting of a **single** housing unit (the Housing Accountability Act applies only to developments of **two or more** units). Therefore, jurisdictions must compile a LORI for applications to build one single-family home.
2. Conversely, in the very next section Gov. Code § 65940.1(b)(4) contains its own definition of "housing development project" that does not reference any other code section and is therefore different from all other definitions of "housing development project" in state law. With the exception that it does not include "farmworker housing" and has a somewhat different definition of "mixed-use developments" it is similar to the definition at Gov. Code § 65589.5(h)(2), and because it refers to "residential units" in the plural, it applies only to projects that propose two or more units.

Other state laws have definitions that differ from both the Permit Streamlining Act and the Housing Accountability Act. For example, the definition of "housing development" in the State Density Bonus Law at Gov. Code § 65915(i) restricts its use to projects consisting of five or more residential units.[19]

To ensure a project qualifies for a provision of law that it intends to use, **practitioners need to check the definition of "housing development project"** that is applicable to that provision.

Simplified Definition of Housing Development Project

All the different definitions of "housing development project" in the various state laws are hard to keep track of, but in practice the term covers projects that are:

1. Multifamily (two units, or a higher minimum number of units under some laws, whether those units are developed on multiple parcels or a single parcel) or for specific provisions, a single single-family home.
2. Residential or Mixed-use (with at least two-thirds of the square footage of the project being residential, or a different percentage under some laws, and sometimes with prohibitions on the other types of uses).
3. Other types of housing (e.g., farmworker housing, etc.) as stated in the particular provision.

---

[19] The five unit minimum has been interpreted by HCD to include ADUs but exclude bonus units granted by the State Density Bonus Law (SDBL). See https://www.hcd.ca.gov/sites/default/files/docs/policy-and-research/adu-handbook-update.pdf page 44: "Can ADUs serve ...." The Author and some other practitioners read the plain text of the SDBL as allowing **bonus** units to count toward the five unit minimum, but it will take a court decision to overcome HCD's interpretation.

Definition of "Housing Development Project" for the HAA — Amended by SB 838

SB 838 (2025) amended the definition of "housing development project," for purposes of the Housing Accountability Act, to exclude hotel/motel uses in mixed-use projects. Per Gov. Code § 65589.5(h)(2), that became effective January 1, 2026 (showing the text amended by SB 838 in red):

(2) "Housing development project" means a use consisting of any of the following:

(A) Residential units only.

(B) Mixed-use developments consisting of residential and nonresidential uses that meet any of the following conditions:

(i) A mixed-use development that meets both of the following:

(I) At least two-thirds of the new or converted square footage is designated for residential use.

(II) (ia) No portion of the project is designated for use as a hotel, motel, bed and breakfast inn, or other transient lodging.

(Ib) The local agency may separately approve the portion of the project that includes a hotel, motel, bed and breakfast inn, or other transient lodging, which shall not be eligible for any benefits conferred on a housing development project by state law, including, but not limited to those available to a development under Section 65913.4.

(ic) For purposes of this subclause, the term "other transient lodging" does not include either of the following:

(Ia) A residential hotel, as defined in Section 50519 of the Health and Safety Code.

(Ib) After the issuance of a certificate of occupancy, a resident's use or marketing of a unit as short-term lodging, as defined in Section 17568.8 of the Business and Professions Code, in a manner consistent with local law.

(ii) At least 50 percent of the new or converted square footage is designated for residential use and the project meets both of the following:

(I) The project includes at least 500 net new residential units.

(II) No portion of the project is designated for use as a hotel, motel, bed and breakfast inn, or other transient lodging, except a portion of the project may be designated for use as a residential hotel, as defined in Section 50519 of the Health and Safety Code.

(iii) At least 50 percent of the net new or converted square footage is designated for residential use and the project meets all of the following:

(I) The project includes at least 500 net new residential units.

(II) The project involves the demolition or conversion of at least 100,000 square feet of nonresidential use.

(III) The project demolishes at least 50 percent of the existing nonresidential uses on the site.

(IV) No portion of the project is designated for use as a hotel, motel, bed and breakfast inn, or other transient lodging, except a portion of the project may be designated for use as a residential hotel, as defined in Section 50519 of the Health and Safety Code.

(C) Transitional housing or supportive housing.

(D) Farmworker housing, as defined in subdivision (h) of Section 50199.7 of the Health and Safety Code.

The primary reason that the legislature has tinkered so much with the definition of "housing development project" for purposes of the Housing Accountability Act is because this law very strictly limits the power of local jurisdictions to disapprove housing development projects. The legislature wants these limitations to apply to housing, but has decided not to extend the provisions of the Housing Accountability Act to certain hotel/motel components of a mixed-use project.

Definition of "Postentitlement Phase Permit" — Amended by AB 301

AB 2234 (2022) added Gov. Code § 65913.3 (**not** part of the Permit Streamlining Act, which begins at Gov. Code § 65920) to regulate "postentitlement phase permits" in a manner similar to how the Permit Streamlining Act regulates development permits. AB 1114 (2023) amended Gov. Code § 65913.3 to strengthen its provisions, for example to ensure that it applies to permits issued under the building codes even if the local jurisdiction treats the building permit as discretionary. AB 301 (2025) was passed as an urgency bill, taking effect on October 13, 2025, to extend the law so that it now covers both local agencies and **state agencies**.

While postentitlement permits are not the topic of this book, it is important to understand three things:

1. **A development permit is, by definition, *not* a postentitlement phase permit**, and a postentitlement phase permit is not a development permit. The Permit Streamlining Act is the state law that applies to development permit applications. Gov. Code § 65913.3 is the state law that applies to postentitlement phase permits.
2. **Postentitlement phase permits are part of the housing development *project*** as defined by the Housing Accountability Act, meaning that a jurisdiction that fails to comply with the postentitlement phase permit requirements and deadlines has violated the Housing Accountability Act. The applicant can petition a court to enforce Gov. Code § 65913.3 under the Housing Accountability Act.
    a. The definition of "postentitlement phase permits" is limited to development projects that are at least **two-thirds residential, including projects consisting of a single unit**. Therefore, the provisions for postentitlement phase permits apply to a project consisting of only one unit. The Housing Accountability Act generally applies to projects with two or more units, however:
        i. The time limits of Gov. Code § 65913.3 are enforceable under the Housing Accountability Act, for projects defined as a "housing development project" under Gov. Code § 65913.3(k)(1) even if the project is a single unit and therefore not generally covered by the Housing Accountability Act. (Gov. Code § 65913.3(f) and Gov. Code § 65589.5(h)(6)(C).)
    b. Conversely, the Housing Accountability Act applies to very large projects (500+ units) that are at least 50% residential (and meet other requirements), whereas the definition of postentitlement phase permit excludes projects that are less than two-thirds residential.
3. **Permits "required and issued"** by a local agency (i.e., a city or county) or a state agency are included in the definition of postentitlement phase permit. However, a Coastal Development Permit is not a postentitlement phase permit because it is required by the California Coastal Commission, even if it is reviewed and approved by a city or county. Permits issued by special districts or by utility providers that are not "owned and operated by a local agency" are also excluded from the definition of a postentitlement phase permit. (Gov. Code § 65913.3(k)(3)(C).)

CHAPTER 3: CALIFORNIA ENVIRONMENTAL QUALITY ACT (CEQA) BASICS

This chapter is intended as a basic overview of the California Environmental Quality Act (CEQA) as it pertains to a privately developed housing project. The intended audience is a person who will manage the entitlement process on behalf of a private developer. It assumes the development manager will consult with attorneys and CEQA experts as needed. Chapter 4: CEQA Review for Housing Projects After AB 130 and SB 131 explains the process of reviewing a housing project for exemption from CEQA, part of the Three-Part Process for Reviewing an Application for a Housing Development Permit.

Where to Find More Information

If the Reader would like to learn more about CEQA, the Governor's Office of Land Use and Climate Innovation provides many useful tools, including a getting started webpage with "CEQA 101 and 102" courses/webinars, technical advisories, the Site Check GIS mapping tool that screens sites for available exemptions, and the State Clearinghouse where notices and documents related to CEQA should be filed.

The Association of Environmental Professionals (AEP) publishes a book (download or order a hard copy) containing the CEQA Statutes and Guidelines, summaries of recent CEQA legislation and case law, appendices, and an index of topics. The book is an excellent reference, but it is unofficial and updated yearly, so always check the official sources for the latest CEQA Statutes and CEQA Guidelines. In addition to the CEQA book, the AEP maintains a portal with access to topic papers and a database of case law. The portal is members-only; membership is $175 per year, or free to students.

As stated in the introduction to Chapter 2: Key Concepts for Projects and Permits, the Institute for Local Government provides resources that, while intended for a public-sector audience, are excellent guides for any land-use practitioner. The CEQA and Environmental Issues chapter of *The Planning Commissioner Handbook* complements the material in this chapter.

CHAPTER CONTENTS

CEQA Statutes and Guidelines

The term "CEQA Statutes" refers to the California Environmental Quality Act (CEQA) as enacted and amended by the California Legislature. When a section of the CEQA Statutes refer to "this division," it means the entirety of the Act (Division 13 of the Public Resources Code). Exemptions from CEQA that are enacted by the Legislature are called **"statutory exemptions."** Most, but not all, statutory exemptions are codified in the Public Resources Code, which this book abbreviates to "PRC." Links in this book to the CEQA Statutes are to the California Legislative Information Website. PRC § 21083 directs the Governor's Office of Land Use and Climate Innovation (abbreviated "LCI" and formerly called the Office of Planning and Research, "OPR") to create guidelines for the implementation of CEQA,[20] which LCI does in coordination with the California Natural Resources Agency.[21]

"CEQA Guidelines" are created and updated as directed by PRC § 21083, and are found in Chapter 3 of Division 6 of Title 14 of the California Code of Regulations (CCR). Although called "guidelines," they are administrative regulations, which have the force of law. The official online source for the CCR is the Thompson Reuters Westlaw website, and links in this book to Guidelines are to this official source. The CEQA Guidelines include a list of **categories** of development projects that are exempt from CEQA if they meet certain criteria and are not barred by certain exceptions. There are 33 of these **"categorical exemptions"** found in the Guidelines §§ 15300 through 15333.[22]

CEQA and Housing

Modeled after the National Environmental Policy Act (NEPA), which was signed by President Nixon on January 1, 1970, CEQA was signed into law by California Governor Ronald Reagan in September of that year. In 1972, the California Supreme Court found that CEQA also applies to projects undertaken by private entities.[23] While other states also have laws modeled on NEPA, California's is recognized as the most restrictive.[24]

All discretionary development projects require CEQA review, at least to determine whether they qualify for an exemption, as part of the permitting process. By 1977, delays and inconsistencies in the processing of permit applications led the Legislature to enact the Permit Streamlining Act to require public agencies to process permits for development in a more predictable and expeditious manner.

The purpose of CEQA has always been to regulate development and prevent environmental damage, but it has long been recognized that CEQA made it harder to house California's growing population.[25] In 1979, SB 606[26] amended several state laws to require consideration of housing needs in adopting zoning regulations and applying environmental laws. It added the words "while providing a **decent home** and satisfying living environment for every Californian" to CEQA's statement of intent at PRC § 21000(g):

Figure 3: A decent home for every Californian.

Ch 947] STATUTES OF 1979 3271

(g) It is the intent of the Legislature that all agencies of the state government which regulate activities of private individuals, corporations, and public agencies which are found to affect the quality of the environment, shall regulate such activities so that major consideration is given to preventing environmental damage, while providing a decent home and satisfying living environment for every Californian

---

[20] https://lci.ca.gov/ceqa/guidelines/.

[21] https://resources.ca.gov/admin/Legal.

[22] It is common practice to refer to sections of Chapter 3 of Division 6 of Title 14 of the California Code of Regulations as, for example, "Section 15000 of the CEQA Guidelines" rather than 14 CCR § 15000, so this book provides links in the form "Guidelines § 15000."

[23] https://scocal.stanford.edu/opinion/friends-mammoth-v-board-supervisors-32943.

[24] Noah DeWitt, *A Twisted Fate: How California's Premier Environmental Law Has Worsened the State's Housing Crisis, and How To Fix It*, 49 Pepp. L. Rev. 413 (2022) Available at: https://digitalcommons.pepperdine.edu/plr/vol49/iss2/3, page 422: "Perhaps the strictest of all little NEPAs is the California Environmental Quality Act (CEQA)."

[25] Ibid, Abstract, page 413.

[26] https://books.google.com/books?id=MvudAJi1mBUC&q=660#v=onepage&q=606&f=false.

(g) It is the intent of the Legislature that all agencies of the state government which regulate activities of private individuals, corporations, and public agencies which are found to affect the quality of the environment, shall regulate such activities so that major consideration is given to preventing environmental damage, while **providing a decent home** and satisfying living environment for every Californian.

In 1980, the legislature enacted the Housing Accountability Act "to significantly increase the approval and construction of new housing." (Gov. Code § 65589.5(a)(2)(K).) The protections of the Housing Accountability Act have been expanded and enhanced in bills passed every legislative session since 2017 when Governor Jerry Brown signed 15 bills to begin addressing California's historic housing and homelessness crisis.

Over the past 9 years,[27] dozens of state laws have chipped away at CEQA's most pernicious unintended environmental consequence: inhibiting the creation of infill housing. In 2025, California passed two major bills, AB 130 and SB 131 that will make far more housing projects exempt from CEQA, reduce the costly documentation required for CEQA exemptions, make it harder for CEQA lawsuits to proceed against housing projects, and generally decrease risk, cost, and time for housing development projects.

Balancing Environmental Risks and Housing Needs

When a development project is subject to CEQA and the project does not qualify for a statutory or categorical exemption, then CEQA requires environmental review of the development project before the project can be approved. If the review finds that a project would have significant adverse environmental impacts, CEQA requires that those impacts be mitigated, and/or that alternatives to the proposed project be considered. If the impacts cannot be mitigated and/or the project alternatives do not achieve the project goals, then the project may still be acceptable and approved if there are "overriding considerations." CEQA Guidelines § 15093(a) and (b) explains:

(a) CEQA requires the decision-making agency to **balance, as applicable, the economic, legal, social, technological, or other benefits, including region-wide or statewide environmental benefits, of a proposed project against its unavoidable environmental risks** when determining whether to approve the project. If the specific economic, legal, social, technological, or other benefits, including region-wide or statewide environmental benefits, of a proposal project outweigh the unavoidable adverse environmental effects, the adverse environmental effects may be considered "acceptable."

(b) When the lead agency approves a project which will result in the occurrence of significant effects which are identified in the final EIR but are not avoided or substantially lessened, the agency shall state in writing the specific reasons to support its action based on the final EIR and/or other information in the record. The **statement of overriding considerations** shall be supported by substantial evidence in the record.

CEQA is a factor in California's housing crisis[28] because CEQA review adds costs to all projects, increases litigation risk for most projects, and delays or stops many projects. Most development projects undertaken by private entities do not require an environmental impact report (EIR) because Most Projects are Exempt from CEQA. CEQA **categorical** exemptions recognize that many classes of development projects can be assumed to have no significant effect on the environment because of their limited scope and their location. **Statutory** exemptions recognize that projects meeting certain criteria (e.g., infill housing projects qualifying for the PRC § 21080.66 Statutory Exemption — New with AB 130) should be exempt from CEQA because their benefits (e.g., providing housing on infill sites) override any environmental impacts that could or would result from the project.

---

[27] https://www.planning.org/planning/2015/oct/ceqa.htm.
[28] https://californialocal.com/localnews/statewide/ca/article/show/94237-ceqa-california-environmental-quality-act-housing-gavin-newsom/.

The Jurisdiction is Usually the "Lead Agency"

Under CEQA, the "lead agency" makes environmental determinations regarding development projects. If the project will be carried out by a nongovernmental person or entity, like a developer, the lead agency will normally be the city or the county with jurisdiction over the location of the project, per Guidelines § 15051(b)(1):

> (b) **If the project is to be carried out by a nongovernmental person or entity**, the lead agency shall be the public agency with the greatest responsibility for supervising or approving the project as a whole.
>
> > (1) The **lead agency will normally be** the agency with general governmental powers, such as a **city or county**, rather than an agency with a single or limited purpose such as an air pollution control district or a district which will provide a public service or public utility to the project.

Any additional agency that also reviews the project is a "responsible agency" that the lead agency will coordinate with. (Guidelines § 15050.)

The Jurisdiction is Accountable for the CEQA Determination

The applicant for a development project does not "apply" for a CEQA exemption or review, per se. Rather the applicant **applies for a permit** to carry out a development project, and the lead agency is required to determine whether the project is exempt, or if not exempt whether the project may have a significant effect on the environment. If a project opponent challenges a CEQA determination in court, it is the **jurisdiction that will be sued** under CEQA, so the conditions of approval for most privately developed projects will require that the developer/owner "hold harmless" and defend the jurisdiction in the event of a CEQA lawsuit.

CEQA Applies to Projects, Broadly Defined

For CEQA purposes, the term "project" has a very broad meaning that includes any activity which may cause a change in the environment. Before a public agency issues an "entitlement for use" to a private entity for an activity that is a "project" as defined by CEQA, that public agency must comply with CEQA. Per PRC § 21065:

> 21065. "Project" means **an activity which may cause either a direct physical change in the environment**, or a reasonably foreseeable indirect physical change in the environment, and which is any of the following:
>
> > (a) An activity directly undertaken by any public agency.
> >
> > (b) An activity undertaken by a person which is supported, in whole or in part, through contracts, grants, subsidies, loans, or other forms of assistance from one or more public agencies.
> >
> > (c) **An activity that involves the issuance to a person of a lease, permit, license, certificate, or other entitlement for use** by one or more public agencies.

For private developers, a project as defined by CEQA is an activity that requires the jurisdiction to issue a development permit, which is an "entitlement for use."

Approval of a Development Permit Grants an "Entitlement"

A development permit is **not** a permit to construct (e.g., a grading or building permit) or a license to conduct business. When a jurisdiction approves a development permit, it grants an **entitlement for use**. An entitlement is a right to use the land for the approved purpose.

For example, when a new commercial development is proposed, the developer requests the jurisdiction to grant the right to use the project site for the commercial purpose. Because the development project will change the environment, the jurisdiction must follow the requirements of CEQA **before** the development permit can be approved. Once the development permit is approved, the project is "entitled" to the approved use. Only **after** granting the entitlement for use, can the jurisdiction issue a permit to construct the commercial building and its associated site improvements. The grading and building permits are not subject to CEQA because they are not an entitlement for use. Building and grading permits to carry out the approved use are virtually always issued ministerially. The jurisdiction has no discretion to deny a grading or building permit for an entitled use if the construction plans comply with the California Building Standards and are consistent with the terms of the entitlement approval as expressed in the development permit with its conditions of approval.

Once the building is constructed, business operations that are compliant with the jurisdiction's codes, and the conditions of approval stipulated in the development permit, can be conducted in the building after obtaining a business license. The business is not a "project" as defined by CEQA, and the business license is ministerial and not subject to CEQA. Except that in cases where the **operations** of a business may change the environment (e.g., operations that discharge air pollutants) these operations constitute a "project" as defined by CEQA and require a permit. Often these operational permits are issued by special districts rather than the city or county.[29]

Uses Permitted by Right

Certain types of development may **already** be "entitled" because the jurisdiction permits the land use "by right." Such development may require a development permit, but issuance of the development permit is not optional. The jurisdiction simply reviews the proposed project against a set of standard criteria and issues the development permit if the project meets the criteria. Development permits for by-right uses are ministerial. **CEQA does not apply to ministerial projects**.

For example, in most jurisdictions, single-family homes in an approved subdivision are a use by right.[30] The approval of the subdivision (which **is** subject to CEQA) already entitles the use of the subdivided lots for single-family homes. The development and construction of the homes within that subdivision are not subject to further CEQA review.

Local jurisdictions have the right to decide whether a land use permit will be granted ministerially or will require discretionary review, unless a state law preempts that authority. Jurisdictions may choose to permit certain land uses by right and may choose to process various development permits ministerially. State law generally allows all jurisdictions to control "local matters," and the California Constitution grants **charter** cities "home rule."[31]

Some Projects are Ministerial by Operation of State Law

Many state housing bills (e.g., SB 330, the Housing Crisis Act of 2019) include findings that the new or amended provisions of state law address "matters of statewide concern" rather than "local matters." Most state housing laws apply to all cities, including charter cities. State laws supersede local code (unless the state law itself is found to be contrary to the California Constitution). State housing laws designate certain types of development permits as ministerial, and certain land uses as by right.

Example 1: Accessory dwelling units (ADUs) specified in Gov. Code § 66323 are a use by right, are processed ministerially, and are not subject to CEQA, throughout California.

Example 2: In jurisdictions that do not issue building permits for enough housing to meet their state-mandated share of housing needs, qualifying housing projects can elect to apply for a development permit under a state-mandated streamlined ministerial approval process (SMAP).[32] Even if the local zoning code says the use is **not** by

---

[29] See, for example, https://www.aqmd.gov/home/rules-compliance/ceqa/ceqa-permit-forms for the South Coast Air Quality Management District.

[30] In jurisdictions where single-family homes are not a use by right, the development permit is usually exempt from CEQA for other reasons.

[31] The California Constitution grants charter cities "home rule" in matters that are included in the city's charter. A discussion of the difference between "charter cities" and "general law cities" is outside the scope of this book.

[32] https://www.hcd.ca.gov/planning-and-community-development/statutory-determinations.

right, and the local code requires discretionary review and approval of the project, the state requires the jurisdiction to follow the SMAP. Because the project is subject to a ministerial approval process it is not subject to CEQA.

CEQA Applies to Discretionary Projects, but Not to Ministerial Projects

If the project requires no discretionary approvals, then it is a ministerial project and is not subject to CEQA at all; no special exemption is required. Per PRC § 21080:

> 21080. (a) Except as otherwise provided in this division, **this division shall apply to discretionary projects** proposed to be carried out or **approved by public agencies**, including, but not limited to, the enactment and amendment of zoning ordinances, the issuance of zoning variances, the issuance of conditional use permits, and the approval of tentative subdivision maps unless the project is exempt from this division.
>
> (b) This division **does not apply to** any of the following activities:
>
> (1) **Ministerial projects** proposed to be carried out or approved by public agencies.
>
> ...

For a discussion of the difference between discretionary and ministerial projects, see Discretionary vs. Ministerial. Any development project that requires **discretionary** approval is subject to CEQA, and at a minimum will require review to determine whether the project qualifies for an exemption.

Most Projects are Exempt from CEQA

Even if the jurisdiction's discretion is very limited (as is the case for housing projects), most development permits/projects are **discretionary** and thus require some level of CEQA review. However, most private development projects, and especially housing development projects, will qualify for a statutory or categorical exemption from CEQA and thus the CEQA review will be limited to determining whether the project meets the qualifications for the exemption.

The PRC § 21080.66 Statutory Exemption — New with AB 130 that became effective July 1, 2025 will ensure that more housing projects are exempt from CEQA and make it harder to challenge the exemption in court. Also effective July 1, 2025, PRC § 21080.1(b) was amended to limit CEQA review when a project **almost** qualifies for an exemption, as explained under But For a Single Condition — New with SB 131.

The CEQA review for exemption process, and initial study process, will be explained in Chapter 4: CEQA Review for Housing Projects After AB 130 and SB 131.

CHAPTER 4: CEQA REVIEW FOR HOUSING PROJECTS AFTER AB 130 AND SB 131

CEQA review is one part of the Three-Part Process for Reviewing an Application for a Housing Development Permit explained in the next chapter. Article 5 of the CEQA Guidelines lays out the process of reviewing projects for a CEQA exemption, and if a project is not exempt the process of conducting an initial study. This book focuses on the CEQA exemption review and determination process, with some discussion of the initial study and other potential CEQA determinations, from the perspective of the applicant/developer.

In 2025, the California Legislature enacted major CEQA reforms. Two key provisions for housing projects are the new PRC § 21080.66 Statutory Exemption for infill housing added by AB 130 (2025), and a provision added by SB 131 (2025) that limits the scope of CEQA review when a housing project would, But For a Single Condition — New with SB 131, qualify for an exemption. This "near-miss" provision, added as subdivision (b) to PRC § 21080.1, will limit the Initial Study and any subsequent environmental determination to a review of only that single condition.

Where to Find More Information

See the introduction to Chapter 3: California Environmental Quality Act (CEQA) Basics for links to some useful CEQA tools and references. The Author recommends that practitioners use the CEQA Statute & Guidelines book by the Association of Environmental Professionals as the comprehensive guide to the CEQA process. This book covers only a small fraction of the topics in the CEQA Statute and Guidelines book.

To get the most benefit from this chapter, the Reader should familiarize themselves with AB 130 (2025) by reading one or more of the summaries provided by various law firms. Among the best annual summaries of new housing laws are those provided by Holland & Knight, which provided a four-part series on the key CEQA reforms enacted as AB 130 (2025) and SB 131 (2025):

- Part 1 covers the PRC § 21080.66 Statutory Exemption — New with AB 130 added by AB 130 (2025) and the "near miss" CEQA provision added by SB 131 (2025) explained under But For a Single Condition — New with SB 131.
- Part 2 covers various provisions of AB 130 (2025), including the new "shot clock" for ministerial projects that was added as Gov. Code § 65950(a)(6), which is discussed under 60-Day Deadline for Approval or Disapproval of a Ministerial Project.
    - The new "shot clock" for the new PRC § 21080.66 statutory CEQA exemption was added by AB 130 (2025), but soon amended by SB 158 (2025); Holland & Knight summarizes the clarified shot clock in their 2026 Housing Laws Alert. This book has a detailed discussion of the issues that the new shot clock, found at Gov. Code § 65950(a)(7), creates for the project review timeline under Deadline for Exempt Projects Using vs. Not Using the New PRC § 21080.66 Exemption.
- Part 3 summarizes a number of limited and specialized CEQA statutory exemptions that were created by SB 131 (2025).
- Part 4 "is intended to explain the nuances of SB 131's impact on CEQA litigation."

CHAPTER CONTENTS

The CEQA Process Runs from Preapplication through Statute of Limitations

All discretionary development projects must be reviewed in accordance with CEQA.[33] However, most projects will qualify for an exemption. A Preapplication CEQA Consultation can be conducted prior to submitting a full development permit application. After the project is approved and its CEQA notice is filed, the CEQA determination can be challenged in court until the Statute of Limitations for CEQA Lawsuits has expired. Thus, the CEQA process runs from preapplication through the statute of limitations, and that entire process requires careful management to avoid unnecessary project delays.

Use a Pre-App Review to Begin CEQA Consultation

This book repeatedly reminds the applicant to always submit an SB 330 preliminary application. As discussed in Chapter 6: SB 330 Preliminary Application, applicants should submit only the minimum required information with the SB 330 preliminary application, and the jurisdiction is not required to provide comments and should not spend time analyzing the SB 330 preliminary application. However, if the applicant wants a preliminary ***review*** of the project, the Author recommends making a **separate** request for a pre-app review under whatever process the jurisdiction provides. This informal pre-app review can include a Preapplication CEQA Consultation, discussed later in this chapter, with the goal of deciding which of the several

PRC § 21080.66 Statutory Exemption — New with AB 130

A brand-new exemption became available on July 1, 2025 with the passage of AB 130 (2025). PRC § 21080.66 is a statutory exemption that is **broadly applicable to infill housing** development projects, with simple qualification requirements. The PRC § 21088.66 statutory exemption will be **difficult to challenge with a CEQA lawsuit**. It does not have an "unusual circumstances" exception or other disqualifiers related to traffic, noise, air quality, or water quality that apply to the Class 32 "Infill" Categorical Exemption and the PRC § 21159.25 Statutory Exemption (Class 32 for Unincorporated County Areas). In most cases, the applicant should not need to hire a consultant to prepare an expensive "CEQA memo" for this new exemption. This new exemption does not require any technical reports or studies, unless further information is needed to confirm that the project site is not disqualified (PRC § 21088.66(a)(6)) by a list of characteristics found at Gov. Code § 65913.4(a)(6), which are the same characteristics that disqualify sites from streamlined ministerial approval processing (SB 35 / SB 423, now known as SMAP).

Like other exemptions, it requires consistency with the general plan and zoning regulations, but unlike other exemptions it uses a "reasonable person standard," per PRC § 21080.66(a)(4)(A):

> (4) (A) The project is consistent with the applicable general plan and zoning ordinance, as well as any applicable local coastal program as defined in Section 30108.6. For purposes of this section, a housing development project shall be deemed consistent with the applicable general plan and zoning ordinance, and any applicable local coastal program, if there is **substantial evidence that would allow a reasonable person to conclude** that the housing development project is consistent.

This exemption will become the most-used CEQA exemption for housing projects because it reduces CEQA risk, reduces costs, and saves time (assuming the required tribal noticing is completed in conjunction with an SB 330 preliminary application, see the next section: PRC § 21080.66 Exemption Requires a Tribal Notification and Consultation Process).

---

[33] Ministerial projects are not subject to CEQA, as explained under CEQA Applies to Discretionary Projects, but Not to Ministerial Projects.

PRC § 21080.66 Exemption Requires a Tribal Notification and Consultation Process

PRC § 21080.66 requires notification to, and if they request it, consultation with California Native American tribes (similar to the requirements for SB 35 / SB 423, now known as SMAP, but with a completely different timeline). The jurisdiction should automatically send the tribal notification within 14 days after receiving the SB 330 preliminary application. (PRC § 21080.66(b)(1)(A)(i).) However, since jurisdictions often need to be prompted to follow state laws, the applicant should notify the jurisdiction that the project likely qualifies for the PRC § 21080.66 statutory exemption, and ask that the tribal notification process be started, as explained under Trigger the Tribal Process for the PRC 21080.66 CEQA Exemption. If the SB 330 preliminary application has not triggered the tribal noticing process, then whenever the applicant decides to pursue the PRC § 21080.66 exemption, they should send an email to the jurisdiction:

> The Project likely qualifies for the CEQA statutory exemption provided by Public Resources Code § 21088.66 (AB 130 effective July 1, 2025). Applicant requests that the jurisdiction "shall provide formal notification via certified mail and email to each California Native American tribe" within 14 days of receipt of this notice, in accordance with PRC § 21088.66(b)(1)(A).

For projects that will use the PRC § 21080.66 exemption, it is **especially important** that an SB 330 preliminary application be submitted, and submitted well before the date the full development permit application is submitted. If no SB 330 preliminary application is submitted, the jurisdiction is not required to start the tribal notification process until the full development permit application is deemed complete. Per PRC § 21080.66(b)(1)(A)(i):

> (b) (1) (A) A local government shall provide formal notification via certified mail and email to each California Native American tribe that is traditionally and culturally affiliated with the project site as an invitation to consult on the proposed project, its location, and the project's potential effects on tribal cultural resources pursuant to one of the following deadlines:
>
> > (i) Within 14 days of the application for the project being deemed complete pursuant to paragraph (5) of subdivision (h) of Section 65589.5 of the Government Code.

The jurisdiction has 14 days to notify the Tribes, and that time period starts on the date the application is "deemed complete" as defined by Gov. Code § 65589.5(h)(i):

> (5) Notwithstanding any other law, "deemed complete" means that the applicant has submitted a preliminary application pursuant to Section 65941.1 or, if the applicant has not submitted a preliminary application, has submitted a complete application pursuant to Section 65943. The local agency shall bear the burden of proof in establishing that the application is not complete.

As will be explained in Overview of the Issue of Ambiguity Regarding the Start of the Compliance Review Period, the deemed complete date for the full development permit application is the date of the final submittal of the application, which the jurisdiction later determines to be complete, or the date that the 30-day time period for the jurisdiction's completeness review expires and the full application is deemed complete as provided by Gov. Code § 65943(a) or (b). If the tribal noticing starts that late, the project approval will almost certainly be delayed by the tribal noticing and consultation process.

Applicants should always submit an SB 330 preliminary application early enough that the tribal process does not delay the overall project timeline. This is illustrated in the next section, and discussed further in Chapter 5: Overall Development Permit Review Process & How AB 130 Changes It.

The Tribal Process Can Take Up to 148 Days

The tribal process **can take up to 148 days** (or longer when deadlines fall on a holiday, see Computation of Time Periods and Deadlines).

- Within 14 days after the jurisdiction receives the SB 330 preliminary application (or if no SB 330 preliminary application is filed, within 14 days of the date the ***complete*** full development permit application is submitted) the jurisdiction must notify "each California Native American tribe that is traditionally and culturally affiliated with the project site" (hereinafter, "Tribe" or "Tribes") as required by PRC § 21080.66(b)(1)(A)(i).
    - If the application was deemed complete prior to July 1, 2026, then the notification must be made within 14 days after the applicant notifies the jurisdiction that the project is eligible for the exemption as per PRC § 21080.66(b)(1)(A)(ii).
    - The Author interprets PRC § 21080.66(b)(1)(A)(i) to mean that jurisdictions, even without a request from the applicant, must notify the Tribes within 14 days of receipt of a complete application (SB 330 preliminary application or full development permit application). Therefore, unless the applicant requests otherwise, the jurisdiction should automatically start the process of applying the PRC § 21080.66 statutory exemption to **all eligible projects**. If the applicant does not want the jurisdiction to apply this exemption, see For Some Projects, Applicants Should "Opt Out" of the PRC § 21088.66 CEQA Exemption.
- Each Tribe has 60 days to accept the invitation to consult, per PRC § 21080.66(b)(2)(A). If no Tribe accepts the invitation within 60 days, the tribal process concludes, per PRC § 21080.66(b)(2)(B).
- Within 14 days after a Tribe notifies the jurisdiction that they accept the invitation to consult, the jurisdiction must initiate the consultation, per PRC § 21080.66(b)(3)(A).
    - Note that this 14-day period starts upon **each** Tribe's notification to the jurisdiction. Multiple Tribes may be involved. The jurisdiction should not wait for the end of the 60-day notice period to initiate consultation with a Tribe; the language of the statute requires that consultation be initiated for ***each*** Tribe within 14 days of ***that*** Tribe's acceptance of the invitation.
- Within 45 days of initiation of consultation with a Tribe, the consultation with that Tribe shall conclude, unless the Tribe extends the consultation for 15 days (which the Tribe can do **unilaterally**). (PRC § 21080.66(b)(3)(F).) Again, the language of the statute indicates that there could be multiple consultations with different Tribes, and each consultation should proceed independently and with a different timeline.

In the Author's experience with the tribal process, there have been multiple California Native American tribes historically associated with a project site. Not all of the Tribes have responded to the notification, so even though some Tribes responded promptly, the process required waiting the full 60-day period, after which Tribes that did not respond are deemed **not** to have accepted the invitation. (PRC § 21080.66(b)(2)(B).) Meanwhile, if at least one of the Tribes accepts the invitation to consult the consultation should **commence** within 14 days of that Tribe's acceptance of the invitation and could **conclude** before the expiration of the 60-day period for other Tribes to respond. In managing this process, both the jurisdiction and the applicant are advised to closely track the schedule. The jurisdiction, applicant, and Tribes all need to work together to ensure that the timelines are met.

On the following pages, the Author has provided screen shots from his Microsoft Project schedule showing the task list and Gantt chart for an example project where three Tribes respond to the invitation at different times (Figure 4); and a timeline from that schedule showing the tribal notification and consultation process (Figure 5). Note that even though the applicant submitted the SB 330 preliminary application on January 5, about 70 days before submitting the full development permit application, the tribal consultation process extends well into the second review of the full development permit application for completeness.

Bottom line: **assume the process will take the full 148 days**. Trigger the Tribal Process for the PRC 21080.66 CEQA Exemption by submitting the SB 330 preliminary application well in advance of the full development permit application (but without missing the 180-Day Deadline for 1st Submittal of the Full Development Permit Application) and carefully track all the dates and deadlines for the tribal process.

Figure 4: Example Microsoft Project schedule tracking each Tribe through the PRC § 21080.66 tribal process.

Task Name	Duration	Predecessors	Actual Start	Start	Finish
PRC § 21080.66 Tribal Process	**95 days**		**Mon 1/5/26**	**Mon 1/5/26**	**Fri 5/22/26**
JURI Receives Request for Tribal Noticing	0 days	7	NA	Mon 1/5/26	Mon 1/5/26
JURI Notifies All Tribes	14 edays	35	NA	Mon 1/5/26	Mon 1/19/26
60-Day Time Period for Tribes to Respond	**42 days**		**NA**	**Mon 1/19/26**	**Fri 3/20/26**
Time Period	59.5 edays	36	NA	Mon 1/19/26	Fri 3/20/26
First Working Day On or After Time Period	1 day	38	NA	Fri 3/20/26	Fri 3/20/26
DEADLINE for Tribes to Respond	0 days	39	NA	Fri 3/20/26	Fri 3/20/26
Tribal Consultation Process	**81.88 days**		**Mon 1/26/26**	**Mon 1/26/26**	**Fri 5/22/26**
Tribe 1	**41.88 days**		**Mon 1/26/26**	**Mon 1/26/26**	**Thu 3/26/26**
TRIBE 1 Accepts Invitation to Consult	0 days	39	Mon 1/26/26	Mon 1/26/26	Mon 1/26/26
14-Day Time Period for Juri to Intiate Tribe 1 Consult	**10.88 days**		**NA**	**Mon 1/26/26**	**Mon 2/9/26**
Juri Initiate Consultation with Tribe 1	13.5 edays	43	NA	Mon 1/26/26	Sun 2/8/26
First Working Day On or After Time Period	1 day	45	NA	Mon 2/9/26	Mon 2/9/26
45-day Tribe 1 Consultation Period (no extension)	**31 days**		**NA**	**Mon 2/9/26**	**Thu 3/26/26**
DATE Tribe 1 Consultation Begins	0 days	46,45	NA	Mon 2/9/26	Mon 2/9/26
Consultation with Tribe 1	44.5 edays	48	NA	Mon 2/9/26	Thu 3/26/26
UNILATERAL Extension of Consultation by Tribe 1	0 edays	49	NA	Thu 3/26/26	Thu 3/26/26
First Working Day on or After Time Period	1 day	49,50	NA	Thu 3/26/26	Thu 3/26/26
DATE Tribe 1 Consult Complete	0 days	50,49,51	NA	Thu 3/26/26	Thu 3/26/26
Tribe 2	**50.88 days**		**Fri 2/20/26**	**Fri 2/20/26**	**Mon 5/4/26**
TRIBE 2 Accepts Invitation to Consult	0 days	39	Fri 2/20/26	Fri 2/20/26	Fri 2/20/26
14-Day Time Period for Juri to Intiate Tribe 2 Consult	**10.88 days**		**NA**	**Fri 2/20/26**	**Fri 3/6/26**
Juri Initiate Consultation with Tribe 2	13.5 edays	54	NA	Fri 2/20/26	Thu 3/5/26
First Working Day On or After Time Period	1 day	56	NA	Fri 3/6/26	Fri 3/6/26
60-day Tribe 2 Consultation Period (w/ extension)	**42.88 days**		**Wed 3/4/26**	**Wed 3/4/26**	**Mon 5/4/26**
DATE Tribe 2 Consultation Begins	0 days	57,56	Wed 3/4/26	Wed 3/4/26	Wed 3/4/26
Consultation with Tribe 2	44.5 edays	59	NA	Wed 3/4/26	Fri 4/17/26
UNILATERAL Extension of Consultation by Tribe 2	15 edays	60	NA	Fri 4/17/26	Sat 5/2/26
First Working Day on or After Time Period	1 day	61,60	NA	Mon 5/4/26	Mon 5/4/26
DATE Tribe 2 Consult Complete	0 days	62	NA	Mon 5/4/26	Mon 5/4/26
Tribe 3	**45.88 days**		**Thu 3/19/26**	**Thu 3/19/26**	**Fri 5/22/26**
TRIBE 3 Accepts Invitation to Consult	0 days	39	Thu 3/19/26	Thu 3/19/26	Thu 3/19/26
14-Day Time Period for Juri to Intiate Tribe 3 Consult	**9.88 days**		**NA**	**Thu 3/19/26**	**Thu 4/2/26**
Juri Initiate Consultation with Tribe 3	13.5 edays	65	NA	Thu 3/19/26	Wed 4/1/26
First Working Day On or After Time Period	1 day	67	NA	Thu 4/2/26	Thu 4/2/26
60-day Tribe 3 Consultation Period (w/ extention)	**43.88 days**		**Mon 3/23/26**	**Mon 3/23/26**	**Fri 5/22/26**
DATE Tribe 3 Consultation Begins	0 days	67,68	Mon 3/23/26	Mon 3/23/26	Mon 3/23/26
Consultation with Tribe 3	44.5 edays	70	NA	Mon 3/23/26	Wed 5/6/26
UNILATERAL Extension of Consultation by Tribe 3	15 edays	71	NA	Wed 5/6/26	Thu 5/21/26
First Working Day On or After Time Period	1 day	71,72	NA	Fri 5/22/26	Fri 5/22/26
DATE Tribe 2 Consult Complete	0 days	73	NA	Fri 5/22/26	Fri 5/22/26
DATE Tribal Process Complete	0 days	36,43,52,54	NA	Fri 5/22/26	Fri 5/22/26
MILESTONE PRC § 21080.66 Tribal Process Complete	0 days	75	NA	Fri 5/22/26	Fri 5/22/26

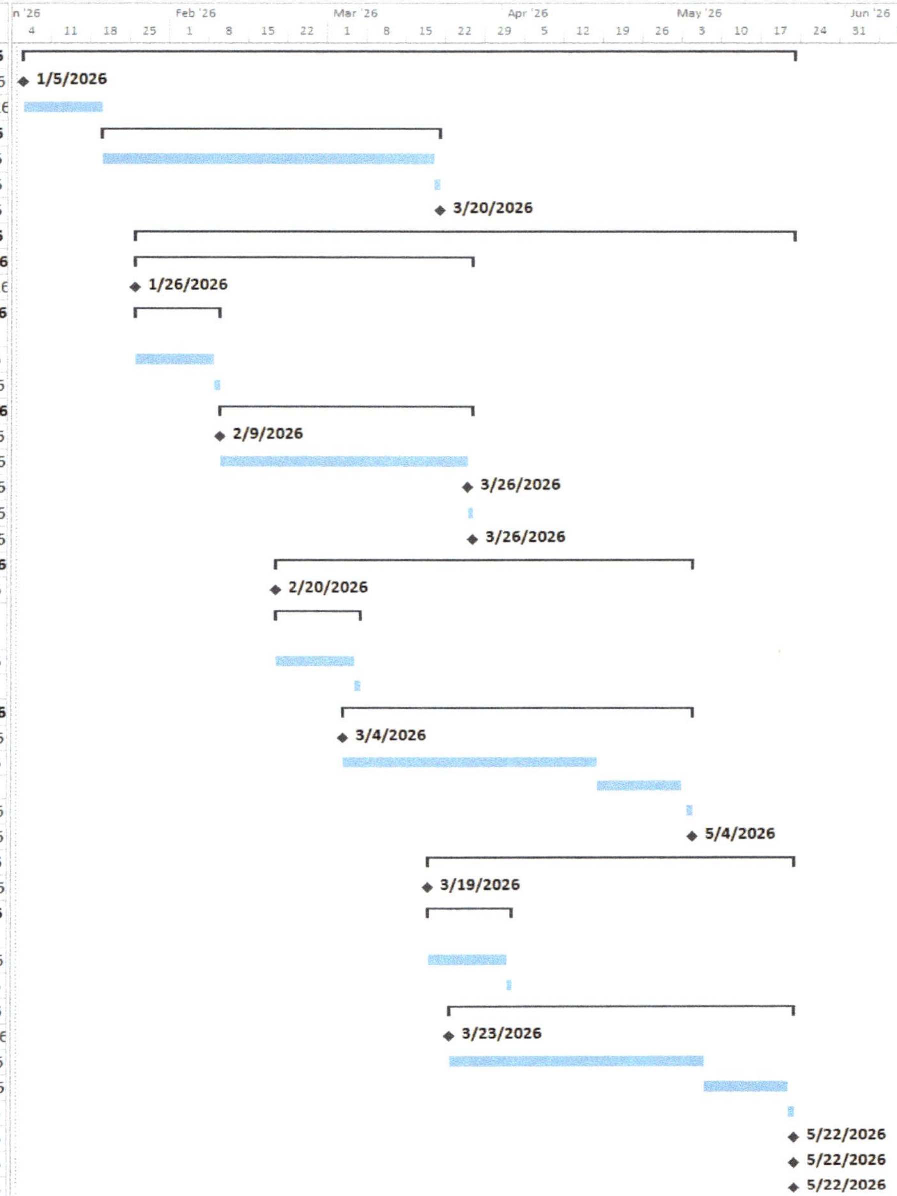

Figure 5: Example timeline of the PRC § 21080.66 tribal process. Each Tribe should be tracked individually.

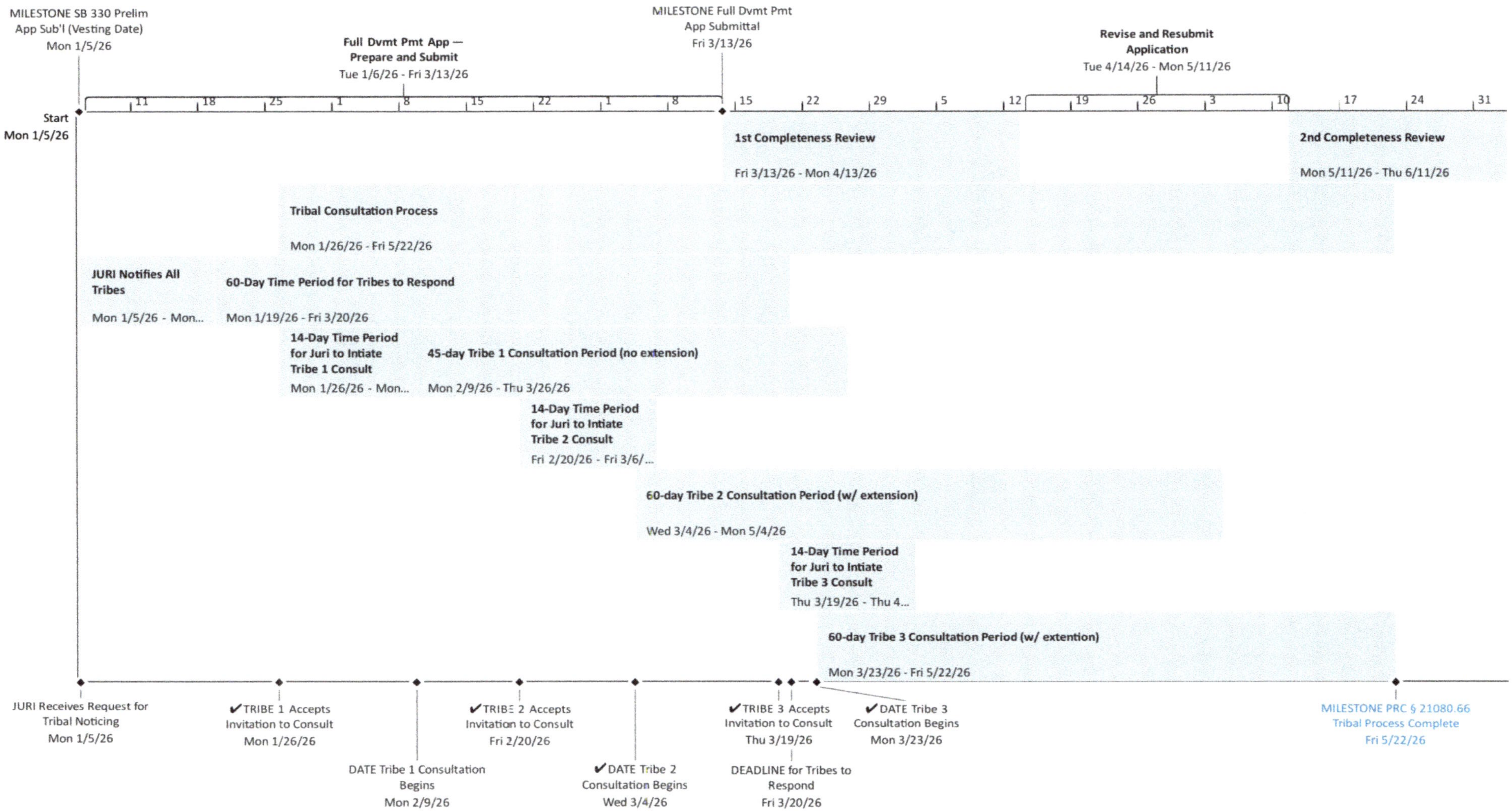

PRC § 21080.66 Exemption Imposes Tribal-Related Conditions of Approval

If a consultation is conducted with a California Native American tribe, the consultation may result in agreements between the Tribe and the developer. The jurisdiction is required to place conditions of approval on the development permit to enforce those agreements. In addition, unless the Tribes and the developer have agreed otherwise, the jurisdiction must impose a set of tribal-related conditions of approval listed under PRC § 21080.66(b)(4):

> (4) The local government shall include, as binding conditions of the project approval, all of the following:
>
> (A) Any enforceable agreements reached during the project consultation.
>
> (B) All of the following measures, unless there is mutual agreement between the California Native American tribe and the project proponent not to include the measure as a binding condition:
>
> (i) Upon request by a California Native American tribe, the project shall include tribal monitoring during all ground-disturbing activities, as follows:
>
> (I) The California Native American tribe shall designate the monitor.
>
> (II) The tribal monitor shall comply with applicant's site access and workplace safety requirements.
>
> (III) The applicant shall compensate the tribal monitor at a reasonable rate, determined in good faith, that aligns with customary compensation for cultural resource monitoring, taking into account factors such as the scope and duration of the project.
>
> (ii) Tribal cultural resources shall be avoided where feasible, in accordance with subdivision (a) of Section 21084.3. In furtherance of this requirement, where feasible, the project applicant shall provide deference to tribal preferences regarding access to spiritual, ceremonial, and burial sites, and incorporate tribal traditional knowledge in the protection and sustainable use of tribal cultural resources and landscapes.
>
> (iii) All treatment and documentation of tribal cultural resources shall be conducted in a culturally appropriate manner, consistent with Section 21083.9.
>
> (iv) A California Historical Resources Information System archaeological records search and a tribal cultural records search shall be completed for the project site.
>
> (v) A Sacred Lands Inventory request shall be submitted to the Native American Heritage Commission.
>
> (vi) The project shall comply with Section 7050.5 of the Health and Safety Code and Section 5097.98, including immediate work stoppage upon discovery of human remains or burial grounds, and treatment in accordance with applicable law and in consultation with the affected California Native American tribe.
>
> (vii) An application of tribal ecological knowledge into habitat restoration efforts undertaken by the project as applicable to the specific environmental context and conditions of the project.

In the Author's experience, after they received the tribal notification, responding Tribes provided proposals for the tribal monitoring during grading and excavation required under PRC § 21080.66(b)(4)(B)(i). That cost is likely to be at least as much as the customary cost for geotechnical observations and testing. The requirements in the event of discovering human remains at PRC § 21080.66(b)(4)(B)(vi) would generally apply regardless of the use of this exemption. The Author recommends working together with any Tribe that responds to the notification, to establish a scope of work and budget, and to regard the tribal monitors as a resource like other consulting professionals required for the successful execution of construction.

PRC § 21080.66 Exemption Imposes a Condition of Approval Requiring a Phase I ESA

It is standard practice in real estate development that a Phase I Environmental Site Assessment (ESA)[34] be conducted and the report obtained and reviewed before closing on the purchase of any real property, and lenders typically require a Phase I ESA prior to closing a loan. Therefore, the requirement at PRC § 21080.66(c) that the local jurisdiction place a condition of approval on the development permit that a Phase I ESA be completed does not place an additional burden on the project. PRC § 21080.66(c) merely imposes a condition of approval; the Phase I ESA can be performed **after** the housing development permit is approved.

In fact, this requirement is more permissive than the requirements imposed by other CEQA exemptions. For example, all of the 33 classes of categorical exemptions are subject to an exception that prohibits their use on sites that are on the Cortese List,[35] such as sites where leaking underground storage tanks have existed. (Guidelines § 15300.2(e).) In other words, contaminated sites typically are not eligible for a categorical exemption. The ability to obtain the PRC § 21080.66 statutory exemption on a site that may be contaminated but will be cleaned up in the course of development is a big advantage of this exemption.

If the Phase I ESA identifies a recognized environmental condition (REC), PRC § 21080.66(c)(1)(B) requires that the developer conduct a preliminary endangerment assessment (PEA) as defined at Health and Safety Code § 78095. If the PEA finds that a hazardous substance exists on the site or that there is potential for exposure from surrounding properties, PRC § 21080.66(c)(1)(C) and (D) require that release or potential exposure to be mitigated in accordance with state and federal standards prior to the issuance of a certificate of occupancy. Again, all of these requirements can be met after the housing development permit is approved.

Under PRC § 21080.66(c)(2), there are certain air conditioning and filtration requirements for housing projects located within 500 feet of a freeway, and balconies of buildings within 500 feet of a freeway may not face the freeway. This, again, is an improvement over other exemptions with restrictions near freeways.[36]

Caution: PRC § 21080.66, in Limited Circumstances, Requires Prevailing Wage

For most projects, the PRC § 21080.66 statutory exemption does not trigger wage or labor requirements. However, for 100% affordable projects, projects over 85 feet in height, and certain projects in San Francisco with 50 or more units, this exemption triggers **prevailing wage**. The applicant should use a different CEQA exemption if their project budget does not support prevailing wage requirements and falls into one of these categories.

Importantly, using the PRC § 21080.66 exemption for these types of projects **extends liability to the developer** for "any debt owed to a wage claimant...." (Labor Code § 218.8(a)(1).) Per PRC § 21080.66(d)(4):

> (4) The provisions of Section 218.8 of the Labor Code shall extend to the development proponent in addition to the direct contractor or subcontractor. For purposes of this paragraph, "development proponent" shall mean a developer who submits the housing development project application to a local government that is exempt from this division pursuant to this section.

Again, jurisdictions will prefer to use this exemption over other available exemptions: it applies to most housing projects, its qualifications are straightforward, and it will be more difficult for project opponents to bring a CEQA

---

[34] The term "Phase I environmental assessment" is defined at Health and Safety Code § 78090. If the Reader is unfamiliar with ESAs, Wikipedia has a short explainer: https://en.wikipedia.org/wiki/Phase_I_environmental_site_assessment.

[35] The "Cortese List" is the common name for what is referred to in state law as "any list compiled pursuant to Section 65962.5 of the Government Code." It is not a single list, but rather a group of data sources prepared by several state agencies. In the preparation of a Phase I ESA, the environmental consultant will obtain a database search that includes all the sources in the Cortese List. The Author recommends requesting from the environmental consultant that the Phase I ESA includes "a clear statement in the executive summary that the site IS/is NOT included on any list compiled pursuant to Section 65962.5 of the Government Code."

[36] For example, the restriction on the statutory exemption at PRC § 21080.40(c)(3)(D) for 100% affordable projects.

lawsuit against this exemption. If a developer contemplates any of these types of projects and does not want to be subject to prevailing wage requirements, the Author recommends that they **consult a qualified attorney** on these questions:

1. If the project does **not** qualify for any ***other*** exemption, should the applicant pursue an ND, MND, or EIR to avoid the prevailing wage requirements?
2. If the project qualifies for ***multiple*** exemptions, should the project pursue **only the *other*** exemption; or should the project pursue the PRC § 21080.66 exemption **plus** another exemption?
    a. The PRC § 21080.66 exemption has the advantage of being very difficult to challenge with a CEQA lawsuit. The Class 32 "Infill" Categorical Exemption, for example, is vulnerable to CEQA lawsuits alleging "unusual circumstances." Could the project obtain both the PRC § 21080.66 statutory exemption and the Class 32 categorical exemption as a way to discourage a CEQA lawsuit?
    b. Could the project later rely only on the Class 32 categorical exemption and modify the project approval to remove the PRC § 21080.66 statutory exemption?
    c. Do the labor and wage requirements apply if the project is exempt per PRC § 21080.66, but is also exempt under a different exemption that does not have labor and wage requirements?

These questions may be addressed when the CEQA Guidelines are updated for 2026, but are likely to be the subject of litigation as labor unions seek to enforce prevailing wage requirements on more projects.

100% Affordable Projects

Prevailing wage requirements are imposed on most projects that receive federal or state funding, and most 100% affordable projects receive such financing. However, it is possible that a 100% affordable project *could* be funded from sources that do not trigger prevailing wage. A 100% affordable project that uses this exemption would be subject to prevailing wage *even if* its funding sources do not trigger wage requirements. Per PRC § 21080.66(d)(1):

> (d) (1) Notwithstanding any other law, all construction workers employed in the execution of a housing development project exempt from this division pursuant to this section where 100 percent of the units within the development project are dedicated to lower income households, as defined by Section 50079.5 of the Health and Safety Code, shall be paid at least the general prevailing rate of per diem wages for the type of work and geographic area, as determined by the Director of Industrial Relations pursuant to Sections 1773 and 1773.9 of the Labor Code, except that apprentices registered in programs approved by the Chief of the Division of Apprenticeship Standards may be paid at least the applicable apprentice prevailing rate, regardless of whether the housing development project is a public work.

Applicants for 100% affordable projects should review the labor and wage requirements of their funding sources to determine whether this exemption would impose any additional requirements.

Buildings Over 85 Feet in Height

Buildings over 85 feet in height are typically subject to the high-rise code, and of Type I, II, or IV construction.[37] Many of the contractors who work on taller buildings are union signatories or pay prevailing wage for other reasons. However, not all projects that exceed 85 feet in height will want to use a CEQA exemption that imposes labor and wage requirements. Per PRC § 21080.66(d)(2):

> (2) Notwithstanding any other law, the labor standards of paragraph (8) of subdivision (a) of Section 65913.4 of the Government Code shall apply to buildings over 85 feet in height above grade in any housing development project exempt from this division pursuant to this section.

---

[37] Type V, Type III, Type IV-C, and Type IV-HT (including podium buildings) cannot exceed 85 feet above grade plane for R-2 occupancies, per CBC Table 504.3.

The labor standards of Gov. Code § 65913.4(a)(8) are those that are applicable to projects requesting streamlined ministerial approval processing (SMAP, formerly known as SB 423 or SB 35). Because the project is over 85 feet, those labor standards include prevailing wage and "skilled and trained workforce" provisions.

The phrase "85 feet in height above grade" is not defined in the CEQA statute. Hopefully, when the CEQA Guidelines are updated in 2026 for the PRC § 21080.66 exemption, this phrase will be interpreted consistent with building height as defined in the California Building Code:

> HEIGHT, BUILDING. The vertical distance from grade plane to the average height of the highest roof surface.

Per CBC 504.3, various non-habitable rooftop structures do not count as building height when they extend above the average height of the roof surface. If the updated CEQA Guidelines follow the CBC in defining building height, the PRC § 21080.66 exemption **should not trigger prevailing wage for typical wood-frame multifamily buildings.**[38] A developer considering a taller building should budget for prevailing wage or use a different exemption.

Certain Projects in San Francisco of 50 Units or More

This exemption includes a complex provision under PRC § 21080.66(d)(3) that applies only to project with 50 units or more that are located in the City and County of San Francisco. The provision applies to specific construction crafts as determined by the Department of Industrial Relations and published on its website.[39] San Francisco is a heavily unionized construction market, and larger projects there are usually union jobs. Developers of 50+ unit projects in San Francisco should consult an attorney before using this exemption.

For Most Projects, Applicants Should Request the PRC § 21088.66 CEQA Exemption

The PRC § 21088.66 exemption will become the default CEQA exemption, preferred by jurisdictions for infill housing projects because it is so simple to apply. In fact, PRC § 21080.66(b)(1)(A)(i) requires the jurisdiction to ***automatically*** send the tribal notification for the PRC § 21088.66 exemption within 14 days after receiving the SB 330 preliminary application, even if the applicant did not explicitly request the PRC § 21088.66 exemption. Likewise, developers will usually prefer this exemption for its simplicity, low cost, and lower litigation risk. For most projects, the Author recommends that applicants specifically request that the jurisdiction apply the PRC § 21088.66 exemption.

Request the PRC § 21080.66 Exemption Even if the Project Does Not Qualify

As explained under But For a Single Condition — New with SB 131, if a project **almost** qualifies for a CEQA exemption, but a **single condition** of that exemption is not met, the initial study and subsequent CEQA analysis will only need to address that one condition. Even if the project does not fully qualify for this exemption, it has such simple criteria that the project will probably miss qualifying due to a single condition, which will narrow the scope of further CEQA review to only that single matter.

For Some Projects, Applicants Should "Opt Out" of the PRC § 21088.66 CEQA Exemption

As explained under Caution: PRC § 21080.66, in Limited Circumstances, Requires Prevailing Wage, 100% affordable projects, projects over 85 feet in height, and certain projects in San Francisco with 50 or more units are subject to labor and wage requirements if they use the PRC § 21088.66 exemption. In addition, the PRC § 21080.66 Exemption Imposes Tribal-Related Conditions of Approval that may add cost during construction of the project. Applicants with projects that would be subject to prevailing wage if they use this exemption, or who wish to avoid

---

[38] Type I, Type IV-A and Type IV-B may exceed 85 feet for R-2 occupancies, and some projects have used "alternative means and methods approvals" to exceed 85 feet with a wood-frame structure.

[39] The Department of Industrial Relations has published this information: https://www.dir.ca.gov/division/List-of-Eligible-Crafts-Classifications-That-Meet-Requirements-of-Assembly-Bill-130.htm.

the tribal-related conditions of approval, may want to "opt out" of this exemption. There is no official "opt out" process; simply ask the jurisdiction **not** to apply this exemption, and request a different exemption or proceed with an Initial Study.

Class 32 "Infill" Categorical Exemption

The Class 32 categorical exemption remains a viable alternative to the new PRC § 21080.66 Statutory Exemption. It has been used for decades and applies not only to housing projects, but all types of infill development projects located within **incorporated city limits**. The Class 32 categorical exemption cannot be used on sites over 5 acres, but there is no limit on the number of units or on mixed uses in the housing project.

However, there are **exceptions** to categorical exemptions in the Guidelines § 15300.2, including a vaguely worded exception that has been a pretext for many CEQA lawsuits (emphasis added):

> (c) Significant Effect. A categorical exemption shall not be used for an activity where there is a reasonable possibility that the activity will have a significant effect on the environment due to **unusual circumstances**.

The CEQA Statutes and Guidelines contain no definition of "unusual circumstances." Project opponents will cite all sorts of allegedly "unusual circumstances" in a CEQA lawsuit. Regardless of the merits of the lawsuit, defending a CEQA exemption can delay or even derail a project.

The PRC § 21088.66 statutory exemption will usually be preferred for its lower CEQA litigation risk when compared to the Class 32 categorical exemption, but the prevailing wage and tribal requirements of the PRC § 21088.66 exemption may make the Class 32 exemption a better option for some projects.

PRC § 21159.25 Statutory Exemption (Class 32 for Unincorporated County Areas)

The PRC § 21159.25 statutory exemption is almost identical to the Class 32 categorical exemption, but it works on sites that are in a Census-designated Urban Area within **unincorporated county** areas. The PRC § 21159.25 statutory exemption has the same "unusual circumstances" language, and essentially the same qualifying requirements and limitations as the Class 32 "Infill" Categorical Exemption.

Projects that are not within an incorporated city and that want to avoid the prevailing wage or tribal requirements of the PRC § 21080.66 Statutory Exemption will likely use this exemption.

Exemptions and Streamlining for Special Situations

Many exemptions (e.g., the Class 3 categorical exemption, and the statutory exemptions at PRC § 21155.4, PRC § 21159.22, PRC § 21159.23, PRC § 21159.24, and Government Code § 65457) apply in limited situations: projects near a major transit stop, projects in a specific plan area, 100% affordable projects, or projects with a limited number of units. This book will not cover these narrowly applicable exemptions, but they sometimes apply on sites, or in situations, that do not allow the PRC § 21080.66, Class 32, or PRC § 21159.25 exemptions.

The Governor's Office of Land Use and Climate Innovation ("LCI," previously called the Office of Planning and Research) published two advisory documents in 2020, one covering CEQA Review of Housing Projects generally, and another specific to CEQA Review of Affordable, Transitional, and Supportive Housing Projects. They are somewhat out of date, but they provide a good overview of the range of potential exemptions and streamlining provisions. CEQA Review of Housing Projects has a useful comparison chart as its Appendix A that can help applicants quickly search for an exemption or streamlining provision that applies to their specific project. Applicants should also use the LCI Site Check tool to **quickly screen the project site** for potential CEQA exemptions and streamlining provisions.

Many special exemptions and streamlining provisions rely on a prior EIR covering the project site, with the project-specific environmental review "tiering" off the earlier EIR. Per PRC § 21068.5:

> 21068.5. "Tiering" or "tier" means the coverage of general matters and environmental effects in an environmental impact report prepared for a policy, plan, program or ordinance followed by narrower or site-specific environmental impact reports which incorporate by reference the discussion in any prior environmental impact report and which concentrate on the environmental effects which (a) are capable of being mitigated, or (b) were not analyzed as significant effects on the environment in the prior environmental impact report.

Even when a full exemption is not available, Article 12 of the CEQA Guidelines explains many special situations where streamlining provisions apply. For example, Guidelines § 15183.63 streamlines review of qualifying infill projects. These provisions can be quite complex, but jurisdictions often have checklists created as part of their housing element EIR to facilitate the use of tiering and streamlining, and to simplify an Initial Study.

Qualifying for Multiple CEQA Exemptions

A project may meet the requirements for several different CEQA exemptions, but a jurisdiction will typically apply only one of the available exemptions. In most cases the new PRC § 21080.66 Statutory Exemption is the best exemption because it has few limitations, it is applicable to most sites, and it is relatively simple to determine whether a project qualifies for the exemption. However, there may be cases where the project site does not qualify for the PRC § 21080.66 exemption but qualifies for a different exemption. For example, the PRC § 21080.66 exemption cannot be used in certain parts of the Coastal Zone; as other options, the PRC § 21159.23 statutory exemption can be used in all areas of the Coastal Zone but only applies to 100% affordable housing projects with 100 units or less, and the Class 32 "Infill" Categorical Exemption applies in all areas of incorporated cities but does not apply in unincorporated county areas. The applicant should guide the jurisdiction to apply the exemption that best suits the needs of the project.

In some cases, however, a developer may want the jurisdiction to apply **more than one** CEQA exemption. One potential reason was given under Caution: PRC § 21080.66, in Limited Circumstances, Requires Prevailing Wage. Another potential strategy is discussed under But For a Single Condition — New with SB 131. These strategies are complex. If the applicant wants the local jurisdiction to review a project for exemption under multiple CEQA provisions, the Author recommends engaging a CEQA attorney or qualified consultant to prepare a CEQA memo and guide the jurisdiction in applying each of the CEQA exemptions.

Preapplication CEQA Consultation

Applicants have the option to request a CEQA consultation prior to submitting the full development permit application. CEQA Guidelines § 15060.5(a) requires the jurisdiction, upon request, to provide a consultation regarding what CEQA requirements and determinations may apply to a project:

> (a) For a potential project involving the issuance of a lease, permit, license, certificate, or other entitlement for use by one or more public agencies, the lead agency shall, upon the request of a potential applicant and prior to the filing of a formal application, **provide for consultation** with the potential applicant to consider the range of actions, potential alternatives, mitigation measures, and any potential significant effects on the environment of the potential project.

Because of the simplicity of the new PRC § 21080.66 Statutory Exemption, jurisdictions should expeditiously complete the review for this exemption. However, the applicant should review the project site against the requirements for the exemption and if any requirement is not obviously met, they should request the CEQA preapplication consultation and work with the jurisdiction to determine what reports or other research are needed.

When using a more complex exemption, or Qualifying for Multiple CEQA Exemptions, the Author recommends applicants engage a CEQA attorney or a qualified CEQA consultant, then request a preapplication consultation to ensure both the jurisdiction and the applicant have the information necessary to determine the project exempt.

CEQA Review During the Review for Completeness

The Author recommends providing clear and complete documentation that the project qualifies for an exemption with the 1st Submittal of the full development permit application. When a development permit application is received, the jurisdiction's first step is to review the submitted materials against a list of required items to determine that the application is complete. During that review, the jurisdiction is advised to be alert for potential environmental issues by the Guidelines § 15060(a):

> (a) A lead agency is allowed 30 days to review for completeness applications for permits or other entitlements for use. **While conducting this review for completeness, the agency should be alert for environmental issues** that might require preparation of an EIR or that may require additional explanation by the applicant. Accepting an application as complete does not limit the authority of the lead agency to require the applicant to submit additional information needed for environmental evaluation of the project. Requiring such additional information after the application is complete does not change the status of the application.

The jurisdiction is not required to start the formal review for exemption until after the jurisdiction accepts the application as complete, but the applicant should provide complete documentation for the requested CEQA exemption as early as practicable to prevent delays.

"Accepted as Complete" — The Trigger for the Review for Exemption from CEQA

The full development permit application is "determined to be complete" at the end of the process described in Chapter 8: Completeness Review. The full application will be "deemed complete" if the jurisdiction fails to meet the deadline prescribed by Gov. Code § 65943 for each round of completeness review.

A different term, "accepted as complete," is used in CEQA. Per PRC § 21080.2:

> 21080.2. In the case of a project described in subdivision (c) of Section 21065 [i.e., when a jurisdiction will issue a development permit to a nongovernmental entity], the determination required by Section 21080.1 shall be made within 30 days from the date on which an application for a project has been received and **accepted as complete** by the lead agency. This period may be extended 15 days upon the consent of the lead agency and the project applicant.

Notwithstanding the discussion under What Triggers the Start of the Compliance Review Period?, the Author does ***not*** think that the CEQA review for exemption starts on the date the complete application was submitted. The 30- or 45-day Time Period for the Review for Exemption starts on the date the full development permit application was "accepted as complete," meaning the date that the jurisdiction affirmatively determines the application to be complete (i.e., the date on the letter of completeness), or if the jurisdiction fails to meet the 30-day deadline under Gov. Code § 65943 the date the full development permit application is deemed complete by operation of state law.

30- or 45-day Time Period for the Review for Exemption

After the jurisdiction accepts the full development permit application as complete, the Guidelines § 15601 require the jurisdiction to determine whether the project is exempt from CEQA:

> (a) Once a lead agency has determined that an activity is a project subject to CEQA, a lead agency shall determine whether the project is exempt from CEQA.
>
> (b) A project is exempt from CEQA if:

(1) The project is exempt by statute (see, e.g. Article 18, commencing with Section 15260).

(2) The project is exempt pursuant to a categorical exemption (see Article 19, commencing with Section 15300) and the application of that categorical exemption is not barred by one of the exceptions set forth in Section 15300.2.

…

The determination of whether the project is or is not exempt is explained under Result of the Review for Exemption. The determination should be made within 30 days from the date the full development permit application is "Accepted as Complete" — The Trigger for the Review for Exemption from CEQA, with the option to mutually extend the deadline by 15 days. Per PRC § 21080.2:

> 21080.2. In the case of a project described in subdivision (c) of Section 21065 [i.e., when a jurisdiction will issue a development permit to a nongovernmental entity], **the determination required by Section 21080.1 shall be made within 30 days** from the date on which an application for a project has been received and accepted as complete by the lead agency. This period **may be extended 15 days** upon the consent of the lead agency and the project applicant.

There is little reason for applicants not to grant the 15-day extension. A jurisdiction that requests the extension is following the law, even though there are no automatic consequences if the jurisdiction misses the deadline. A request for an extension shows that the jurisdiction is acting in good faith, and the applicant should cooperate and support the jurisdiction's diligent CEQA review.

If the project qualifies for the new PRC § 21080.66 Statutory Exemption — New with AB 130, and/or the applicant and jurisdiction had a Preapplication CEQA Consultation, the review for exemption could easily be finished by the time the application is determined to be complete, and the determination of exemption could be included in the completeness letter.

Deadline to Determine if the Project is Exempt is Not Self-Enforcing

When the full development permit application is accepted as complete, it triggers the start of the 30- or 45-day Time Period for the Review for Exemption, but if the jurisdiction misses the deadline at the end of the review for exemption, **nothing happens**. The deadline for the review for exemption is **not** self-enforcing; it does not result in deemed exemption. At the end of the time period, the jurisdiction is required to either determine that the project is exempt from CEQA or require an Initial Study to further investigate the potential for the project to have a significant environmental impact. If the jurisdiction fails to make the determination that the project is exempt within 30 or 45 days, the applicant can complain, but the jurisdiction could simply decide to require an Initial Study.

Subject to the conditions at Gov. Code § 65589.5.1, failure to make the determination of exemption is one of the things that meets the definition of "disapprove the housing development project" and is therefore a violation of the Housing Accountability Act. (Gov. Code § 65589.5(h)(6)(I)(i).) The applicant *could* bring an action in court pursuant to Gov. Code § 65589.5(k), but unless the jurisdiction is intentionally obstructing the project, bringing a court action would probably just delay the CEQA determination.

If more information is needed to complete the CEQA review, the jurisdiction can ask for additional items **after** determining that the application is complete, even if the items were not listed on the LORI. Per Gov. Code § 65944:

> 65944. (a) After a public agency accepts an application as complete, the agency shall not subsequently request of an applicant any new or additional information which was not specified in the list prepared pursuant to Section 65940. The agency may, in the course of processing the application, request the applicant to clarify, amplify, correct, or otherwise supplement the information required for the application.
>
> …

> (c) This section shall not be construed as limiting the ability of a public agency to request and obtain information which may be needed in order to comply with the provisions of Division 13 (commencing with Section 21000) of the Public Resources Code.

There may not be enough time for the applicant to obtain the additional specialized CEQA reports, and for the jurisdiction to review them, within the 30- or 45-day Time Period for the Review for Exemption. The applicant really has little option but to provide the requested information and give the jurisdiction more time to review it. Again, the Author recommends early and cooperative engagement with the jurisdiction to work through the CEQA review process.

Result of the Review for Exemption

The 30- or 45-day Time Period for the Review for Exemption is prescribed by PRC § 21080.2, and results in the "determination required by Section 21080.1," which refers to PRC § 21080.1(a):

> 21080.1. (a) The lead agency shall be responsible for determining whether the project is exempt from this division and whether an environmental impact report, a negative declaration, or a mitigated negative declaration shall be required for any project that is subject to this division. That determination shall be final and conclusive on all persons, including responsible agencies, unless challenged as provided in Section 21167.

In other words, the review for exemption results in a determination that either:

A. The project is exempt from CEQA; or

B. The project will require an environmental impact report, a negative declaration, or a mitigated negative declaration.

The CEQA Guidelines implement PRC § 21080.1(a), and provide that the result of the review for exemption is either a preliminary determination that the project is exempt from CEQA (Guidelines § 15601, titled "Review for Exemption") or that an Initial Study should be prepared (Guidelines § 15603, titled "Initial Study") to determine which of the Environmental Determinations Other Than Exemptions is appropriate and necessary for the project.

The language of PRC § 21080.1(a) and the Guidelines § 15601 and § 15603 suggests that the review for exemption always concludes with a yes/no determination of whether the project is exempt from CEQA. However, in the real world, there is sometimes a period of further investigation — after the 30- or 45-day Time Period for the Review for Exemption has concluded but before commencing an Initial Study — during which additional studies and reviews are conducted to resolve any outstanding questions or uncertainties about whether the project is exempt. See Result of the Initial Study for more information.

If the Project is Exempt

If the project **is exempt** from CEQA, the determination made during staff review of the project is "preliminary" in the sense that it is not effective until the project has been **approved**. The jurisdiction will not "file" the determination of CEQA exemption until the development permit application itself is approved (see Filing a Notice of Exemption). Per the Guidelines § 15061(d):

> (d) After determining that a project is exempt, the agency may prepare a notice of exemption as provided in Section 15062. Although the notice may be kept with the project application at this time, the **notice shall not be filed** with the Office of Planning and Research or the county clerk **until the project has been approved**.

And, the determination is "preliminary" in the sense that a determination made by a lesser decisionmaker can be appealed, per Guidelines § 15061(e):

> (e) When a non-elected official or decisionmaking body of a local lead agency decides that a project is exempt from CEQA, and the public agency approves or determines to carry out the project, **the decision that the project is exempt may be appealed** to the local lead agency's elected decisionmaking body, if one exists. A local lead agency may establish procedures governing such appeals.

However, despite being technically "preliminary," the date of the preliminary determination that a project is exempt from CEQA is extremely important because it triggers the 60-Day Deadline for Approval or Disapproval of Exempt Projects that Do Not Use PRC § 21080.66. It may (depending on interpretation of the law) also figure into the Unclear Deadline for Approval or Disapproval of Projects that are Exempt Pursuant to PRC § 21080.66.

The "Preliminary" Determination that the Project is Exempt Triggers the Deadline for Approval/Disapproval

The fact that the **preliminary** determination of exemption triggers the 60-Day Deadline for Approval or Disapproval of Exempt Projects that Do Not Use PRC § 21080.66 is not disputed by knowledgeable practitioners. It would make no sense to base the deadline for approval or disapproval of the project on the **final** determination of exemption, since the final determination of exemption ***is*** the date of final approval. For those who need more convincing, the following law citations lead to this fact. Per PRC § 21080.1(a):

> 21080.1. (a) **The lead agency shall be responsible for determining whether the project is exempt** from this division and whether an environmental impact report, a negative declaration, or a mitigated negative declaration shall be required for any project that is subject to this division. **That determination shall be final and conclusive on all persons**, including responsible agencies, unless challenged as provided in Section 21167.

Per PRC § 21080.2:

> 21080.2. In the case of a project described in subdivision (c) of Section 21065, **the determination** required by Section 21080.1 **shall be made within 30 days from the date on which an application for a project has been received and accepted as complete by the lead agency**. This period may be extended 15 days upon the consent of the lead agency and the project applicant.

Per PRC § 21065(c):

> 21065. "Project" means an activity which may cause either a direct physical change in the environment, or a reasonably foreseeable indirect physical change in the environment, and which is any of the following:
>
> ...
>
> (c) **An activity that involves the issuance to a person** of a lease, **permit**, license, certificate, **or other entitlement for use** by one or more public agencies.

And per Gov. Code § 65950(a)(5):

> 65950. (a) A public agency that is **the lead agency for a development project shall approve or disapprove the project** within whichever of the following periods is applicable:
>
> ...
>
> (5) **Sixty days from the determination by the lead agency that the project is exempt** from the California Environmental Quality Act (Division 13 (commencing with Section 21000) of the Public Resources Code), if the project is exempt from that act.

In other words, for projects that are developed by private entities (PRC § 21065(c): "issuance to a **person**"), "The lead agency shall be responsible for determining whether the project is exempt" (PRC § 21080.1) and that determination "shall be made within 30 days from the date on which an application for a project has been received and accepted as complete by the lead agency" (PRC § 21080.2). And "Sixty days from the determination by the lead agency that the project is exempt" (Gov. Code § 65950(a)(5)) "the lead agency for a development project shall approve or disapprove the project" (Gov. Code § 65950(a)).

Final Acknowledgement of the CEQA Exemption

After the jurisdiction's staff makes the preliminary determination that the project is exempt, that determination is "acknowledged" as part of the resolution the jurisdiction makes to approve the project. Because approvals by lesser decisionmakers can be appealed, the jurisdiction will often **wait** before Filing a Notice of Exemption, until the appeal period expires, or until unappealable final approval of the project by the city council or county board of supervisors.

It is possible that the preliminary determination that the project is exempt will be challenged during a hearing or in and appeal of an approval. The jurisdiction's local code prescribes the decisionmakers and decisionmaking bodies that are authorized to approve the project and make the CEQA determination (see Decisionmakers and Decisionmaking Bodies). A determination by a lesser decisionmaker that a project is exempt from CEQA can be appealed to the city council or county board of supervisors. Per the Guidelines § 15061(e):

> (e) When a non-elected official or decisionmaking body of a local lead agency decides that a project is exempt from CEQA, and the public agency approves or determines to carry out the project, **the decision that the project is exempt may be appealed** to the local lead agency's **elected** decisionmaking body, if one exists. A local lead agency may establish procedures governing such appeals.

Each jurisdiction will have its own appeals process. Applicants are advised to consult a CEQA attorney or qualified CEQA consultant if the staff makes a preliminary determination that the project is exempt from CEQA and that determination is either not acknowledged (i.e., approved) at a hearing, or is appealed by a project opponent.

If the Project is Not Exempt

If the project is **not** exempt, then CEQA review proceeds to an Initial Study. Per the Guidelines § 15063(a):

> (a) Following preliminary review, the lead agency shall conduct an initial study determine if the project may have a significant effect on the environment. If the lead agency can determine that an EIR will clearly be required for the project, an initial study is not required but may still be desirable.

The Initial Study will determine what type of CEQA determination will be required (EIR, MND, ND, or potentially a determination that the project really did qualify for an exemption). For housing projects, a full environmental impact report is rarely needed. Even projects that are not exempt from CEQA will usually be subject to various streamlining provisions, including the "near miss" provision explained in the next section.

But For a Single Condition — New with SB 131

Among many other CEQA reforms in 2025, SB 131 (2025) added a new provision that will significantly reduce the scope and cost of CEQA review for housing projects "that meet all but one eligibility criteria for specified CEQA exemptions ("near-miss")."[40] A housing development project that would have qualified for a CEQA exemption **but for a single condition** can limit CEQA review to that single issue. SB 131 added subdivision (b) to PRC § 21080.1:

> (b) (1) If a proposed housing development project **would otherwise be exempt** from this division pursuant to a statutory exemption, or categorical exemption pursuant to Class 1 to 5, inclusive, 12, 15, 20, 27, 30, or 32 that is adopted before January 1, 2026, **but for a single condition** detailed in the statutory exemption or in Section 15300.2, 15301, 15302, 15303, 15304, 15305, 15312, 15315, 15320, 15322, 15327, 15330, or 15332 of Title 14 of the California Code of

[40] SB 131 (2025) *06/30/25- Senate Floor Analyses* https://leginfo.legislature.ca.gov/faces/billAnalysisClient.xhtml?bill_id=202520260SB131.

> Regulations, as applicable, the application of this division to the approval of the proposed housing development project shall be limited to effects upon the environment that are caused solely by that single condition.

This new provision applies to all statutory exemptions, and to categorical exemptions of Classes 1 through 5, 12, 15, 20, 27, 30, and 32. The words "that is adopted before January 1, 2026" refer to the adoption (by the Secretary of the Natural Resources Agency) of CEQA Guidelines that create categorical exemptions pursuant to PRC § 21084. That is, PRC § 21080.1(b) applies to all of the listed Classes of categorical exemptions **as they exist on January 1, 2026**, and it continues to apply to them after January 1, 2026.

PRC § 21080.1(b) does **not** mean that a near-miss project is exempt. It means that when the Result of the Review for Exemption is that the project is **not** exempt because a **single** condition disqualifies the project from using the exemption, then the subsequent CEQA review process is limited to the environmental effects "caused solely by that single condition." PRC § 21080.1(b) continues:

> (2) An initial study or environmental impact report prepared for a housing development project subject to this subdivision is only required to examine those effects that the lead agency determines, based upon substantial evidence in the record, are **caused solely by the single condition that makes the proposed housing development project ineligible** for the statutory exemption or categorical exemption.
>
> (3) An environmental impact report for a housing development project subject to this subdivision is not required to include any discussion of alternatives to the housing development project or the growth-inducing impacts of the housing development project.

Near-miss projects will proceed to an Initial Study **focusing *only* on the sole disqualifying condition.**

Definitions specific to this provision are found at PRC § 21080.1(b)(5):

> (5) For purposes of this subdivision, the following definitions apply:
>
> > (A) "Condition" means a physical or regulatory feature of the project or its setting or an effect upon the environment caused by the project.
> >
> > (B) "Housing development project" has the same meaning as defined in Section 65589.5 of the Government Code.

The above definition of a "condition" that disqualifies a project from an exemption is very broad, covering "physical," "regulatory," "setting," and "effect upon the environment" conditions. New CEQA Guidelines in 2026 will need to address how the near-miss rule will be implemented. A focused review of some disqualifying conditions could be quite simple to implement. Other disqualifying conditions could require significant time and cost for studies and reports.

The definition of "housing development project" is the same as in the Housing Accountability Act, but certain types of housing development projects are **not eligible** for the "near-miss" provision, per PRC § 21080.1(b)(4):

> (4) This subdivision does not apply to any of the following housing development projects:
>
> > (A) A proposed housing development project that is not similar in kind to the projects listed in the statutory or categorical exemption.
> >
> > (B) A proposed housing development project that is ineligible for the statutory exemption or categorical exemption due to two or more conditions.
> >
> > (C) A proposed housing development project that includes a distribution center or oil and gas infrastructure.
> >
> > (D) (i) A proposed housing development project located on natural and protected lands, as defined pursuant to Section 21067.5.

(ii) The definition of "natural and protected lands" described in clause (i) does not include the lands described in subdivision (o) of Section 21067.5.

(E) The project site or the parcel size exceeds four acres, and either of the following occurred:

(i) The project is a builder's remedy project, as defined in paragraph (11) of subdivision (h) of Section 65589.5 of the Government Code.

(ii) The project applicant applied pursuant to paragraph (5) of subdivision (d) of Section 65589.5 of the Government Code as it read before January 1, 2025.

These exceptions add complexity when applying the "near-miss" rule. For example, per PRC § 21080.66(a)(6), a project using this new statutory exemption must satisfy the conditions specified at Gov. Code § 65913.4(a)(6), including that it "is not located on a site that is ... (C) Wetlands, as defined in the United States Fish and Wildlife Service Manual, Part 660 FW 2 (June 21, 1993)." If the sole disqualifying condition is that the site is wetlands, then one might think the "near-miss" rule applies, but PRC § 21080.1(b)(4)(D) is an exception that excludes "(i) A proposed housing development project located on natural and protected lands, as defined pursuant to Section 21067.5." PRC § 21067.5(l) includes in the definition of "natural and protected lands," sites that are located "(l) On, or within a 300-foot radius of, a wetland, as defined in the United States Fish and Wildlife Service Manual, Part 660 FW 2 (June 21, 1993)." Therefore, a site that contains wetlands as defined would not qualify for the new PRC § 21080.66 exemption, and the "near-miss" rule does not apply to housing development projects that contain wetlands by the same definition. Unless some other exemption or streamlining provision applied, the Initial Study would have to consider the full range of potential environmental impacts, not just those related to the wetland.

Initial Study

If the project is not determined to be exempt, then further CEQA review will be required. If it is clear that an environmental impact report (EIR) is required then the jurisdiction can proceed directly to preparing the EIR, but Guidelines § 15063(a) encourages the jurisdiction to conduct an initial study even when an EIR will be prepared. Therefore, when a project is not exempt, an initial study is the next step in the CEQA review process.

Ostensibly, the initial study is prepared after the development permit application has been determined to be complete and the jurisdiction has determined that the project is not exempt from CEQA. In the real world, if the applicant *knows* that the project does not qualify for a CEQA exemption, they can (and likely should) start working on the documentation necessary for the initial study even before making the 1st Submittal of the full development permit application. The potential need for, and requirements of, an initial study should be discussed during a Preapplication CEQA Consultation. Of course, there will be situations where an applicant *thinks* that a project is exempt from CEQA, but a disqualifying condition is uncovered in the course of reviewing the development permit application, leading to an unexpected initial study.

If it is determined that an initial study is required, the jurisdiction will begin consulting with other agencies in accordance with the Guidelines § 15063(g):

> (g) Consultation. As soon as a lead agency has determined that an initial study will be required for the project, the lead agency shall consult informally with all responsible agencies and all trustee agencies responsible for resources affected by the project to obtain the recommendations of those agencies as to whether an EIR or a negative declaration should be prepared. During or immediately after preparation of an initial study for a private project, the lead agency may consult with the applicant to determine if the applicant is willing to modify the project to reduce or avoid the significant effects identified in the initial study.

This is another reason for engaging in Preapplication CEQA Consultation: it gives the jurisdiction time to consult with other agencies, without delaying the project.

Purposes of an Initial Study

The Guidelines § 15063(c) describes the reasons for conducting an initial study, which are primarily to avoid *unnecessarily* preparing an EIR, and if preparation of an EIR cannot be avoided, *focusing the scope* of the EIR:

> (c) Purposes. The purposes of an initial study are to:
>
> (1) Provide the lead agency with information to use as the basis for deciding whether to prepare an EIR or negative declaration;
>
> (2) Enable an applicant or lead agency to modify a project, mitigating adverse impacts before an EIR is prepared, thereby enabling the project to qualify for a negative declaration;
>
> (3) Assist the preparation of an EIR, if one is required, by:
>
> (A) Focusing the EIR on the effects determined to be significant,
>
> (B) Identifying the effects determined not to be significant,
>
> (C) Explaining the reasons for determining that potentially significant effects would not be significant, and
>
> (D) Identifying whether a program EIR, tiering, or another appropriate process can be used for analysis of the project's environmental effects.
>
> (4) Facilitate environmental assessment early in the design of a project;
>
> (5) Provide documentation of the factual basis for the finding in a negative declaration that a project will not have a significant effect on the environment;
>
> (6) Eliminate unnecessary EIRs;
>
> (7) Determine whether a previously prepared EIR could be used with the project.

Paragraph (7) notes that one purpose of the initial study is to "Determine whether a previously prepared EIR could be used with the project." In most cases, the location of a housing development project will have already been subject to an EIR covering a specific plan area, the jurisdiction's housing element, or the jurisdiction's general plan. There are many types of EIRs as outlined in Article 11 of the CEQA Guidelines. A full "Project EIR" is rarely required for housing projects, which can rely on a previously adopted EIR covering the project site to limit the scope of CEQA review. Prior EIRs are often the basis for Exemptions and Streamlining for Special Situations, and EIRs often include initial study templates or forms to facilitate streamlining.

Preparation of the Initial Study

The CEQA Guidelines § 15063(a) introduces the initial study and the requirements for its preparation:

> (a) Following preliminary review, the lead agency shall conduct an initial study determine if the project may have a significant effect on the environment. If the lead agency can determine that an EIR will clearly be required for the project, an initial study is not required but may still be desirable.
>
> (1) All phases of project planning, implementation, and operation must be considered in the initial study of the project.
>
> (2) To meet the requirements of this section, the lead agency may use an environmental assessment or a similar analysis prepared pursuant to the National Environmental Policy Act.
>
> (3) An initial study may rely upon expert opinion supported by facts, technical studies or other substantial evidence to document its findings. However, an initial study is neither intended nor required to include the level of detail included in an EIR.

> > (4) The lead agency may use any of the arrangements or combination of arrangements described in Section 15084(d) to prepare an initial study. The initial study sent out for public review must reflect the independent judgment of the Lead Agency.

As stated in paragraph (4), the initial study can be prepared using any of the same "arrangements" as can be used for preparation of a draft EIR, per the Guidelines § 15084(d):

> (d) The lead agency may choose one of the following arrangements or a combination of them for preparing a draft EIR [or, per Guidelines § 15063(a)(4), an initial study].
>
> > (1) Preparing the draft EIR [or initial study] directly with its own staff.
> >
> > (2) Contracting with another entity, public or private, to prepare the draft EIR [or initial study].
> >
> > (3) Accepting a draft [EIR or initial study] prepared by the applicant, a consultant retained by the applicant, or any other person.
> >
> > (4) Executing a third party contract or memorandum of understanding with the applicant to govern the preparation of a draft EIR [or initial study] by an independent contractor.
> >
> > (5) Using a previously prepared EIR.

By engaging the jurisdiction in a Preapplication CEQA Consultation, the applicant can begin arrangements for the preparation of the initial study as early as possible. When using a previously prepared EIR, the initial study will "tier" off that EIR (see Exemptions and Streamlining for Special Situations).

In cases where the **jurisdiction** will prepare the initial study, but the project is being developed by a private entity, the developer will need to provide information to the jurisdiction, as provided in Guidelines § 15084(e):

> (e) Submission of Data. If the project is to be carried out by a private person or private organization, the lead agency may require such person or organization to submit data and information which will enable the lead agency to prepare the initial study. Any person may submit any information in any form to assist a lead agency in preparing an initial study.

In cases where the **applicant** will prepare the initial study, the CEQA Guidelines **do** allow for an applicant to prepare it themselves, but it is typically prepared by a CEQA consultant that the jurisdiction has approved in advance.

Contents and Format of the Initial Study

If the housing development project is eligible for the "near-miss" provision under PRC § 21080.1(b), the initial study will focus solely on the single condition that disqualified the project from being exempt from CEQA. If the project is ineligible for the "near-miss" provision due to the reasons listed at PRC § 21080.1(b)(4), the range of potential environmental impacts to be studied will be limited by the applicable CEQA streamlining provisions. The initial study will determine whether those impacts are significant, and how they might be mitigated.

The required contents of the initial study are found at Guidelines § 15063(d):

> (d) Contents. An initial study shall contain in brief form:
>
> > (1) A description of the project including the location of the project;
> >
> > (2) An identification of the environmental setting;
> >
> > (3) An identification of environmental effects by use of a checklist, matrix, or other method, provided that entries on a checklist or other form are briefly explained to indicate that there is some evidence to support the entries. The brief explanation may be either through a narrative or a reference to another information source such as an

attached map, photographs, or an earlier EIR or negative declaration. A reference to another document should include, where appropriate, a citation to the page or pages where the information is found.

(4) A discussion of ways to mitigate the significant effects identified, if any;

(5) An examination of whether the project would be consistent with existing zoning, plans, and other applicable land use controls;

(6) The name of the person or persons who prepared or participated in the initial study.

As explained under Exemptions and Streamlining for Special Situations, if an initial study is required for a housing project, it will likely be based on a prior EIR for the housing element, the general plan, or a specific plan. Jurisdictions often have a checklist or template initial study form that is adopted as part of the prior EIR, which greatly simplifies the preparation of the initial study. Where the jurisdiction does not have their own checklist or template, Appendices G and H of the CEQA Guidelines provide sample forms that constitute the format for an initial study, per Guidelines § 15063(f):

> (f) Format. Sample forms for an applicant's project description and a review form for use by the lead agency are contained in Appendices G and H. When used together, these forms would meet the requirements for an initial study, provided that the entries on the checklist are briefly explained pursuant to subdivision (d)(3). These forms are only suggested, and public agencies are free to devise their own format for an initial study. A previously prepared EIR may also be used as the initial study for a later project.

Because of various streamlining provisions of the CEQA Statutes and Guidelines, the variety of types of previous EIRs that may apply, and regional programs such as transportation plans that must be referenced, the Author advises applicants to seek the advice of the CEQA consultant that **prepared** the jurisdiction's most recent EIR for the housing element, the general plan, or a specific plan; or a CEQA consultant that has successfully **obtained** streamlined CEQA determinations in the jurisdiction. These consultants will already understand the required content and format of the initial study and will have developed relationships with the jurisdiction's staff.

Result of the Initial Study

It is possible that during or after the preparation of the initial study the jurisdiction will determine that the project actually **is** exempt from CEQA. There are many potential CEQA exemptions, and in the course of further review a different exemption may be found to apply, or the condition that seemed to disqualify the exemption may not actually exist or may not be significant; or the applicant could make a change to the project that resolves the condition that barred the exemption. In such cases, the jurisdiction would simply make the preliminary determination that the project is exempt from CEQA and proceed to approve the project and acknowledge the CEQA exemption.

When the project is not exempt from CEQA, the intent of the initial study is to identify any significant impacts that the project **may** have on the environment and consider ways to mitigate those impacts. The potential results of an initial study are summarized at Guidelines § 15063(b):

> (b) Results.
>
> (1) If the agency determines that there is substantial evidence that any aspect of the project, either individually or cumulatively, may cause a significant effect on the environment, regardless of whether the overall effect of the project is adverse or beneficial, the lead agency shall do one of the following:
>
> (A) Prepare an EIR or
>
> (B) Use a previously prepared EIR which the lead agency determines would adequately analyze the project at hand, or

> (C) Determine, pursuant to a program EIR, tiering, or another appropriate process, which of a project's effects were adequately examined by an earlier EIR or negative declaration. Another appropriate process may include, for example, a master EIR, a master environmental assessment, approval of housing and neighborhood commercial facilities in urban areas, approval of residential projects pursuant to a specific plan as described in section 15182, approval of residential projects consistent with a community plan, general plan or zoning as described in section 15183, or an environmental document prepared under a State certified regulatory program. The lead agency shall then ascertain which effects, if any, should be analyzed in a later EIR or negative declaration.
>
> (2) The lead agency shall prepare a negative declaration if there is no substantial evidence that the project or any of its aspects may cause a significant effect on the environment.

Put simply, the initial study results in a document that narrows down the scope of the CEQA determination that follows. Essentially, the initial study will have one of three potential results:

1. There is **not** substantial evidence that the project may cause a significant environmental impact, in which case a Negative Declaration (ND) is prepared and circulated for public review.
2. There **is** substantial evidence of one or more potential significant environmental impacts, but **mitigation measures** will be implemented to reduce those impacts to a less-than-significant level, in which case a Mitigated Negative Declaration (MND) is prepared and circulated for public review.
3. There **is** substantial evidence of one or more potential significant impacts on the environment that **will *not* be mitigated**, and an Environmental Impact Report (EIR) must adequately examine the impact(s).
    a. Particularly for a housing project, a prior EIR or ND/MND has likely already examined the impact(s), and the initial study will simply rely on the prior environmental document to address the impact.
    b. If the potential impact is significant (after applying any available mitigation) and has not been studied by a prior EIR or ND, the initial study will determine the scope of analysis required for a subsequent EIR.

The purpose of the initial study is **not** to determine whether the project taken as a whole is beneficial, or to weigh the potential environmental impacts against the project's benefits (environmental or otherwise). That analysis is the purpose of the EIR.

Environmental Determinations Other Than Exemptions

At the conclusion of the initial study, the lead agency (again, usually the jurisdiction) will determine what further CEQA process is required, and that determination, duly adopted by the lead agency's decisionmaker, is final unless challenged in court, per PRC § 21080.1(a):

> 21080.1. (a) The lead agency shall be responsible for determining whether the project is exempt from this division and whether an environmental impact report, a negative declaration, or a mitigated negative declaration shall be required for any project that is subject to this division. That determination shall be final and conclusive on all persons, including responsible agencies, unless challenged as provided in Section 21167.

While a detailed discussion of the preparation and processing of environmental determinations other than exemptions is beyond the scope of this book, the applicant should be aware of the general process and how the process extends the timeline to approve a housing development permit application.

Negative Declarations and Mitigated Negative Declarations

With the new "near-miss" rule at PRC § 21080.1(b), it will be even less likely that housing projects will require an EIR, and more likely that the initial study for a housing project will result in an ND or MND, because the scope of review will be limited to the single disqualifying condition. Within the scope of the initial study (as narrowed by the "near-miss" rule and any streamlining provisions that apply to the project) if the analysis does not produce substantial evidence of significant environmental impacts, or if the impacts are less-than-significant when mitigation measures are implemented, then the jurisdiction can make the "negative declaration" that the project would **not** have a significant environmental impact.

Article 6 of the CEQA Guidelines describes the negative declaration process, starting with the decision to prepare the ND or MND, per the Guidelines § 15070:

> 15070. A public agency shall prepare or have prepared a proposed negative declaration or mitigated negative declaration for a project subject to CEQA when:
>
> (a) The initial study shows that there is no substantial evidence, in light of the whole record before the agency, that the project may have a significant effect on the environment, or
>
> (b) The initial study identifies potentially significant effects, but:
>
> (1) Revisions in the project plans or proposals made by or agreed to by the applicant before a proposed mitigated negative declaration and initial study are released for public review would avoid the effects or mitigate the effects to a point where clearly no significant effects would occur, and
>
> (2) There is no substantial evidence, in light of the whole record before the agency, that the project as revised may have a significant effect on the environment.

The contents of the ND or MND are prescribed in the Guidelines § 15071:

> 15071. A negative declaration circulated for public review shall include:
>
> (a) A brief description of the project, including a commonly used name for the project, if any;
>
> (b) The location of the project, preferably shown on a map, and the name of the project proponent;
>
> (c) A proposed finding that the project will not have a significant effect on the environment;
>
> (d) An attached copy of the initial study documenting reasons to support the finding; and
>
> (e) Mitigation measures, if any, included in the project to avoid potentially significant effects.

For a housing project, the "near-miss" rule or other streamlining provisions will limit the scope and contents of the ND or MND. Nevertheless, the public noticing, review, and comment process — which can result in consideration of new evidence, revision, and recirculation of the ND or MND — adds a significant and unpredictable amount of time to the process.

Time Period for Completion and Adoption of the ND or MND

For privately developed projects, there is a time limit of 180 days to adopt the ND or MND, starting from the date the full development permit application is accepted as complete. However, PRC §§ 21100.2(a)(4) and 21151.5(a)(4) allow the jurisdiction's local code to provide for a "reasonable extension" of that deadline, which the Guidelines § 15107 interprets as "not more than 90 days upon consent of the lead agency and the applicant." Just as with the Deadline to Determine if the Project is Exempt is Not Self-Enforcing, this 180- to 270-day time limit is not self-enforcing — nothing happens if the lead agency fails to adopt the ND or MND by the end of the time period.

After preparing the ND or MND, to circulate it for public review, the jurisdiction will file a notice of intent (NOI) to adopt the proposed ND or MND, as outlined in the Guidelines § 15072. Although a shorter review period is possible, the public review period will typically be at least 30 days per the Guidelines § 15105(b). If the ND or MND is substantially revised, the revised version must be recirculated for another round of public review. (Guidelines §

15073.5.) Public comments become part of the record, and the lead agency must consider them when deciding whether to adopt the ND or MND.

The process for consideration and adoption of the ND or MND at Guidelines § 15074 mirrors the development permit approval process, where the local jurisdiction may have lesser decisionmakers review the ND or MND and recommend adoption/rejection to a decisionmaking body, and/or lesser decisionmakers may have the authority to adopt/reject an ND or MND, with their decision subject to appeal. As with the development permit application, the decision of the jurisdiction's legislative body cannot be appealed.

The ND / MND process is complete when the negative declaration is adopted by the lead agency. Failure to adopt an ND / MND for a housing development project meets the definition of "disapprove the housing development project," per Gov. Code § 65589.5(h)(6)(J), if the conditions and restrictions at Gov. Code § 65589.5.2 are met. Therefore, if a jurisdiction improperly fails to adopt an ND / MND the applicant or others with standing can file a lawsuit to enforce the Housing Accountability Act and compel the jurisdiction to adopt the ND / MND.

Project Approval *Concurrent* with the Adoption of an ND or MND

Because the ND / MND adoption process mirrors the development permit approval process, in most cases, the ND / MND is considered at the **same hearing** as the development permit application, and the ND / MND is **adopted concurrently** with the project approval. When the development permit approval occurs at the same hearing as the adoption of the ND / MND, the jurisdiction cannot miss the 60-Day Deadline for Approval or Disapproval of Projects Requiring a Negative Declaration.

Project Approval *After* the ND or MND is Adopted

The Jurisdiction is Usually the "Lead Agency" and the ND / MND is usually adopted concurrently with the jurisdiction's approval of the project. However, the ND / MND **can** be adopted first, with the project approved later, in which case the deadline at Gov. Code § 65950(a)(4) applies:

> 65950. (a) A public agency that is the lead agency for a development project shall **approve or disapprove the project** within whichever of the following periods is applicable:
>
> > …
> >
> > (4) Sixty days from the date of adoption by the lead agency of the negative declaration, if a negative declaration is completed and adopted for the development project.
> >
> > …

When this deadline applies because the ND / MND was adopted **before** the project is approved, there is a 60-Day Deadline for Approval or Disapproval of Projects Requiring a Negative Declaration and missing this deadline will result in Deemed Approval — New with AB 130.

Environmental Impact Reports

In most cases, a prior EIR will have weighed the potential environmental impacts of the project against the need for housing. Even if the project has significant environmental impacts, the jurisdiction **can** approve the project with a Statement of Overriding Considerations, but the impacts must be studied in the EIR, and presented to the public as part of the CEQA review process, prior to approving the project.

The preparation of a new EIR is very rarely required for housing projects. Five common reasons that a new EIR might be prepared are:

1. When a general plan amendment is necessary for the approval of the project.
2. When a new specific plan is proposed.

3. When the project is not located in an urban area.
4. When the project significantly impacts historic or cultural resources, or has other unmitigable impacts.
5. As a means to reduce the risk of a CEQA lawsuit.

When a proposed housing project is not consistent with the general plan designation of the project site, a general plan amendment is often (but not always) required. For a general plan amendment, an EIR of some kind is virtually always required. It is also possible that a zone change will require an EIR, but housing projects that are consistent with the general plan designation seldom require a zone change.

If the developer is proposing a new specific plan (as when developing, for example, a master planned community or a major redevelopment project) the specific-plan EIR will usually "tier" from the general plan EIR. Subsequent projects within the specific plan area will rely on the specific plan EIR and will typically be exempt from CEQA if they are consistent with the specific plan.

Most CEQA exemptions and streamlining provisions apply only within urban areas, and rural areas typically have habitat or other natural features that would be impacted by the project. When a housing project is proposed in a rural area it is far more likely to require an EIR. Such locations may also require a general plan amendment or a new specific plan. In urban settings, the demolition of a historic building is a common reason for preparing an EIR. The initial study and streamlining provisions will focus the EIR on the specific impact or impacts that may be caused by the project.

There are many types of EIRs (see Article 11 of the CEQA Guidelines) and the use of "tiering" (Guidelines § 15152) means that an EIR for a specific project need only study the impacts that were not addressed in a prior EIR. Every EIR is unique, and this book will not attempt to provide recommendations, except that practitioners should always engage an attorney with deep knowledge of the housing laws and how they limit the scope of environmental review, along with CEQA consultants that have expertise in the specific impacts at issue with the project.

Time Period for Completion and Certification of the EIR

For a privately developed project, the lead agency has a time limit to complete and certify an EIR of one year, per the Guidelines § 15108. As with the Time Period for Completion and Adoption of the ND or MND, the time starts from the date the full development permit application was accepted as complete, a reasonable extension of "not more than 90 days upon consent of the lead agency and the applicant" is allowed, and the time limit is not self-enforcing.

Upon deciding that an EIR will be prepared, the lead agency must file a notice of preparation (NOP), as explained in the Guidelines § 15082, which starts the process of consultation with other agencies. EIRs, unlike an ND or MND, are required to be **prepared by the lead agency** itself or under contract directly to the lead agency; the applicant cannot prepare the EIR or directly contract for its preparation. (Guidelines § 15084.)

Upon completing the draft EIR, the lead agency files a Notice of Completion, which starts the public review of the draft EIR (Guidelines § 15087) and further consultation with other agencies (Guidelines § 15086). Comments on the draft EIR are reviewed (Guidelines § 15088) and significant new information that is added to the EIR requires recirculation of a revised EIR (Guidelines § 15088.5).

Before approving the project, the lead agency prepares the final EIR (Guidelines § 15089) and certifies that it is in compliance with CEQA, that the decisionmaking body reviewed and considered its contents before approving the project, and that the final EIR "reflects the lead agency's independent judgement and analysis." If the EIR was certified by a lesser decisionmaker, it can be appealed to the elected body of the lead agency. (Guidelines § 15090.)

The EIR process is complete when the final EIR is certified by the lead agency. As with a negative declaration, failure to certify an environmental impact report for a housing development project meets the definition of "disapprove the housing development project," per Gov. Code § 65589.5(h)(6)(J), but subject to the conditions specified in Gov. Code § 65589.5.2.

Deadline for Approval of a Project that Requires an EIR

The Jurisdiction is Usually the "Lead Agency" and the EIR is sometimes certified concurrently with the jurisdiction's approval of the project. However, it is not unusual for the EIR to be certified first and the project to be approved at a later hearing. If the project is not approved concurrently with the EIR, the deadline to approve or disapprove a **housing** development project after the EIR is certified is shorter than for a non-housing project, per Gov. Code § 65950(a)(1) through (3) and (c):

> 65950. (a) A public agency that is the lead agency for a development project shall **approve or disapprove the project** within whichever of the following periods is applicable:
>
> (1) One hundred eighty days from the date of certification by the lead agency of the environmental impact report, if an environmental impact report is prepared pursuant to Section 21100 or 21151 of the Public Resources Code for the development project.
>
> (2) Ninety days from the date of certification by the lead agency of the environmental impact report, if an environmental impact report is prepared pursuant to Section 21100 or 21151 of the Public Resources Code for a development project defined in subdivision (c).
>
> (3) Sixty days from the date of certification by the lead agency of the environmental impact report, if an environmental impact report is prepared pursuant to Section 21100 or 21151 of the Public Resources Code for a development project defined in subdivision (c) and all of the following conditions are met:
>
> (A) At least 49 percent of the units in the development project are affordable to very low or low-income households, as defined by Sections 50105 and 50079.5 of the Health and Safety Code, respectively. Rents for the lower income units shall be set at an affordable rent, as that term is defined in Section 50053 of the Health and Safety Code, for at least 30 years. Owner-occupied units shall be available at an affordable housing cost, as that term is defined in Section 50052.5 of the Health and Safety Code.
>
> (B) Prior to the application being deemed complete for the development project pursuant to Article 3 (commencing with Section 65940), the lead agency received written notice from the project applicant that an application has been made or will be made for an allocation or commitment of financing, tax credits, bond authority, or other financial assistance from a public agency or federal agency, and the notice specifies the financial assistance that has been applied for or will be applied for and the deadline for application for that assistance, the requirement that one of the approvals of the development project by the lead agency is a prerequisite to the application for or approval of the application for financial assistance, and that the financial assistance is necessary for the project to be affordable as required pursuant to subparagraph (A).
>
> (C) There is confirmation that the application has been made to the public agency or federal agency prior to certification of the environmental impact report.
>
> ...
>
> (c) For purposes of paragraphs (2) and (3) of subdivision (a) and Section 65952, "development project" means a **housing** development project, as defined in paragraph (3) of subdivision (b) of Section 65905.5.

Paragraph (1), with a deadline of 180 days after EIR certification, applies to projects that do not meet the definition of a housing development project at Gov. Code § 65905.5(b)(3) (which is somewhat different from the definition in the Housing Accountability Act). Paragraphs (2) and (3) apply to **housing** development projects as defined at

Gov. Code § 65905.5(b)(3). The deadline for housing development projects is 90 days per paragraph (2), except that projects with at least 49% affordable units meeting the requirements of paragraph (3) have a 60-day deadline.

As with exemptions, and negative declarations, missing the deadline will result in **deemed approval**, as explained under Deemed Approval — New with AB 130.

Assuming that the project is not deemed approved, the jurisdiction must make the required findings about the EIR described in Guidelines § 15091, including adopting a monitoring program to ensure that mitigation measures are enforced. Approval of a project must conform to the requirements of the Guidelines § 15092:

> 15092. (a) After considering the final EIR and in conjunction with making findings under Section 15091, the lead agency may decide whether or how to approve or carry out the project.
>
> (b) A public agency shall not decide to approve or carry out a project for which an EIR was prepared unless either:
>
> (1) The project as approved will not have a significant effect on the environment, or
>
> (2) The agency has:
>
> (A) Eliminated or substantially lessened all significant effects on the environment where feasible as shown in findings under Section 15091, and
>
> (B) Determined that any remaining significant effects on the environment found to be unavoidable under Section 15091 are acceptable due to overriding concerns as described in Section 15093.
>
> (c) With respect to a project which includes housing development, the public agency shall not reduce the proposed number of housing units as a mitigation measure if it determines that there is another feasible specific mitigation measure available that will provide a comparable level of mitigation.

Statement of Overriding Considerations

When approving a project that has a significant effect on the environment, the jurisdiction must include a **statement of overriding considerations** in accordance with the Guidelines § 15093:

> 15093. (a) CEQA requires the decision-making agency to balance, as applicable, the economic, legal, social, technological, or other benefits, including region-wide or statewide environmental benefits, of a proposed project against its unavoidable environmental risks when determining whether to approve the project. If the specific economic, legal, social, technological, or other benefits, including region-wide or statewide environmental benefits, of a proposal project outweigh the unavoidable adverse environmental effects, the adverse environmental effects may be considered "acceptable."
>
> (b) When the lead agency approves a project which will result in the occurrence of significant effects which are identified in the final EIR but are not avoided or substantially lessened, the agency shall state in writing the specific reasons to support its action based on the final EIR and/or other information in the record. The **statement of overriding considerations** shall be supported by substantial evidence in the record.
>
> (c) If an agency makes a statement of overriding considerations, the statement should be included in the record of the project approval and should be mentioned in the notice of determination. This statement does not substitute for, and shall be in addition to, findings required pursuant to Section 15091.

The statement of overriding consideration can only be made after the findings at Guidelines § 15091 have been adopted for the project:

> 15091. (a) No public agency shall approve or carry out a project for which an EIR has been certified which identifies one or more significant environmental effects of the project unless the public agency makes one or more written findings for each of those significant effects, accompanied by a brief explanation of the rationale for each finding. The possible findings are:

(1) Changes or alterations have been required in, or incorporated into, the project which avoid or substantially lessen the significant environmental effect as identified in the final EIR.

(2) Such changes or alterations are within the responsibility and jurisdiction of another public agency and not the agency making the finding. Such changes have been adopted by such other agency or can and should be adopted by such other agency.

(3) Specific economic, legal, social, technological, or other considerations, including provision of employment opportunities for highly trained workers, make infeasible the mitigation measures or project alternatives identified in the final EIR.

(b) The findings required by subdivision (a) shall be supported by substantial evidence in the record.

(c) The finding in subdivision (a)(2) shall not be made if the agency making the finding has concurrent jurisdiction with another agency to deal with identified feasible mitigation measures or alternatives. The finding in subdivision (a)(3) shall describe the specific reasons for rejecting identified mitigation measures and project alternatives.

(d) When making the findings required in subdivision (a)(1), the agency shall also adopt a program for reporting on or monitoring the changes which it has either required in the project or made a condition of approval to avoid or substantially lessen significant environmental effects. These measures must be fully enforceable through permit conditions, agreements, or other measures.

(e) The public agency shall specify the location and custodian of the documents or other material which constitute the record of the proceedings upon which its decision is based.

(f) A statement made pursuant to Section 15093 does not substitute for the findings required by this section.

Notes on EIR Risks and CEQA Litigation Risks

During the EIR process and subsequent project approval process, it is quite common for jurisdictions to require substantial changes to the project. Because they are in response to environmental impacts, jurisdictions have much more discretion to impose changes, or to disapprove the project, than would be the case for a project that is exempt from CEQA or that qualifies for a negative declaration. The biggest risk, the greatest cost, and the primary delay incurred for a project that requires an EIR are usually due to the project changes and mitigations, not the preparation and adoption of the EIR itself.

Despite the significant time required for an EIR, some developers (usually only for a large and controversial project) will choose to have a full EIR prepared **even though** the project is exempt from CEQA or would qualify for an ND or MND. The time and cost of a "defensive EIR" may be well spent if it prevents a long and expensive CEQA lawsuit. Such lawsuits are more common when a project relies on a categorical exemption, or the PRC § 21159.25 exemption, which are subject to exceptions (e.g., the "unusual circumstances" exception). The PRC § 21080.66 Statutory Exemption — New with AB 130 should be less exposed to CEQA lawsuits.

Applicants should consider carefully the risks of pursuing a project that will require an EIR and discuss CEQA litigation risk with a CEQA attorney.

Statute of Limitations for CEQA Lawsuits

A "statute of limitations" is a law (i.e., a "statute") that limits the time period during which a lawsuit can be filed for a specified cause of action. The *time period* specified by the law is *also* called the statute of limitations.

The statute of limitations for a CEQA lawsuit is **not** an "appeal period" and the applicant does not need to wait for the statute of limitations to end before continuing the development process. CEQA prescribes statutes of limitations with different time periods (primarily at PRC § 21167) depending on the type of CEQA determination. They are summarized by the Guidelines § 15112:

§ 15112. Statutes of Limitations.

(a) CEQA provides unusually short statutes of limitations on filing court challenges to the approval of projects under the act.

(b) The statute of limitations periods are not public review periods or waiting periods for the person whose project has been approved. The project sponsor may proceed to carry out the project as soon as the necessary permits have been granted. The statute of limitations cuts off the right of another person to file a court action challenging approval of the project after the specified time period has expired.

(c) The statute of limitations periods under CEQA are as follows:

(1) Where the public agency **filed a notice of determination** in compliance with Sections 15075 or 15094, **30 days** after the filing of the notice and the posting on a list of such notices.

(2) Where the public agency **filed a notice of exemption** in compliance with Section 15062, **35 days** after the filing of the notice and the posting on a list of such notices.

(3) Where a certified state regulatory agency files a notice of decision in compliance with Public Resources Code Section 21080.5(d)(2)(E), 30 days after the filing of the notice.

(4) Where the Secretary for Resources certifies a state environmental regulatory agency under Public Resources Code Section 21080.5, the certification may be challenged only during the 30 days following the certification decision.

(5) **Where none of the other statute of limitations periods in this section apply, 180 days** after either:

(A) The public agency's decision to carry out or approve the project, or

(B) Commencement of the project if the project is undertaken without a formal decision by the public agency.

If the CEQA determination notice is *not* properly filed and posted, the statute of limitations is 180 days from the date of final approval of the project. When the CEQA determination notice **is** properly filed and posted, the statute of limitations is shortened. For exemptions, **filing the NOE shortens the statute of limitations to 35 days.**[41] As explained by the Guidelines § 15062(d):

(d) The filing of a Notice of Exemption and the posting on the list of notices start a 35 day statute of limitations period on legal challenges to the agency's decision that the project is exempt from CEQA. If a Notice of Exemption is not filed, a 180 day statute of limitations will apply.

Note the language, "The filing of a Notice of Exemption **and the posting** ...." Always check to confirm proper Posting by the County Clerk and State Clearinghouse.

The applicant and jurisdiction both have a strong incentive to properly file the CEQA notice. Until the statute of limitations expires, a lawsuit to challenge the CEQA determination can be brought against the jurisdiction (i.e., the "lead agency" that made the determination) and will name and involve the applicant/developer. Such lawsuits are, unfortunately, a common tactic used by project opponents to delay or stop housing projects.

Filing and Posting CEQA Notices

The CEQA State Clearinghouse is the statewide repository for all CEQA documents. In addition, the county clerk is required to properly post CEQA filings for projects located in that county.

For most CEQA notices, the **lead agency** (The Jurisdiction is Usually the "Lead Agency") is **required** to file the notice with both the State Clearinghouse and the county clerk. For projects that are exempt from CEQA, the lead

[41] With the rare exception of a project that is exempt pursuant to Gov. Code § 65457, for which the statute of limitations is 30 days.

agency may or may not be mandated to file the notice of exemption (depending on which exemption is applied), and the applicant may be involved in the filing, as explained under Filing a Notice of Exemption.

CEQA notices (e.g., the notice of preparation of an EIR; notice of determination of an EIR, MND, or ND; notice of exemption; etc.) are **filed** with the county clerk of the county (or counties, if the project crosses county lines) where the project is located. CEQA notices are ***not* recorded** with the county recorder. In some counties, the clerk and recorder are the same entity, referred to as the "County Clerk-Recorder," but in many counties they are separate entities. The county clerk is sometimes called the "Clerk of the Board of Supervisors."

Posting by the County Clerk and State Clearinghouse

When CEQA notices are filed, the county clerk and State Clearinghouse are required to **post** them in accordance with PRC § 21152(c):

> (c) (1) A notice filed pursuant to this section, including any subsequent or amended notice, shall be available for public inspection, and shall be posted within 24 hours of receipt in the office and on the internet website of the county clerk. A notice shall remain posted for a period of 30 days. Thereafter, the clerk shall return the notice to the local agency with a notation of the period it was posted. The local agency shall retain the notice for not less than 12 months.
>
> > (2) A notice filed pursuant to this section, including any subsequent or amended notice, shall be posted by the Office of Planning and Research within 24 hours of receipt on the State Clearinghouse internet website. A notice shall remain posted for a period of 30 days. Provided that notices have been filed in accordance with subdivision (a) or (b), as applicable, nothing in this paragraph shall affect the time limitations contained in Section 21167.

Notices are required to be posted, by both the county clerk and State Clearinghouse, within 24 hours of receipt, and each of the postings must remain posted for 30 **full** days (midnight to midnight). This means that the notice might be delivered on one day and not posted until the next day, and the day of the posting would be a partial day and not count toward the 30 full days.

An improper or incomplete posting could cause the Statute of Limitations for CEQA Lawsuits to be 180 days, rather than the shorter statute of limitations that would apply if the notice were properly posted (see Example 2: Latinos Unidos de Napa v. City of Napa (2011) — 30 Day NOD Posting Requirement for an example).

The **filing *and* posting** of the notice with the county clerk ***and*** State Clearinghouse triggers the beginning of the shorter statute of limitations.[42] Check and keep a record of the dates of the ***postings*** by the county clerk and State Clearinghouse and count the statute of limitations from the first **full** day of the **later** of the two postings. Then check that the notice remains posted for the **full** 30 days. For the county clerk, visit the office to check for the physical posting and search the website to check for the online posting. For the State Clearinghouse, anyone can search the CEQAnet web portal to confirm the posting of the CEQA notice. For more information, see Computation of Time Periods and Deadlines.

Filing a Notice of Determination

The notice filed after an ND, MND, or EIR has been adopted is called a Notice of Determination (NOD). The ***lead agency*** that approves the project is ***required*** to file the NOD with **both** the county clerk and the State Clearinghouse within five (5) working days after the approval of the project becomes final (i.e., after the expiration of the appeal period, if any). (Guidelines § 15075.) **There is no option for the applicant to file an NOD.**

[42] The CEQA Statutes may refer only to the ***filing*** (for example, PRC § 21167(d) "... within 35 days from the date of the filing ...."), but the CEQA Guidelines clearly indicate that the ***posting*** is required to trigger the beginning of the statute of limitations (for example, Guidelines § 15112(c)(2) "... 35 days after the filing of the notice ***and the posting*** ...").

Filing a Notice of Exemption

For some, but not all exemptions, the state mandates that a notice of exemption (NOE) be filed (for example, see PRC § 21152.1). For exemptions that are not mandated to file an NOE, the jurisdiction and/or the applicant have the option to file the NOE.

For the PRC § 21080.66 Statutory Exemption — New with AB 130, as amended by SB 158 (2025), the jurisdiction is **required** to file the NOE with **both** the county clerk and the State Clearinghouse, per PRC § 21080.66(f):

> (f) If a lead agency determines that this division does not apply to an activity pursuant to this section and determines to approve or carry out the activity, **the lead agency shall file a notice of exemption with the Governor's Office of Land Use and Climate Innovation and the county clerk** of the county in which the activity will occur in the manner specified in subdivisions (b) and (c) of Section 21108 or subdivisions (b) and (c) of Section 21152, as applicable.

The applicant should remind the jurisdiction of this requirement. For PRC § 21080.66 exemptions, this alleviates the issue that At This Time, the NOE Cannot be Filed by the Applicant and Should be Filed by the Jurisdiction.

Always Ensure that the NOE is Filed Even if Filing is Optional

Filing the NOE provides for a shorter Statute of Limitations for CEQA Lawsuits, so applicants should **always ensure that the NOE is filed.** A sample Notice of Exemption form is provided as Appendix E of the CEQA Guidelines, however, as explained below The Applicant Should Not Fill Out and Sign Their Own NOE.

The NOE is Filed After Approval of the Project

The approval of a project by the legislative body (i.e., the city council or the county board of supervisors) is final and has no appeal period, but approvals by decisionmakers other than the legislative body are appealable. The NOE may not be filed until **after approval** of the project, but the CEQA Statutes and Guidelines do **not** stipulate that the approval must be final before the NOE may be filed. (Guidelines § 15062(a), and its referenced sections of the Public Resources Code.)

For example, after a planning commission approves a project there will be an appeal period during which the planning commission's approval can be appealed to the city council or county board of supervisors. If the NOE was filed after planning commission approval, and the project approval is appealed, then the NOE must be re-filed after the city council approval. To avoid this situation, many jurisdictions will wait until the appeal period expires before filing the NOE or providing the applicant with the signed NOE to deliver to the county clerk. In the event that the approval is not appealed, waiting until the end of the appeal period before filing the NOE delays the expiration of the Statute of Limitations for CEQA Lawsuits by approximately two weeks.[43] For this reason, the Author recommends asking the jurisdiction to file the NOE immediately after the first approval of the project, and then if the approval is appealed, ask the jurisdiction to re-file the NOE after the final approval of the project.

At This Time, the NOE Cannot be Filed by the Applicant and Should be Filed by the Jurisdiction

Always ensure the notice of exemption (NOE) is **filed in strict compliance with CEQA**. State law requires that if the NOE is filed with **either** the State Clearinghouse or with the county clerk, it must be filed with ***both***. PRC § 21152(b) begins:

> (b) If a local agency determines that a project is not subject to this division [i.e., CEQA] pursuant to subdivision (b) of Section 21080 [i.e., the projects is exempt from CEQA for any of a long list of reasons], and the local agency approves or determines to carry out the project, the local agency or the person specified in subdivision (b) or (c) of Section 21065 [i.e., a "person" who undertakes an activity subject to CEQA, such as a developer] **may** file a notice of exemption with

[43] Appeal periods are typically fourteen (14) calendar days but vary by jurisdiction.

> the county clerk of each county in which the project will be located **and with the State Clearinghouse in the Office of Planning and Research**. A notice filed pursuant to this subdivision shall identify the person or persons in subdivision (b) or (c) of Section 21065, as reflected in the agency's record of proceedings. ...

The Guidelines § 15062 provide an overview of the NOE process. However, as of this writing the CEQA Guidelines have not been updated to reflect the underlined text above, which was added by SB 69 (2024). The text of Guidelines § 15062 remains mostly correct, but its subdivision (c) does not explain that the NOE **must** be filed with the State Clearinghouse, and assumes that the **applicant** is ***able*** to file the NOE with the State Clearinghouse.

As of this writing it is ***not possible*** for the applicant alone to comply with the underlined text in the above quotation of PRC § 21152(b). **Applicants are currently not able to file CEQA documents with the State Clearinghouse**; only public agencies are currently eligible to use the "CEQA Submit" function of the State Clearinghouse. It is possible to register a non-public-agency email with CEQA Submit, but the automated response requires that "To begin our CEQA Documents and Notices process, you must first request and be approved for a Lead/Public Agency role." The Author confirmed with a representative of the Governor's Office of Land Use and Climate Innovation (LCI) that **only** public agencies are currently able to file documents with the State Clearinghouse. Per an email from LCI on November 24, 2025:

> The State Clearinghouse (SCH) is still working on a solution regarding project applicants filing NOEs with the SCH as coordination with state and local agencies is necessary to fine tune an appropriate process.

The next version of this book will have an update.

In the meantime, applicants will need to **rely on the jurisdiction** to file the NOE with the State Clearinghouse, which is an online filing that the jurisdiction can do from their office through the CEQA Submit portal. If the county clerk also offers electronic filing, then the jurisdiction's standard process should be to file online with both the State Clearinghouse and the county clerk, in accordance with PRC § 21152(d):

> (d) A notice filed by a local agency pursuant to this section shall be filed electronically with the State Clearinghouse in the Office of Planning and Research and with the county clerk if that option is offered by the county clerk.

However, not all county clerks have an electronic filing option, and there is usually a fee to file. Therefore, jurisdictions quite often have the **applicant** deliver the NOE to the county clerk and pay the filing fee. This is not an issue so long as the NOE form is **completed and signed by the jurisdiction**; in such cases the applicant is merely a courier. Because the **jurisdiction** prepared and signed the NOE, it is jurisdiction that is filing the NOE even if the applicant delivers the NOE to the county clerk and pays the fee.

It is important to both the jurisdiction and the applicant that CEQA documents are properly filed because doing so shortens the Statute of Limitations for CEQA Lawsuits. Jurisdictions want to avoid CEQA lawsuits as much as applicants. If for some reason the jurisdiction refuses to file the NOE, the applicant should check the CEQA Submit portal to see if it has become possible for the applicant to file CEQA documents with the State Clearinghouse. Applicants can request assistance from LCI; a contact person is listed at the bottom of https://lci.ca.gov/sch/document-submission.html.

The Applicant Should Not Fill Out and Sign Their Own NOE

The Author recommends that applicants **do not** fill out and sign their own NOE. If the applicant is delivering the NOE to the county clerk, **always file the NOE provided and signed by the jurisdiction**. As explained above, it is not currently possible for the applicant to file the NOE with CEQA Submit, and it is better for the **same** NOE form to be filed with the county clerk as was filed with the State Clearinghouse.

PRC § 21152(b) ***allows*** the applicant (i.e., "a person specified in subdivision (b) or (c) of Section 21065") to file the NOE, but in order for the **applicant** to file the NOE (whether with the county clerk or the State Clearinghouse) a ***certified*** copy of the determination of exemption (i.e., the final, signed resolution approving the project and accepting the environmental determination) must be attached to the NOE. Per PRC § 21152(b):

> ... A notice filed pursuant to this subdivision by a person specified in subdivision (b) or (c) of Section 21065 shall have **a certificate of determination attached to it** issued by the local agency responsible for making the determination that the project is not subject to this division pursuant to subdivision (b) of Section 21080. The certificate of determination may be ***in the form of a certified copy*** of an existing document or record of the local agency.

It can take quite a while for the jurisdiction to sign the final resolution and make it available to the applicant, which could delay the filing of the NOE and thus delay the end of the Statute of Limitations for CEQA Lawsuits. The **jurisdiction** can file the NOE ***without*** providing this additional document.

Bottom line: Ensure that the jurisdiction files the NOE with the State Clearinghouse, and if the jurisdiction will not file it with the county clerk, then ensure that the applicant transmits the same jurisdiction-signed NOE to the county clerk on behalf of the jurisdiction.

CHAPTER 5: OVERALL DEVELOPMENT PERMIT REVIEW PROCESS & HOW AB 130 CHANGES IT

When state law refers to an "application for a development project" it means an **application** for a **permit** to **develop** a **project**, as those terms are used in CEQA and the Permit Streamlining Act, and as discussed in Chapter 2: Key Concepts for Projects and Permits. The development community uses the term "***full*** development permit application" to distinguish the application for approval to develop a project, from the SB 330 **preliminary** application (and other types of "preliminary" or informal applications).

This chapter is the most complex in the book, discussing difficult legal interpretations that create uncertainty about important deadlines for the review and approval of the full development permit application. It covers:

1. An overview of the three-part process of reviewing the full application for a housing development permit: completeness review, CEQA review, and compliance review. Although there are time limits and determinations associated with each of the three parts, most jurisdictions review the application and the project for all three parts after each submittal during completeness review.
2. Typical project timelines under various assumptions and interpretations of state law, showing them graphically using the timeline feature from a Microsoft Project schedule.
3. How AB 130 (2025) has changed the approval timeline, with new deadlines for the PRC § 21080.66 Statutory Exemption — New with AB 130, and Deemed Approval — New with AB 130 if those deadlines are missed.
4. How AB 1294 (2026?) ***could*** change the timeline if, after being introduced but not yet passed in 2025, it becomes law in 2026.
5. A tricky question of What Triggers the Start of the Compliance Review Period?, the answer to which has become critically important with the passage of AB 130 (2025), new deadlines for approval or disapproval of projects that use the PRC § 21080.66 Statutory Exemption — New with AB 130, and the consequence of missing the deadline being Deemed Approval — New with AB 130.
6. A detailed review of the time limits for approval or disapproval of development permit applications depending on the type of CEQA determination.
7. Details on the amendment to Gov. Code § 65956 passed with AB 130 (2025) that makes the Deadline for Initial Approval or Disapproval of the Project self-enforcing, such that if the jurisdiction misses this deadline the consequence will be Deemed Approval — New with AB 130.
8. The Author's perception of The Real World of Development Permit Review and how it fails to follow the process required by state law.

Where to Find More Information

Find helpful resources for the three-part process of development permit review in the chapter introductions for Chapter 8: Completeness Review, Chapter 4: CEQA Review for Housing Projects After AB 130 and SB 131, and Chapter 9: Compliance Review.

CHAPTER CONTENTS

Three-Part Process for Reviewing an Application for a Housing Development Permit

State law prescribes three determinations that a jurisdiction must make as it reviews the full housing development permit application. In summary, the jurisdiction must:

1. Review the full development permit application to **determine whether the application is complete.** If the application is *not* complete, send a letter to the applicant with an exhaustive list of what information is missing (The "Real" LORI). If it *is* complete, send a letter accepting the application as complete.
    a. The jurisdiction has 30 days to review the application for completeness. If a written determination is not provided within 30 days, the application is **deemed complete**. (Gov. Code § 65943.)
    b. When the jurisdiction either accepts the application as complete or time expires and the application is deemed complete, it triggers the start of the 30- or 45-day Time Period for the Review for Exemption.
2. Review the project as described in the application to **determine whether the project is exempt from CEQA**. (See Result of the Review for Exemption.)
    a. The jurisdiction has a 30- or 45-day Time Period for the Review for Exemption, but this deadline is not self-enforcing. The project is ***not*** deemed exempt if the jurisdiction fails to meet the deadline.
    b. If the project is not exempt or if the jurisdiction cannot determine whether the project is exempt without further investigation, provide written notice to the applicant that the project has not been determined to be exempt, and that the project will require an Initial Study.
    c. If the project is exempt from CEQA, provide written notice to the applicant that the jurisdiction has made the preliminary determination that the project is exempt from CEQA. This determination is the most important milestone in the review process for a project that is exempt from CEQA, because it **triggers** the Deadline for Initial Approval or Disapproval of the Project.
3. Review the project as described in the application to **determine whether the project is compliant**. The project is compliant, if it "... complies with applicable, objective general plan, zoning, and subdivision standards and criteria, including design review standards, in effect at the time that the application [was vested]." (Gov. Code 65589.5(j)(1). Also see Chapter 7: Vesting the Development Standards.)
    a. There is a 30- or 60-day Time Period Allowed for Compliance Review, depending on whether the project has 150 units or less (30 days), or more than 150 units (60 days).
        i. The jurisdiction is required to provide the applicant with an exhaustive list of compliance comments, with reference to specific objective development standards, by the end of the compliance review period. The project is **deemed compliant** with any development standard not included in the exhaustive list. However, jurisdictions generally ignore this deadline and continue to conduct compliance review until they publish the staff report a few days before the hearing.
        ii. The end of the compliance review period does not trigger any other deadlines, ***except*** for projects that use the PRC § 21080.66 Statutory Exemption — New with AB 130, for which the end of the compliance review period is ***one of*** **the triggers** for the Deadline for Initial Approval or Disapproval of the Project. (Gov. Code § 65950(a)(7).)
    b. If the project is compliant, the jurisdiction **must approve the project** unless it can make certain findings related to public health or safety. (Gov. Code § 65589.5(j) and (d).)
    c. If the project is not compliant, then the jurisdiction is **still** required to approve the project if state law preempts the offended development standards (e.g., for the reasons in Gov. Code § 65915(e) in the State Density Bonus Law); or if the jurisdiction is prohibited from disapproving the project (e.g., for the reasons in Gov. Code § 65589.5(d) in the Housing Accountability Act).

Typical Project Timeline with No Delays (Not Showing Effect of New Laws)

Although there is a three-part process, with three time periods, that results in three key determinations, in practice jurisdictions review ***each*** submittal and resubmittal of the development permit for completeness, compliance, and CEQA. Figure 6 shows a typical process and timeline. In the example, the SB 330 preliminary application is submitted on January 5, 2026. The applicant spends the next three months gathering all the plans, reports, and studies required by the jurisdiction's list of required information (LORI). The full development permit application is submitted on April 6, starting the first completeness review. The jurisdiction responds with a letter of incompleteness within 30 days, which is required to include a complete list of remaining LORI items that must be submitted for the application to be complete. The applicant revises the application and resubmits on June 5. Despite the applicant's best efforts, the jurisdiction again finds the application to be incomplete, and the applicant must make a third submittal.

This timeline assumes that the third submittal is determined to be complete (aka, "accepted as complete") at the end of the third 30-day completeness review period. The CEQA review period (shown without the 15-day extension that is allowed by mutual agreement between the applicant and jurisdiction) is triggered and begins when the application is "Accepted as Complete" — The Trigger for the Review for Exemption from CEQA.

If the project proposes more than 150 units, there is a 60-day compliance review period (for projects of 150 units or less, the compliance review period is 30 days). After the compliance review period ends, the jurisdiction notices the public hearing while preparing the staff report. Although the compliance review ***should*** be started when the **complete** application was ***submitted,*** there is some dispute about What Triggers the Start of the Compliance Review Period?, and in this example, the 60-day compliance review is shown as starting on the date the jurisdiction ***determines*** the application to be complete. Jurisdictions have generally ignored the deadline for compliance review, because until AB 130 (2025) there were effectively no consequences for missing the deadline.

The timeline assumes the project is appealed, which is very common, but that the appeal hearing is conducted quickly. The notice of exemption is filed and posted, and the CEQA statute of limitations expires 35 days later. In The Real World of Development Permit Review, the process can be somewhat jumbled and rarely takes less than a year.

Figure 6: Timeline for a project over 150 units. Compliance review period after determination of completeness.

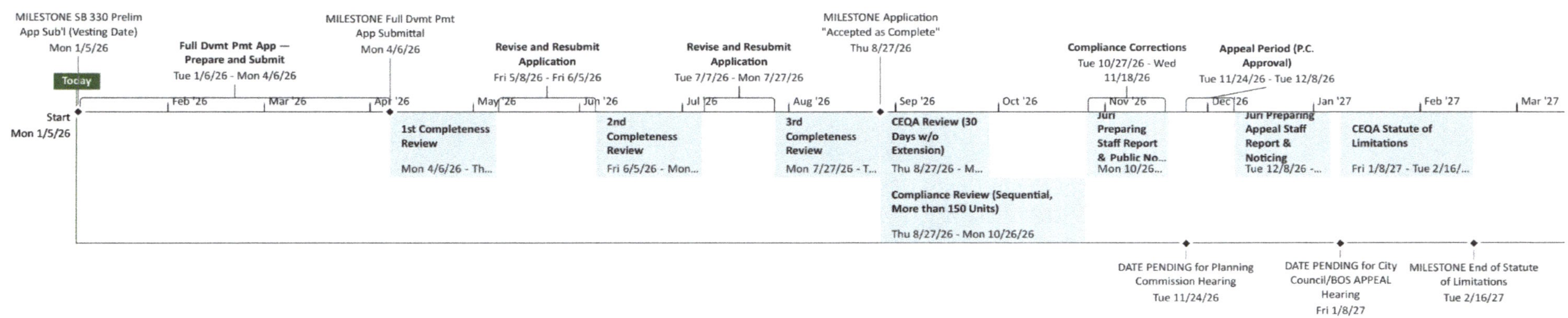

Shortening the Project Approval Timeline with SB 130 (2025) and AB 1294 (2026?)

Despite a decade of reforms passed by the State Legislature, it still takes far too long to obtain a permit to develop a housing project. For various types of streamlined ministerial projects, the timeline has been reduced significantly, but for discretionary permits it still takes most projects over a year from first submittal of the development permit application to final approval. Two bills that have the potential to significantly reduce the entitlement timeline for discretionary projects were introduced in the State Assembly in 2025. AB 130 (2025) passed the Legislature as an urgency bill, was signed by the Governor, and became effective on July 1, 2025. AB 1294 passed the Assembly, but did not make it through the Senate during 2025; it will be taken up as a "two-year bill" during 2026.

How AB 130 Changes the Entitlement Timeline

For decades the Permit Streamlining Act has stipulated deadlines for the initial approval or disapproval of development permit applications. The time limits depend on the type of CEQA determination and are triggered by that determination. However, jurisdictions could and usually did ignore the deadlines, because there were no consequences for exceeding the time limits. With the passage of AB 130 (2025) the deadlines are now self-enforcing, and are sometimes referred to as "shot clocks" — if the jurisdiction fails to act by the Deadline for Initial Approval or Disapproval of the Project, the project is **deemed approved**. As will be discussed under Deemed Approval — New with AB 130.

For most projects, the approval/disapproval deadlines are found at Gov. Code § 65950(a). Along with the creation of the PRC § 21080.66 statutory exemption, AB 130 (2025) added paragraph (7) to Gov. Code § 65950(a) to provide a new time limit for the initial approval or disapproval of projects that use the new exemption. Gov. Code § 65950(a)(7) was later amended by SB 158 (2025) and now reads:

> 65950. (a) A public agency that is the lead agency for a development project **shall approve or disapprove the project** within whichever of the following periods is applicable:
>
> ...
>
> (7) If a development project is exempt from the California Environmental Quality Act (Division 13 (commencing with Section 21000) of the Public Resources Code) pursuant to Section 21080.66 of the Public Resources Code, **30 days from the later of the following dates**:
>
> (A) The conclusion of the process outlined in subdivision (b) of Section 21080.66 of the Public Resources Code.
>
> (B) The expiration of the applicable time limit in paragraph (2) of subdivision (j) of Section 65589.5.

Subparagraph (A) refers to the tribal notification and consultation process required for the new PRC § 21080.66 exemption. The Tribal Process Can Take Up to 148 Days, so subparagraph (A) ensures that the deadline for approval or disapproval of the project cannot be earlier than 30 days after the conclusion of the tribal process. Subparagraph (B) refers to the 30- or 60-day Time Period Allowed for Compliance Review, and the approval/disapproval deadline cannot be earlier than 30 days after the compliance review period has ended. As will be explained later in this chapter, there is disagreement about What Triggers the Start of the Compliance Review Period?, and therefore ambiguity about what is the "expiration" date under subparagraph (B).

It is unclear whether the Legislature intends that the time limit for approval or disapproval of a project that is exempt pursuant to PRC § 21080.66 is **shorter** than the time limit for projects that use other exemptions, or if paragraph (7) applies only if its deadline is **later** than the deadline under paragraph (5) of Gov. Code § 65950(a) that applies to ***all*** CEQA-exempt projects. This uncertainty will be explained in detail under Deadline for Exempt Projects Using vs. Not Using the New PRC § 21080.66 Exemption.

How AB 1294 Could Greatly Reduce the Entitlement Timeline

The Deadline for Initial Approval or Disapproval of the Project is triggered by the CEQA determination, and most housing projects will be determined to be exempt from CEQA. As detailed under Deadline for Exempt Projects Using vs. Not Using the New PRC § 21080.66 Exemption, once the determination has been made that the project is **exempt** from CEQA, the jurisdiction has no more than 60 days to approve or disapprove the project, or it will be deemed approved. The jurisdiction is allowed a 30- or 45-day Time Period for the Review for Exemption. Per PRC § 21080.2, the start of that time period is the "date on which an application for a project has been received and **accepted as complete** by the lead agency" (in most cases the jurisdiction is the lead agency). To shorten the timeline for approval of discretionary housing projects, the time it takes for jurisdictions to review the development permit application and accept it as complete needs to be reduced.

State law requires that each jurisdiction create a list of required information for a complete application and post it on their website, though oftentimes Jurisdictions Fail to Post a Complete List of Required Items (LORI) on their Website. There are some state-law limits on what can be included in the LORI, but jurisdictions can and do require dozens of studies, reports, and plans, many of which are not necessary to determine whether the housing project is consistent with the applicable objective development standards. Each jurisdiction creates their own application forms and jurisdictions have various requirements for submittal of the forms (by-appointment, via email, or through the jurisdiction's web portal).

AB 1294, as currently proposed, would create a **statewide LORI** and a **statewide application form** for housing development projects that would apply in all jurisdictions; most importantly the full development permit application would be **deemed complete upon *submittal*** if it contains the information required by the statewide LORI. The entire completeness review process would be **eliminated**, and jurisdictions would be required to return a comprehensive written ***compliance*** review within 30 or 60 days[44] from the ***submittal*** date of the full development permit application, rather than conducting three or more rounds of 30-day completeness reviews. Because the application would be deemed complete upon submittal, that submittal would immediately trigger the 30- or 45-day Time Period for the Review for Exemption. The end of the time limit for the review for exemption is not self-enforcing, but with the PRC § 21080.66 Statutory Exemption — New with AB 130, the review will be relatively straightforward and jurisdictions should generally be able to complete the review for exemption by the deadline. Once the project is determined to be exempt from CEQA, failure to approve or disapprove the project by the applicable deadline (Deadline for Exempt Projects Using vs. Not Using the New PRC § 21080.66 Exemption) would result in Deemed Approval — New with AB 130.

AB 1294 would fundamentally change the process of reviewing the full development permit application, by eliminating the completeness review process. The Author estimates that AB 1294 would reduce the typical development review timeline for most discretionary housing projects by about six months.

What Triggers the Start of the Compliance Review Period?

If AB 1294 has passed, you can finish this paragraph and skip to Deadline for Initial Approval or Disapproval of the Project, because if AB 1294 passed the way it was in July of 2025 (when it became a "two-year bill" that may become law in 2026) the full development permit application is **deemed complete upon submittal**, and the deadline for the jurisdiction to provide the comprehensive compliance determination required by Gov. Code § 65589.5(j)(2) is 30 days after the date you ***submit*** the full development permit application for a project of 150 units or less, or 60 days for a project of more than 150 units.

[44] 30 days for a project of 150 units or less, or 60 days for a project of more than 150 units, per Gov. Code § 65589.5(j)(2).

If AB 1294 has not passed, the discussion below explains an ambiguous detail of the law that leads not only to disagreement in interpretation, but contributes to the significant problem of jurisdictions failing to provide the applicant with the single, comprehensive compliance determination required by Gov. Code § 65589.5(j)(2):

> (2) (A) If the local agency considers a proposed housing development project to be inconsistent, not in compliance, or not in conformity with an applicable plan, program, policy, ordinance, standard, requirement, or other similar provision as specified in this subdivision, **it shall provide the applicant with written documentation identifying the provision or provisions, and an explanation of the reason or reasons it considers the housing development to be inconsistent, not in compliance**, or not in conformity as follows:

Many attorneys will argue the opposite of the Author's interpretation (as explained below) of the law that sets the start of the 30- or 60-day Time Period Allowed for Compliance Review and therefore the deadline for the determination required by by Gov. Code § 65589.5(j)(2). Hopefully some policymakers will read this and provide clarity by passing a bill.

Overview of the Issue of Ambiguity Regarding the Start of the Compliance Review Period

The trigger for the **start** of the 30- or 60-day Time Period Allowed for Compliance Review is less than clear in the law. It is either:

A. The date the ***complete*** application was ***submitted*** (i.e., the date of the *final* ***submittal*** of the development permit application that the jurisdiction *later* determines to be complete).
B. The date the application is affirmatively ***determined*** to be complete by the jurisdiction (i.e., the date the jurisdiction sends the "completeness letter").

The ambiguity arises because Gov. Code § 65589.5(j)(2)(A) uses the phrase "determined to be complete" ...

> (2) (A) If the local agency considers a proposed housing development project to be inconsistent, not in compliance, or not in conformity with an applicable plan, program, policy, ordinance, standard, requirement, or other similar provision as specified in this subdivision, it shall provide the applicant with written documentation identifying the provision or provisions, and an explanation of the reason or reasons it considers the housing development to be inconsistent, not in compliance, or not in conformity as follows:
>
>> (i) Within 30 days of the date that the application for the housing development project is **determined to be complete**, if the housing development project contains 150 or fewer housing units.
>>
>> (ii) Within 60 days of the date that the application for the housing development project is **determined to be complete**, if the housing development project contains more than 150 units.

... however, the ***definition*** of "determined to be complete" is that the applicant has ***submitted*** a complete application. Gov. Code § 65589.5(h)(10):

> (10) Notwithstanding any other law, "determined to be complete" means that the applicant **has *submitted* a complete application** pursuant to Section 65943.

Many practitioners read the plain language in Gov. Code § 65589.5(j)(2)(A) — "date that the application for the housing development project is **determined to be complete**" — and believe that the answer is B: the date the application is affirmatively ***determined*** to be complete. But the definition of "determined to be complete" is that "the applicant **has submitted** a complete application." That definition indicates that the answer is A: the date the **complete** application was ***submitted***. The Author believes that the wording in the **definition** is deliberate, and therefore the compliance review period starts upon the *final* ***submittal*** of the development permit application that the jurisdiction *later* affirmatively determines to be complete.

If the Author is right, the **compliance** review period runs **concurrently** with the **completeness** review of the final, ***complete*** resubmittal of the development permit. For example, if the project proposes 150 units or less there is a 30-day period for compliance review, and the time period for completeness review is always 30 days, so the deadline for both compliance and completeness review is the same. The jurisdiction "shall provide the applicant with written documentation identifying the provision or provisions, and an explanation of the reason or reasons it considers the housing development to be inconsistent, not in compliance, or not in conformity" (Gov. Code § 65589.5(j)(2)(A)) within 30 days after ***submittal***. (Figure 7(A) assumes the 3rd submittal is *complete*.)

Figure 7(A):[45] If the Author is right, the compliance period runs concurrently with the final completeness review.

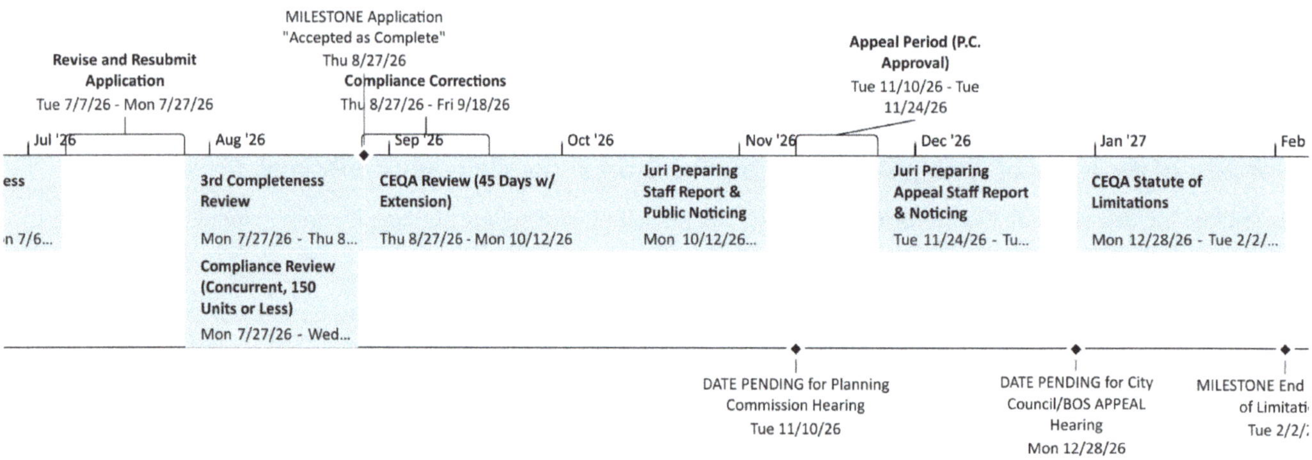

Figure 8(B): If the Author is wrong, the compliance period runs sequentially after the final completeness review.

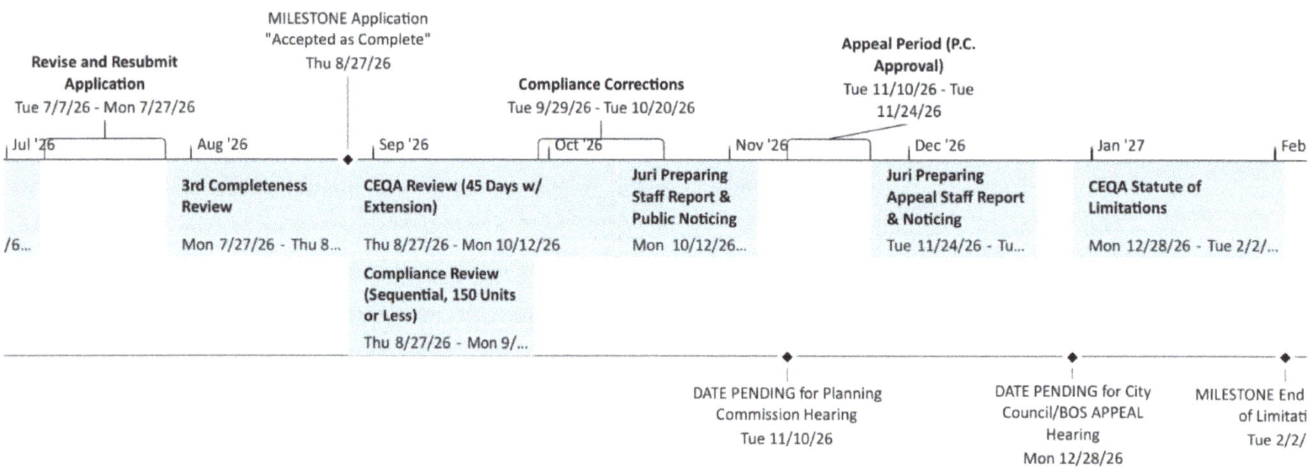

If the Author is wrong, then the completeness and compliance periods run **sequentially**. For a project with 150 units or less, the deadline to provide compliance documentation is 30 days after the application is affirmatively ***determined*** to be complete (i.e., 30 days after the date of the letter of completeness). (Figure 8(B).)

Why Does it Matter?

Before the addition of paragraph (7) to Gov. Code § 65950(a) (see How AB 130 Changes the Entitlement Timeline), the question of when the 30- or 60-day Time Period Allowed for Compliance Review legally begins was mostly

[45] The (A) or (B) in a figure number indicates whether the timeline assumes the compliance review period is A: The date the complete application was ***submitted*** or B: The date the application is affirmatively ***determined*** to be complete by the jurisdiction.

academic. Jurisdictions typically review each submittal for completeness and compliance, include compliance comments with each review letter, and continue to review the application as they write the staff report. The applicant responds to the compliance comments with each resubmittal until the application is complete and makes any compliance revisions necessary to obtain approval of the project.

But as explained under How AB 130 Changes the Entitlement Timeline, for projects that use the PRC § 21080.66 Statutory Exemption — New with AB 130, a new deadline for approval or disapproval of the project may depend on "The expiration of the applicable time limit in paragraph (2) of subdivision (j) of Section 65589.5." (Gov. Code § 65950(a)(7)(B).) In other words, the Deadline for Initial Approval or Disapproval of the Project may be 30 days after the end of the 30- or 60-day Time Period Allowed for Compliance Review, and if the jurisdiction misses the deadline the project will be **deemed approved**. The ambiguity about the start of the compliance review period is no longer academic. **The approval of the project could depend on the proper legal interpretation.**

Furthermore, providing compliance comments with each incompleteness letter usually has the effect of extending the completeness review process and delays the date that the application is "Accepted as Complete" — The Trigger for the Review for Exemption from CEQA. The sooner the completeness review process is concluded, the sooner the applicant can enforce all the other deadlines leading to approval of the project.

Finally, the ambiguity about the start of the compliance review period means that applicants and jurisdictions are unsure of the date that the jurisdiction is required to provide the final, detailed, substantiated list of compliance comments with reference to specific code provisions, that is required by Gov. Code § 65589.5(j)(2)(A). At least in part due to this ambiguity, the applicant is never quite sure what compliance issues the jurisdiction might find, until the staff report is published a few days before the hearing.

Deadline for Approval or Disapproval of Projects with More than 150 Units

If the project proposes more than 150 units, the compliance review period is 60 days. If the answer is B: the compliance review period starts **sequentially** after the jurisdiction accepts the application as complete, then the 60-day compliance review period will end later than the end of the CEQA review period (regardless of whether the CEQA review is mutually extended by 15 days), as shown in Figure 9(B).

Figure 9(B): Compliance review running sequentially. Large project using an "*old*" CEQA exemption.

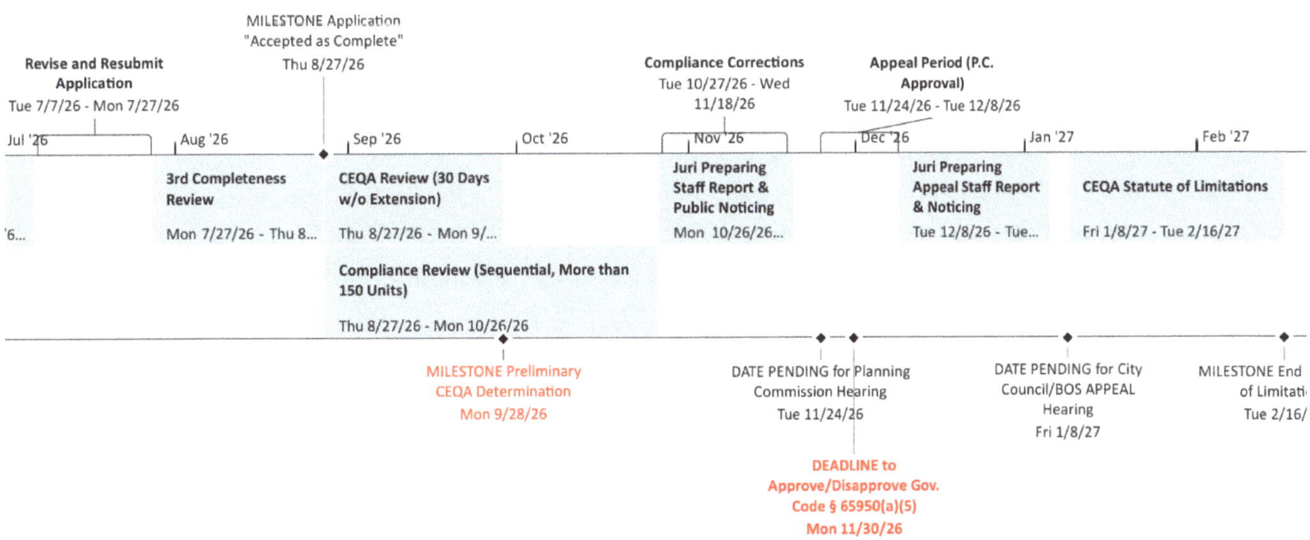

For any CEQA exemption other than the PRC § 21080.66 exemption, there is a 60-day deadline for approval or disapproval of the project. The 60-Day Deadline for Approval or Disapproval of Exempt Projects that Do Not Use PRC § 21080.66 is prescribed by paragraph (5) of Gov. Code § 65950(a). That time period starts on the date of the preliminary CEQA determination (shown in red), and the 60-day deadline for the jurisdiction to hold the planning commission hearing is shown in **bold red** in Figure 9(B). The jurisdiction has enough time to meet this deadline, even if completeness review, compliance review, and staff report preparation / public noticing run sequentially.

And, for projects using the **new** PRC § 21080.66 exemption created by AB 130 (2025), if the project is over 150 units (and therefore the compliance review period is 60 days) the jurisdiction can follow the same timeline and meet the Unclear Deadline for Approval or Disapproval of Projects that are Exempt Pursuant to PRC § 21080.66 prescribed by paragraph (7) of Gov. Code § 65950(a), shown in **bold blue** in Figure 10(B). The deadline for approval/disapproval of the project will be (roughly, depending on holidays) the same under paragraph (5) or (7) of Gov. Code § 65950(a), because the trigger for the 60-day deadline under paragraph (5) (shown in red) will be about 30 days earlier than the trigger for the 30-day deadline under paragraph (7) (shown in blue). As shown in Figure 10(B), deadline in **bold red** is the same date as the deadline in **bold blue**.

Figure 10(B): Compliance review running sequentially. Large project using the *PRC § 21080.66* CEQA exemption.

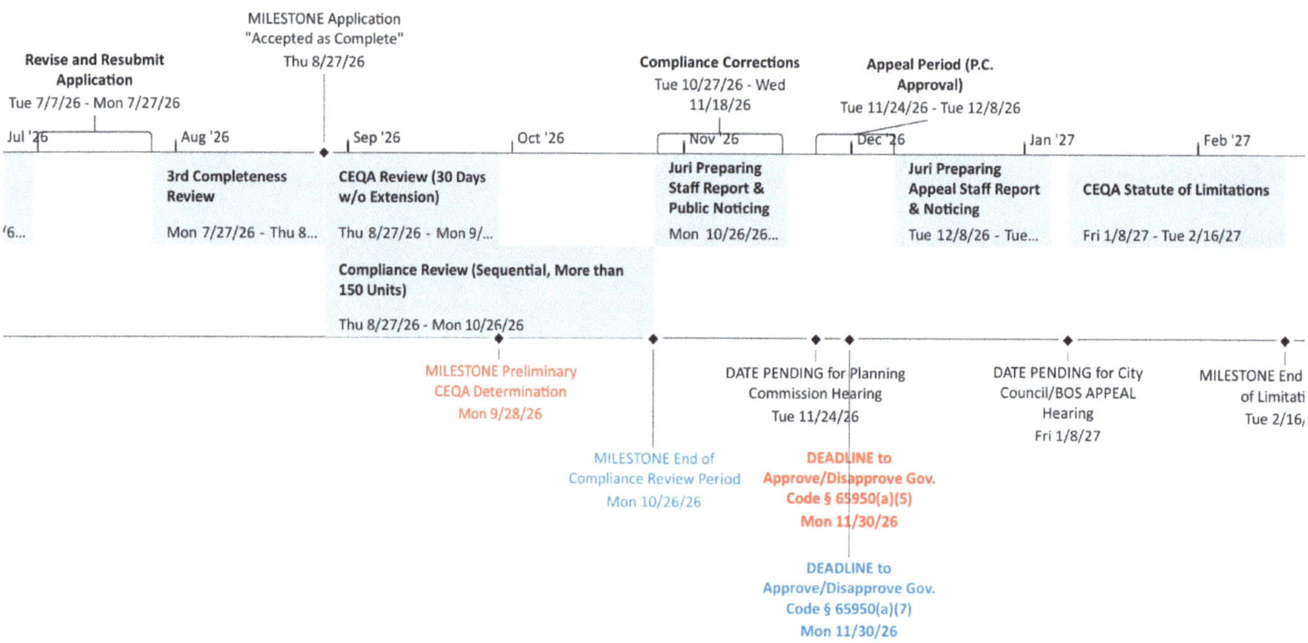

Next, we consider the timeline if the Author is right and the answer is A: the compliance review period starts on the date the ***complete*** application was ***submitted***. Figure 11(A) shows the timeline for the same over-150-unit project, using the **new** PRC § 21080.66 exemption, and assuming the compliance review period runs concurrently with the final review for completeness. The deadline for approval/disapproval of the project under paragraph (7) in **bold blue** is about 30 days earlier than the deadline under paragraph (5) shown in **bold red**. As explained under Unclear Deadline for Approval or Disapproval of Projects that are Exempt Pursuant to PRC § 21080.66, the law is not clear about whether the blue deadline or the red deadline apply in this case.

Figure 11(A): Compliance review running *concurrently*. Large project using the PRC § 21080.66 CEQA exemption.

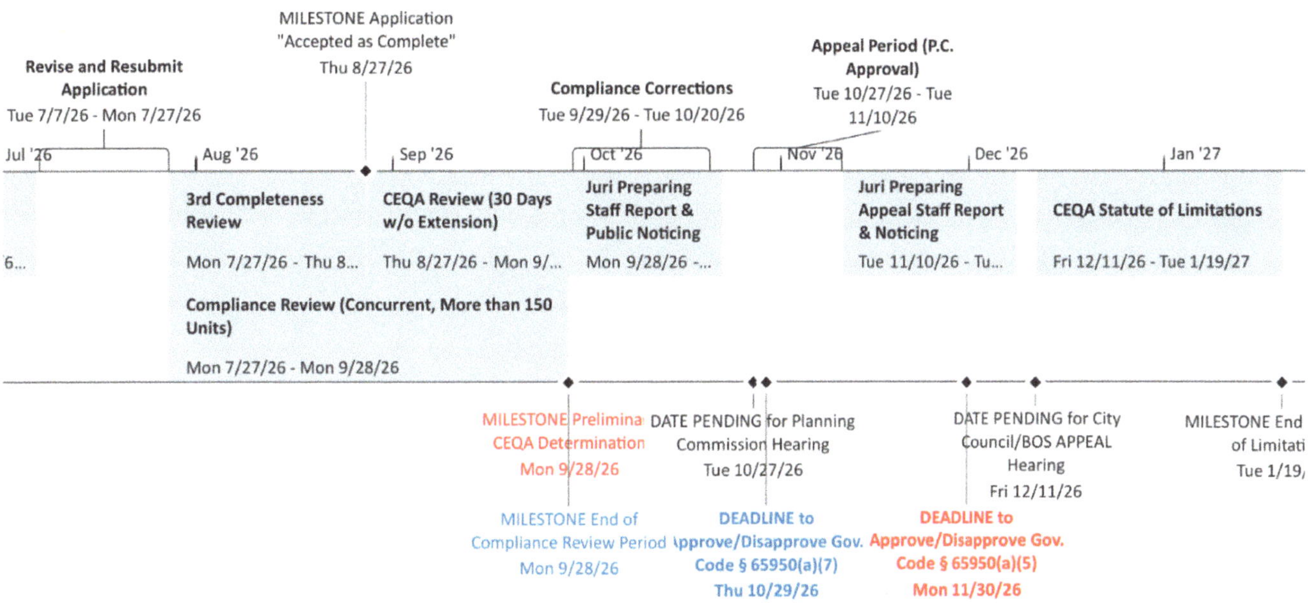

Figure 11(A) illustrates that the question of what triggers the **start** of the 30- or 60-day Time Period Allowed for Compliance Review may be material to the deadline for approval or disapproval of the project. Again, the Author interprets state law to mean that the answer is as shown in Figure 11(A):

A. The date the ***complete*** application was ***submitted*** (i.e., the date of the *final* ***submittal*** of the development permit application that the jurisdiction *later* determines to be complete).

But other practitioners argue that the answer is as shown in in Figure 10(B):

B. The date the application is affirmatively ***determined*** to be complete by the jurisdiction (i.e., the date the jurisdiction sends the "completeness letter").

The answer becomes even more critical when a project proposes 150 units or less, and the compliance review period is only 30 days as shown in Figure 12(A) in the next section.

Deadline for Approval or Disapproval of Projects with 150 Units or Less

What is unclear about the Unclear Deadline for Approval or Disapproval of Projects that are Exempt Pursuant to PRC § 21080.66 is the proper interpretation of Gov. Code § 65950(a) for projects using the **new** PRC § 21080.66 exemption. Either the deadline for approval/disapproval of the project is the ***later*** of the deadlines under paragraphs (5) and (7), or ***only*** the deadline under paragraph (7) applies.

Figure 11(A) under the previous sub-heading, shows a project with over 150 units, and therefore a 60-day compliance review period. In that figure, the planning commission hearing is shown as occurring before **both** the deadlines under paragraphs (5) and (7) that occur on the same date.

But as shown below in Figure 12(A), if the project has 150 units or less, the compliance review period is only 30 days, and the jurisdiction will miss the deadline under paragraph (7) but can hold the planning commission hearing before the deadline under paragraph (5). If the intent of Gov. Code § 65950(a) for projects using the **new** PRC § 21080.66 exemption is that the deadline for approval/disapproval of the project is the ***later*** of the deadlines under paragraphs (5) or (7), the jurisdiction can hold the planning commission hearing on October 27 and the project will not be deemed approved prior to that date.

Figure 12(A): Compliance review running concurrently. *Small* project using the PRC § 21080.66 CEQA exemption.

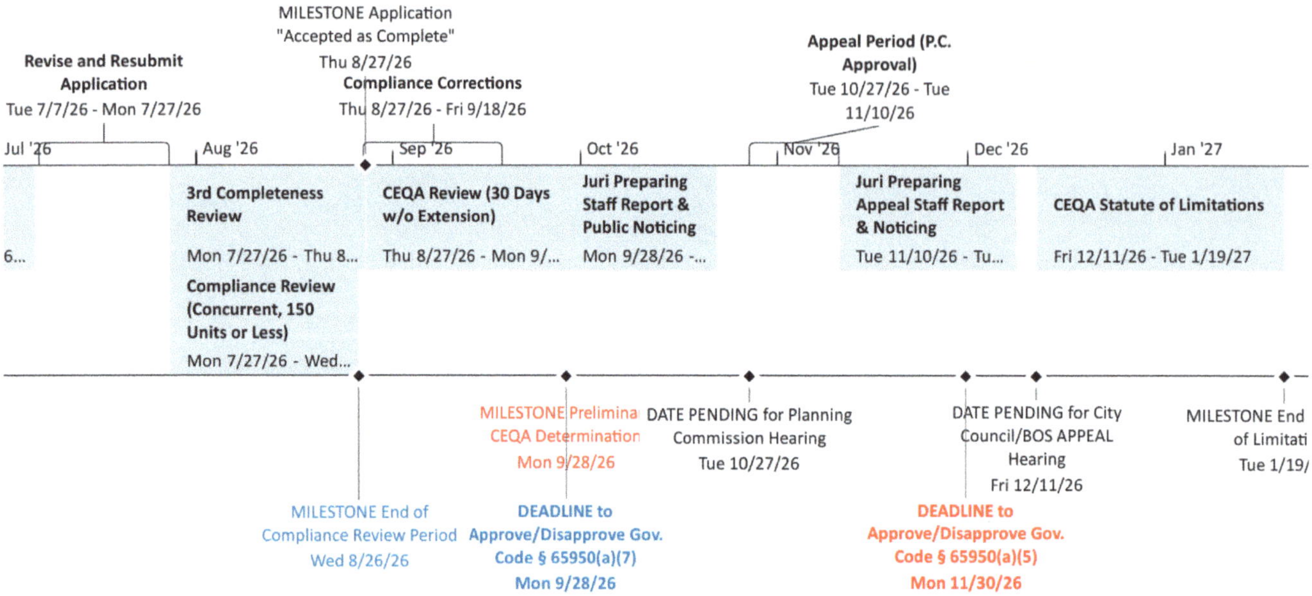

However, if ***only*** the deadline under paragraph (7) applies, then the project shown in Figure 12(A) was **deemed approved** on September 28, 2026, because the jurisdiction had failed to approve or disapprove the project by that **blue** deadline. This uncertainty around the deadline in paragraphs (5) versus (7), and several examples of timelines where it matters are discussed in detail under Unclear Deadline for Approval or Disapproval of Projects that are Exempt Pursuant to PRC § 21080.66.

To avoid Deemed Approval — New with AB 130, if ***only*** the deadline under paragraph (7) applies, the jurisdiction reviewing the project in Figure 12(A) would need to change their process, for example as shown in Figure 13(A) where the jurisdiction begins preparing the staff report and public noticing while the CEQA review period is running and holds the hearing 30 days after the end of the compliance review period to meet the **blue** deadline.

Figure 13(A): Timeline to *avoid deemed approval* of a small project using the PRC § 21080.66 CEQA exemption.

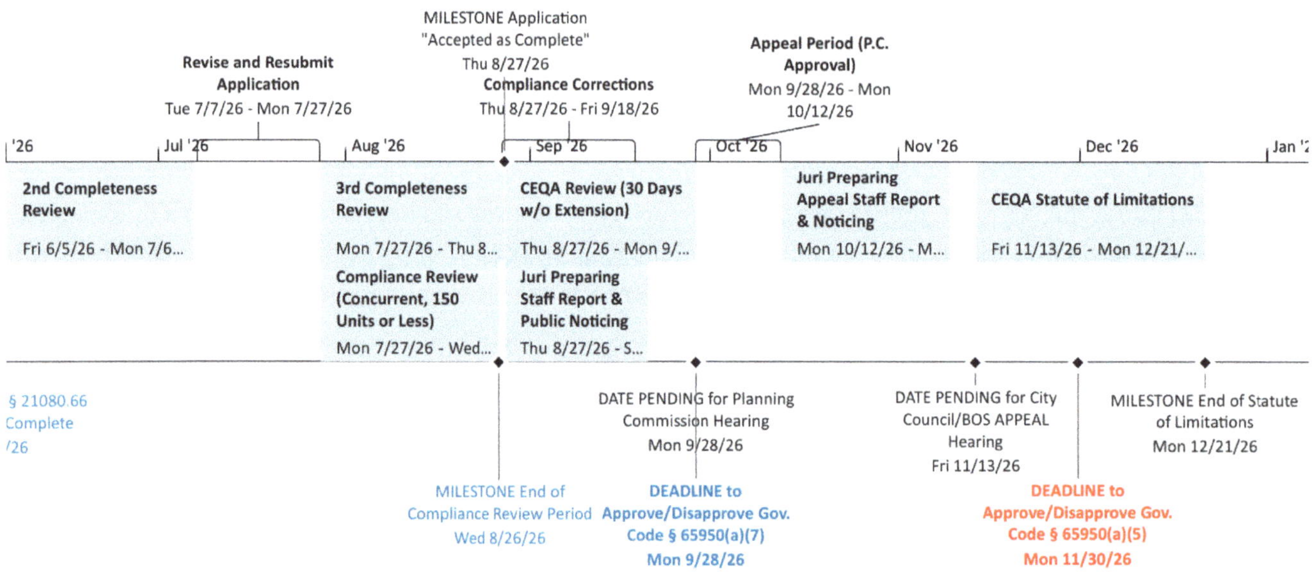

The timeline in Figure 13(A) assumes the jurisdiction takes the entire legally allowed time period (with the applicant agreeing to no extensions) for completeness review, compliance review, and CEQA review. It assumes the answer to the question "what triggers the start of the compliance review period" is A: the date the ***complete*** application was ***submitted*** (i.e., the date of the **final** submittal of the development permit application that is **later** determined to be complete by the jurisdiction). If the correct interpretation of the Unclear Deadline for Approval or Disapproval of Projects that are Exempt Pursuant to PRC § 21080.66 is that ***only*** the deadline under paragraph (7) of Gov. Code § 65950(a) applies, the jurisdiction would have a deadline of September 28, 2026 to approve or disapprove the project, and would be making the determination that the project is exempt from CEQA pursuant to PRC § 21080.66 on the date of the planning commission hearing.

It is very possible that this is exactly what the Legislature intended when it passed AB 130 (2025), but if this ***is*** the correct legal interpretation, jurisdictions need to process projects that use the new exemption much more quickly than has been typical.

Why the Author Believes the Answer is A: the Date the Complete Application was *Submitted*

Up to now, jurisdictions have pretty much **ignored the compliance review deadline**. They provide compliance comments with every round of completeness review, they continue to review the application for compliance after the date the compliance review period has expired, and they never provide a comprehensive compliance determination until they publish the staff report recommending approval or disapproval of the project, a few days before the hearing. Jurisdictions generally do not start writing the staff report or scheduling the hearing until they have made the CEQA determination and are satisfied that the project is compliant with the applicable development standards. This is partially because the ambiguity about the start of the compliance review period makes it very hard for applicants to enforce the deadline for compliance review, and partly because the deemed approval provision of Gov. Code § 65956(b) was virtually impossible to enforce until AB 130 (2025) amended it (see Deemed Approval — New with AB 130).

The development community needs clarity on the question posed at the beginning of this section: what triggers the start of the compliance review period? Is it A or B:

A. The date the ***complete*** application was ***submitted*** (i.e., the date of the **final** submittal of the development permit application that is **later** determined to be complete by the jurisdiction).
B. The date the application is affirmatively ***determined*** to be complete by the jurisdiction (i.e., the date the jurisdiction sends the "completeness letter").

The Author believes answer is A: The date the *complete* application was ***submitted***. His arguments for why this is the correct interpretation follow.

Achieving a Complete Application is Imperative

The first major issue that boondoggles the review process, delaying projects and undermining the protections of the Housing Accountability Act, is that the application cannot move forward until it is **determined to be complete** by the jurisdiction, or **deemed complete** by operation of state law.

The completeness review process creates a big problem: it allows the jurisdiction to undermine the limits on their discretion to disapprove the project by delaying the applicant's ability to enforce the Housing Accountability Act. Until the application is determined to be complete, the jurisdiction does not have to make the determination whether the project is exempt from CEQA, which triggers the deadline to approve or disapprove the project.

Achieving a complete application is *imperative* because it starts the decision-making process and leads to either approval or disapproval of the project. If the project is disapproved by a planning commission, the applicant can appeal the disapproval, and then if the city council or county board of supervisors upholds the disapproval, the applicant can file an action in court to compel the jurisdiction to comply with the Housing Accountability Act.

Achieving a Compliant Project is Secondary

Compliance review is the process of determining whether the housing development project is compliant with the "applicable, objective general plan, zoning, and subdivision standards and criteria, including design review standards" that were in effect on the vesting date. (Gov. Code § 65589.5(j)(1).) Unlike the completeness review process that is prescribed by the Permit Streamlining Act and applies to all types of development permit applications, the compliance review process is prescribed by the Housing Accountability Act and applies ***only*** to housing development projects. Housing projects are special. The preamble to the Housing Accountability Act explains why it strictly limits the discretion of local governments when it comes to housing projects. Gov. Code § 65589.5(a), paraphrased:

> The Legislature finds ... that the lack of housing ... is a critical problem that threatens the ... quality of life in California. ... Many local governments do not give adequate attention to the economic, environmental, and social costs of decisions that result in disapproval of housing development projects, reduction in density of housing projects, and excessive standards for housing development projects.
>
> ...
>
> The consequences of failing to effectively and aggressively confront this crisis are hurting millions of Californians, robbing future generations of the chance to call California home, stifling economic opportunities for workers and businesses, worsening poverty and homelessness, and undermining the state's environmental and climate objectives. [T]he absence of meaningful and effective policy reforms to significantly enhance the approval and supply of housing affordable to Californians of all income levels is a key factor.
>
> ...
>
> The Legislature's intent in enacting this section in 1982 and in expanding its provisions since then was to significantly increase the approval and construction of new housing for all economic segments of California's communities by meaningfully and effectively curbing the capability of local governments to deny, reduce the density for, or render infeasible housing development projects and emergency shelters. That intent has not been fulfilled.

Because of the housing crisis, the Legislature has essentially **prohibited** jurisdictions from disapproving housing projects that provide affordable units or imposing conditions that would make those projects infeasible. Gov. Code § 65589.5(b):

> (b) It is the policy of the state that a local government not reject or make infeasible housing development projects, including emergency shelters, that contribute to meeting the [jurisdiction's share of the Regional Housing Needs Assessment] without a thorough analysis of the economic, social, and environmental effects of the action and without complying with subdivision (d).

For projects that qualify for subdivision (d) of the Housing Accountability Act, including Builder's Remedy Projects and projects located on sites that are listed in the jurisdiction's housing element (which the Author calls Mini Builder's Remedy Projects), the jurisdiction "**shall not disapprove** the housing development project" (Gov. Code § 65589.5(d)) even if it is ***not*** compliant. And, for projects that qualify for the State Density Bonus Law, "In no case may a city, county, or city and county apply any development standard that will have the effect of physically precluding the construction of a development ..." (Gov. Code § 65915(e)(1)). The jurisdiction's discretion to disapprove a project is extremely limited, and full compliance with local development standards is ***not*** required.

Even for projects that do not qualify under subdivision (d), the Housing Accountability Act requires that "standards and criteria shall be applied to facilitate and accommodate development at the density allowed on the site by the general plan and proposed by the proposed housing development project." (Gov. Code § 65589.5(j)(4).) So, for ***all*** housing projects, **achieving a compliant project is *secondary*.**

Unsurprisingly, jurisdictions do not like these limits on their discretion. Applicants and jurisdictions often vehemently disagree about which development standards can be imposed on the project and which are preempted by state law. The responsibility of the jurisdiction's planning department is to review the project and "provide the applicant with written documentation identifying the provision or provisions, and an explanation of the reason or reasons it considers the housing development to be inconsistent, not in compliance, or not in conformity." (Gov. Code § 65589.5(j)(2)(A).) Once the jurisdiction provides comprehensive compliance comments, the applicant can respond to each of them and explain why the offended development standards do not apply to the project or apply a waiver or reduction of the development standards as allowed by the State Density Bonus Law.

The problem is that jurisdictions **ignore** the requirement of Gov. Code § 65589.5(j)(2)(A) to provide a compliance determination within 30 or 60 days of receiving a complete application. The staff report, coming long after the compliance review period expired and just days before the hearing, is typically the first time the applicant receives **comprehensive** compliance comments with code citations and general plan references and a legal rationale for why the project is considered not to be compliant with each offended development standard. Jurisdictions have been able to ignore this requirement because of the uncertainty as to when the compliance review period starts, and because there was effectively no enforceable deadline for the approval or disapproval of the project until the passage of AB 130 (2025). Compliance review could just drag on and on, undermining the special protections afforded to housing projects.

Definition of Determined to be Complete

Which date triggers the start of the 30- or 60-day Time Period Allowed for Compliance Review depends on the definition of the term "determined to be complete" because Gov. Code § 65589.5(j)(2)(A) reads:

> (2) (A) If the local agency considers a proposed housing development project to be inconsistent, not in compliance, or not in conformity with an applicable plan, program, policy, ordinance, standard, requirement, or other similar provision as specified in this subdivision, it shall provide the applicant with written documentation identifying the provision or provisions, and an explanation of the reason or reasons it considers the housing development to be inconsistent, not in compliance, or not in conformity as follows:
>
> > (i) Within 30 days of the date that the application for the housing development project is **determined to be complete**, if the housing development project contains 150 or fewer housing units.
> >
> > (ii) Within 60 days of the date that the application for the housing development project is **determined to be complete**, if the housing development project contains more than 150 units.

The term "determined to be complete" appears three times in the Housing Accountability Act: in clauses (i) and (ii) above, and in the **definition** at Gov. Code § 65589.5(h)(10):

> (10) Notwithstanding any other law, "**determined** to be complete" **means** that the applicant **has *submitted*** a complete application pursuant to Section 65943.

The **full** development permit application (the "application pursuant to Section 65943) is the relevant in the definition of "determined to be complete."

Definition of Deemed Complete

Contrast the full development permit application that must be "determined to be complete" with the SB 330 preliminary application that is "deemed complete" upon submittal per this definition at Gov. Code § 65589.5(h)(5):

> (5) Notwithstanding any other law, "**deemed** complete" means that the applicant has submitted a preliminary application pursuant to Section 65941.1 or, if the applicant has not submitted a preliminary application, has submitted a complete application pursuant to Section 65943. The local agency shall bear the burden of proof in establishing that the application is not complete.

Deemed complete very clearly means the date that the SB 330 preliminary application is **submitted.** The SB 330 preliminary application is deemed complete upon submittal because Gov. Code § 65941.1(a) says:

> 65941.1. (a) An applicant for a housing development project, as defined in paragraph (3) of subdivision (b) of Section 65905.5, **shall be deemed to have submitted a preliminary application upon providing all of the following information** …

Gov. Code § 65941.1 goes on to prescribe a list of 17 items that constitute a complete SB 330 preliminary application (see What Are the 17 Required Items?), and so long as it includes those items the SB 330 preliminary application is deemed complete when submitted. There is no requirement that the jurisdiction provide any determination as to the completeness of the SB 330 preliminary application. (Gov. Code § 65941.1(e)(3).)

The SB 330 preliminary application is deemed complete upon submittal because Gov. Code § 65941.1(a) says:

> 65941.1. (a) An applicant for a housing development project, as defined in paragraph (3) of subdivision (b) of Section 65905.5, **shall be deemed to have submitted a preliminary application upon providing all of the following information** …

Gov. Code § 65941.1 goes on to prescribe a list of 17 items that constitute a complete SB 330 preliminary application (see What Are the 17 Required Items?), and so long as it includes those items the SB 330 preliminary application is deemed complete when submitted. There is no requirement that the jurisdiction provide any determination as to the completeness of the SB 330 preliminary application. (Gov. Code § 65941.1(e)(3).)

But look at the definition of deemed complete when there is ***no*** SB 330 preliminary application. From the definition at Gov. Code § 65589.5(h)(5) quoted above, remove the part about the SB 330 preliminary application (which is what "pursuant to Section 65941.1" refers to):

> (5) Notwithstanding any other law, "**deemed** complete" **means** that the applicant **has submitted** … a complete application pursuant to Section 65943. The local agency shall bear the burden of proof in establishing that the application is not complete.

That bit about the "burden of proof" in the definition of "deemed complete" also applies to the completeness determination for the full development permit application, per Gov. Code § 65589.5(h)(6)(g) "The local agency shall bear the burden of proof …" for determinations the full development permit application is incomplete.

Therefore, if the applicant **did not submit an SB 330 preliminary application**, there is ***no*** **difference** between Gov. Code § 65589.5(h)(5) and (10):

> (5) Notwithstanding any other law, "deemed complete" means that the applicant has submitted … a complete application pursuant to Section 65943. The local agency shall bear the burden of proof in establishing that the application is not complete.
>
> (10) Notwithstanding any other law, "determined to be complete" means that the applicant has submitted a complete application pursuant to Section 65943. [The local agency shall bear the burden of proof … (Gov. Code § 65589.5(h)(6)(g))]

When no SB 330 preliminary application applies to the project, the terms "deemed complete" and "determined to be complete" mean exactly the same thing: the applicant ***submitted*** the **complete** full development permit application.

The Full Application Was Complete Upon Submittal if the Jurisdiction Later Determines it to be Complete

The **full** development permit application requires an **affirmative determination** of completeness, per Gov. Code § 65943(a):

> 65943. (a) Not later than 30 calendar days after any public agency has received an application for a development project, the agency **shall determine in writing whether the application is complete** and shall immediately transmit the determination to the applicant for the development project. **If the application is determined to be incomplete, the lead agency shall provide the applicant with an exhaustive list** of items that were not complete. ...

Unlike the SB 330 preliminary application with its 17 required items, the local jurisdiction decides what items are required for a complete application (i.e., the jurisdiction compiles its own LORI in accordance with Gov. Code § 65940). Therefore, the jurisdiction has to make a **determination** whether the full development permit application includes the items on the LORI created by that jurisdiction. Only if the jurisdiction **fails** to make the determination is the application deemed complete in accordance with Gov. Code § 65943.

But here's the key: **if** the jurisdiction makes the affirmative determination that the application is complete, then that application ***was*** **complete *when* it was submitted.**

The "Determined to be Complete" Date is the (Final) Submittal Date of the Complete Application

The **submittal** of a development permit application starts the clock for the completeness review period (always 30 days), and **only if** that submittal was complete, it starts the clock for the compliance review period (30 days for a project of up to 150 units, or 60 days for a project over 150 units). Each **re**submittal of the application resets the clock. Upon the **final** submittal the time periods run **concurrently**. When the jurisdiction receives an application that ***is*** complete (i.e., that it later determines to be complete), the clocks for both completeness review and compliance review run from the submittal date until their respective deadlines.

Take another look at the definition of "determined to be complete," Gov. Code § 65589.5(h)(10):

> (10) Notwithstanding any other law, "determined to be complete" means that **the applicant has submitted a complete application** pursuant to Section 65943.

If we replace the term "determined to be complete" with its definition, Gov. Code § 65589.5(j)(2)(A) reads:

> (2) (A) If the local agency considers a proposed housing development project to be inconsistent, not in compliance, or not in conformity with an applicable plan, program, policy, ordinance, standard, requirement, or other similar provision as specified in this subdivision, it shall provide the applicant with written documentation identifying the provision or provisions, and an explanation of the reason or reasons it considers the housing development to be inconsistent, not in compliance, or not in conformity as follows:
>
> > (i) Within 30 days of the date [**that the applicant has submitted a complete application** pursuant to Section 65943], if the housing development project contains 150 or fewer housing units.
> >
> > (ii) Within 60 days of the date [**that the applicant has submitted a complete application** pursuant to Section 65943], if the housing development project contains more than 150 units.
>
> (B) If the local agency fails to provide the required documentation pursuant to subparagraph (A), the housing development project shall be deemed consistent, compliant, and in conformity with the applicable plan, program, policy, ordinance, standard, requirement, or other similar provision.

"Determined to be complete" means "has submitted a complete application." The 30- or 60-day clock starts on the date the application is submitted, but **only if** that application was "complete." If the jurisdiction determines that the application was ***in***complete, then the clock for the compliance review period gets reset because the applicant **had not submitted** a complete application.

Keep in mind that it routinely takes three submittals before the jurisdiction will determine that an application is complete, and as explained in Chapter 8: Completeness Review, Gov. Code § 65943 anticipates three rounds of completeness review. By the third submittal, if the applicant ***has* submitted a complete application**, it should take very little time to confirm that the third submittal is complete. The jurisdiction could send a letter of completeness on day one saying, "your application is complete, but we're still reviewing the application for compliance," then take the next 29 or 59 days to review the application for compliance, and send the comprehensive compliance review required by Gov. Code § 65589.5(j)(2)(A) by the deadline. There really is no excuse for a jurisdiction to ignore the compliance review deadline, or to fail to provide comprehensive and detailed compliance comments meeting the letter and intent of Gov. Code § 65589.5(j)(2)(A).

Complete Application on the First Try

Let's look at what happens if an applicant submits a complete application on the very first try. The jurisdiction takes in the application, including the required fee, and the completeness review and compliance review clocks start running. Let's say that after 15 days the jurisdiction sends the applicant a "letter of completeness." That application was determined to be complete on the 15th day, but the applicant had submitted a complete application on the 1st day.

By the time the jurisdiction sent the letter of completeness, the clock had been running on the **compliance** review period for 15 days. If the application was for a project of over 150 units, the jurisdiction would have 45 more days (60 days total) to provide the comprehensive compliance determination required by Gov. Code § 65589.5(j)(2)(A). If the application was for a project of 150 or fewer units, the jurisdiction would have 15 days left to make the compliance determination.

Complete on Day One — Would be the case with AB 1294

Taking this complete-on-the-first-try example just a little further, let's say the applicant walks up to the planning counter, hands the jurisdiction the application materials and a check for the fee, and the planner signs a form, right then and there, determining that the application is complete.

In this case there is no ambiguity. The applicant has submitted a complete application that has been determined to be compete pursuant to Gov. Code § 65943, and the 30- or 60-day clock is running for the jurisdiction to determine whether or not the application is compliant. This is the way it **should** work. The LORI is a checklist of items and information that constitute a complete application. It should not take any special skills, or a long time, to review the application for completeness. Nobody needs a master's degree in urban planning to run a checklist. In fact, **any *reasonable person* can review an application for completeness**. If "a reasonable person would conclude that the applicant has submitted all of the items required on the local agency's submittal requirement checklist" the application ***is*** complete. (Gov. Code § 65589.5(h)(6)(F)(iii).)

This is essentially what will happen if AB 1294 passes: the full development permit application will be deemed complete upon submittal if it includes all the items specified in a new statewide LORI. The submittal of the complete application will trigger the compliance review, and there will be no doubt as to the deadline for the comprehensive compliance determination required by Gov. Code § 65589.5(j)(2).

What does HCD Say?

HCD has enforcement authority over most housing laws,[46] and their Housing Accountability Unit answers dozens of the thorniest questions every year. However, HCD has never provided a clear answer to the question of what triggers the start of the compliance review period, except in cases where the full development permit application was ***deemed*** complete because the jurisdiction **failed** to make the determination required by Gov. Code § 65943 within 30 days.

In a letter to the City of Santa Ana *RE: 1212 E Fourth Street Application – Letter of Technical Assistance*, dated April 27, 2023,[47] HCD explained that the City had missed the 30-day deadline to determine the application was incomplete, and therefore the 1212 E Fourth Street development permit application had been **deemed complete** due to the expiration of the time limit. Furthermore, Santa Ana had also missed the 30-day deadline for compliance review, and the project had been **deemed compliant**. In the letter, HCD indicates that the time periods run ***sequentially***. Here is a condensation of that letter:

> This letter presents the Project's permitting history in three distinct phases, punctuated by key milestones ...
>
> **Phase 1: Application Submittal to Application Completeness Determination**
>
> On November 10, 2021, the applicant submitted the full development application. ...
>
> The City failed to inform the applicant in writing that the application was not complete by December 10, 2021 (i.e., 30 days from the date of submittal). Therefore, on December 10, 2021, the application was deemed complete by operation of law.
>
> **Phase 2: Application Completeness Determination to Project Consistency Determination**
>
> The HAA requires that for housing development projects containing 150 or fewer housing units, the local agency has 30 days from the date the development application is deemed complete to provide the applicant with written documentation of any inconsistency, incompliance, or inconformity ...
>
> The City failed to inform the applicant in writing of any inconsistencies by January 9, 2022 (i.e., 30 days from the date that the application was deemed complete by operation of law). Therefore, on January 9, 2022, the Project was deemed consistent and compliant with the applicable plan, ordinance, and standards by operation of law. On the same date, the Project became vested under the HAA (Gov. Code, § 65589.5, subd. (j)(1)). Note that the Project's vesting is not based on the submittal of a Preliminary Application (Gov. Code, § 65941.1) because the applicant did not submit a Preliminary Application. The Project's vesting occurred when the application was deemed consistent by operation of law (Gov. Code, § 65589.5, subd. (h)(5)).
>
> **Phase 3: Project Consistency Determination to Project Consideration**
>
> [Santa Ana sent its first letter to the applicant on January 18, 2022, determining the project **not** to be compliant. Even though the project had already been deemed compliant on January 9, 2022, the applicant attempted to resolve the purported inconsistencies for 14 months, until March 15, 2023. The applicant resolved all but one specific item, which the applicant continued to contest as not applicable to the project because that item had been adopted by the city on April 19, 2022, **after** the development standards had been vested by the complete application (again, the applicant had not submitted an SB 330 preliminary application). This led to the request for Technical Assistance from HCD. HCD agreed with the applicant that the item did not apply.]

So, in this Letter of Technical Assistance, HCD's guidance is that the project was **deemed** complete on day 30 because the jurisdiction failed to send written notice that the application was incomplete. The project was 150 units or less, and the jurisdiction failed to send written notice that the application was not compliant within 30

[46] https://www.hcd.ca.gov/hau.
[47] https://www.hcd.ca.gov/sites/default/files/docs/planning-and-community/HAU/SantaAna-TA-04272023.pdf.

days **after** the deemed complete date and was therefore deemed compliant on the 60th day. HCD is saying that the **time periods run sequentially *if* an application is *deemed* compliant**.

Some practitioners argue that this HCD letter means that the compliance period ***always*** starts after the completeness review, even when the jurisdiction determines the application to be complete. If they are right, then the Author is wrong. And maybe the Author ***is*** wrong, but not because of this letter. This case in Santa Ana certainly indicates that the 30-day time period for compliance review starts the day after an application is ***deemed*** complete due to expiration of the 30-day deadline for the completeness determination. The Author **agrees** with HCD in the case of a ***deemed*** complete application. The HCD letter did not address the timeline when the jurisdiction affirmatively **determines** that the application they received was complete when it was submitted.

Start of the Compliance Period When the Application is *Deemed* Complete by State Law

In the case where the jurisdiction has failed to respond within 30 days, the application may **not** have been complete when it was submitted. In fact, jurisdictions often send a letter of ***in***completeness ***late***, after the completeness review period has expired, and despite that determination that the development permit application was **not** complete in accordance with the jurisdiction's LORI when it was submitted, it ***became*** complete (was deemed complete by operation of the Permit Streamlining Act) **when** the jurisdiction failed to respond within 30 days. The compliance review period, in this case, starts the moment the application ***becomes/is deemed*** complete at midnight on the date the completeness review period expires.

Again, the full development permit application is not like the SB 330 preliminary application for which the **presumption** is that it included the 17 items and was complete when submitted, and the law explicitly says that no affirmative determination is required. (Gov. Code § 65941.1(e)(3).) The jurisdiction ***can*** make a determination (if they can prove it) that the SB 330 preliminary application is **in**complete, in which case it will **not** have vested the development standards. By contrast, for the full development permit application, Gov. Code § 65943 pretty clearly **presumes multiple submittals** before the application will be complete. The full development permit application is not deemed complete ***unless*** the 30-day completeness review period expires without a determination by the jurisdiction.

In short, the Author's interpretation is that, in the event the jurisdiction fails to find it incomplete within 30 days, the full development permit application ***becomes*** complete at the end of the 30th day and triggers the start of the compliance review period.

What if The Author is Wrong?

The Author acknowledges that he may be wrong. Maybe the correct interpretation of the definition at Gov. Code § 65589.5(h)(10) is that the date the application is determined to be complete is the **date of the determination** (i.e., the date at the top of the "letter of completeness").

But if the Author is wrong, there's no reason for the words "has submitted" to be in that definition. If the Legislature had intended for the compliance review period to start on the date of the determination, they could have made everyone's life a lot easier and said:

> (10) Notwithstanding any other law, "determined to be complete" means that ~~the applicant has submitted a complete application~~ the jurisdiction has determined the application to be complete, or that the application has been deemed complete pursuant to Section 65943."

Until the passage of AB 130 (2025) added paragraph (7) to Gov. Code § 65950(a), and that paragraph was later amended by SB 158 (2025), the end of the compliance review period did not trigger **any** other deadlines. Nor did the project being deemed compliant trigger any deadlines. In scheduling terms, the tasks *receipt of compliance comments* or *deemed compliant due to expiration of time* have no successors.

Whether the Author is right or wrong, he hopes that the Legislature will clarify this issue, because with the passage of AB 130 (2025) the correct legal interpretation of when the compliance review period starts is potentially of critical importance — it may determine the deadline for approval or disapproval of a project using the new PRC § 21080.66 CEQA exemption, and lead to Deemed Approval — New with AB 130.

Deadline for Initial Approval or Disapproval of the Project

As explained under The Path to Final Approval, the CEQA determination is, for projects that are exempt from CEQA, the single most important milestone for the timely approval of the project. Article 5. Approval of Development Permits of the Permit Streamlining Act sets time limits for initial approval or disapproval of a project, depending on the type of CEQA determination. For most housing development projects, the time limits for the jurisdiction to approve or disapprove a project (subject to appeals, which can extend far beyond this time limit) are specified in Gov. Code § 65950(a), which begins:

> 65950. (a) A public agency that is the lead agency for a development project **shall approve or disapprove the project** within whichever of the following periods is applicable: ...

Under Gov. Code § 65950(a) are paragraphs (1) through (7) that prescribe deadlines based on the type of project and CEQA determination. The deadlines are summarized in the numbered list below, with further explanation under the subheadings that follow.

1. For projects that are ministerial (see Discretionary vs. Ministerial), and thus not subject to CEQA, the 60-day time limit for approval/disapproval starts on the date the jurisdiction ***receives*** the complete development permit application. Except that projects that are ministerial pursuant to the Affordable Housing and High Road Jobs Act of 2022 (AB 2011) follow the time periods in that Act. (Gov. Code § 65950(a)(6), which was added by AB 130 (2025).) See 60-Day Deadline for Approval or Disapproval of a Ministerial Project.
2. For projects that are exempt from CEQA pursuant to any exemption other than the PRC § 21080.66 Statutory Exemption — New with AB 130, the jurisdiction must act to approve or disapprove the project within 60 days from the date the jurisdiction's staff ***makes the determination*** that the project is exempt (i.e., the date of the preliminary CEQA exemption determination letter). (Gov. Code § 65950(a)(5).) See 60-Day Deadline for Approval or Disapproval of Exempt Projects that Do Not Use PRC § 21080.66.
3. For the new PRC § 21080.66 exemption, AB 130 (2025) added a new deadline as paragraph (7) of Gov. Code § 65950(a), and SB 158 (2025) quickly amended that new paragraph (7). The proper interpretation of that paragraph is not entirely clear. Please review Unclear Deadline for Approval or Disapproval of Projects that are Exempt Pursuant to PRC § 21080.66 for a detailed discussion, and consult a qualified attorney.
4. For projects that require a CEQA negative declaration or mitigated negative declaration, there is also a 60-day time limit for approval/disapproval of the project, but that time period starts when the lead agency ***adopts*** the ND or MND. (Gov. Code § 65950(a)(4).) See 60-Day Deadline for Approval or Disapproval of Projects Requiring a Negative Declaration.
5. For projects that require a CEQA environmental impact report, the time limit starts when the lead agency ***certifies*** the EIR. The time limit could be 60, 90, or 180 days depending on the type of project. (Gov. Code § 65950(a)(1) through (3).) EIRs are not covered in detail in this book, but see Environmental Impact Reports for a general discussion of the time limits.

Deadlines for special cases are prescribed in other Sections of Article 5 of the Permit Streamlining Act. This book does not provide details on the deadlines prescribed by these Sections:

- Gov. Code § 65950.1, which states that when "there has been an extension of time pursuant to Section 21100.2 or 21151.5 of the Public Resources Code to complete and certify the environmental impact report, the lead agency shall approve or disapprove the project within 90 days after certification of the environmental impact report."
- Gov. Code § 65951 applies when "a combined environmental impact report-environmental impact statement is being prepared" under both CEQA and the National Environmental Policy Act (NEPA).
- Gov. Code § 65952 applies when the project has already been approved by the lead agency, but a "**responsible** agency" must also approve the project.

The Deadline for Initial Approval or Disapproval of the Project is Now *Self-Enforcing*

The jurisdiction is required to approve or disapprove the project within the applicable time period specified in Article 5 of the Permit Streamlining Act. The amendment made to Gov. Code § 65956(b) by AB 130 (2025) has made those deadlines **self-enforcing**. If the jurisdiction fails to approve or disapprove the project by the end of the time period, the project is **deemed approved**, as explained under Deemed Approval — New with AB 130. This does **not** mean that ***final*** approval/disapproval must be achieved by the deadline. If the initial decisionmaker's approval/disapproval is subject to appeal, then the appeal process can extend beyond the prescribed time period.

The jurisdiction cannot extend the time period by "continuing" a hearing to a later date. If the jurisdiction "continues" the hearing, the continued hearing must be concluded with an initial approval/disapproval before the deadline. Likewise, holding an advisory hearing to "recommend" approval or disapproval does not extend the time period. The law requires that the jurisdiction "shall approve or disapprove the project" by the deadline.

The Jurisdiction Shall Not Disapprove the Application Just to Meet the Deadline

Compliance with the deadline requires approval or disapproval of the project, including making the relevant findings if the project is disapproved. Per Gov. Code § 65952.2:

> 65952.2. No public agency shall disapprove an application for a development project in order to comply with the time limits specified in this chapter. Any disapproval of an application for a development project shall specify reasons for disapproval other than the failure to timely act in accordance with the time limits specified in this chapter.

Public agencies are prohibited from simply disapproving the project to comply with the time limits prescribed in the Permit Streamlining Act ("this chapter" refers to Chapter 4.5. Review and Approval of Development Projects, which is the Permit Streamlining Act).

The Deadline is a Maximum and Cannot Exceed the Time Limits Established by Any Other Law

AB 130 (2025) added subdivision (b) to Gov. Code 65953:

> 65953. (a) All time limits specified in this article are maximum time limits for approving or disapproving development projects. All public agencies shall, if possible, approve or disapprove development projects in shorter periods of time.
>
> (b) All time limits specified in this article shall only apply to the extent that the time limits are **equal to or shorter than** the applicable time limits for public agency review established in **any other law**.

"This article" refers to Article 5 of the Permit Streamlining Act, and therefore Gov. Code 65953 applies to all of the time limits for approval or disapproval of the development application summarized above. If any other law prescribes a shorter time limit, the shorter time limit applies.

Extending the Deadline

Gov. Code § 65950(b) allows the deadline for initial approval/disapproval of the project to be extended:

> (b) This section does not preclude a project applicant and a public agency from mutually agreeing in writing to an extension of any time limit provided by this section pursuant to Section 65957.

Per Gov. Code § 65957, the deadline can only be extended **once** for up to **90 days**, and only by **mutual written agreement** between the applicant and the public agency:

> 65957. The time limits established by Sections 65950, 65950.1, 65951, and 65952 **may be extended *once* upon mutual written agreement** of the project applicant and the public agency **for a period not to exceed 90 days** from the date of the extension. No other extension, continuance, or waiver of these time limits either by the project applicant or the lead agency shall be permitted, except as provided in this section and Section 65950.1. Failure of the lead agency to act within these time limits may result in the project being deemed approved pursuant to the provisions of subdivision (b) of Section 65956.

In most cases, the applicant should not agree to this extension, since pursuant to Gov. Code § 65956(b) expiration of the deadline results in Deemed Approval — New with AB 130.

60-Day Deadline for Approval or Disapproval of a Ministerial Project

The next section, Deadline for Exempt Projects Using vs. Not Using the New PRC § 21080.66 Exemption, applies when a project is (statutorily or categorically) ***exempt*** from CEQA, and therefore Gov. Code § 65950(a)(5) and/or (7) apply. **Ministerial** projects, although sometimes referred to as "exempt," are ***not subject*** to CEQA, because CEQA Applies to Discretionary Projects, but Not to Ministerial Projects.

To make it clear that ministerial projects are subject to a 60-day approval/disapproval deadline, triggered by a complete development permit application ***submittal***, AB 130 (2025) added paragraph (6) to Gov. Code § 65950(a):

> 65950. (a) A public agency that is the lead agency for a development project **shall approve or disapprove the project** within whichever of the following periods is applicable:
>
> > ...
> >
> > (6) Except as provided in subdivision (a) of Section 65912.114 and subdivision (a) of Section 65912.124, **sixty days from the *date of receipt* of a complete application if the project is subject to ministerial review** by the public agency.

"Section 65912.114 and ... Section 65912.124" refer to the Affordable Housing and High Road Jobs Act of 2022 (AB 2011), which prescribes the deadlines for projects using its ministerial process. For all other ministerial projects, the deadline to approve/disapprove the project is 60 days from the date a complete application is submitted.

Deadline for Exempt Projects Using vs. Not Using the New PRC § 21080.66 Exemption

The process for determining which type of CEQA determination will be required for a project is covered in Chapter 4: CEQA Review for Housing Projects After AB 130 and SB 131. That process begins with a review to determine whether or not the project is exempt from CEQA. If the Result of the Review for Exemption is that the project is not exempt, or that more information is necessary to determine whether the project is exempt, the jurisdiction's staff will make a written preliminary determination that the project is not exempt from CEQA and require the applicant to provide more information or to prepare an Initial Study. Further review of the project may result in a revised preliminary determination that the project actually is exempt.

If the project is determined to be exempt, that determination triggers a time limit for approval or disapproval of the project. (See If the Project is Exempt for more information.) For projects that are exempt from CEQA, the jurisdiction must either approve or disapprove the project (subject to any appeal) by the 60-day deadline specified in Gov. Code § 65950(a)(5), or for the PRC § 21080.66 Statutory Exemption — New with AB 130, by the deadline specified in Gov. Code § 65950(a)(7), as explained under the following subheadings.

60-Day Deadline for Approval or Disapproval of Exempt Projects that Do *Not* Use PRC § 21080.66

For a project that is exempt from CEQA pursuant to any exemption ***other than*** the PRC § 21080.66 Statutory Exemption — New with AB 130, the deadline to approve or disapprove the project is 60 days from the date the jurisdiction makes the **preliminary determination** (see If the Project is Exempt) that the project is exempt (i.e., the date of the CEQA determination letter). The 60-day deadline is prescribed by Gov. Code § 65950(a)(5):

> 65950. (a) A public agency that is the lead agency for a development project **shall approve or disapprove the project** within whichever of the following periods is applicable:
>
> ...
>
> (5) **Sixty days from the determination** by the lead agency **that the project is exempt from the California Environmental Quality Act** (Division 13 (commencing with Section 21000) of the Public Resources Code), if the project is exempt from that act.

If the jurisdiction fails to approve or disapprove the project by the deadline, it is **deemed approved** as explained under Deemed Approval — New with AB 130.

Unclear Deadline for Approval or Disapproval of Projects that are Exempt Pursuant to PRC § 21080.66

Gov. Code § 65950(a) directs that the lead agency "shall approve or disapprove the project within whichever of the following periods is applicable." Paragraph (5) is applicable to projects that are exempt from CEQA and has been the law for decades. Paragraph (7) was added by AB 130 (2025) and amended by SB 158 (2025), and is applicable to a project that uses the PRC § 21080.66 Statutory Exemption — New with AB 130:

> 65950. (a) A public agency that is the lead agency for a development project **shall approve or disapprove the project** within whichever of the following periods is applicable:
>
> ...
>
> (5) **Sixty days from the determination** by the lead agency **that the project is exempt from the California Environmental Quality Act** (Division 13 (commencing with Section 21000) of the Public Resources Code), if the project is exempt from that act.
>
> ...
>
> (7) If a development project is exempt from the California Environmental Quality Act (Division 13 (commencing with Section 21000) of the Public Resources Code) **pursuant to Section** 21080.66 of the Public Resources Code, **30 days from the later of the following dates**:
>
> (A) The conclusion of the process outlined in subdivision (b) of Section 21080.66 of the Public Resources Code.
>
> (B) The expiration of the applicable time limit in paragraph (2) of subdivision (j) of Section 65589.5.

A project that is exempt "pursuant to Section 21080.66 of the Public Resources Code" per paragraph (7) is also "exempt from the California Environmental Quality Act" per paragraph (5), and therefore both paragraph (5) and paragraph (7) appear to be "applicable," leading to two potential interpretations of paragraph (7):

1. **Both** time periods under paragraphs (5) and (7) apply and the deadline is the ***later*** of the two deadlines.
2. ***Only*** the deadline under paragraph (7) applies. (I.e., the deadline is the later of subparagraph (A) or (B), irrespective of the time period of 60 days from the CEQA determination specified in paragraph (5).)

There is not yet case law, CEQA Guidelines, or HCD guidance on this question. However, the Legislative Counsel's Digest for SB 158 (2025), which was a clean-up bill that became effective upon the Governor's signature on October 11, 2025, seems to indicate that **only** the deadline under paragraph (7) applies:[48]

> CEQA exempts from its requirements housing projects that meet certain conditions. Under the exemption for housing projects, CEQA requires a local government to notify and consult, as specified, with each California Native American tribe that is traditionally and culturally affiliated with the project site on the proposed project, as specified. For a development project exempt from CEQA pursuant to this exemption, existing law, the Permit Streamlining Act, requires that a public agency that is the lead agency for the development project approve or disapprove the project within 30 days from the conclusion of the consultation process.
>
> Existing law, the Housing Accountability Act (HAA), among other things, prohibits a local agency from disapproving a housing development project that complies with applicable objective general plan, zoning, and subdivision standards and criteria, or from imposing a condition that it be developed at a lower density, unless the local agency bases its decision on written findings supported by a preponderance of the evidence on the record that specified conditions exist, as provided. When a local agency makes a decision as described above, existing law requires the local agency to provide the applicant documentation describing the reason for the decision within a specified time period.
>
> For a development project exempt from CEQA pursuant to the exemption for housing projects, this bill would instead require the public agency to approve or disapprove the project within 30 days from the later of the conclusion of the above-specified consultation process or the above-specified time period under the HAA.

Likewise, the Senate Floor Analyses dated September 13, 2025,[49] suggests that only the deadline in paragraph (7) applies:

> Modifies the deadline for a lead public agency to approve or disapprove specified infill housing development projects that are exempt from the California Environmental Quality Act (CEQA) from 30 days after the conclusion of the applicable tribal consultation process to 30 days from the later of:
>
> a) The conclusion of the applicable tribal consultation process; or
>
> b) The time period specified under the Housing Accountability Act.

However, if only the deadline in paragraph (7) applies, it would be possible for a project to be **deemed approved** ***before*** the jurisdiction determines that the project actually qualifies for the PRC § 21080.66 exemption. That could be the Legislature's intent, or it could be that the Legislature did not anticipate situations where the project would be approved before the jurisdiction makes the preliminary determination that the project is exempt pursuant to PRC § 21080.66. This potential situation is explained in Example 1: A Real-Life Project with the Determination of PRC § 21080.66 CEQA Exemption Delayed Beyond the Deadline at Gov. Code § 65950(a)(7).

In addition, the time period for approval or disapproval of the project will in many situations be very short, necessitating a change to the timeline by which most jurisdictions review projects (as in the example under Deadline for Approval or Disapproval of Projects with 150 Units or Less). Otherwise, jurisdictions will miss the deadline, resulting in Deemed Approval — New with AB 130 of a large number of projects.

[48] https://leginfo.legislature.ca.gov/faces/billTextClient.xhtml?bill_id=202520260SB158.
[49] https://leginfo.legislature.ca.gov/faces/billAnalysisClient.xhtml?bill_id=202520260SB158.

Example 1: A Real-Life Project with the Determination of PRC § 21080.66 CEQA Exemption Delayed Beyond the Deadline at Gov. Code § 65950(a)(7)

While writing this book, the Author was managing entitlements for a project that requested the PRC § 21080.66 exemption soon after AB 130 took effect on July 1, 2025. The application had already been determined to be complete, and the jurisdiction was in the midst of the 30- or 45-day Time Period for the Review for Exemption for a *different* CEQA exemption. On July 31, 2025, the jurisdiction issued a preliminary CEQA determination that the project may not meet the qualifications for the PRC § 21080.66 exemption (**bold black text** in Figure 14(A)).

For the next several months additional reports were obtained and reviewed, culminating in a revised determination on December 16, 2025 (red milestone) that the project actually did meet all of the requirements for the PRC § 21080.66 exemption. Therefore, the project is exempt "pursuant to Section 21080.66 of the Public Resources Code," and paragraph (7) of Gov. Code § 65950(a) applies. Paragraph 7 sets a deadline of October 30, 2025 (**bold blue**) 30 days after the later of the dates in subparagraphs (A) and (B) shown in the two blue milestones.

However, the **bold blue** deadline falls during a time period ***after*** the project had been determined **not to be exempt** from CEQA (**bold black**), and ***before*** the *revised* determination that the project is exempt pursuant to PRC § 21080.66 (red). If the correct legal interpretation of Gov. Code § 65950(a) is that ***only*** paragraph (7) applies, then the project would be deemed approved on the date in **bold blue**, despite the fact that, as of that date, the jurisdiction had determined that the project was **not** exempt from CEQA.

In addition, paragraph (5) of Gov. Code § 65950(a) applies "if the project is exempt," and the deadline under paragraph (5) is 60 days after the CEQA determination (red milestone). That deadline is February 17, 2026 (considering the President's Day holiday, see Computation of Time Periods and Deadlines) shown in **bold red**. The jurisdiction did **not** approve or disapprove the project at the planning commission hearing on January 14, 2026 (that hearing was *continued* to a "date uncertain"), and the jurisdiction did not act to approve or disapprove the project by the deadline in **bold red**.

When was this project deemed approved?

Figure 14(A): Timeline for a real-life project with a delayed determination of PRC § 21080.66 exemption

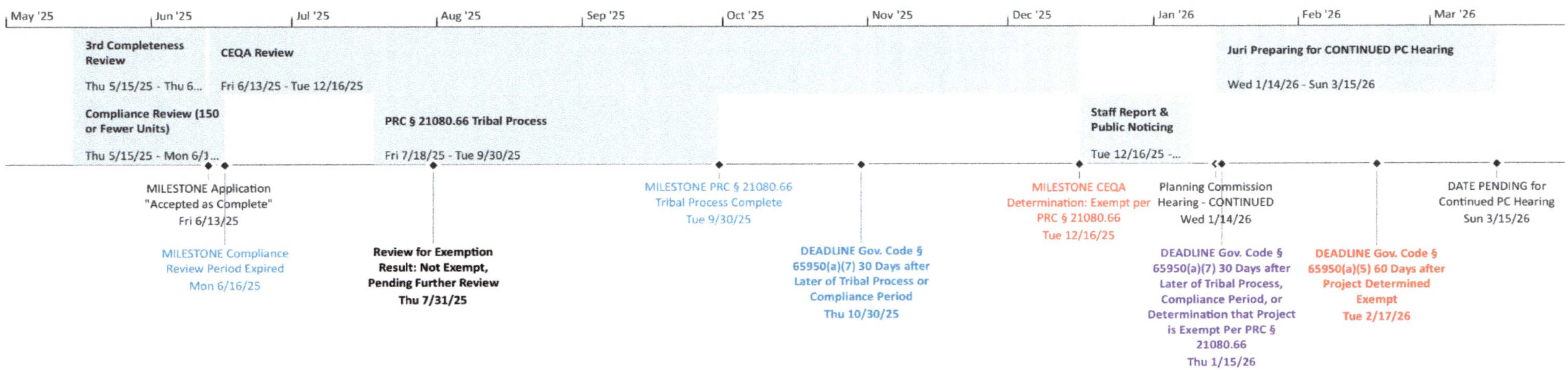

If the project in Example 1 had used a CEQA exemption *other than* the PRC § 21080.66 Statutory Exemption — New with AB 130, the deadline for approval/disapproval of the project would not be in question; the deadline would be February 17, 2026. But AB 130 (2025) added paragraph (7) to Gov. Code § 65950(a), and SB 158 (2025) amended paragraph (7) to read:

> (7) If a development project is exempt from the California Environmental Quality Act (Division 13 (commencing with Section 21000) of the Public Resources Code) **pursuant to Section** 21080.66 of the Public Resources Code, **30 days from the later of the following dates**:
>
> (A) The conclusion of the process outlined in subdivision (b) of Section 21080.66 of the Public Resources Code.
>
> (B) The expiration of the applicable time limit in paragraph (2) of subdivision (j) of Section 65589.5.

For the real-life project in Figure 14(A):

A. The "process outlined in subdivision (b) of Section 21080.66 of the Public Resources Code" for **tribal noticing and consultation** concluded (without any tribe requesting a consultation) on August 30, 2025. (Second blue milestone.)

B. The "time limit in paragraph (2) of subdivision (j) of Section 65589.5" for **compliance review** had expired on either June 16, 2025 (first blue milestone) if the Author is *right* about What Triggers the Start of the Compliance Review Period? or July 14, 2025 if the Author is *wrong*.[50]

Therefore, the deadline under paragraph (7), "30 days from the later" of the two dates in blue, was October 30, 2025, shown in **bold blue** in Figure 14(A). But as of that date, the project had not yet been determined to be exempt from CEQA, and in fact a letter preliminarily determining the project **not** to qualify for the PRC § 21080.66 exemption had been issued on July 31, 2025 (**bold black text**).

The jurisdiction held a planning commission hearing on January 14, 2026, but ***continued*** the hearing to a "date uncertain." That continuance did **not** constitute a decision to approve or disapprove the project, and the jurisdiction did not hold another hearing or otherwise act to approve or disapprove the project by the deadline pursuant to paragraph (5) of Gov. Code § 65950(a) (shown in **bold red**) of February 17, 2026. Regardless of what deadline applied, the jurisdiction failed to act in time, and the project was deemed approved. One of the first deemed approvals (if not ***the first***) to occur in the state after AB 130 (2025).

Although there is no question that this project was deemed approved not later than midnight on February 17, 2026, the Author and the project owner are uncertain as to the **deemed approval *date*** pursuant to Gov. Code § 65956(b) and Gov. Code § 65950(a). The potential interpretations are:

1. The project was deemed approved on October 30, 2025 (**bold blue**), in accordance with the deadline at Gov. Code § 65950(a)(7), regardless of the fact that the project had been determined **not** to be exempt from CEQA (subject to further studies and review) on July 31, 2025 (**black**).
   a. This interpretation is likely incorrect for this specific project, because paragraph (7) requires that the "project is exempt from the California Environmental Quality Act ... pursuant to Section 21080.66 of the Public Resources Code," and as of October 30, 2025 the jurisdiction had made a written determination that the project was **not** exempt from CEQA, subject to further investigation.

[50] In Figure 14(A) the compliance review period is shown beginning **concurrently** with the final round of completeness review, after the application had ***submitted*** a complete application. (Per the definition at Gov. Code § 65589.5(h)(10).) See Overview of the Issue of Ambiguity Regarding the Start of the Compliance Review Period for more information. The Author's interpretation, in this case, has no effect on the approval/disapproval deadline, because the tribal process was not complete until later.

2. The project was deemed approved on the date the jurisdiction made the written determination that the project was exempt, December 16, 2025 (red), because all the conditions in paragraph (7) had been satisfied by that date. This is a plausible interpretation, however:
    a. If this interpretation is correct, the only way the jurisdiction could comply with the law and avoid deemed approval of the project would be to **withhold** the written determination that the project is exempt from CEQA pursuant to PRC § 21080.66 until the date of the planning commission hearing.
        i. Project Approval Concurrent with the Adoption of an ND or MND is common, but If the Project is Exempt, the preliminary determination that the project is exempt from CEQA is typically made by the staff during the 30- or 45-day Time Period for the Review for Exemption and later **acknowledged** upon approval of the project.
    b. The 30- or 45-day Time Period for the Review for Exemption is **not** self-enforcing. If the jurisdiction does not provide an affirmative determination of whether the project is or is not exempt, there is no "deemed exempt" provision. If this second potential interpretation is correct, then jurisdictions could, and probably would, simply withhold the CEQA determination until the jurisdiction approves the project, thereby avoiding deemed approval of the project.
3. The deemed approval date is **30 days after *all*** of the conditions in paragraph (7) — including a determination that the project is exempt pursuant to PRC § 21080.66 — have been satisfied. This would make the deemed approval date January 15, 2026 (**purple**). This is a plausible interpretation, but it does not follow the letter of Gov. Code § 65950(a)(7). If this is the intent, the Legislature should amend paragraph (7) to read:

    > (7) If a development project is exempt from the California Environmental Quality Act (Division 13 (commencing with Section 21000) of the Public Resources Code) pursuant to Section 21080.66 of the Public Resources Code, 30 days from the later of the following dates:
    >
    > (A) The conclusion of the process outlined in subdivision (b) of Section 21080.66 of the Public Resources Code.
    >
    > (B) The expiration of the applicable time limit in paragraph (2) of subdivision (j) of Section 65589.5.
    >
    > *(C) The date the lead agency makes the determination required by subdivision (a) of Section 21080.1 of the Public Resources Code.*

4. The project was deemed approved at the end of February 17, 2026 (**bold red**), because the deadline for approval or disapproval of a project that is exempt pursuant to PRC § 21080.66 is the ***later*** of the dates calculated under paragraph (5) or paragraph (7). If this is the intent, the Legislature should amend paragraph (7) to read:

    > (7) If a development project is exempt from the California Environmental Quality Act (Division 13 (commencing with Section 21000) of the Public Resources Code) pursuant to Section 21080.66 of the Public Resources Code, *the later of the date calculated pursuant to paragraph (5) or* 30 days from the later of the following dates:
    >
    > (A) The conclusion of the process outlined in subdivision (b) of Section 21080.66 of the Public Resources Code.
    >
    > (B) The expiration of the applicable time limit in paragraph (2) of subdivision (j) of Section 65589.5.

Hopefully the 2026 CEQA Guidelines will address this issue and clarify the approval/disapproval deadline under various timelines, or the Legislature will pass clean-up legislation as an urgency bill early in 2026.

Example 2: Hypothetical Project Using the PRC § 21080.66 CEQA Exemption with a Typical Jurisdiction Process

The real-life project described in Example 1 was not typical of projects that qualify for the PRC § 21080.66 Statutory Exemption — New with AB 130. It did not request the new exemption until the review for exemption was already in progress, because PRC § 21080.66 only became effective on July 1, 2025. Moreover, the project required additional CEQA studies to confirm eligibility for the exemption, which took several months to prepare and review. The result was a CEQA review process that lasted far longer than normal, and a long gap between the deadline calculated under paragraph (7) and the deadline calculated under paragraph (5).

A more typical project is shown in Figure 15(A). The project is exempt pursuant to PRC § 21080.66, and the tribal process is complete well before the compliance review period. The jurisdiction follows a typical process where preparation of the staff report and public noticing for the planning commission hearing does not start until after compliance review is complete and the 30- or 45-day Time Period for the Review for Exemption has expired.

In Figure 15(A), if ***only*** the deadline under paragraph (7) applies, the deadline to approve/disapprove the project (**bold blue**) will fall during the CEQA review period, in this case extended by 15 days. It will be common for the deadline under paragraph (7) to occur before the planning commission hearing, and thus deemed approval will occur frequently if the Legislature's intent is that ***only*** paragraph (7) sets the deadline.

Perhaps it is the Legislature's intent that jurisdictions must conduct the review for the PRC § 21080.66 exemption during the tribal process? Perhaps the intent is that projects are presumed to qualify for the PRC § 21080.66 exemption unless the jurisdiction determines that they are not?

Figure 15(A): Typical jurisdiction process — timeline for a project that is exempt pursuant to PRC § 21080.66.

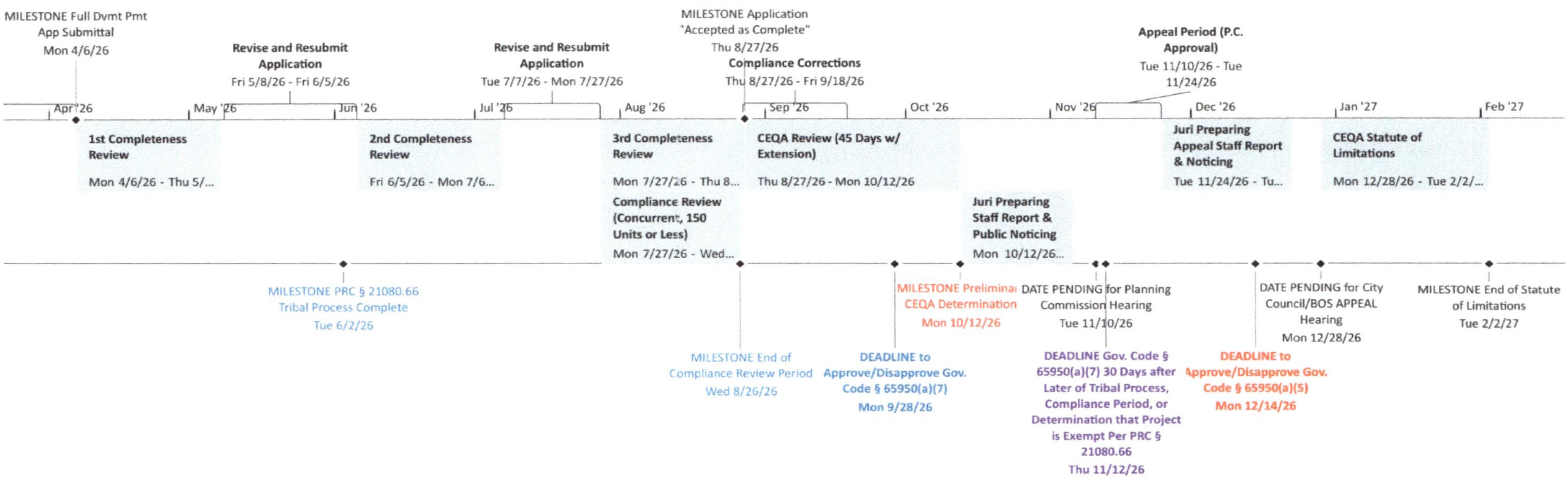

In The Real World of Development Permit Review, jurisdictions do things sequentially and only when faced with a deadline. Jurisdictions will typically use the entire 30- or 45-day Time Period for the Review for Exemption, which does not start until the application has been "accepted as complete by the lead agency." (PRC § 21080.2.) If the Legislature intends that the review for the PRC § 21080.66 exemption be conducted during the tribal process, or during the compliance review process, some sort of new legislation will be needed (a clean-up bill?).

If ***only*** paragraph (7) of Gov. Code § 65950(a) applies to a project that is exempt pursuant to PRC § 21080.66 (and the proper interpretation is that the later deadline in paragraph (5) does **not** apply), then the 30-day time period calculated under paragraph (7) leaves the jurisdiction very little time to get the project to a hearing, especially for a project with 150 units or fewer, that has only a 30-day compliance review period. An example of how a jurisdiction could meet the deadline, by not extending the CEQA review by 15 days, and completing the staff report and public noticing concurrently with the CEQA review was given under Deadline for Approval or Disapproval of Projects with 150 Units or Less, and the figure in that section is repeated as Figure 16(A), below.

Figure 16(A): Timeline to *avoid deemed approval* of a small project using the PRC § 21080.66 CEQA exemption.

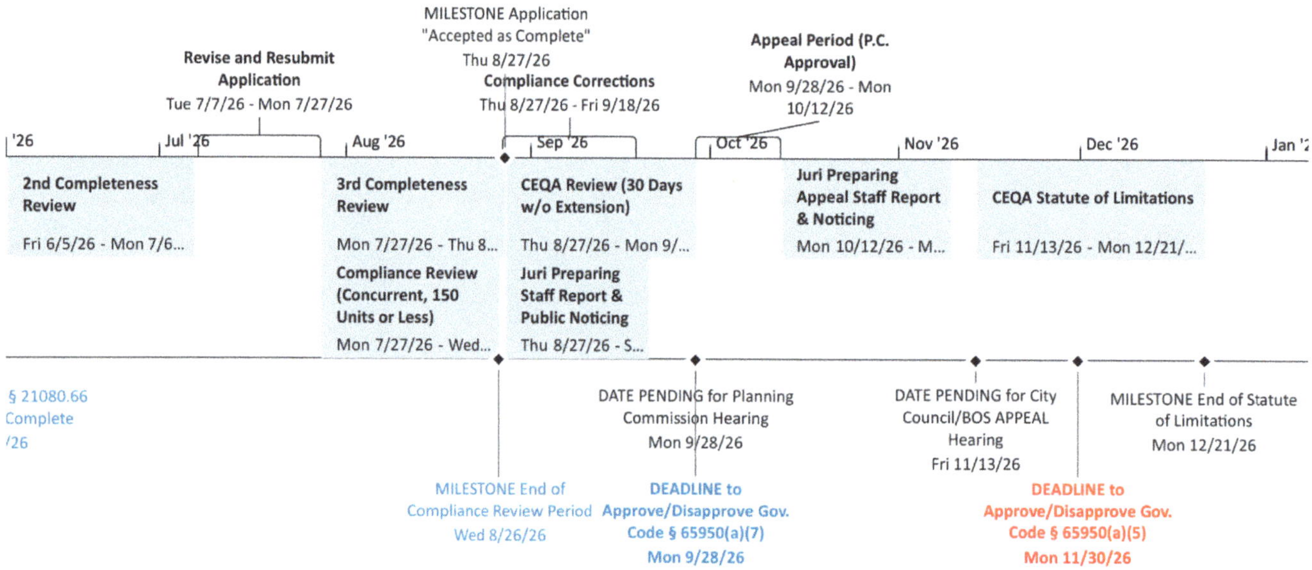

Example 3: Hypothetical Project Using the PRC § 21080.66 Exemption with a Late Tribal Process

The Legislature, by adding Gov. Code § 65950(a)(7), may simply have been addressing the potential situation where the new tribal process required for the new PRC § 21080.66 exemption does not finish in time to meet the deadline for CEQA-exempt projects under paragraph (5). The proper interpretation may be that ***both*** time periods under paragraphs (5) and (7) apply and the deadline is the ***later*** of the two deadlines.

This potential situation would arise when applicants do not submit an SB 330 preliminary application, or when the SB 330 preliminary application does not trigger the tribal process. PRC § 21080.66(b)(1)(A)(ii) anticipates that projects that are deemed complete prior to July 1, 2026 may be in this situation, and that the jurisdiction must send the tribal notification "within 14 days of [the applicant] notifying the local government that the project is eligible to be exempt" pursuant to PRC § 21080.66.

In Figure 17(A), the applicant notifies the jurisdiction that the project is eligible for the PRC § 21080.66 exemption on July 13, 2026. The Tribal Process Can Take Up to 148 Days, and Figure 17(A) assumes it takes the maximum time. The preliminary CEQA determination (red text) is made long before the tribal process is complete, so the deadline under paragraph (5) of Gov. Code § 65950(a) (**bold red**) expires before the deadline under paragraph (7) (**bold blue**). The planning commission hearing is on December 23, before the deadline of January 11, 2027. Therefore, the project will not be deemed approved in this example.

Figure 17(A): Late tribal process — timeline for a project that is exempt pursuant to PRC § 21080.66.

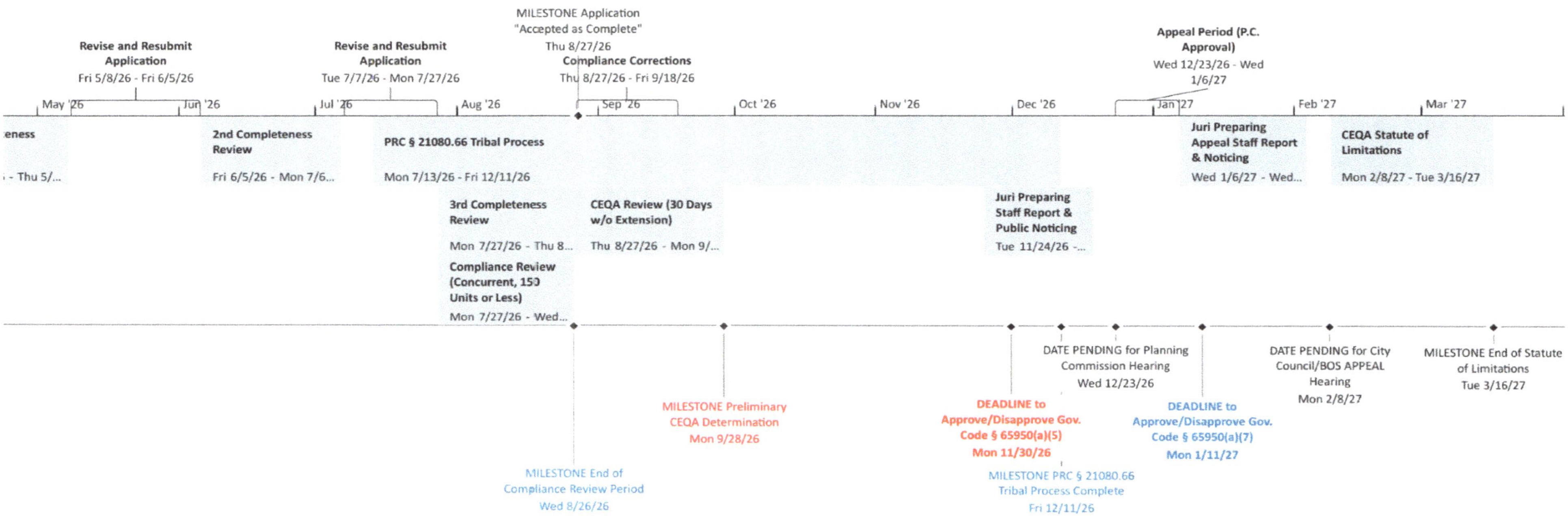

Bottom Line: What is the Deadline for Projects that are Exempt Pursuant to PRC § 21080.66?

The bottom line is that there are several potential interpretations of Gov. Code § 65950(a)(7), there are many possible permutations of project timelines, and it is not clear what the Legislature intended. Hopefully the 2026 CEQA Guidelines will address this issue. (CEQA Guidelines are regulations with the force of law. See CEQA Statutes and Guidelines). When it becomes available, applicants can download the new edition of the Association of Environmental Professionals 2026 CEQA book from https://www.califaep.org/statute_and_guidelines.php.

In the meantime, applicants and jurisdictions should be aware of the potential for a project to meet the requirements of Gov. Code § 65950(a)(7)(A) and (B) ***before*** a CEQA determination has been made. Without a clear legal interpretation from an authoritative source (a court, the CEQA Guidelines, or HCD), the most conservative and defensible interpretation is that, for projects that use the PRC § 21080.66 Statutory Exemption — New with AB 130, the deadline is the **later** of the dates calculated under Gov. Code § 65950(a)(5) and (7).

60-Day Deadline for Approval or Disapproval of Projects Requiring a Negative Declaration

As explained under Project Approval After the ND or MND is Adopted, in most cases where a project requires the preparation of a Negative Declaration or Mitigated Negative Declaration, the ND or MND will be adopted, and the project approved, **at the same hearing**. In such cases, the deadline at Gov. Code § 65950(a)(4) does not matter. Occasionally, the ND or MND will be adopted first, and a hearing to approve the project will be held later, in which case the jurisdiction must approve or disapprove the project within 60 days of the **adoption** of the ND or MND, per Gov. Code § 65950(a)(4):

> (4) Sixty days from the date of adoption by the lead agency of the negative declaration, if a negative declaration is completed and adopted for the development project.

Deadline for Projects Requiring an Environmental Impact Report

Very few housing projects will require an EIR. As explained under Deadline for Approval of a Project that Requires an EIR, the time period between certification of the EIR and the deadline varies depending on the type of project, and can be 60, 90, or 180 days.

Deemed Approval — New with AB 130

As explained under Deadline for Initial Approval or Disapproval of the Project, there are different deadlines by which the jurisdiction is required to either approve or disapprove a project. The deadlines depend on the type of project and the type of CEQA determination. Especially for projects that are exempt from CEQA (or are ministerial and therefore not subject to CEQA), the time limits for initial approval/disapproval are quite short. If the jurisdiction fails to approve the project by any of the deadlines described under Deadline for Initial Approval or Disapproval of the Project, the jurisdiction's failure to act results in **deemed approval** of the development permit application. While this deemed approval provision has been in Gov. Code § 65956 for decades, it used to be almost impossible to enforce.

AB 130 (2025) amended Gov. Code § 65956 to remove a noticing prerequisite that used to be required before a project would be deemed approved, as shown below with the deleted ~~text stricken~~ and the added text in blue:

> 65956. (a) If any provision of law requires the lead agency or responsible agency to provide public notice of the development project or to hold a public hearing, or both, on the development project and the agency has not provided the public notice or held the hearing, or both, at least 60 days prior to the expiration of the time limits established by Sections 65950 and 65952, the applicant or ~~his or her~~ the applicant's representative may file an action pursuant to Section 1085 of the Code of Civil Procedure to compel the agency to provide the public notice or hold the hearing, or both, and the court

shall give the proceedings preference over all other civil actions or proceedings, except older matters of the same character.

(b) In the event that a lead agency or a responsible agency fails to act to approve or to disapprove a development project within the time limits required by this article, the failure to act shall be deemed approval of the permit application for the development project. ~~However, the permit shall be deemed approved only if the public notice required by law has occurred. If the applicant has provided seven days advance notice to the permitting agency of the intent to provide public notice, then no earlier than 60 days from the expiration of the time limits established by Sections 65950 and 65952, an applicant may provide the required public notice using the distribution information provided pursuant to Section 65941.5. If the applicant chooses to provide public notice, that notice shall include a description of the proposed development substantially similar to the descriptions which are commonly used in public notices by the permitting agency, the location of the proposed development, the permit application number, the name and address of the permitting agency, and a statement that the project shall be deemed approved if the permitting agency has not acted within 60 days. If the applicant has provided the public notice required by this section, the time limit for action by the permitting agency shall be extended to 60 days after the public notice is provided. If the applicant provides notice pursuant to this section, the permitting agency shall refund to the applicant any fees which were collected for providing notice and which were not used for that purpose.~~

(c) Failure of an applicant to submit complete or adequate information pursuant to Sections 65943 to 65944, inclusive, may constitute grounds for disapproving a development project.

(d) Nothing in this section shall diminish the permitting agency's legal responsibility to provide, where applicable, public notice and hearing before acting on a permit application.

That long section of deleted text in subdivision (b), which required public notice before the deemed approval could occur, had made it exceedingly rare[51] for any project to be deemed approved due to the expiration of a time limit. By deleting that of text, AB 130 (2025) made the Deadline for Initial Approval or Disapproval of the Project self-enforcing and the deemed approval self-executing. As explained in the Legislative Counsel's Digest of the bill:

> In the event that a lead agency or a responsible agency fails to act to approve or to disapprove a development project within the time limits required by the act, existing law deems the failure to act as an approval of the permit application for the development project, only if the public notice required by law has occurred, as specified.
>
> This bill would remove the requirement that the public notice required by law has occurred, in order for the failure to act to be deemed as an approval of the permit application for the development project.

Thus, the intent of the Legislature is clear, the deemed approval no longer requires public notice. Prior to the passage of AB 130 (2025) in *Linovitz Capo Shores LLC v. California Coastal Commission* the court found:[52]

> The Coastal Commission's failure to act on appellants' applications for costal development permits, however, resulted in the applications being deemed approved under the Streamlining Act. Aside from passage of the necessary amount of time, which is not disputed, the only precondition to a permit being deemed approved by operation of law is provision of "the public notice required by law."

With the notice requirement deleted from Gov. Code § 65956(b) the only precondition for deemed approval is the passage of time period without the jurisdiction taking action to approve or disapprove the project.

Note that Gov. Code § 65956 applies not just to housing development projects, but to any project subject to the Permit Streamlining Act. This means that for every discretionary project that is exempt from CEQA, whether a housing project or not, jurisdictions must take action to approve or disapprove the project within 60 days of

---

[51] See *Linovitz Capo Shores LLC v. California Coastal Commission*, No. G058331 (4th Dist. June 25, 2021) https://law.justia.com/cases/california/court-of-appeal/2021/g058331.html.
[52] Ibid.

providing written notice that the project is exempt, or the project will be deemed approved. It will be very challenging for jurisdictions to meet this deadline across all the CEQA-exempt projects.

Deadlines for Approval or Disapproval are now Self-Enforcing, and Deemed Approval is Automatic

Per Gov. Code § 65956(b), if the jurisdiction "fails to act to approve or to disapprove a development project ... the failure to act shall be **deemed approval**" upon the expiration of the time limit prescribed for the relevant CEQA determination by Article 5 of the Permit Streamlining Act. That statement, "failure to act shall be deemed approval," is now **unqualified**. By deleting the long section of text from Gov. Code § 65956(b), AB 130 (2025) made "the time limits required by this article" **self-enforcing.**[53]

A deemed approval by operation of Gov. Code § 65956(b) is **unappealable.**[54] Further, the Author's interpretation is that the deemed approval is **ministerial**, because the jurisdiction has not exercised, and was not permitted by state law to exercise, any discretion. CEQA **does not apply** to projects that are ministerially approved. (See Discretionary vs. Ministerial.) An alternative interpretation is that the CEQA determination that triggered the Deadline for Initial Approval or Disapproval of the Project remains in effect because the project was approved, and the CEQA statute of limitations of 180 days runs from the date of the deemed approval (which is final and unappealable) unless the Notice of Exemption or Notice of Determination is filed and posted to establish a shorter statute of limitations. (See Statute of Limitations for CEQA Lawsuits.) There is no option for the applicant to file an NOD, and while PRC § 21152(b) allows the applicant to file an NOE, the applicant must attach a **certified** copy of the determination of exemption, which the jurisdiction may be unwilling to provide in the case of a deemed-approved project. (See Filing and Posting CEQA Notices.)

This is a very consequential change to the law. Major questions remain about implementation of the deemed approval, including whether conditions of approval may apply, whether a CEQA lawsuit can be brought against a deemed-approved project at all, and how to file CEQA notices. The Author expects there to be litigation related to this amended deemed approval provision, and the applicant is advised to ***consult an attorney*** with deep expertise in California housing law if it appears that the jurisdiction has missed or may miss the Deadline for Initial Approval or Disapproval of the Project.

A Cross-Reference to the Deleted Text in Gov. Code § 65956(b) Remains

AB 130 (2025) did **not** amend Gov. Code § 65956.5, which cross-references to the deleted text in Gov. Code § 65956(b):

> 65956.5. (a) Prior to an applicant providing advance notice to an environmental agency of the intent to provide public notice pursuant to subdivision (b) of Section 65956 for action on an environmental permit, the applicant may submit an appeal ...

The appeal process described in Gov. Code § 65956.5 no longer appears to serve any purpose, because "the advance notice ... pursuant to subdivision (b) of Section 65956" has been deleted from Gov. Code § 65956(b). The process under Gov. Code § 65956.5 whereby the Applicant would first submit a written appeal requesting, essentially, that the jurisdiction explain its failure to meet the time limits, and to specify a date by which the jurisdiction will act to approve or disapprove the project, was and is ***optional*** ("the applicant *may*"). There should be no reason to use this appeal process since the project will automatically be deemed approved upon the expiration of the deadline. Perhaps the Legislature will remove this cross-reference in a clean-up bill?

---

[53] "This article" means Article 5. Approval of Development Permits within the Permit Streamlining Act. See Deadline for Initial Approval or Disapproval of the Project for more information about the different time limits in Article 5 for different types of CEQA determinations.
[54] See *Ciani v. San Diego Trust Savings Bank* (1991) 233 Cal.App.3d.

The Real World of Development Permit Review

The rest of the book focuses on how jurisdictions are **required by state laws** to process housing development permits. Many of those laws have existed for decades but had no effective enforcement mechanism, so jurisdictions simply ignored them. Over the past decade, the State Legislature has passed dozens of housing bills, steadily if somewhat slowly improving the enforcement of these laws.

While the intent of the state housing laws is to increase the supply of housing, a byproduct of all these new laws and their enforcement provisions is a significant increase on the compliance burden shouldered by the staff, appointed decisionmakers, and elected officials of jurisdictions. This section will point out many failings of jurisdictions, but the applicant should always remember that the jurisdiction is working with limited resources in a rapidly changing regulatory environment. The staff, decisionmakers, and officials all have a duty to the community they serve and must balance the competing wants and needs of residents, developers, and other interests.

In this section, the Author shares his experience and perceptions about how jurisdictions review development permits in the real world. Faced with diminished authority and discretion over housing development projects, jurisdictions often use procedural obstacles to slow down projects and to try and *negotiate* for the subjective standards and personal preferences that, in the past, they could *demand*. Applicants generally see procedural delay as an effort to undermine the intent of the Permit Streamlining Act, Housing Accountability Act, and State Density Bonus Law, while jurisdictions want a robust public process with many levels of review so that developers must engage with the community and hear their priorities and concerns.

Jurisdictions Fail to Post a Complete List of Required Items (LORI) on their Website

Jurisdictions are required to "compile one or more lists that shall specify in detail the information that will be required from any applicant for a development project" and make that list "available to all applicants for development projects and to any person who requests the information." These are the "LORIs" that Gov. Code § 65940 requires each jurisdiction to create and Gov. Code § 65943(f) requires to be on the jurisdiction's website. The intent is that the applicant can **know in advance what is required, so that the *first* submittal is complete**. Many jurisdictions comply with this requirement, but many others have a hodge-podge of application forms, handouts, webpages, and pre-application processes that they claim are all part of the required information, making it impossible for the applicant to know what is required before submitting.

The LORI and the process of reviewing the development permit application to determine whether it is complete with all the required information is covered in Chapter 8: Completeness Review. There you will read how Gov. Code § 65943 presumes that there will be three rounds of completeness review before the application is accepted as complete. Those three rounds of review generally take about six months to complete. The Author provides some tips on getting through the process as quickly as possible, but the reality is that completeness review is, in many cases, a way that jurisdictions try to force projects to conform to local standards that state laws preempt.

AB 1294 would solve this problem by creating a statewide LORI and a statewide application form for housing projects. Housing application requirements would be standardized across the entire state, and the application would be deemed complete upon submittal, eliminating the entire completeness review process.

Jurisdictions Fail to Post Clear Fee Information

Jurisdictions are required to post on their website "A current schedule of fees, exactions, and affordability requirements" so that the applicant can **calculate the proper fee to submit with the application**, and plan for the other fees that will be imposed on the project later. (Gov. Code § 65940.1.)

The Author has found that even when a "master fee schedule" is posted, it is usually impossible to calculate the required application fee and pay it along with the first submittal of the development permit application. The jurisdiction calculates the fee **after** submittal, the fee can be hundreds of thousands of dollars, and the application is not considered submitted until the fee is paid. Between the time it takes the jurisdiction to calculate the fee and provide an invoice for payment, and the time it takes the developer to cut a very large check, the commencement of the completeness review is often delayed by a few weeks.

A 2024 report by California YIMBY[55] investigated the websites of 60 jurisdictions to see if they complied with this requirement. They found that only 46% of the 60 jurisdictions had a fee schedule that was easy to locate on their website; 24% did not post the fee schedule at all. Only 18% posted the reports (called "nexus" studies) justifying the imposition of impact fees in an easy to access location, and 67% did not post nexus studies at all. There needs to be an effective enforcement mechanism to ensure that jurisdictions comply with fee transparency requirements, but there is little the applicant can do except request the information in writing. (See How to Ensure You Have the Entire LORI and the Fee Amount for a Complete 1st Submittal.)

Jurisdictions Combine Compliance Review with Completeness Review

After reviewing the complete housing development permit application, Gov. Code § 65589.5(j)(2)(A) requires that the jurisdiction provide comprehensive compliance comments "identifying the provision or provisions, and an explanation of the reason or reasons it considers the housing development to be inconsistent, not in compliance, or not in conformity." In practice, the completeness review and compliance review are conducted simultaneously. Each "incompleteness letter" contains a list of items that the jurisdiction says are necessary to **complete** the application, and a **partial** list of ***compliance*** items. Conducting compliance review on an incomplete application contributes to the long time it takes for a jurisdiction to determine the application is complete. Oftentimes, the compliance review comments are just repeated over and over again; the applicant does not make the changes demanded by the jurisdiction because state law preempts the imposition of the offended development standard.

AB 1294 would solve this problem by deeming the full development permit application complete upon submittal. The compliance review period would start immediately upon submittal of the application. Jurisdictions would have to complete their compliance review and provide a fill list of compliance matters in accordance with Gov. Code § 65589.5(j)(2)(A), within 30 days for projects of 150 units or less, or 60 days for project over 150 units.

Jurisdictions Confuse Compliance Matters with Incompleteness

The various departments of the jurisdiction routinely confuse **compliance** matters as **completeness** items. For example, the public works department might say the application is *incomplete* because the preliminary geotechnical report doesn't include an infiltration test to support the calculations in the preliminary stormwater management report. If the LORI did not specifically list "infiltration test" as a required item, the application is not incomplete, and the public works comments is actually a compliance matter, not a completeness matter. Unfortunately, the applicant can't just insist that "no, the application is complete, the LORI did not include "infiltration test" as a required item of information." The applicant would have to submit a written appeal of the incompleteness determination and wait 60 days for a response to the appeal. (Gov. Code § 65943(c).) Because it takes so much time to get through the completeness review process, applicants generally just "work with" the jurisdiction to address compliance matters as they make resubmittals for several rounds of completeness review. Once the application is determined to be complete, a series of deadlines are triggered and the project proceeds to the decisionmakers (see The Path to Final Approval).

[55] https://cayimby.org/reports/the-impact-of-fees/.

See Jurisdictions Should Not Combine and/or Confuse Completeness and Compliance for some guidance on addressing this issue.

Jurisdictions Perform Building Code and CEQA Review During Completeness Review

Perhaps a more significant problem than just confusing compliance matters for incompleteness, is that jurisdictions often require plans to have a level of detail that is simply not necessary at the entitlement phase and should only be required with the grading and building permit submittal. The planning department typically sends each submittal of the application to various departments and other agencies for their review. For example, the building department often reviews the plans for building-code compliance, even though the plans are only conceptual and are not for construction. A building department might review the conceptual plans for ADA compliance and say the application is incomplete or not compliant because the floor plans don't show the dimensions for ADA clearances. There is no reason for the plans to have any accessibility information at the entitlement phase, because the approval of an entitlement is *always* conditioned on compliance with state and federal laws. ADA clearances are simply not applicable **development standards** found in the jurisdiction's general plan or zoning code.

The review of a development permit should be limited to the "general plan, zoning, and subdivision standards and criteria, including design review standards" (Gov. Code § 65589.5(j)(1)) and the review required by CEQA. The building and grading code reviews, including ADA, should be deferred to the building permit phase.

Jurisdictions routinely require and review many different environmental reports even when CEQA explicitly exempts a project from environmental review. If the project is exempt from CEQA, all that is necessary is for the application to show that the project qualifies for the CEQA exemption. For example, a traffic study is not required for ***any*** CEQA exemption — all that is required is a screening for Vehicle Miles Traveled (Guidelines § 15064.3) — but many jurisdictions still include a comprehensive traffic study as a LORI requirement. Contrary to popular belief, traffic studies do **not** study traffic *safety*, they study traffic *delay*. Traffic delay is not an applicable development standard for housing projects under state law. If the traffic study was not listed on the LORI, projects would not be required to spend thousands of dollars on an unnecessary study.

Jurisdictions Almost Never Provide the Required Compliance Documentation

Gov. Code § 65589.5(j)(2)(A) requires that the jurisdiction provide "written documentation identifying the provision or provisions, and an explanation of the reason or reasons it considers the housing development to be inconsistent, not in compliance, or not in conformity...." But even after multiple rounds of review, when the jurisdiction finally sends the letter of completeness, it routinely includes a vague blanket statement that "we are still reviewing the application and there are other compliance issues with the project," without specifying exactly which development standards the jurisdiction contends the project doesn't comply with or why the jurisdiction thinks the project is inconsistent with those standards.

If the jurisdiction fails to identify a development standard and explain why it considers the project not to be compliant with that standard, in the written determination required by Gov. Code § 65589.5(j)(2)(A), then Gov. Code § 65589.5(j)(2)(B) says that the project is **deemed *compliant*** with that development standard. The problem is that the jurisdiction provided written documentation (however vague and unsubstantiated) that the project is **not** compliant, in the letter of completeness. Is the application deemed compliant because the jurisdiction didn't send the full documentation required by Gov. Code § 65589.5(j)(2)(A)? Or does the vague and partial list of compliance issues in the completeness letter constitute the determination that the project is not compliant? The jurisdiction will argue that the project can't be *deemed* compliant, because they already *determined* that the project was *not* compliant.

The Author's experience is that jurisdictions just ignore Gov. Code § 65589.5(j)(2)(A) entirely. After providing the letter of completeness with the statement that "we are still reviewing the application," they never provide a second letter with "written documentation identifying the provision or provisions, and an explanation of the reason or reasons it considers the housing development to be inconsistent, not in compliance, or not in conformity…." The applicant does not receive a comprehensive compliance review until the staff report is issued, typically the Friday before the jurisdiction takes action to approve or disapprove the project on a Tuesday or Wednesday. The applicant has just one-to-three working days to respond to any allegations of non-compliance, or to challenge conditions of approval proposed by the staff report.

AB 1294 would solve this problem, because there would be no completeness review process. The jurisdiction would have to meet the 30- or 60-day Time Period Allowed for Compliance Review and provide the "written documentation identifying the provision or provisions, and an explanation of the reason or reasons it considers the housing development to be inconsistent, not in compliance, or not in conformity…" as required by Gov. Code § 65589.5(j)(2)(A) or the project will be deemed compliant in accordance with Gov. Code § 65589.5(j)(2)(B).

Jurisdictions Take More than 30 Days for the Determination of Exemption — SB 130 Improvement

If the project is exempt from CEQA, then PRC § 21080.2 requires that the jurisdiction make the determination of exemption within "30 days from the date on which an application for a project has been received and accepted as complete." That deadline can be extended by up to 15 days, and applicants have little choice but to grant the extension. However, the deadline for determination whether the project is exempt is **not** self-enforcing; nothing happens if the jurisdiction simply ignores the deadline. (See Deadline to Determine if the Project is Exempt is Not Self-Enforcing.) As explained in Chapter 8: Completeness Review, it routinely takes three rounds of submittals before the jurisdiction determines that an application is complete, jurisdictions then have 30 additional days to make the determination that the project is exempt from CEQA, and jurisdiction ***still*** fail to meet that deadline.

Another problem is that a jurisdiction can skirt the deadline for the review for exemption, even after the applicant grants them a 15-day extension, by finding that the project **might** be exempt from CEQA but that the jurisdiction needs more information. If the jurisdiction does not find the project to be exempt, an Initial Study is required and can take many months and tens, if not hundreds, of thousands of dollars to complete. No applicant wants to enforce the deadline for the determination of exemption if it means starting an unnecessary initial study. In practice, the jurisdiction can take as long as it needs to review the project for exemption.

Fortunately, AB 130 (2025) added a **statutory exemption with simple qualifying criteria** (PRC § 21080.66), and that exemption comes with a new, potentially shorter deadline, that may not require the jurisdiction to affirmatively determine that the project is exempt from CEQA. (The possible interpretations of the new approval/disapproval deadline for the new PRC § 21080.66 statutory exemption were discussed earlier in this chapter. See Unclear Deadline for Approval or Disapproval of Projects that are Exempt Pursuant to PRC § 21080.66.)

Jurisdictions Ignore the Deadline for Approving the Project — Fixed by SB 130

The determination that the application is complete triggers the 30- or 45-day Time Period for the Review for Exemption. Next, the determination that the project is exempt from CEQA triggers a Deadline for Initial Approval or Disapproval of the Project. Until the passage of AB 130 (2025), that deadline was essentially unenforceable, and a jurisdiction could simply ignore it. AB 130 (2025) amended Gov. Code § 65956(b) to make it **self-enforcing**, such that a project will be **deemed approved** ***unless*** the jurisdiction acts to approve or disapprove the application by the deadline. (See Deemed Approval — New with AB 130.)

CHAPTER 6: SB 330 PRELIMINARY APPLICATION

When state law refers to a "preliminary application" it means a preliminary application meeting the requirements of Gov. Code § 65941.1, which was added by SB 330 (2019). The development community uses the term "SB 330 preliminary application" to distinguish a preliminary application submitted pursuant to Gov. Code § 65941.1 and **vests** the development standards, from the sort of informal "pre-app" or "preliminary review application" that local jurisdictions have used for decades to provide feedback on a contemplated development project before a formal submittal, but which had no legal effect whatsoever.

The only legal effect of an SB 330 preliminary application is to **"lock in" or "vest" the applicable local ordinances, policies, and standards on the date the SB 330 preliminary application was submitted.** (Gov. Code § 65589.5(o)(1).) Note that an SB 330 preliminary application vests the jurisdiction's general plan, including its housing element. The vesting of development standards can be of paramount importance to the viability of a project, for example projects that submit an SB 330 preliminary application when a jurisdiction's housing element is not in compliance can qualify as Builder's Remedy Projects and remain subject to builder's remedy throughout the vesting period. (Gov. Code § 65589.5(h)(11)(B).)

Always submit an SB 330 preliminary application. The Author cannot think of any situation where a preliminary application should not be submitted. The Author recommends that applicants do not disclose or discuss a project with a jurisdiction prior to submitting an SB 330 preliminary application. Especially when a development project may face opposition from the local jurisdiction itself, it is best that the jurisdiction does not know about a potential project until the development standards are locked in by an SB 330 preliminary application.

This Chapter details the requirements to ensure that SB 330 preliminary applications are complete and valid. The lock-in or "vesting" of development standards is fully explained in Chapter 7: Vesting the Development Standards, including tips to ensure that all the SB 330 vesting rights continue through certificate of occupancy.

Where to Find More Information

For a good overview of the material in this chapter, watch or listen to *SB 330 Preliminary Application: Why It's Essential For Every Infill Housing Project*, which was Episode 1 of The Infill Insiders,[56] a podcast created by Santa Cruz California based real estate firm, Workbench.

One of the reasons the Author decided to write this book is that he could not find a relatively thorough guide to the SB 330 preliminary application. None of the sources recommended in the "Where to Find More Information" section of other chapters have published a guide that explains any of the complexities that are explained in this chapter and in Chapter 7: Vesting the Development Standards.

[56] https://www.workbenchbuilt.com/theinfillinsiders.

CHAPTER CONTENTS

What Did SB 330 Actually Do?

SB 330 (2019) was titled "Housing Crisis Act of 2019" and created Chapter 12 of the Planning and Zoning Law, which is *also* titled "Housing Crisis Act of 2019." However, that Chapter 12 has little to do with individual projects and nothing to do with an SB 330 preliminary application. It is the changes SB 330 (2019) made to **other** parts of the Government Code, primarily the Permit Streamlining Act and the Housing Accountability Act, that are applicable to **individual projects**. The passage of SB 330 (2019):

1. Added Gov. Code § 65905.5 (the Five Hearing Rule).
2. Amended Gov. Code § 65940 (part of the Permit Streamlining Act) with new requirements related to the "list of required items" (LORI) for development project applications (see Lists of Required Information).
3. Added Gov. Code § 65941.1 (part of the Permit Streamlining Act) to **create the SB 330 preliminary application**, that is automatically **deemed complete** upon submittal if it contains **17 required items**.
4. Amended Gov. Code § 65943 (part of the Permit Streamlining Act) related to the process of reviewing a full development permit application for completeness (see Chapter 8: Completeness Review).
5. Amended Gov. Code § 65950 (part of the Permit Streamlining Act), shortening the deadline for approval of housing projects after EIR certification (see Deadline for Approval of a Project that Requires an EIR).
6. Amended the Housing Accountability Act, under Gov. Code § 65589.5(h)(5) and (o)(1), to **vest** the local ordinances, policies, and standards (aka "development standards") **as of the date the SB 330 preliminary application is *submitted*** (see Chapter 7: Vesting the Development Standards).
7. Amended the Housing Accountability Act, under Gov. Code § 65589.5(j)(2) related to the process of reviewing a full development permit application for compliance (see Chapter 9: Compliance Review).

The addition of Gov. Code § 65941.1 creating the SB 330 preliminary application, and the associated changes in the Housing Accountability Act to vest development standards on the date the preliminary application is submitted, are the part of SB 330 (2019) most important to the processing of housing development permits in California.

What Are the 17 Required Items?

The SB 330 preliminary application consists of a specified list of **17 required items**. Upon the date the preliminary application is submitted, with **payment of a fee** (set by the jurisdiction), the SB 330 preliminary application is **deemed complete** in accordance with Gov. Code § 65941.1(a):

> 65941.1. (a) An applicant for a housing development project, as defined in paragraph (3) of subdivision (b) of Section 65905.5, shall be deemed to have submitted a preliminary application upon providing all of the following information about the proposed project to the city, county, or city and county from which approval for the project is being sought and upon payment of the permit processing fee:
>
> (1) The specific location, including parcel numbers, a legal description, and site address, if applicable.
>
> (2) The existing uses on the project site and identification of major physical alterations to the property on which the project is to be located.
>
> (3) A site plan showing the location on the property, elevations showing design, color, and material, and the massing, height, and approximate square footage, of each building that is to be occupied.
>
> (4) The proposed land uses by number of units and square feet of residential and nonresidential development using the categories in the applicable zoning ordinance.
>
> (5) The proposed number of parking spaces.
>
> (6) Any proposed point sources of air or water pollutants.

(7) Any species of special concern known to occur on the property.

(8) Whether a portion of the property is located within any of the following:

(A) A very high fire hazard severity zone, as determined by the Department of Forestry and Fire Protection pursuant to Section 51178.

(B) Wetlands, as defined in the United States Fish and Wildlife Service Manual, Part 660 FW 2 (June 21, 1993).

(C) A hazardous waste site that is listed pursuant to Section 65962.5 or a hazardous waste site designated by the Department of Toxic Substances Control pursuant to Article 5 (commencing with Section 78760) of Chapter 4 of Part 2 of Division 45 of the Health and Safety Code.

(D) A special flood hazard area subject to inundation by the 1 percent annual chance flood (100-year flood) as determined by the Federal Emergency Management Agency in any official maps published by the Federal Emergency Management Agency.

(E) A delineated earthquake fault zone as determined by the State Geologist in any official maps published by the State Geologist, unless the development complies with applicable seismic protection building code standards adopted by the California Building Standards Commission under the California Building Standards Law (Part 2.5 (commencing with Section 18901) of Division 13 of the Health and Safety Code), and by any local building department under Chapter 12.2 (commencing with Section 8875) of Division 1 of Title 2.

(F) A stream or other resource that may be subject to a streambed alteration agreement pursuant to Chapter 6 (commencing with Section 1600) of Division 2 of the Fish and Game Code.

(9) Any historic or cultural resources known to exist on the property.

(10) The number of proposed below market rate units and their affordability levels.

(11) The number of bonus units and any incentives, concessions, waivers, or parking reductions requested pursuant to Section 65915.

(12) Whether any approvals under the Subdivision Map Act, including, but not limited to, a parcel map, a tentative map, or a condominium map, are being requested.

(13) The applicant's contact information and, if the applicant does not own the property, consent from the property owner to submit the application.

(14) For a housing development project proposed to be located within the coastal zone, whether any portion of the property contains any of the following:

(A) Wetlands, as defined in subdivision (b) of Section 13577 of Title 14 of the California Code of Regulations.

(B) Environmentally sensitive habitat areas, as defined in Section 30240 of the Public Resources Code.

(C) A tsunami run-up zone.

(D) Use of the site for public access to or along the coast.

(15) The number of existing residential units on the project site that will be demolished and whether each existing unit is occupied or unoccupied.

(16) A site map showing a stream or other resource that may be subject to a streambed alteration agreement pursuant to Chapter 6 (commencing with Section 1600) of Division 2 of the Fish and Game Code and an aerial site photograph showing existing site conditions of environmental site features that would be subject to regulations by a public agency, including creeks and wetlands.

(17) The location of any recorded public easement, such as easements for storm drains, water lines, and other public rights of way.

Most of the 17 items are simply information that is entered on the Form for the SB 330 Preliminary Application.

Only the 17 Items Can Be Required

The jurisdiction cannot require any items or information, other than the 17 specified items, for an SB 330 preliminary application to be deemed complete. The jurisdiction **can** charge a fixed fee for processing the SB 330 preliminary application but cannot require that the applicant enter into any sort of agreement or contract. No studies or reports are required. The jurisdiction cannot require the applicant to submit any evidence to support the information provided. **There is no requirement that the information be correct.**

In a letter to the Town of Los Gatos *RE: 405 Alberto Way Preliminary Application – Letter of Technical Assistance*, dated February 16, 2023,[57] HCD made clear that nothing other than the 17 items can be required:

> The purpose of a Preliminary Application is to increase certainty for developers with development projects in the early stages of the entitlement process. ... The Preliminary Application process allows a developer to "freeze" the applicable ordinances, policies, and standards and prevent changes to development requirements that could impact the project. A Preliminary Application becomes vested upon the submittal of **exactly** 17 items enumerated in statute along with the permit processing fee payment (Gov. Code, § 65941.1, subd. (a)).

Applicants should always retain the receipt for payment of the processing fee as evidence of the vesting date of the SB 330 preliminary application.

Plans Required for the SB 330 Preliminary Application

The Author recommends that applicants keep the SB 330 preliminary application very simple. The only project plans required are at Gov. Code § 65941.1(a)(3):

> (3) A site plan showing the location on the property, elevations showing design, color, and material, and the massing, height, and approximate square footage, of each building that is to be occupied.

To ensure that the jurisdiction does not question the completeness of the SB 330 preliminary application, the minimum plan-set submittal is a **site plan** that shows the location of the property (i.e., a site plan with a location map), **elevations** (plural, with the minimum design detail of colors, materials, massing, and height), and the approximate square footage of the buildings. ***Each*** existing or future **building** proposed to be part of the project should have its approximate square footage listed, and ***each*** **building should have at least two elevations** in the plan set. In the same letter to Los Gatos, HCD clarified:[58]

> As commonly understood in the field of planning, an "elevation" typically refers to a two-dimensional drawing of a building which visually demonstrates the finished appearance and dimensions of a given side of a building. While the general intent for providing elevations in a Preliminary Application is to share a visual representation of each proposed building that is to be occupied (Gov. Code, § 65941.1, subd. (a)(3)), the statute explicitly states that "elevations" are to be provided. This should not be construed to prohibit local agencies from accepting alternative visual representations (e.g., architectural renderings) if they so choose, but it does not obligate a local agency to accept an alternative to conventional building elevations. It should be noted that elevations submitted for Preliminary Application purposes are expected to be conceptual in nature and need not contain a level of detail associated with construction drawings. **Requiring elevations for all sides of each building seems excessive** for meeting the purpose of the statute, which is to communicate the "design, color, and material, massing, and height" of the primary side of the proposed structures.

---

[57] https://www.hcd.ca.gov/sites/default/files/docs/planning-and-community/HAU/los-gatos-TA-021623.pdf.
[58] Ibid.

The Author recommends that the applicant submit all of the items required for the SB 330 preliminary application, as itemized in Gov. Code § 65941.1(a) and as indicated in the official form provided by the Department of Housing and Community Development (HCD), and **not significantly more** than what is required. Local jurisdictions may want to be helpful in meticulously reviewing the SB 330 preliminary application to advise the applicant of local code requirements, but the applicant will not want the jurisdiction to find some pretense to find the SB 330 preliminary application "incomplete." Applicants should provide only the required items and make clear that the intent is to vest the development standards rather than to obtain a detailed review of a project.

No Review of the SB 330 Preliminary Application is Required

The preliminary application is automatically deemed complete upon the date the 17 required items and the fee are submitted pursuant to Gov. Code §§ 65941.1(a) and 65589.5(h)(5). State law is explicit that **an affirmative determination of completeness is not required**. Per Gov. Code § 65941.1(e)(3):

> (3) This section **shall not require an affirmative determination** by a city, county, or city and county regarding the completeness of a preliminary application or a development application for purposes of compliance with this section.

If the preliminary application contains the 17 items, the jurisdiction is not required to take any action, but should acknowledge the receipt of the SB 330 preliminary application and the associated fee, and note the date that the development standards have been vested.

The Jurisdiction Should Check for Completeness, but Not "Analyze" the Preliminary Application

Jurisdictions should check to ensure that the SB 330 preliminary application contains the 17 required items, but they should not spend time analyzing the preliminary application. Detailed analysis of an SB 330 preliminary application is a waste of resources. In the February 16, 2023, letter to Los Gatos referenced above, HCD explained:[59]

> The statute provides that an "affirmative determination" is not required to be made by a local agency when processing a Preliminary Application (Gov. Code, § 65943, subd. (d)(3)). This provision does not prohibit a local agency from reviewing the contents of the Preliminary Application. Indeed, a local agency must review the application to confirm that the two vesting eligibility criteria are met: (1) All 17 items are included in the application and (2) the processing fee is paid. On the date that both criteria are met, the application is considered vested. An application that does not contain all 17 items is not vested and will not become vested until all items are submitted. The primary focus of local agencies, therefore, should be on verifying the presence of all application materials – without analyzing the substance of the materials submitted. **Analyzing the application materials is contrary to the purpose of the Preliminary Application**. Applicants, for their part, should be fastidious in their preparation and submittal of Preliminary Application materials.

If the jurisdiction finds that the preliminary application is incomplete, the jurisdiction bears the burden of proof to show that one or more of the 17 required items are missing from the submittal. Per Gov. Code § 65589.5(h)(5):

> (5) Notwithstanding any other law, "deemed complete" means that the applicant has submitted a preliminary application pursuant to Section 65941.1 or, if the applicant has not submitted a preliminary application, has submitted a complete application pursuant to Section 65943. **The local agency shall bear the burden of proof** in establishing that the application is not complete.

Jurisdictions are not prohibited from providing comments, but the preliminary application is not intended to provide sufficient detail for the jurisdiction to determine whether the project is compliant with applicable development standards. Furthermore, the plans in the full development permit application may bear little resemblance to the plans in the SB 330 preliminary application.

---

[59] Ibid.

The Sole Purpose of the Preliminary Application is to Vest Development Standards

The sole legal purpose of submitting an SB 330 preliminary application is to **vest the local development standards** in effect on the date of submittal. Changes to the ordinances, policies, and standards of any local agency ***after*** the SB 330 preliminary application is submitted do not apply to the project. (See Which Development Standards are "Vested" by an SB 330 Preliminary Application?) Vesting is covered in detail in Chapter 7: Vesting the Development Standards.

There are times when the vesting date is critical to the project. For example, if the jurisdiction is in the process of revising its local development standards, but the new standards have not yet been adopted, submitting an SB 330 preliminary application locks in the old standards. If the applicant decides they want to use a new development standard adopted by the jurisdiction **after** the vesting date, the applicant can ask the jurisdiction to apply that new, more favorable standard. The jurisdiction is neither required nor prohibited from **allowing** a project to use newer standards; the jurisdiction is prohibited from **requiring** the project to follow the newer standards. (Gov. Code §§ 65589.5(f)(5) and (j)(1).)

If the applicant wants to use new, more favorable development standards, and there are no new unfavorable development standards that the project would have to comply with, then the applicant could simply withdraw the SB 330 preliminary application and submit a new SB 330 preliminary application under the new standards.

What If the Applicant *Wants* a Preliminary *Review*?

If the applicant **wants** the jurisdiction to complete a preliminary **review** of the project and provide informal comments on the conceptual plans, the Author recommends that the applicant make two separate submittals:

1. An SB 330 preliminary application containing only the minimum requirements (the 17 items).
2. A request for pre-app review of a more complete submittal package with whatever plans, reports, and studies the developer would like the jurisdiction to review and provide informal comments on. This can be combined with a request for Preapplication CEQA Consultation.

Only *after* submitting the SB 330 preliminary application and vesting the development standards does the Author recommend engaging with staff, elected officials, and neighbors. The pre-app review will be more useful if the applicant provides more information than is required for the SB 330 preliminary application.

Form for the SB 330 Preliminary Application

HCD created a **template** SB 330 preliminary application form for jurisdictions to customize or adapt. Jurisdictions can create their own forms so long as their forms are consistent with Gov. Code § 65941.1. If the jurisdiction does not have its own form the applicant can use the form provided by HCD. Per Gov. Code § 65941.1(c):

> (c) (1) Each local agency shall compile a checklist and application form that applicants for housing development projects may use for the purpose of satisfying the requirements for submittal of a preliminary application.
>
> > (2) The Department of Housing and Community Development shall adopt a standardized form that applicants for housing development projects may use for the purpose of satisfying the requirements for submittal of a preliminary application if a local agency has not developed its own application form pursuant to paragraph (1). Adoption of the standardized form shall not be subject to Chapter 3.5 (commencing with Section 11340) of Part 1 of Division 3 of Title 2 of the Government Code.
> >
> > (3) A checklist or form shall not require or request any information beyond that expressly identified in subdivision (a).

Figure 18: Cover page of HCD's standard form for submitting an SB 330 preliminary application.

HOUSING CRISIS ACT of 2019 – SB 330

PRELIMINARY APPLICATION FORM

PURPOSE

This form serves as the preliminary application for housing development projects seeking vesting rights pursuant to SB 330, the Housing Crisis Act of 2019.

GENERAL INFORMATION

An applicant for a housing development project that includes (1) residential units (2) a mix of commercial and residential uses with two-thirds of the project's square footage used for residential purposes; or (3) transitional or supportive housing, shall be deemed to have submitted a preliminary application upon provision of all of the information listed in this Preliminary Application form and payment of the permit processing fee to the agency from which approval for the project is being sought.

After submitting this Preliminary Application to the local agency, an applicant has 180 days to submit a full application or the Preliminary Application will expire.

Submittal Date Stamp*[1,2]:

*[1]Submittal of all the information listed and payment of the permit processing fee freezes fees and development standards as of this date, unless exceptions per Government Code § 65889.5(o) are triggered.

*[2]Note: Record keeping pertaining to which standards and fees apply at date of submittal is imperative, as **penalties may apply for imposing incorrect standards**

If the jurisdiction uses a form of its own creation, the Author recommends reviewing the form and confirming that it requires nothing more than:

1. The "payment of the permit processing fee" (Gov. Code § 65941.1(a).) The jurisdiction may not require the applicant to enter into a contract or agreement to pay an indeterminate amount, hold the jurisdiction harmless, or other impose other conditions on the acceptance of the SB 330 preliminary application.
2. The 17 items (see What Are the 17 Required Items?).
3. The affidavit on page 8 of the form provided by HCD, or an equivalent used by the jurisdiction to ensure that the property owner has consented to the submission of the SB 330 preliminary application.

The form provided by HCD is fairly straightforward, and most of the information is merely advisory. The information does not need to be correct, and can be revised and updated throughout the process of reviewing the full development permit application. The only change that can cause the project to lose its SB 330 vesting is a 20% or greater change to the density of the project **exclusive of any density bonus**, as explained in the next section; or the failure to meet the deadlines explained under Deadlines to Maintain SB 330 Vesting.

Maximum Density and the State Density Bonus Law

The terms "base density" and "maximum allowable residential density" are synonymous. When a project will apply for the benefits of the State Density Bonus Law, the term "base density" means the number of units allowed, exclusive of the bonus units that the project qualifies for. Per Gov. Code § 65915(o)(6):

> (6) "Maximum allowable residential density" or "base density" ... means the greatest number of units allowed by the specific zoning range, specific plan, or land use element of the general plan applicable to the project. Density shall be determined using dwelling units per acre. ...

In most cases, the maximum allowable residential density for a site is expressed by the development standards in terms of dwelling units per acre. If the local development standards applicable to the project site do not specify density in units per acre, then the maximum density must be estimated by the jurisdiction, and the applicant may provide a "base density study" in accordance with Gov. Code § 65915(o)(6)(A) and (B), as explained under Base Density in Units per Acre (DUA) vs. Form-Based Density. In cases where the maximum density is not specified in units per acre, the preliminary application is virtually always submitted **before** the applicant has received a determination of the base density of the project site. This uncertainty could potentially lead to the full development permit application losing its SB 330 vesting if the base density changes by 20% or more between the SB 330 preliminary application and the full development permit application.

The project is not required to use the entire maximum density to qualify for the other benefits of the SDBL (e.g., waivers or reductions of development standards), but with few exceptions (e.g., Builder's Remedy Projects), the project must first use the **entire** base density allowed for the site ***before*** adding **bonus** units.

The State Density Bonus Law (SDBL) is not the subject of this book, because it needs an entire book of its own. For assistance with a density bonus project, contact the Author or an attorney with expertise in the SDBL.

Only "Base Density" Matters for the SB 330 Preliminary Application

Nothing in a preliminary application is binding. The full development permit application can be completely different from the SB 330 preliminary application. However, the ***vesting*** of the SB 330 preliminary application can be ***lost*** if the **base** density of the project changes.

If the number of units or the square footage of construction, **exclusive of any density bonus**, in the full development permit application (as acted upon to approve or disapprove the project) is **20% or more different** (higher or lower than) from the **base** dwelling units of density or **base** square footage of construction shown in the SB 330 preliminary application, then the full development permit application will be considered **as if *no* SB 330 preliminary application had been submitted**. (Gov. Code § 65941.1(d): "... shall not be deemed to have submitted a preliminary application ...".)

This "20% change rule" is found in two places. First in the Permit Streamlining Act at Gov. Code § 65941.1(d):

> (d) After submittal of all of the information required by subdivision (a), if the development proponent revises the project such that the number of residential units or square footage of construction **changes by 20 percent or more, *exclusive* of any increase resulting from the receipt of a density bonus**, incentive, concession, waiver, or similar provision, the housing development project **shall not be deemed to have submitted a preliminary application** that satisfies this section until the development proponent resubmits the information required by subdivision (a) so that it reflects the revisions. For purposes of this subdivision, "square footage of construction" means the building area, as defined by the California Building Standards Code (Title 24 of the California Code of Regulations).

And second in the Housing Accountability Act at Gov. Code § 65589.5(o):

(o) (1) Subject to paragraphs (2), (6), and (7), and subdivision (d) of Section 65941.1, a housing development project shall be subject only to the ordinances, policies, and standards adopted and in effect when a preliminary application including all of the information required by subdivision (a) of Section 65941.1 was submitted.

(2) Paragraph (1) shall not prohibit a housing development project from being subject to ordinances, policies, and standards adopted after the preliminary application was submitted pursuant to Section 65941.1 in the following circumstances:

...

(E) The housing development project is revised following submittal of a preliminary application pursuant to Section 65941.1 such that the number of residential units or square footage of construction **changes by 20 percent or more, *exclusive* of any increase resulting from the receipt of a density bonus**, incentive, concession, waiver, or similar provision, including any other locally authorized program that offers additional density or other development bonuses when affordable housing is provided. For purposes of this subdivision, "square footage of construction" means the building area, as defined by the California Building Standards Code (Title 24 of the California Code of Regulations).

Again, the 20% change **only** applies to **base** density. It does not apply to "any increase resulting from the receipt of a density bonus, incentive, concession, waiver, or similar provision." This includes local bonus density programs as well as the State Density Bonus Law. The change must be ***less* than 20%**; it cannot be 20% or more. So, a project changed from 10 to 12 units of base density would not be vested by the SB 330 preliminary application.

Only Base Density Matters

The only information that actually matters in the SB 330 preliminary application is **base** density in units or square footage of construction. The SB 330 vesting **does not apply** if the base density of the project proposed by the full development permit application is a change of **20% or more** (higher or lower) compared to the base units or base square footage indicated in the SB 330 preliminary application.

If the jurisdiction makes a written determination to invalidate the vesting rights of an SB 330 preliminary application **for any reason other than** a change of 20% or more to the base density, or the expiration of one of the Deadlines to Maintain SB 330 Vesting, that written finding is one of the Things that Constitute Disapproval of a Housing Development Project, and is grounds for a lawsuit to enforce the Housing Accountability Act. Per Gov. Code § 65589.5(h)(6)(I):

(I) Makes a written determination that a preliminary application described in subdivision (a) of Section 65941.1 has expired or that the applicant has otherwise lost its vested rights under the preliminary application for any reason other than those described in subdivisions(d) and (e) of Section 65941.1.

Only base density matters. No other details in the SB 330 preliminary application matter to its vesting rights.

Does the SB 330 Preliminary Application Go Poof if the Applicant "Revises the Project"

The "20% change rule" found in the Permit Streamlining Act at Gov. Code § 65941.1(d) reads:

(d) After submittal of all of the information required by subdivision (a), if the development proponent **revises the project** such that the number of residential units or square footage of construction changes **by 20 percent or more**, exclusive of any increase resulting from the receipt of a density bonus, incentive, concession, waiver, or similar provision, **the housing development project shall not be deemed to have submitted a preliminary application** ...

In the Housing Accountability Act at Gov. Code § 65589.5(o)(2)(E), the rule reads:

> (E) The housing development **project is revised** following submittal of a preliminary application pursuant to Section 65941.1 such that the number of residential units or square footage of construction changes **by 20 percent or more** ...

These provisions are often paraphrased with language like, "the project loses its SB 330 vesting if the project is revised such that its base density differs by 20% or more from the SB 330 preliminary application." However, "revises the project" or "project is revised" does not mean that the SB 330 preliminary application is extinguished, or its vesting is invalidated, merely by ***submitting*** a full development permit application that breaks the 20% change rule.

As explained in Chapter 8: Completeness Review, the full development permit application goes through multiple rounds of review before it is determined to be complete. With each review the jurisdiction will typically provide compliance comments, and these comments might flag that the project has been revised such that it violates the 20% change rule. The SB 330 preliminary application does not go "poof" simply because the applicant makes a submittal that differs by 20% or more. The applicant can bring the project within the 20% limit by revising and resubmitting the application.

If the **intent** of the applicant is to proceed with a project that differs by 20% or more from the base density in the preliminary application, then the applicant should **submit a *new* SB 330 preliminary application** reflecting the new base density and establishing a new vesting date.

Number of Units Exclusive of Density Bonus

For the unit count (but *not* for the square footage of construction, see the next section) determining whether the base density has changed by 20% or more is fairly simple. Surprisingly, the SB 330 preliminary application form created by HCD and used or adapted by most local jurisdictions does not explicitly ask for the number of units exclusive of a density bonus, but it is simple arithmetic to calculate from the unit count table in Question 5.a.:

a. **RESIDENTIAL DWELLING UNIT COUNT:**

Please indicate the number of dwelling units proposed, including a breakdown of levels by affordability, set by each income category.

	Number of Units
Market Rate	
Managers Unit(s) – Market Rate	
Extremely Low Income	
Very Low Income	
Low Income	
Moderate Income	
Total No. of Units	
Total No. of Affordable Units	
Total No. of Density Bonus Units	

Other notes on units:

The **Total No. of Units** minus the **Total No. of Density Bonus Units** equals the "number of units ... exclusive of any increase resulting from the receipt of a density bonus, incentive, concession, waiver, or similar provision" or **base** density. When completing Question 5.a., the applicant should take care to set the base density within 20% of the base density that is likely to be included in the full development permit application.

First consider an example where the applicant is **not applying for a density bonus**:

1. The maximum base density of the project site is 120 units.
2. The applicant submits an SB 330 preliminary application with Question 5.a. showing **Total No. of Units** is 100, and **Total No. of Density Bonus Units** is zero (0).
3. If the developer later decides to apply for a project with 120 units of base density, that is a change of 20% or more **exclusive** of any density bonus. The SB 330 preliminary application will not apply to the revised project, and the jurisdiction could subject the project to development standards adopted after the SB 330 preliminary application was submitted.
4. But if the developer proposes a project with 119 base units, the change in base density is less than 20%, and the jurisdiction could not apply development standards adopted more recently.

If the developer wanted to ensure they could use the maximum allowable density of 120 units, they should have submitted an application with at least 101 base units, then an additional 19 units would be less than a 20% change. By submitting an SB 330 with 101 base units, any project from 81 to 120 units would be vested by the SB 330 preliminary application.

Now consider a project for which the applicant **does** intend to request a density bonus:

1. The maximum base density of the project site is 120 units.
2. If the applicant had submitted an SB 330 preliminary application with 100 base units, the project **could not use** the State Density Bonus Law (SDBL) and maintain the project's vesting under SB 330 because the SDBL ***requires*** projects to use their **entire** base density before applying any density bonus, and the site's base density is 120 units. A full development permit application with 120 units of base density would not be vested because it would be a change of 20%.
3. To avoid this situation, the applicant submitted an SB 330 preliminary application with 101 base units and no density bonus units.
4. The applicant can submit a **full** development permit application with the entire 120 units of base density (less than a 20% change from the 101 base units in the SB 330 preliminary application), and qualify for the SDBL by providing affordable units.
5. The project could qualify for up to a 50% "first" density bonus of 60 units, plus a 50% "second" density bonus for another 60 units. (Gov. Code § 65915(f) and (v).)
6. The project with 120 units of **base** density plus 120 units of bonus density would have 240 units, but the SB 330 preliminary application would continue to vest the development standards for the much larger project because the 120 units of base density is less than a 20% change from the SB 330 preliminary application's **base** density of 101 units.

Remember that the "20% change rule" applies to either an increase *or a decrease* in the base number of units, so take care in selecting the numbers you enter in Question 5.a. Also remember that the 17 required items do not include any requirement to show floor plans or unit mix, so leave that information out of the plan set; don't tempt the jurisdiction to count the number of units in the plans.

Square Footage of Construction Exclusive of Density Bonus

The **square footage of construction** "exclusive of any increase resulting from the receipt of a density bonus, incentive, concession, waiver, or similar provision" is much more difficult to calculate. The 20% rule explicitly states that the square footage of construction is the "building area" as defined by the California Building Code (CBC section 202):

> AREA, BUILDING. The area included within surrounding exterior walls, or exterior walls and fire walls, exclusive of vent shafts and courts. Areas of the building not provided with surrounding walls shall be included in the building area if such areas are included within the horizontal projection of the roof or floor above.

The **building area** as defined by the CBC is seldom the same as the **floor area** as defined in the local ordinance that is used to calculate the Floor Area Ratio (FAR) limits under the general plan or zoning code. Also, Gov. Code § 65941.1(a)(3) requires that the square footage "of each building that is to be occupied" must be separately approximated:

> (3) A site plan showing the location on the property, elevations showing design, color, and material, and the massing, height, and approximate square footage, **of each building** that is to be occupied.

Question 6 in the form provided by HCD requests the **Floor Area (Zoning)** separately from the **Square Footage of Construction** and says to "attached relevant information by building and [enter] totals here." Many housing projects will have multiple buildings; the applicant should carefully **prepare a table of areas and uses by building**.

6. **FLOOR AREA** - Provide the proposed floor area and square footage of residential and nonresidential development, by building (attach relevant information by building and totals here):

	Residential	Nonresidential	Total
Floor Area (Zoning)			
Square Footage of Construction			

Note that Question 6. does not request a breakout of **square footage of construction** "exclusive of any increase resulting from the receipt of a density bonus, incentive, concession, waiver, or similar provision." It only asks for the breakout for **residential** and **nonresidential** areas, and a **total** of the two. It is probably best for the applicant **not** to provide any information about the "base" square footage of construction with the SB 330 preliminary application, but to make a rough calculation for the applicant's own use.

Remember, there is no place in the standard HCD form to enter the base square footage of construction, and it is not one of the 17 required items of information. The applicant should not volunteer this information. It would be challenging for a project opponent to convince a jurisdiction (or a court) to invalidate a project's SB 330 vesting on the basis of a change in base square footage of construction unless the project was **obviously** revised by 20% or more, and it was obviously ***not*** due to "a density bonus, incentive, concession, waiver, or similar provision."

Base Density in Units per Acre (DUA) vs. Form-Based Density

The density allowed by a jurisdiction's local development standards can be expressed in terms of:

1. Dwelling units per acre ("DUA"), and/or
2. Floor area ratio ("FAR," which is the ratio of building floor area to gross site area), and/or
3. Limitations on the "building envelope" or "building form" (height, setbacks, stepbacks, plane changes, articulation, lot coverage ratio, etc.).

If the local development standards applicable to the project **do *not* specify a DUA limit** and instead limit density ***only*** by form or FAR, the State Density Bonus Law provides a method to convert the FAR-based and/or form-based density limitation to a maximum base density expressed in units by creating a base density study. (Gov. Code § 65915(o)(6).) When a base density study is used to establish the allowable base density of the site, the square footage of construction contained in the base density study ***is*** the square footage of construction "exclusive of any increase resulting from the receipt of a density bonus, incentive, concession, waiver, or similar provision."

The number of units that fit in the base density study depends on the **size** of the units. (Gov. Code § 65915(O)(6)(B).) Therefore, when the maximum base density is not expressed in DUA, the number of base units in the SB 330 preliminary application ***should*** **not matter**.

Conversely, when the maximum allowable base density of a site **is** expressed in terms of **DUA**, the calculation of square footage of construction exclusive of any density bonus is academic and ***should*** **not matter**.

However, the 20% change rule found in both Gov. Code § 65941.1(d) and Gov. Code § 65589.5(o) uses the phrase "the number of residential units ***or*** square footage of construction." That little word "or" could mean that ***both*** **the base units *and* the base square footage matter**.

Possible Interpretations of the Word "Or"

The SB 330 vesting does not apply to a project that differs by 20% or more from the base density specified in the SB 330 preliminary application. This 20% rule is found at Gov. Code § 65941.1(d):

> (d) After submittal of all of the information required by subdivision (a), if the development proponent revises the project such that the **number of residential units *or* square footage of construction** changes by 20 percent or more, exclusive of any increase resulting from the receipt of a density bonus, incentive, concession, waiver, or similar provision, the housing development project shall not be deemed to have submitted a preliminary application that satisfies this section until the development proponent resubmits the information required by subdivision (a) so that it reflects the revisions. For purposes of this subdivision, "square footage of construction" means the building area, as defined by the California Building Standards Code (Title 24 of the California Code of Regulations).

And at Gov. Code § 65589.5(o)(2)(E), the rule reads:

> (E) The housing development project is revised following submittal of a preliminary application pursuant to Section 65941.1 such that the **number of residential units *or* square footage of construction** changes by 20 percent or more ...

Jurisdictions (and project opponents) might interpret the word "or" in a number of different ways, and their interpretation could lead them to challenge the vesting rights of the project under SB 330.

First, the word "or" **could** be interpreted to mean that the SB 330 preliminary application does **not** vest the development standards if the full development permit application changes ***either*** the base number of units ***or*** the base square footage of construction by 20% or more. Applicants should be aware of this potential interpretation and use care to avoid a situation where their SB 330 vesting could be challenged under the 20% rule for either base **units** or base **square footage** of construction.

Second, the word "or" **could** be interpreted to mean that there are two options:

1. If the base density is expressed in DUA, then the limitation is 20% of base **units**.
2. If the base density is expressed in FAR or by limiting the building envelope (i.e., there is **no** DUA limitation specified in the applicable zoning or general plan designation), then the limitation is 20% of base **square footage** of construction.

Third, the word "or" **could** be interpreted to mean that the SB 330 preliminary application **does** vest the development standards if ***either one*** (base units or base square footage) remains within 20%.

Interpreting the word "or" in a more **permissive** manner is in keeping with the Housing Accountability Act, Gov. Code § 65589.5(a)(2)(L):

> (L) It is the policy of the state that this section be interpreted and implemented in a manner to afford the fullest possible weight to the interest of, and the approval and provision of, housing.

And in keeping with the State Density Bonus Law, Gov. Code § 65915(r):

> (r) This chapter shall be interpreted liberally in favor of producing the maximum number of total housing units.

These rules of interpretation should lead jurisdictions and courts to a permissive interpretation, that SB 330 preliminary applications continue to vest projects that stay within 20% of ***either*** base density ***or*** base square footage.

Unfortunately, the Author is not aware of any guidance from HCD, nor any case law, pertaining to the word "or" in the 20% change rule. **If the SB 330 vesting date is critical to the approval of the project**, the developer should use caution to ensure they can defend against any attempt to invalidate the SB 330 preliminary application. If a jurisdiction or project opponent attempts to invalidate a project's SB 330 vesting, the applicant should contact a qualified attorney.

Submitting a Base Density Study *As* the SB 330 Preliminary Application

When a project is seeking the benefits of the State Density Bonus Law, ***and*** neither the zoning, specific plan, nor land use element of general plan[60] specify density in dwelling units per acre, the applicant has the option to submit a base density study,[61] as defined in Gov. Code § 65915(o)(6):

> (6) "Maximum allowable residential density" or "base density" means the greatest number of units allowed under the zoning ordinance, specific plan, or land use element of the general plan, or, if a range of density is permitted, means the greatest number of units allowed by the specific zoning range, specific plan, or land use element of the general plan applicable to the project. Density shall be determined using dwelling units per acre. **However, if the applicable zoning ordinance, specific plan, or land use element of the general plan *does not provide* a dwelling-units-per-acre standard for density, then the local agency shall calculate the number of units by:**
>
> > (A) Estimating the realistic development capacity of the site based on the objective development standards applicable to the project, including, but not limited to, floor area ratio, site coverage, maximum building height and number of stories, building setbacks and stepbacks, public and private open-space requirements, minimum percentage or square footage of any nonresidential component, and parking requirements, unless not required for the base project. Parking requirements shall include considerations regarding number of spaces, location, design, type, and circulation. **A developer may provide a base density study and the local agency shall accept it, provided that it includes all applicable objective development standards.**
> >
> > (B) Maintaining the same average unit size and other project details relevant to the base density study, excepting those that may be modified by waiver or concession to accommodate the bonus units, in the proposed project as in the study.

If the developer intends to provide a base density study, the applicant could **submit the base density study *as* the SB 330 preliminary application**. Since Only "Base Density" Matters for the SB 330 Preliminary Application,

[60] Note that the housing element of the general plan is not mentioned here, meaning that if ***only*** the housing element specifies a density in dwelling units per acre, the applicant may still provide a base density study.
[61] This option was added by AB 2334 (2022).

the applicant could submit an SB 330 preliminary application **using the base density study** in a plan set meeting the minimum requirements of Gov. Code § 65941.1(a)(3):

> (3) A site plan showing the location on the property, elevations showing design, color, and material, and the massing, height, and approximate square footage, of each building that is to be occupied.

After submitting the "base project" as the SB 330 preliminary application, the applicant can submit the "density bonus project" with all the benefits of the SDBL as the full development permit application. The base density study will clearly show the base number of residential units and base square footage of construction. If the applicant needs to change the base density in the full development permit application, it will be easy to compare the base density study in the full development permit application to the version submitted as the SB 330 preliminary application and show that it meets the 20% rule.

Good Faith Estimate of Fees at Preliminary Application

The jurisdiction is required to provide a good faith estimate of fees within 30 *business* days from a request made **along with the SB 330 preliminary application**, in accordance with Gov. Code § 65941.1(b):

> (b) (1) A development proponent that submits a preliminary application providing the information required by subdivision (a) may include in its preliminary application a request for a preliminary fee and exaction estimate, which the city, county, or city and county shall provide within 30 **business** days of the submission of the preliminary application. ...

The good faith estimate is not binding but should at least identify what fees have been adopted by the jurisdiction as of the SB 330 preliminary application submittal date.

Request a Good Faith Estimate of Fees

The Author includes this request with the SB 330 preliminary application:

> Applicant requests a preliminary fee and exaction estimate and a fee schedule, which the jurisdiction shall provide within 30 business days of the submission of this preliminary application, in accordance with Gov. Code § 65941.1(b)(1) and (6).

Note that the deadline is 30 business days, rather than calendar days.

Jurisdictions are not required to review the SB 330 preliminary application, but they will base the good faith estimate on the information provided by the applicant in the SB 330 preliminary application.

Notice of Intent to Submit a SMAP Project and Commence Tribal Consultation

SB 423 (2023) revised and replaced the streamlined ministerial approval process created by SB 35 (2017). Now referred to as "SMAP," SB 423 / SB 35 is available for qualifying projects that are located in a jurisdiction that is subject to this process because the jurisdiction has not made adequate progress toward its state-mandated housing goals. HCD has a web page where the applicant can find information on SMAP.

Special state laws that require ministerial processing of housing development permits are beyond the scope of this book. However, the applicant should be aware that the jurisdiction cannot accept an application for SMAP until the jurisdiction has completed a notification and consultation process with California Native American tribes regarding the contemplated development project. Per the HCD SMAP Guidelines[62] Section 400 (page 16):

[62] As of this writing, HCD had not updated the SMAP Guidelines since 2021, before SB 423 was enacted, so they are out of date. Check this website for the SMAP Guidelines: https://www.hcd.ca.gov/planning-and-community-development/statutory-determinations.

> (a) Prior to submitting an application for the Streamlined Ministerial Approval Process, the development proponent must submit to the local government a notice of intent to submit an application and the local government must have completed the tribal consultation process outlined in Government Code section 65913.4(b). The notice of intent shall be in the form of a preliminary application that includes all of the information described in Government Code section 65941.1.

Per Gov. Code § 65913.4(b), the notice of intent must be "in the form of" an SB 330 preliminary application. The law does not require the notice of intent to be submitted at the same time as the SB 330 preliminary application; it would be permissible to submit the SB 330 preliminary application and then later submit the SMAP notice of intent with all the same information as the preliminary application. But the easiest way to provide the notice of intent is to include it with the submission of the SB 330 preliminary application. Some jurisdictions have added a checkbox to their SB 330 preliminary application form, but HCD's standard form does not include a checkbox for the notice of intent.

Notice of Intent to Submit a SMAP Application

To provide the notice of intent that must be "in the form of" an SB 330 preliminary application, which triggers consultation with California Native American tribes that must be completed before the jurisdiction can accept an application for streamlined ministerial approval process (SMAP), the Author includes this request with the SB 330 preliminary application:

> Applicant hereby provides Notice of Intent to submit an application for streamlined ministerial approval pursuant to Gov. Code § 65913.4(b)(1)(A)(i). The jurisdiction "shall engage in a scoping consultation regarding the proposed development with any California Native American tribe" within 30 days of receipt of this notice of intent."

If the applicant has already submitted an SB 330 preliminary application that has vested the development standards, and later decides to apply for SMAP, the applicant does not need to submit a new SB 330 preliminary application (nor pay the fee again). The applicant can simply use the same SB 330 form and submittal material and replace any reference to "SB 330 preliminary application" with a statement that "This is a SMAP notice of intent. The SB 330 preliminary application date remains [date]."

As always, the Author recommends submitting the SB 330 preliminary application as early as possible, which fpr SMAP projects will help ensure that the tribal process is complete before the applicant is ready to submit the full development permit application. Remember that the jurisdiction **cannot officially accept the SMAP application until after the tribal process** has concluded. (Gov. Code § 65913.4(b)(3).)

Note that the timeline for the tribal process required for SMAP is completely different from the tribal process timeline for the PRC 21080.66 CEQA exemption explained under PRC § 21080.66 Exemption Requires a Tribal Notification and Consultation Process.

Trigger the Tribal Process for the PRC 21080.66 CEQA Exemption

The PRC § 21080.66 Exemption Requires a Tribal Notification and Consultation Process. The tribal process under PRC § 21080.66(b) can take up to 148 days to complete, so approval of projects that use this statutory exemption could be delayed if an applicant fails to submit an SB 330 preliminary application that triggers the tribal notification process. If the SB 330 preliminary application is submitted on or after July 1, 2026, the jurisdiction should automatically start the notification process within 14 days of receiving the preliminary application. (PRC § 21080.66(b)(1)(A)(i).) However, when submitting the SB 330 preliminary application, the Author recommends explicitly requesting that the jurisdiction start the tribal notification process (see the following text box).

Request to Commence Tribal Noticing for PRC 21080.66 CEQA Exemption

To ensure that jurisdictions review the project for the new PRC 21080.66 statutory CEQA exemption, trigger the required tribal notification process, and avoid delays in the processing of a housing development permit, the Author includes this request with the SB 330 preliminary application:

> The project likely qualifies for the CEQA statutory exemption provided by Public Resources Code § 21088.66 (AB 130 effective July 1, 2025). Applicant requests that the jurisdiction "shall provide formal notification via certified mail and email to each California Native American tribe" within 14 days of receipt of this preliminary application, in accordance with PRC § 21088.66(b)(1)(A).

CHAPTER 7: VESTING THE DEVELOPMENT STANDARDS

Prior to the passage of SB 330 (2019), jurisdictions could subject projects to new ordinances, policies, and standards adopted **after** the project was submitted. In extreme cases, a jurisdiction would adopt new local regulations with the **intent to stop a housing project** that was already under review. Now, applicants can submit an SB 330 preliminary application to "lock-in" or "vest" the ordinances, policies, and standards as of the date the preliminary application is submitted. SB 330 (2019) made it possible to ***know in advance*** **the rules and requirements that apply to a project**.

The advice throughout this book is to **ensure your project is *always* protected by an SB 330 preliminary application**. Unfortunately, project opponents may find flaws in the preliminary application during the approval process, deadlines can be missed causing the preliminary application to expire, and applicants are not always aware that their project has changed in a way that invalidates the preliminary application. In such cases, the **full** development permit application does provide some vesting rights, but they are inferior to the vesting of an SB 330 preliminary application.

This chapter explains the vesting of development standards when an SB 330 preliminary application is submitted, how to maintain that vesting through construction and certificate of occupancy, and what happens if the project loses the SB 330 vesting. It also covers the less-comprehensive vesting rights provided by the full development permit application when no SB 330 preliminary application applies to the project.

Where to Find More Information

The Author could find no source with a detailed explanation of the vesting rights provided by an SB 330 preliminary application or how the vesting rights (based on the full development permit application) differ if no preliminary application applies to the project. As explained in the introduction to Chapter 6: SB 330 Preliminary Application, this is one of the reasons the Author decided to write this book.

CHAPTER CONTENTS

What is the "Vesting Date" When a Preliminary Application Applies to the Project?

The vesting date of a project is the date on which an SB 330 preliminary application is **submitted**, with the 17 items required by Gov. Code § 65941.1 and the fee paid, on which date the preliminary application is ***deemed* complete**. (Gov. Code §§ 65941.1(a) and 65589.5(o).)

The following sections explain the vesting rights when an SB 330 preliminary application applies to the project. If no SB 330 preliminary application applies to the project, see Vesting of the Full Development Permit Application for the vesting date and the vesting rights provided by the full application.

Which Development Standards are "Vested" by an SB 330 Preliminary Application?

The term "development standard" is not used or defined in the Housing Accountability Act but is used by the development community in a generic sense to apply to any sort of standard that applies to development.[63] The term used for the development standards vested by an SB 330 preliminary application is "ordinances, policies, and standards" as defined at Gov. Code § 65589.5(o)(4). If there is no SB 330 preliminary application that applies to a project, then only the "general plan, zoning, and subdivision standards and criteria, including design review standards" are vested, as explained under Which Development Standards are Vested by the Full Housing Development Permit Application.

On the date of submittal of an SB 330 preliminary application, the "**ordinances, policies, and standards**" of the local jurisdiction are "vested." The vesting is provided by the Housing Accountability Act, in accordance with Gov. Code § 65589.5(o)(1) and (4):

> (o) (1) Subject to paragraphs (2), (6), and (7), and subdivision (d) of Section 65941.1, a housing development project shall be subject only to the **ordinances, policies, and standards** adopted and in effect when a **preliminary application** including all of the information required by subdivision (a) of Section 65941.1 was submitted.
>
>> (4) For purposes of this subdivision, "**ordinances, policies, and standards**" includes general plan, community plan, specific plan, zoning, design review standards and criteria, subdivision standards and criteria, and **any other rules, regulations, requirements, and policies of a local agency**, as defined in Section 66000, including those relating to development impact fees, capacity or connection fees or charges, permit or processing fees, and other exactions.

The definition of "ordinances, policies, and standards" at Gov. Code § 65589.5(o)(4) applies "for purposes of this subdivision" meaning subdivision (o) of the Housing Accountability Act. As quoted above, "... a housing development project shall be subject only to the **ordinances, policies, and standards** adopted and in effect when a **preliminary application** ... was submitted." So, this definition is **not** applicable to the vesting rights of a full development permit application when **no** SB 330 preliminary application applies to the project.

The definition of "ordinances, policies, and standards" is exhaustive. It applies to **all** "rules, regulations, requirements, and policies" adopted by a "local agency" as the term is defined at Gov. Code § 66000(c):

> (c) "Local agency" means a county, city, whether general law or chartered, city and county, school district, special district, authority, agency, any other municipal public corporation or district, or other political subdivision of the state.

Ordinances, policies, or standards of the state, state agencies, or at the federal level are **not** vested. But everything below the state level is vested by an SB 330 preliminary application. This means that the vesting of development standards applies not only to the ordinances, policies, and standards of the city or county that is processing the development permit application but also those of any local agency such as a water, sewer, or stormwater district;

[63] There is a definition of "development standard" in the State Density Bonus Law at Gov. Code § 65915(o)(2), but that definition does not apply in the context of the vesting rights afforded by the Housing Accountability Act.

air quality management district or regional water quality control board; parks and recreation district, fire district, or police district; etc. When the project is located in a city, the vesting also applies to the ordinances, policies, and standards of the county (for example, many cities adopt the county's roadway standards).

Vesting Does Not Apply to Tribal Cultural Resources

One exception from the vesting rights is that tribal cultural resources can be listed on a register **after** the date the SB 330 preliminary application was submitted, per Gov. Code § 65941.1(f):

> (f) Notwithstanding any other law, submission of a preliminary application in accordance with this section shall not preclude the listing of a tribal cultural resource on a national, state, tribal, or local historic register list on or after the date that the preliminary application is submitted. For purposes of Section 65589.5 or any other law, the listing of a tribal cultural site on a national, state, tribal, or local historic register on or after the date the preliminary application was submitted shall not be deemed to be a change to the ordinances, policies, and standards adopted and in effect at the time that the preliminary application was submitted.

This means that if a tribal cultural resource is located on the site or would be impacted by the project, submitting an SB 330 preliminary application does not prevent the tribal cultural resource from being listed in a register, and the project would be subject to the relevant requirements.

The Vesting of the SB 330 Preliminary Application Applies to *New* Fees

Jurisdictions generally have the authority to impose fees in accordance with various state laws, including the Mitigation Fee Act (see Gov. Code § 66000.5 for the sections of the Government Code that constitute the Mitigation Fee Act), and the Housing Accountability Act preserves this general authority per Gov. Code § 65589.5(f)(3):

> (3) Except as provided in subdivision (o), nothing in this section shall be construed to prohibit a local agency from imposing fees and other exactions otherwise authorized by law that are essential to provide necessary public services and facilities to the housing development project or emergency shelter.

However, in accordance with Gov. Code § 65589.5(o)(4) the vesting of an SB 330 preliminary application applies to ***new* fees and exactions** adopted by the local jurisdiction after the date the preliminary application is submitted. Such new fees cannot be imposed on the project:

> (4) For purposes of this subdivision, "ordinances, policies, and standards" includes general plan, community plan, specific plan, zoning, design review standards and criteria, subdivision standards and criteria, and any other rules, regulations, requirements, and policies of a local agency, as defined in Section 66000, **including those relating to development impact fees, capacity or connection fees or charges, permit or processing fees, and other exactions**.

Note that this definition includes "other exactions," not just fees. For example, Gov. Code § 66477 (a part of the Subdivision Map Act known as the "Quimby Act") allows jurisdictions to adopt an ordinance requiring dedication of parkland when a project involves subdividing property to create one or more new parcels. A Quimby ordinance adopted after the date the SB 330 preliminary application was submitted would not apply to the project.

Keep in mind that an SB 330 preliminary application continues to vest the project through the date of certificate of occupancy. (Gov. Code § 65589.5(o)(7).) Any **new** fees created by any local agency after the date the SB 330 preliminary application was submitted cannot be imposed on the project, nor can the jurisdiction apply **increases** to fees unless the increase is an automatic annual adjustment, as explained below.

Automatic Annual Fee Adjustments are Allowed

When a fee ordinance adopted prior to the SB 330 vesting date includes **automatic annual adjustments** tied to an independent cost index, the automatic adjustments **can** be applied to the fee, per Gov. Code § 65589.5(o)(2)(A):

> (2) Paragraph (1) **shall not prohibit** a housing development project from being subject to ordinances, policies, and standards adopted after the preliminary application was submitted pursuant to Section 65941.1 in the following circumstances:
>
> > (A) In the case of a fee, charge, or other monetary exaction, to **an increase resulting from an automatic annual adjustment** based on an **independently published cost index** that is referenced in the ordinance or resolution establishing the fee or other monetary exaction.
> >
> > ...

Vesting is about locking in the rules that apply to a project. A fee ordinance, including its automatic inflation adjustment provisions, applies to the project if it was adopted prior to the SB 330 vesting date.

However, not all fee increases satisfy the requirements of Gov. Code § 65589.5(o)(2)(A). Sometimes a local agency will use a new ordinance each year to adopt annual increases, or the amount of the fee increase will be determined by something other than an independent cost index. In a letter *RE: Berkeley Unified School District Housing Accountability Act Fee Vesting – Letter of Technical Assistance*, dated August 19, 2025,[64] HCD emphasized the three criteria necessary to impose a fee increase (page 2):

1. The fee increase must be an automatic annual adjustment.
2. The automatic annual adjustment must be based on a current independently published cost index.
3. The automatic annual adjustment must be established through an ordinance or resolution.

With respect to the school development fee increase that was the subject of this letter, HCD wrote:

> School district fees in California are regulated by the State Allocation Board. Every two years, the Board adjusts the maximum fee per square foot of floor area that can be charged in the state.[footnote omitted] In fact, the District's resolution indicates that the District affirmatively adopted the increased fee of $5.17 and did not rely on an automatic annual adjustment.[footnote omitted] Therefore, the District's impact fee does not qualify for the exemption from the statutory requirement that the Project is subject only to the fees, charges, and exactions in effect at the time of the preliminary application's submission. Therefore, the District is not authorized to impose a higher fee on the Project under this HAA exemption.

The fee increase was not an automatic annual adjustment, but rather an increase adopted by a new ordinance after the vesting date and therefore could not be imposed on the project.

---

[64] https://www.hcd.ca.gov/sites/default/files/docs/planning-and-community/HAU/berkeley-hau-1602-ta-081925.pdf.

SB 937 Restrictions on Increases to Fees for Public Improvements or Facilities

With the passage of SB 937 (2024), for a "designated residential development project" certain fees are not due until certificate of occupancy (with very limited exceptions), and even automatic annual increases to those fees cannot be applied after the date of building permit issuance. As defined at Gov. Code § 66007(c)(4):

> (4) For purposes of this subdivision, "**designated residential development project**" means a residential development project that meets any of the following conditions:
>
> (A) The project dedicates 100 percent of units, exclusive of a manager's unit or units, to lower income households, as defined by Section 50079.5 of the Health and Safety Code. [**100% affordable projects**.]
>
> (B) The project meets the requirements described in Section 65662. [**Low Barrier Navigation Center**.]
>
> (C) The project is approved by a local government pursuant to Article 2 (commencing with Section 65912.110) or Article 3 (commencing with Section 65912.120) of Chapter 4.1. [**Affordable Housing and High Road Jobs Act of 2022, AKA AB 2011 projects**.]
>
> (D) The project meets the requirements described in subdivision (a) of Section 65913.4. [**SMAP, AKA SB 35 / SB 423 projects**.]
>
> (E) The project meets the criteria described in subdivision (c) of Section 65913.16. [**Affordable Housing on Faith and Higher Education Lands Act of 2023, AKA SB 4 projects**.]
>
> (F) The project is entitled to a density bonus pursuant to subdivision (b) of Section 65915. [**State Density Bonus Law projects**.]
>
> (G) The project includes 10 or fewer units. [**Projects with 10 or fewer units**.]

For these "designated residential development projects" fees "for the construction of public improvements or facilities" are **not due until certificate of occupancy**, and the amount of the fee is frozen at building permit issuance, per Gov. Code § 66007(c)(1):

> (c) All of the following apply to designated residential development projects:
>
> (1) If a local agency imposes any fees or charges on the residential development **for the construction of public improvements or facilities** [the fees subject to this provision would be mitigation "fees" as defined at Gov. Code § 66000(b), but with the limitation at Gov. Code § 66007(e)], then all of the following conditions apply:
>
> (A) (i) Notwithstanding any other law, **the local agency shall not require the payment of those fees or charges until the date the first certificate of occupancy** or first temporary certificate of occupancy is issued, whichever occurs first.
>
> (ii) Notwithstanding clause (i), utility service fees related to connections may be collected at the time an application for service is received, provided that those fees do not exceed the costs incurred by the utility provider resulting from the connection activities.
>
> (iii) Clause (i) shall not apply if construction of the residential development does not begin within five years of the date upon which the building permit is issued.
>
> (B) **The amount of the fees and charges shall be the same amount as would have been paid had the fees and charges been paid prior to the issuance of building permits**, and the local agency shall not charge interest or other fees on any amount deferred pursuant to this paragraph.
>
> …

There are exceptions under Gov. Code § 66007(c)(2), and the Mitigation Fee Act is quite complex. The Author recommends reviewing the provisions in detail, as applicable to specific fees imposed on a project.

Fees and Exactions to Mitigate CEQA Impacts are Allowed

Two different exceptions to the vesting of an SB 330 preliminary application apply to CEQA mitigations. First, in accordance with Gov. Code § 65589.5(o)(2)(C):

> (2) Paragraph (1) **shall not prohibit** a housing development project from being subject to ordinances, policies, and standards adopted after the preliminary application was submitted pursuant to Section 65941.1 in the following circumstances:
>
> > ...
> >
> > (C) Subjecting the housing development project to an ordinance, policy, standard, or any other measure, beyond those in effect when a preliminary application was submitted is **necessary to avoid or substantially lessen an impact of the project under the California Environmental Quality Act** (Division 13 (commencing with Section 21000) of the Public Resources Code).

Ordinances, policies, and standards adopted after the vesting date can be applied when they are "necessary to avoid or substantially lessen" a CEQA impact of the project. This first CEQA exception applies to impact fees that are **adopted by ordinance**, and applicable to projects that meet the criteria in the ordinance.

Not all CEQA mitigations are adopted by ordinance. If a project is subject to an Environmental Impact Report or a Mitigated Negative Declaration that imposes mitigations, those mitigations are allowed by the second CEQA exception at Gov. Code § 65589.5(o)(6):

> (6) This subdivision shall not restrict the authority of a public agency or local agency to **require mitigation measures to lessen the impacts of a housing development project under the California Environmental Quality Act** (Division 13 (commencing with Section 21000) of the Public Resources Code).

This provision means that regardless of any ordinance, policy, or standard, project-specific mitigations can be imposed to lessen CEQA impacts.

However, the exceptions at Gov. Code § 65589.5(o)(2)(C) and (6) apply only in the case of **CEQA impacts arising from the project**. Returning to the school development fee that was the subject of the HCD letter referenced in the previous section, the Berkeley Unified School District argued that the fee increase was necessary to lessen the impact of the project under CEQA. HCD rejected this argument, concluding (page 4):

> The District's reliance on a CEQA exemption to impose an additional $1.69 per square foot on the Applicant's Project approximately one year after the Applicant's submission of its preliminary application has no legal basis. The fee is not charged to mitigate specific impacts that arise from the Project. Therefore, the District is not authorized to impose a higher fee on the Project under this HAA exemption.

As an example of a non-monetary exaction using the same logic as in HCD's conclusion, jurisdictions often adopt tree-replacement ordinances requiring planting of new trees when a project will remove existing trees from the project site. Most housing projects will be exempt from CEQA under a statutory or categorical exemption that has no qualifications related to trees; any tree-replacement requirements would not be to mitigate a CEQA impact and could not be imposed if the tree-replacement requirement was adopted after the SB 330 vesting date.

How Can the Applicant Know Which Fees Were Adopted *After* the Vesting Date?

Applicants should obtain and file all of the fee-related documents available from the jurisdiction on the date the SB 330 preliminary application was submitted. The developer can then check this fee information, perhaps several years later when the various fees are collected, to ensure no **new** fees are being applied. Gov. Code § 65940.1 imposes many fee-transparency requirements on jurisdictions, including fee-related disclosures that must be posted on the jurisdiction's website. Fee transparency may improve in the future. For example, Gov. Code §

65940.2, added by AB 3012 (2024), requires jurisdictions to have a fee *estimation* tool on their website by July 1, 2031, or for a city or county with 500,000 or fewer population by July 1, 2032.

In the Author's experience, however, most jurisdictions have not complied with the fee-transparency requirements. Rather than rely solely on the information from the jurisdiction's website, the Author recommends that developers obtain a "good faith estimate" of fees for the SB 330 preliminary application, and a second estimate for the approved project. AB 1820 (2024) amended Gov. Code § 65941.1 and added Gov. Code § 65943.1 to require jurisdictions to provide these project-specific estimates. The first Good Faith Estimate of Fees is requested along with the SB 330 preliminary application, and should at least identify what fees have been adopted by the jurisdiction as of the SB 330 vesting date. A second estimate is required within 30 *business* days **after final approval** of the project, by Gov. Code § 65943.1(a):

> (a) (1) Upon final approval of a housing development project, the city, county, or city and county shall provide the development proponent with an itemized list and a good faith estimate of the total sum amount of all fees and exactions that will apply to the project within 30 business days.

The applicant can compare the estimate provided after final approval to the one provided on the basis of the SB 330 preliminary application. If the itemized list of fees provided after final approval includes fees that were not in the estimate provided for the SB 330 preliminary application, the applicant should question whether the fee was created after the vesting date.

Duration of Vesting When an SB 330 Preliminary Application Applies

When an SB 330 preliminary application applies to a project, state law is very clear that the vesting of development standards continues to apply to that **project** even after its development **permit** is approved. The SB 330 preliminary application locks in the local ordinances, policies, and standards applicable to a ***project***, throughout the life of that project, not just during the review and approval of the application. Per Gov. Code § 65589.5(o)(1):

> (o) (1) Subject to paragraphs (2), (6), and (7), and subdivision (d) of Section 65941.1, a housing development **project** shall be subject only to the **ordinances, policies, and standards** adopted and in effect when a **preliminary application** including all of the information required by subdivision (a) of Section 65941.1 was submitted.

So long as the applicant meets the Deadlines to Maintain SB 330 Vesting, and no other event or condition causes the vesting to expire or become invalid, the vesting continues to apply through the date the project is issued its **certificate of occupancy**, per Gov. Code § 65589.5(o)(7):

> (7) With respect to completed residential units for which the project approval process is complete and a **certificate of occupancy has been issued**, nothing in this subdivision shall limit the application of later enacted ordinances, policies, and standards that regulate the use and occupancy of those residential units, such as ordinances relating to rental housing inspection, rent stabilization, restrictions on short-term renting, and business licensing requirements for owners of rental housing.

Or, if construction of the project has not commenced, until the deadline specified in Gov. Code § 65589.5(o)(2)(D):

> (2) Paragraph (1) shall not prohibit a housing development project from being subject to ordinances, policies, and standards adopted after the preliminary application was submitted pursuant to Section 65941.1 in the following circumstances:
>
> > ...
> >
> > (D) The housing **development project has not commenced construction** within **two and one-half years, or three and one-half years** for an affordable housing project, following the date that the project received **final approval**.

Note that construction must **commence** within the 2.5-year (or 3.5-year for a 100% affordable project) time period, or the vesting will expire.[65] It is not unusual for approved development projects to wait years before starting construction. Developers should consider the potential consequences of allowing the SB 330 vesting to expire, which could include the imposition of significant new fees.

Vesting of the SB 330 Preliminary Application Applies to Modifications of an Approval

Many jurisdictions have adopted ordinances that provide for processing an application to modify an approved project. A modification (often classified as a Major or Minor Modification) is just a process, adopted by a local jurisdiction, to review and approve a type of development permit application. If the project applied for in the modification meets the definition of a "housing development project" under the Housing Accountability Act, then the modification is protected by the HAA in the same way as any other housing development project.

Because an SB 330 preliminary application's vesting continues to apply to a **project** after the development **permit** is approved, when a developer submits an application for a modification of an approved housing development permit, the **modification** is subject only to the ordinances, policies, and standards that were in effect on the vesting date of the SB 330 preliminary application. However, if the modification includes a change of 20% or more to the base density, then the SB 330 preliminary application's vesting no longer applies, as explained under Only "Base Density" Matters for the SB 330 Preliminary Application.

As explained in the previous section, Gov. Code § 65589.5(o)(2)(D) provides that the vesting expires if construction is not commenced within 2.5 years (or 3.5 years for a 100% affordable project) after **final approval**. The Author interprets this provision to mean that a modification that is **approved** within 2.5 (or 3.5) years after the original final approval will continue the SB 330 vesting rights until 2.5 (or 3.5) years after the final approval of the **modification**. However, the Author knows of no case law or HCD guidance on this matter.

Deadlines to Maintain SB 330 Vesting

The vesting of the SB 330 preliminary application can only be lost due to the 20% rule (see Only "Base Density" Matters for the SB 330 Preliminary Application), due to not commencing construction within 2.5 or 3.5 years as explained in the previous section, or due to missing one of the deadlines described below.

180-Day Deadline for 1st Submittal of the Full Development Permit Application

After submitting an SB 330 preliminary application, the applicant has 180 days to submit the full development permit application, per Gov. Code § 65941.1(e)(1):

> (e) (1) **Within 180 calendar days** after submitting a preliminary application with all of the information required by subdivision (a) to a city, county, or city and county, the development proponent shall submit an application for a development project that includes all of the information required to process the development application consistent with Sections 65940, 65941, and 65941.5.

Remember that most jurisdictions do not consider the application submitted until the application **fee is paid**. It can take several days for the jurisdiction to calculate the fee and issue an invoice for the applicant to pay. **Submit early**, to avoid losing the vesting. As noted in an HCD letter *RE: Town of Los Gatos – Saratoga Road Project – Letter of Technical Assistance*, dated August 30, 2024:[66]

---

[65] The expiration of the **vesting** does not mean that the **entitlement** expires. Local codes determine the time period after which entitlement approvals in the jurisdiction expire, generally providing 12 to 36 months for the developer to submit a building permit application. Time periods can often be extended in accordance with the local code. State laws, for various reasons, may provide extensions of local time periods. For example, AB 2729 (2024) extended housing entitlement approvals that were to expire before December 31, 2025.

[66] https://www.hcd.ca.gov/sites/default/files/docs/planning-and-community/HAU/losgatos-hau891-ta-08302024.pdf.

> HCD understands that when development project applications are submitted to the Town, a Town staff person first checks to verify the appropriate type of permit being sought, then generates the invoice accordingly. Because this process requires action on the part of the staff person, it is not procedurally possible for an applicant to submit an application and associated fee at the same time. While in most instances this practice creates an insignificant delay, it is a matter of great concern to an applicant that is attempting to submit a full application with the 180-day submittal window to maintain vesting under a Preliminary Application. ...

That text suggests that HCD interprets Gov. Code § 65941.1(e)(1) to mean that the SB 330 preliminary application **expires** if the 180-day deadline is missed. This interpretation may or may not be correct. Gov. Code § 65941.1(e)(1) does not specify a consequence for missing the 180-day deadline. A court might not agree with HCD that failure to submit a full development permit application within 180 days would cause the SB 330 preliminary application to expire, **especially** in a case where the jurisdiction's delay in providing a fee invoice caused the applicant to miss the deadline. However, the next paragraph, Gov. Code § 65941.1(e)(2) specifies that the SB 330 preliminary application "shall expire and have no further force or effect" if that **90-day** deadline is not met. (See 90-Day Deadline for Each Resubmittal of the Full Development Permit Application, below.) To be safe, applicants should ensure they comply with all time limits associated with the SB 330 preliminary application. (See also, Extending SB 330 Preliminary Application Deadlines by Mutual Agreement.)

Lessons Learned: Submit Early!

The Los Gatos – Saratoga Road project had submitted an SB 330 preliminary application on June 30, 2023, which made the full development permit application due no later than December 27, 2023. The applicant transmitted the full development permit application to the jurisdiction on December 15, 2023, but the Town of Los Gatos did not provide a fee invoice until December 19, and the applicant paid the fee on the 173rd day, December 20, 2023. It is common practice for jurisdictions not to consider the application submitted until the fee is paid. A deadline can easily be missed due to a jurisdiction not timely providing a means to pay the fee. Deadlines are especially easy to miss over a holiday period!

90-Day Deadline for Each Resubmittal of the Full Development Permit Application

Once the full development permit application has been submitted, it is common for jurisdictions to send two or more incompleteness letters, before finally determining that the application is complete (see Chapter 8: Completeness Review). The applicant must resubmit the full development permit application within 90 days of receiving **each** written notice that the application is incomplete. If the applicant fails to resubmit within 90 days, the SB 330 preliminary application expires and its vesting is lost. Per Gov. Code § 65941.1(e)(2):

> (2) If the public agency determines that the application for the development project is not complete pursuant to Section 65943, the development proponent shall submit the specific information needed to complete the application within 90 days of receiving the agency's written identification of the necessary information. **If the development proponent does not submit this information within the 90-day period, then the preliminary application shall expire and have no further force or effect.**

Note that even when the application contains all of the required items for completeness, there have been cases where a jurisdiction repeatedly issued letters of incompleteness in an effort to kill a project that the jurisdiction did not want to approve (see The Real World of Development Permit Review and the lawsuit brought by the Town of Los Gatos against developers of two builder's remedy projects described in the next section). Therefore, although Extending SB 330 Preliminary Application Deadlines by Mutual Agreement is possible, applicants should not count on the jurisdiction extending any deadlines.

The 90-Day Deadline Restarts After *Each* Incompleteness Letter

Some jurisdictions have argued that there is only a **single** 90-day period from the **first** incompleteness letter until the project ***loses*** its vesting rights. For the Los Gatos – Saratoga Road project discussed above, HCD's August 2024 letter[67] responded to a question about the 90-day time limit, answering:

> The 90-day deadline restarts with each subsequent resubmittal by the applicant. ... An interpretation that there is a single finite 90-day review period is inconsistent with both the intent of the PSA and the Legislature when it introduced this system in Senate Bill 330 (Chapter 654, Statutes of 2019). This interpretation is also inconsistent with a recent Los Angeles Superior Court ruling which concluded "that when an applicant receives an incompleteness determination pursuant to section 65943 – not just the first incompleteness determination – an applicant has 90 days to respond." (Janet Jha v. City of Los Angeles, et al., (Super. Ct. L.A. County, 2024, No. 23STCP03499).)

The 155-unit project at 50 Los Gatos – Saratoga Road was approved by the Town Council March 4, 2025.[68]

However, rather than accepting HCD's interpretation that the 90-day deadline restarts each time the applicant resubmits, in a **different** case pertaining to a 68-unit townhome project, as related in an HCD letter *RE: Town of Los Gatos – 980 University Avenue Project – Notice of Potential Violation*, dated February 12, 2025:[69]

> ... on October 23, 2024, the Town informed an applicant for a development at 980 University Avenue (Project) that it interprets the PSA [Permit Streamlining Act] to provide a single 90-day period to achieve completeness and will treat applications not meeting this deadline as expired.
>
> ...
>
> Failure by the Town to allow for an additional 90-day resubmittal period after each of its incompleteness determinations would be a violation of the PSA. The Town must allow the applicant to resubmit the application within 90 days of any incompleteness determination.

HCD gave the Town of Los Gatos until February 26, 2025, to respond to the Notice of Potential Violation. The Town issued a letter of completeness to the Los Gatos – 980 University Avenue Project on February 12, 2025.[70] That project is a builder's remedy project and as of November 3, 2025, the project was still working toward a hearing.[71]

Then, on March 28, 2025, the Town sued the developers of two builder's remedy projects, Arya Properties, LLC (developing 15300-15330 Los Gatos Boulevard) and Boulevard Properties, LLC (developing 14849 Los Gatos Boulevard), in Santa Clara County Superior Court and issued a press release stating:[72]

> The Town of Los Gatos announced today that it has filed a declaratory relief action in Santa Clara County Superior Court to seek a judicial clarification of the Town's and property owners' legal rights and obligations under Government Code Section 65941.1, a state housing law. That section provides that applicants for land use approvals have 90 days after an initial 180-day deadline to submit any missing information needed to complete a formal application for a so-called "builder's remedy" housing project. That section further stipulates that if the missing information is not submitted "within the 90-day period, then the preliminary application shall expire and have no further force or effect." The Town interprets this section to mean there is a single 90-day cure period following an initial 180-day application deadline. In an apparently conflicting reading, in letters dated August 30, 2024 and February 12, 2025, the California Department of Housing and Community Development (HCD) stated its view that there is not just one 90-day period but that successive 90-day periods can run indefinitely. By filing this lawsuit, the Town is acting in good faith so that it will know how to comply with the law and ensure it can continue to serve its residents and property owners, while lawfully processing land use applications.

---

[67] Ibid.
[68] https://losgatos-ca.municodemeetings.com/bc-towncouncil/page/town-council-meeting-2.
[69] https://www.hcd.ca.gov/sites/default/files/docs/planning-and-community/HAU/losgatos-hau-1398-nopv-02122025.pdf.
[70] https://www.losgatosca.gov/DocumentCenter/View/42441/Re-Issued-Planning-Comment-Letter---980-University-Ave-PDF.
[71] https://www.losgatosca.gov/DocumentCenter/Index/2243.
[72] https://www.losgatosca.gov/DocumentCenter/View/41775/Press-Release_Declaratory-Relief-32825.

In an amicus brief filed September 9, 2025,[73] three housing advocacy groups (California Housing Defense Fund, Californians for Homeownership, Inc., and Patterson & O'Neill, PC for Yes in My Back Yard) opined:

> What is going on? Certainly more than "a simple and straightforward question of statutory interpretation," as the Town attempts to frame it. ... If one steps back to assess the Town's choices in the context of state housing law, a more nuanced picture emerges. In that picture, local governments like the Town have produced a devastating statewide crisis by refusing to permit new housing. The Legislature has responded by passing laws that revoke the Town's power to stop housing construction. These laws carry stiff penalties for violations.
>
> The Town, then, was in a bind when it received the applications at issue in this case. It lacked the power to reject the applications, and it knew that trying to do so risked serious consequences. But it wanted to stop the projects. So it came up with a clever strategy. It would not reject the applications outright. It would, instead, solicit law firms for a legal argument it could use to claim the applications had "expired." It would then refuse to process the applications and deny the applicants the right to file an administrative appeal. The final step was to file this action for declaratory relief. This strategy held several tactical advantages. First, it gave the Town plausible deniability against accusations that it is trying to stop new housing. The Town, wide-eyed and earnest, pleads that it likes new housing, but — wouldn't you know it! — its hands are tied by procedural technicalities. Second, the Town's strategy left room to muddy the waters about whether it has violated the powerful and punitive legal regime established by the Legislature. The Town "has not denied" the applications; the applications have simply "expired" through no fault of the Town's. (Town's Brief, 10:1 - 2.) Third, by filing a preemptive declaratory relief action, the Town could try to evade strict procedural rules and penalties that would apply if the applicants had sued the Town first. Finally, even if the Town loses this lawsuit, it will have wasted months of the applicants' time and cost them a good deal of money.
>
> But as cunning as the Town is — and it is cunning — it is wrong about the law. The defendants' applications have not "expired." The applications remain live, and any reasonable interpretation of the law confirms this conclusion. The courts agree, and so does the state agency charged with interpreting and enforcing state housing law. ...

On November 14, 2025, the Office of the California Attorney General issued a legal alert[74] stating:

> Recently, and despite ample guidance from the Department of Housing and Community Development (HCD), several jurisdictions have denied housing development applications based on an incorrect application of the "90-Day Rule" set forth in subdivision (e)(2) of Government Code section 65941.1. The purpose of this legal alert is to assist California local officials, such as county supervisors and councilmembers, planning directors, city attorneys, and county counsel, in the consistent application of Government Code section 65941.1, subdivisions (c) and (e) 1, as amended by the Housing Crisis Act. By providing both the Attorney General and HCD's interpretation of the law, this advisory strives to provide clarity and consistency in the expeditious and fair processing of housing development project applications.
>
> In short, for purposes of determining whether a housing development project application is complete, **an applicant is entitled to as many 90-day review and resubmission periods as necessary** and, throughout the process, retains the rights that vest upon the submission of a preliminary application under the Housing Crisis Act.

However, the Town and its attorneys objected in a court filing on November 26, 2025, that the Court "should decline to afford any deference to the Alert ...."

The Author's intent in sharing this case is to help practitioners understand that some jurisdictions will not accept interpretations of housing law from HCD or the California Attorney General (let alone the Author!) and are willing to undertake extremely costly lawsuits to stop housing projects. One purpose of this book is to make practitioners aware of disagreements in interpretation. Applicants should take care in documenting their compliance with all

---

[73] *The Town of Los Gatos, a California municipal corporation vs Arya Properties, LLC et al* — Case Number 25CV462276 at https://portal.scscourt.org/search.

[74] https://oag.ca.gov/system/files/media/legal-alert-oag-2025-04.pdf.

housing laws, and keep date-stamped records (of payment, submittal, mailings, postings, etc.) for proof of meeting all deadlines.

On January 29, 2026, the Town of Los Gatos lost its case. The Superior Court concluded:[75]

> [S]ection 65941.1(e)(2), by its express cross-reference to section 65943, allows for multiple 90-day resubmission periods for a project proponent to respond to successive incompleteness determinations without losing the project vesting conferred by a preliminary application as provided at section 65941.1, subdivision (e)(1).

The Town has indicated that it will appeal the court's decision.

Extending SB 330 Preliminary Application Deadlines by Mutual Agreement

In its August 2024 letter about the Los Gatos – Saratoga Road project,[76] HCD answered a question about **extending** the 90-Day Deadline for Each Resubmittal of the Full Development Permit Application (emphasis in original):

> **Can a housing development project applicant and a city or county mutually agree to an extension of the 90-day time limit provided in Government Code section 65941.1, subdivision [e](2)[77]?**
>
> Yes. As mentioned above, subdivision [e](1)[78] links its process to that of section 65943, which provides in its subdivision [e][79] that the timelines for submittal do not preclude "an applicant and a public agency from mutually agreeing to an extension of any time limit provided by this section." It logically follows that if a project is in a situation where section 65943 is applicable because the application is not complete, then the local government and the applicant should be able to extend the submittal timelines by mutual agreement. HCD encourages local governments and applicants to work together to successfully realize residential development projects.

Rules for extending deadlines are not consistent across various sections of state law. Some laws allow unilateral extension (for example, a Tribe can extend a consultation period unilaterally, see PRC § 21080.66 Exemption Requires a Tribal Notification and Consultation Process); some laws allow for mutual extension a single time (see, for example, 30- or 45-day Time Period for the Review for Exemption); and some do not provide clear rules about extensions. In the case of this 90-day deadline, HCD's guidance interprets the law to allow mutual extension of the deadline. By the same logic, the 180-Day Deadline for 1st Submittal of the Full Development Permit Application can also be extended by mutual agreement.

Granting an extension can build good will and facilitate orderly review of projects without unnecessary new submittals or resubmittals. However, both applicants and jurisdictions should remember that Missing a Deadline (Usually) Has Consequences and ***avoid*** being in a situation where they need to ask for an extension.

Vesting of the *Full* Development Permit Application

It is somewhat counterintuitive that, in cases where no SB 330 preliminary application applies to a project, the submittal of a full development permit application does **not** automatically provide the same vesting rights. As compared to the vesting provided by a full development permit application, an SB 330 preliminary application vests development standards earlier, its vesting applies to a broader range of development standards, and the vesting continues after the approval of the development permit application through certificate of occupancy. The superior vesting rights of the preliminary application are enumerated in Gov. Code § 65589.5(o), which begins:

---

[75] *The Town of Los Gatos, a California municipal corporation vs Arya Properties, LLC et al* — Case Number 25CV462276 at https://portal.scscourt.org/search Order RE: Motion for Summary Judgement documents filed January 29, 2026.
[76] https://www.hcd.ca.gov/sites/default/files/docs/planning-and-community/HAU/losgatos-hau891-ta-08302024.pdf.
[77] Note that the HCD letter refers to subdivision (d) here, but Gov. Code § 65941.1 has been amended since the August 2024 letter and subdivision (d) was renumbered to subdivision (e).
[78] Ibid.
[79] Ibid.

> (o) (1) Subject to paragraphs (2), (6), and (7), and subdivision (d) of Section 65941.1, a housing development project shall be subject only to the ordinances, policies, and standards adopted and in effect **when a preliminary application** including all of the information required by subdivision (a) of Section 65941.1 **was submitted**.

Only the preliminary application provides the vesting described previously in this chapter, because Gov. Code § 65589.5(o) only applies "when a **preliminary application** ... was submitted."

A Full Development Permit Application Is Not Automatically a Preliminary Application

A complete full development permit application will almost certainly contain the 17 items required for a preliminary application, and a permit processing fee will be paid for the full development permit application, so some practitioners will argue that the full development permit application qualifies as a preliminary application, in accordance with Gov. Code § 65941.1(a):

> (a) An applicant for a housing development project, as defined in paragraph (3) of subdivision (b) of Section 65905.5, shall be deemed to have submitted a preliminary application upon providing all of the following information about the proposed project to the city, county, or city and county from which approval for the project is being sought and upon payment of the permit processing fee:

However, applicants should not rely on that argument, and should instead submit a separate SB 330 preliminary application using the proper form (see Form for the SB 330 Preliminary Application) and paying a separate fee. The preliminary application can even be submitted on the same day as the full development permit application, if necessary. This will remove any need for interpretation and clearly establish the SB 330 vesting date.

Reasons Why a Preliminary Application Would Not Apply to a Project

The vesting rights provided by the full development permit application ***only*** matter when no SB 330 preliminary application applies to the project, either because no preliminary application was submitted, or because the preliminary application became inapplicable to the project. A preliminary application can become inapplicable for four main reasons:

1. The SB 330 preliminary application is determined not to meet the requirements of Gov. Code § 65941.1. Applicants are "deemed to have submitted a preliminary application" upon providing the 17 items listed at Gov. Code § 65941.1(a) and the processing fee. However, the jurisdiction is expected to check that the preliminary application does in fact include the 17 items. (See No Review of the SB 330 Preliminary Application is Required.) If the preliminary application did **not** contain the 17 items, then it could be determined to be incomplete and therefore be inapplicable.
2. The project changes by 20% or more. (See Only "Base Density" Matters for the SB 330 Preliminary Application.)
3. The applicant misses a deadline. (See Deadlines to Maintain SB 330 Vesting.)
4. The vesting of the preliminary application expires before construction commences. (See Duration of Vesting When an SB 330 Preliminary Application Applies.)

When a preliminary application becomes inapplicable to a project, in most cases the applicant should submit a new SB 330 preliminary application. The submittal date of the new preliminary application sets the new vesting date, and the project can be subjected to new development standards adopted by a local agency up to the submittal date of the new preliminary application.

However, practitioners should be aware of the **limited** vesting rights provided by the full development permit application if a preliminary application does not apply to the project.

Which Development Standards are Vested by the Full Housing Development Permit Application

If no SB 330 preliminary application is submitted, or if the SB 330 vesting is lost as explained above, the development standards that are vested are limited to the "general plan, zoning, and subdivision standards and criteria, including design review standards" vested by the **full** development permit in accordance with Gov. Code § 65589.5(j)(1):

> (j) (1) When a proposed housing development project complies with applicable, objective **general plan, zoning, and subdivision standards and criteria, including design review standards**, in effect at the time that the application was deemed complete, but the local agency proposes to disapprove the project or to impose a condition that the project be developed at a lower density, the local agency shall base its decision regarding the proposed housing development project upon written findings supported by a preponderance of the evidence on the record that both of the following conditions exist: ...

Compare this vesting of "general plan, zoning, and subdivision standards and criteria, including design review standards" to the vesting of "ordinances, policies, and standards" provided by an SB 330 preliminary application, in accordance with Gov. Code § 65589.5(o)(1) and (4):

> (o) (1) Subject to paragraphs (2), (6), and (7), and subdivision (d) of Section 65941.1, a housing development project shall be subject only to the ordinances, policies, and standards adopted and in effect **when a preliminary application** including all of the information required by subdivision (a) of Section 65941.1 **was submitted**.
>
>> (4) For purposes of this subdivision, "ordinances, policies, and standards" includes **general plan, community plan, specific plan, zoning, design review standards and criteria, subdivision standards and criteria, and any other rules, regulations, requirements, and policies of a local agency**, as defined in Section 66000, including those relating to **development impact fees, capacity or connection fees or charges, permit or processing fees, and other exactions**.

The vesting of the preliminary application applies to a broader set of development standards than the vesting of the full development permit application. Specifically, Gov. Code § 65589.5(j)(1) that vests the full development permit application does not list "other rules, regulations, requirements, and policies of a local agency ... including ... development impact fees, capacity or connection fees or charges, permit or processing fees, and other exactions." Not having an SB 330 preliminary application that vests these "other rules, regulations, requirements and policies" could be a costly mistake.

Duration of Vesting When *No* SB 330 Preliminary Application Applies

As explained under Duration of Vesting When an SB 330 Preliminary Application Applies, when the project is vested by an SB 330 preliminary application, the project continues to be vested until certificate of occupancy or 2.5 years after final approval of the project if construction is not started (3.5 years for affordable housing projects).

When **no** SB 330 preliminary application was submitted or its vesting was **lost** for some reason, then unlike under Gov. Code § 65589.5(o) which continues to provide vesting rights based on the preliminary application, Gov. Code § 65589.5(j)(1) applies **only** to the approval of the project:

> (j) (1) When a proposed housing development project complies with applicable, objective general plan, zoning, and subdivision standards and criteria, including design review standards, in effect at the time that the application was deemed complete, **but the local agency proposes to disapprove the project or to impose a condition that the project be developed at a lower density**, the local agency shall base its decision regarding the proposed housing development project upon written findings supported by a preponderance of the evidence on the record that both of the following conditions exist: ...

Subdivision (j) pertains entirely to the review and approval of the project. Therefore, the full development permit application vests the project only through the date of final approval. It only vests the "general plan, zoning, and subdivision standards and criteria, including design review standards" as of the "deemed complete" date, which if no SB 330 preliminary application applies to the project, is established by the full development permit application in accordance with Gov. Code § 65589.5(h)(5), as explained in the next section.

What is the "Vesting Date" For a Full Development Permit Application?

The vesting that applies to subdivision (j) for the approval of the project begins on the date the "application was deemed complete." The definition of "deemed complete" applies to either the SB 330 preliminary application or a full development permit application, per Gov. Code § 65589.5(h)(5):

> (5) Notwithstanding any other law, "**deemed complete**" means that the applicant has submitted a **preliminary application** pursuant to Section 65941.1 or, if the applicant has not submitted a preliminary application, has submitted a ***complete* application** pursuant to Section 65943. The local agency shall bear the burden of proof in establishing that the application is not complete.

The reference to Gov. Code § 65941.1 is to the SB 330 preliminary application, which is deemed complete upon submittal. The preliminary application is **presumed** to be complete, and the jurisdiction must **prove** that it is not. By contrast, the reference to Gov. Code § 65943 is to the full development permit application, for which there is a lengthy review process, and the jurisdiction must make a determination that the application is complete (or if the 30-day deadline expires, the application is deemed complete, see Chapter 8: Completeness Review).

As the Author explains under What Triggers the Start of the Compliance Review Period?, there are three alternatives that cause an application to be "deemed complete," and each alternative establishes a different vesting date:

1. If an SB 330 preliminary application pursuant to Gov. Code § 65941.1 applies to the project, then the SB 330 preliminary application is deemed complete on the date it was **submitted** and the development standards are vested on that date.
2. If **no** SB 330 preliminary application applies, then the date a **complete** full housing development permit application was **submitted** (if that submittal is ***later* determined to be complete** in accordance with Gov. Code § 65943) is the deemed complete date that vests the development standards. In practical terms:
   a. It typically takes several rounds of resubmittals before the jurisdiction makes the affirmative determination that the full development permit application is complete, in accordance with Gov. Code § 65943.
   b. The full development permit application is deemed complete upon submittal ***if*** that submittal was complete in accordance with Gov. Code § 65943. The vesting date is the ***(re)submittal* date** of the full application that is determined to be complete, **not** the date of the completeness determination.
3. If no SB 330 preliminary application applies to the project, ***and*** the jurisdiction **fails** to provide the applicant with a written determination by the 30-day deadline in accordance with Gov. Code § 65943, then the application **becomes** complete by operation of state law at the expiration of the 30-day deadline. The date that the project is deemed complete by operation of Gov. Code § 65943 is the vesting date of the full application in this case.

This is all quite simple if an SB 330 preliminary application applies to the project: the vesting date is the date the preliminary application was submitted (alternative 1, above). However, when no SB 330 preliminary application applies to a project it could take many months of resubmittals before the full development permit application is deemed complete. The jurisdiction could adopt and apply new development standards while the project is going through multiple rounds of completeness review.

Therefore, even if the applicant submits the full development permit application on the **same date** as the preliminary application the SB 330 preliminary application will establish an **earlier** vesting date than the full development permit application.

Legislative History of Vesting — Full Application vs. Preliminary Application

Some historic context may be helpful to understand how and why the vesting dates of the full development permit application and preliminary application are different. With the passage of a series of bills, the vesting date applicable to a housing project has evolved:

1. Prior to the passage of SB 330 (2019), the vested development standards would be based on:
   a. A **full development permit application**, consisting of **whatever the jurisdiction asked for at any time** during their application review process. The vesting date was either:
      i. The date the jurisdiction **determined the application to be complete**.
      ii. Or, very rarely, the date the application was **deemed complete** by operation of state law.
2. With the passage of SB 330, the vested development standards could be based on **either**:
   a. A **preliminary application** consisting of a **list of 17 specified items** in Gov. Code § 65941.1.
      i. The vesting date is the date the preliminary application was **submitted** with the fee paid.
      ii. The SB 330 preliminary application **does not require review** by the local jurisdiction. It is automatically **deemed** complete upon submittal. (Gov. Code § 65589.5(h)(5).)
   b. Or, a full development permit application, consisting of everything on a **list of required information ("LORI")**[80] **created and published by the jurisdiction in advance.**[81] The vesting date was either:
      i. The date the jurisdiction determined the application to be complete.
      ii. Or the date the application was deemed complete by operation of state law, because the jurisdiction did not comply with Gov. Code § 65950 as amended with **shorter deadlines.**[82]
3. With the passage of SB 1030 (2020), Gov. Code § 65589.5(h)(5) was revised such that the vested development standards could be based on either:
   a. As in 2.a., above, submittal of a preliminary application with the 17 items.
   b. Or, a **full** development permit application, that was complete with all the LORI items, as in 2.b. above, but the vesting date would be the date that the full application was either:
      i. **Submitted**, and ***later*** determined by the jurisdiction to be complete.
         - Note that there could be **multiple rounds of submittals** before the application is complete. The vesting date is the date of the *last* of the submittals (the submittal that the jurisdiction determined to be complete).
      ii. Or, as in 2b., above, the date the application was deemed complete by operation of state law, because the jurisdiction did not comply with Gov. Code § 65950.

Today, just as in 2019 prior to the passage of SB 330, a **complete** full development permit application vests the "general plan, zoning, and subdivision standards and criteria, including design review standards" for purposes of Gov. Code § 65589.5(j), through the date of final approval of the project.

---

[80] SB 330 and subsequent bills placed some limitations on the items that can be required by the jurisdiction's LORI.
[81] Jurisdictions often fail to comply with the requirement to post a document with a comprehensive list of required items on their website.
[82] SB 330 and subsequent bills have shortened the deadlines and made other changes to strengthen the rules pertaining to the "completeness review" process.

Perhaps someday the Legislature will add to Gov. Code § 65589.5(o) the same language found in Gov. Code § 65589.5(h)(5): "or, if the applicant has not submitted a preliminary application, has submitted a complete application pursuant to Section 65943." Until then, to obtain the full vesting rights provided by Gov. Code § 65589.5(o), ***always*** submit an SB 330 preliminary application. If for any reason the SB 330 preliminary application becomes invalid, it is usually best to submit a **new** SB 330 preliminary application.

CHAPTER 8: COMPLETENESS REVIEW

The first part of the Three-Part Process for Reviewing an Application for a Housing Development Permit is to review the application for **completeness**. This chapter explains the list of required information (LORI) that jurisdictions must post on their website for each type of development permit application that jurisdiction reviews. It then details the requirements for submitting a complete full housing development permit application. Each step in the completeness review process is described in detail with the Author's advice on keeping the process as short as possible. Jurisdictions Should Not Combine and/or Confuse Completeness and Compliance, but unfortunately, they usually do exactly that. This chapter has recommendations for working with jurisdictions to clearly separate completeness items from compliance matters. When the jurisdiction accepts the application as complete, it triggers the second part of the three-part process, which is the CEQA review for exemption that was explained in Chapter 4: CEQA Review for Housing Projects After AB 130 and SB 131.

Where to Find More Information

Because each jurisdiction has its own types of applications, application forms, submittal requirements, and review processes, applicants must carefully review the development code for the city or county that has jurisdiction over the project, obtain the LORI and the proper forms from the jurisdiction's planning department, and follow the procedures specified in the local code. There are few good resources for understanding the state-law requirements for conducting completeness review other than the many HCD Technical Assistance and Enforcement letters that have addressed these requirements, which can be found at HCD's Housing Accountability and Enforcement website.

CHAPTER CONTENTS

Overview of Completeness Review

Gov. Code § 65940 requires that each jurisdiction create lists of required information (LORIs) for each type of development permit application that the jurisdiction processes. Gov. Code § 65943 requires that jurisdictions review the materials submitted as the full development permit application and (if it includes the items and information listed in the LORI) affirmatively **determine that the application is complete**. If the jurisdiction determines that the application is **not** complete, it must provide "an exhaustive list of items" necessary to complete the application. (Gov. Code § 65943(a).) The list of incomplete items is limited to the items that were **included in the LORI** but were not included in the application. If the jurisdiction fails to provide the list of incomplete items within 30 days, the application is **deemed complete**.

The Housing Accountability Act is clear that a LORI for a housing project is a "submittal requirements ***checklist***." (Gov. Code § 65589.5(h)(6)(F).) The completeness review should be limited to checking that each of the items listed in the LORI is included in the application. In the real world, however, few jurisdictions process housing development permits the way that state law intends. As explained under The Real World of Development Permit Review, jurisdictions often fail to post a clear and comprehensive LORI on their websites, perform compliance review during the completeness review process, confuse compliance matters for incompleteness, and perform building code and CEQA review during the completeness review process. This leads to significant delays in processing housing development permits.

Figure 19(A): Typical project timeline through completeness.

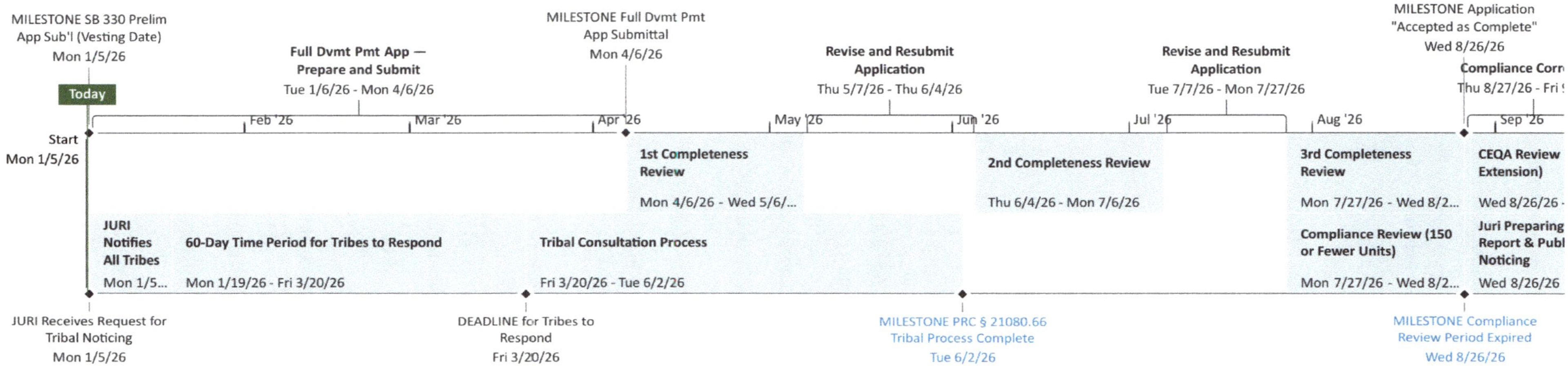

In Figure 19(A), the project is using the PRC § 21080.66 Statutory Exemption — New with AB 130, with a tribal process triggered by the SB 330 preliminary application. The full development permit application is submitted three months after the SB 330 preliminary application, on April 6, 2026. The jurisdiction takes the full 30 days for each of three rounds of completeness review. The 30-day compliance review starts on July 27, concurrently with the 3rd completeness review, upon submittal of the **complete** development permit application later determined to be complete on August 26. As always, the (A) in the figure number means that this timeline follows the Author's interpretation of the law, with the compliance review period starting when the complete full development permit application is submitted. See What Triggers the Start of the Compliance Review Period?.

This chapter includes recommendations for managing the completeness review process to minimize delays, but unfortunately Gov. Code § 65943 that prescribes the process jurisdictions must follow for completeness review is written in a way that assumes three rounds of review before the applicant can appeal the staff's incompleteness determinations, and that appeal process takes 60 days (see Appeal of the Staff's Determination that an Application is Incomplete.)

Development Permit Application Form

State law has no specific requirements for the format of a full application for a development permit. Each jurisdiction creates its own form or forms, and its own submittal requirements and process. However, state law requires that the forms be posted on the jurisdiction's website and limits the information that a jurisdiction can require for a complete application.

If AB 1294 passes in 2026, there will be a standard, **statewide application form** for housing development permits (see How AB 1294 Could Greatly Reduce the Entitlement Timeline).

Lists of Required Information

Gov. Code § 65940 requires that each jurisdiction clearly disclose, in advance, the information required to be submitted with an application for a development permit:

> 65940. (a) (1) Each public agency shall compile one or more **lists that shall specify in detail the information that will be required from any applicant for a development project**. Each public agency shall revise the list of information required from an applicant to include a certification of compliance with Section 65962.5, and the statement of application required by Section 65943. Copies of the information, including the statement of application required by Section 65943, shall be made available to all applicants for development projects and to any person who requests the information.

Jurisdictions are required to provide these lists of required information (LORIs) to any person who requests them (Gov. Code § 65940(a)), and if the jurisdiction has a website it must publish the LORIs there (Gov. Code § 65940.1(a)(1)(C)). These requirements apply to all LORIs, not just those for housing projects.

For housing development projects, the most common way that jurisdictions have addressed these requirements is to publish a "universal LORI" that applies to all housing development permit applications in the jurisdiction. LORIs often require several dozen costly reports, studies, and plan sets; including items that are not actually necessary to establish that the project is compliant with the applicable development standards. For example, LORIs typically include a geotechnical report, a stormwater management report, detailed civil and utility plans, and ADA accessibility plans, none of which should be required until the building permit phase because they are related to grading and building standards rather than to the standards of the general plan and zoning code.

If AB 1294 passes in 2026, there will be a standard, **statewide LORI** for housing development permits (see How AB 1294 Could Greatly Reduce the Entitlement Timeline).

Criteria for Application Completeness

The jurisdiction's LORI is also required to explain the **criteria** a jurisdiction will apply to determine whether the application is complete. Gov. Code § 65941(a):

> 65941. (a) The information compiled pursuant to Section 65940 shall also indicate the criteria which the agency will apply in order to determine the completeness of any application submitted to it for a development project.

The criteria for completeness should be related to the type of development permit application, and the applicable standards for that application. The criteria should not include things that would be checked in a **building** permit application, because this is a **development** permit application. And, because this is a **housing** development permit application, the criteria should be limited to the information that the jurisdiction needs for it to determine whether the "proposed housing development project complies with applicable, objective general plan, zoning, and subdivision standards and criteria, including design review standards." (Gov. Code 65589.5(j)(1).)

If AB 1294 passes in 2026, the full development permit application will be **deemed complete upon submittal** if it includes all the items required by the **statewide LORI** (see How AB 1294 Could Greatly Reduce the Entitlement Timeline).

Limitation on LORI Items Related to CEQA

With respect to CEQA, the LORI may only include the information necessary for the jurisdiction to complete the review to determine **whether** the project is **exempt** from CEQA; it cannot require studies that will not be necessary if the project is exempt. Gov. Code § 65941(b):

> (b) If a public agency is a lead or responsible agency for purposes of the California Environmental Quality Act, Division 13 (commencing with Section 21000) of the Public Resources Code, that criteria **shall not require** the applicant to submit the **informational equivalent of an environmental impact report** as part of a complete application, or to otherwise require proof of compliance with that act as a prerequisite to a permit application being deemed complete. However, that criteria **may require sufficient information** to permit the agency to make the determination required by Section 21080.1 of the Public Resources Code [i.e., **whether the project is exempt from CEQA**].

Gov. Code § 65941(b) limits the LORI to items required for the jurisdiction to make the determination, pursuant to PRC § 21080.1 of whether the project is exempt from CEQA (see Chapter 4: CEQA Review for Housing Projects After AB 130 and SB 131). Environmental reports that are not required for the jurisdiction to determine whether the project is exempt from CEQA cannot be included in the LORI and are not required for a complete development permit application. If the jurisdiction accepts the application as complete and later finds that additional information is necessary to complete the CEQA review, the applicant must provide those additional items and information that are required for CEQA purposes. (Gov. Code § 65944(c).)

For example, the PRC § 21080.66 Statutory Exemption — New with AB 130 — does not require a noise study, because it has no criteria related to noise. Unlike **categorical** exemptions that cannot be used if the project **may** have significant environmental impacts due to "unusual circumstances" (see Class 32 "Infill" Categorical Exemption), **statutory** exemptions like the one provided by PRC § 21080.66 provide an exemption from CEQA ***even if*** the project could have significant impacts. As another example, the PRC § 21080.66 statutory exemption does not require a biotic study **unless** the project site has the potential to be habitat for protected species. (PRC § 21080.66(a)(6) and Gov. Code § 65915.4(a)(6)(J).)

The applicant should identify the CEQA exemption or exemptions that they believe the project qualifies for and meet with the jurisdiction for a Preapplication CEQA Consultation if there is any question as to what documentation the jurisdiction will need to make the CEQA determination. The applicant should provide the necessary information and evidence of eligibility for the exemption(s) with the 1st Submittal. Providing the necessary CEQA documentation will help the jurisdiction review the 1st Submittal and reduce the chance that the jurisdiction will demand unnecessary studies before determining the application is complete.

How to Ensure You Have the Entire LORI and the Fee Amount for a Complete 1st Submittal

It is the applicant's responsibility to ensure that they know what the LORI requires and to submit all the LORI items. Unfortunately, no matter how diligent the applicant is, jurisdictions virtually never determine that an application is complete on the 1st Submittal.

In addition to the requirements of Gov. Code § 65940(a)(1) that apply to LORIs for all types of projects, Gov. Code § 65943(f) applies specifically to **housing** development permit applications, and requires that:

> (f) Each city and each county shall make copies of any list compiled pursuant to Section 65940 with respect to information required from an applicant for a housing development project, as that term is defined in paragraph (2) of subdivision (h) of Section 65589.5, available both (1) **in writing** to those persons to whom the agency is required to make information available under subdivision (a) of that section, and (2) publicly available **on the internet website** of the city or county.

Even when the applicant has obtained a LORI from the jurisdiction's website, they should email a request to the jurisdiction's planning department and/or clerk's office to formally request a copy of the LORI for the type of application being submitted and all of the approvals being requested. The applicant should insist that the jurisdiction confirm in writing that the response constitutes the entire list of required items for a complete application. This formal request and response can help ensure that the applicant and the jurisdiction understand the submittal requirements; and it should help the applicant to include all the required items thereby reducing the number of resubmittals. These inquiries should be made **after** the SB 330 preliminary application has been submitted and well **before** the anticipated date that the full development permit application will be submitted.

The applicant should have requested a Good Faith Estimate of Fees with the SB 330 preliminary application. When preparing the full development permit application, the applicant should ask that the fee estimate be updated, especially if the project has changed since the SB 330 preliminary application.

The Author recommends that applicants inquire with the jurisdiction to determine the **amount of the fee** required to be paid at time of development permit application, and the process and requirements for submitting the application materials and paying the fee.

Example of Email to Request a Jurisdiction's LORI

Applicants should formally request the list of required information (LORI) for a complete submittal and ask the jurisdiction to confirm that the response constitutes the entire LORI. Applicants can send an email to this effect:

> On [date], Applicant submitted an SB 330 preliminary application for [identify the project] ("Project"). We are preparing to submit a housing development permit application for this Project, which will seek:
>
> [list of approvals requested]
>
> In accordance with Gov. Code § 65940(a)(1), the jurisdiction is required to provide, upon the request of any person, "lists that shall specify in detail the information that will be required from any applicant for a development project" ("LORI"). In accordance with Gov. Code § 65943(f), the LORI for a housing development project shall be provided "in writing" at the request of any person, in addition to being made publicly available on the internet.
>
> Please provide the LORI applicable to the Project and confirm in writing that your response constitutes the entire list of required information, and that the application will be determined to be complete in accordance with Gov. Code § 65943(a) if all of the information is provided.
>
> In addition, please provide instructions for submitting the application materials and paying the application fee. A good faith estimate of fees was requested with the SB 330 preliminary application pursuant to Gov. Code § 65941.1(b). Please update the estimate based on the attached Project parameters and provide an exact fee amount for this housing development permit application, to be paid simultaneously with our transmittal of the application materials.

The applicant should carefully review the LORI and request clarification of any items that are not clear or that the applicant believes should **not** be included in the LORI. For example, if any item is impossible to submit with the initial application (e.g., evidence that a community meeting has been held to obtain comments on the full submittal, or an affidavit that the applicant has posted a sign stating the scheduled hearing date), the applicant should protest those items and explain that they cannot be required for the application to be considered complete.

LORIs as Lists of *Potential* Requirements

One common way that jurisdictions create their LORI is as a list of **potential** requirements. Basically, this is the same as a "universal LORI", but the "potential LORI" implicitly acknowledges that not all of the items are required for a complete submittal. Either the applicant decides which items are necessary for their particular project (sometimes called "self-certifying") and submits only those items, or the jurisdiction requires some sort of pre-application appointment, during which planning staff identify which items on the list are required. The Author knows of no HCD guidance or case law that has challenged the use of a "potential LORI."

The "Real" LORI

Partly because state law allows every jurisdiction to create its own unique LORIs and application forms, applications are virtually never determined to be complete after the first submittal. As explained under 1st Letter of Incompleteness (The Real LORI), when the jurisdiction reviews the application and determines it to be incomplete, the jurisdiction is required to send a written determination that the application is incomplete with a list of items required to complete the application. The list of incomplete items in the 1st letter of incompleteness is final; the jurisdiction is prohibited from adding other items later in the review process. (Gov. Code § 65943(a).) So, the list of items in the 1st letter of incompleteness is the final ("real") LORI.

Jurisdictions Should Not Combine and/or Confuse Completeness and Compliance

A major delay in the processing of the development permit application is caused when jurisdictions do not separate the compliance review process from the completeness review process. More often than not, Jurisdictions Combine Compliance Review with Completeness Review and provide compliance comments in each letter of incompleteness and in the final letter of completeness. The applicant should **discourage jurisdictions from combining compliance comments with completeness comments** or even including compliance comments in the same letter as the incompleteness or completeness determination. When the compliance comments are included in the same letter as completeness items, Jurisdictions Confuse Compliance Matters with Incompleteness.

In a letter *RE: City of El Cerrito – 921 Kearney Street and 10167 San Pablo Avenue Projects – Letter of Technical Assistance*, dated August 5, 2025,[83] HCD addressed this issue:

> **1. What standards apply for application completeness versus consistency review?**
>
> The PSA mandates transparency in the local review process, among other provisions, requiring publicly available planning entitlement application checklists and prompt determination regarding the completeness of a development project application. The PSA requires that local agencies begin the review of proposed development projects by determining the completeness of the submitted application before proceeding with continued processing. In making this determination, local agencies may only consider those submittal items identified in the applicable publicly available application checklists. Specifically, the PSA provides the following:

HCD then quotes the first half of Gov. Code § 65943(a), and HCD emphasizes the text in bold:

[83] https://www.hcd.ca.gov/sites/default/files/docs/planning-and-community/HAU/el-cerrito-hau-1459-ta-080525.pdf.

> (a) Not later than 30 calendar days after any public agency has received an application for a development project, the agency shall determine in writing whether the application is complete and shall immediately transmit the determination to the applicant for the development project. If the application is determined to be incomplete, the lead agency shall provide the applicant with an exhaustive list of items that were not complete. ***That list shall be limited to those items actually required on the lead agency's submittal requirement checklist***. ...

The HCD letter continues:

> To date, the City has issued multiple incompleteness letters to the Projects. HCD would like to remind the City that during a project application completeness review, the City must ensure its determination is "limited to those items actually required on the lead agency's submittal requirement checklist."[footnote omitted] When a local jurisdiction improperly characterizes consistency review comments as incomplete items, the jurisdiction unlawfully raises the bar to achieving a complete application, in violation of the PSA. If the City chooses to conduct the PSA completeness review and HAA consistency review concurrently, rather than doing so in sequence as the HAA allows, it must ensure that its response letter specifically differentiates the two reviews with clear written responses to the applicant pursuant to Government Code sections 65589.5, subdivision (j) and 65943, respectively. Additionally, the HAA consistency review must not act as a barrier to achieving an otherwise complete application under the PSA.

While it can be beneficial for both the applicant and the jurisdiction to review each submittal for *compliance*, the purpose of the completeness review process prescribed by Gov. Code § 65943 is to achieve a **complete** application. Noting prevents the jurisdiction from sending a letter of incompleteness identifying the missing LORI items and ***then*** continuing to review that submittal for compliance. Providing the letter of incompleteness ***earlier*** than the 30-day deadline would help the applicant keep the project moving forward by identifying missing LORI items so that the applicant can obtain them. For example, if the applicant neglects to provide a geotechnical report that the LORI requires, it will take quite a while for the applicant to hire a geotechnical engineer, complete the soil borings, and write and review the report. Letting the applicant know, in less than 30 days, that they need to submit a geotechnical report simply saves time.

The jurisdiction should review the application for completeness and provide written notice determining whether the application is complete or not, ***then*** begin compliance review. This would help jurisdictions avoid missing the 30-day deadline for completeness review, resulting in a **deemed complete** application that does not actually contain the items in the LORI. The jurisdiction really loses nothing by separating the completeness review from the compliance review. When an application is determined to be ***in***complete, the clock for that submittal stops. The jurisdiction can take as much time to review that submittal for compliance as it needs. The jurisdiction can facilitate meetings between the applicant and various departments that are reviewing the submittal materials so that the compliance issues can be discussed and worked out, rather than describing the compliance issues in the incompleteness letter.

In the Author's experience, incompleteness letters often consist of a cover letter discussing completeness and compliance matters, with a series of attachments from various departments and technical reviewers containing both compliance and completeness comments. The Author is suggesting that the jurisdiction should have a member of the planning staff determine whether the application is complete with all the items required by the LORI, ***then*** send the submitted materials to the appropriate people for compliance review. There is no need for those reviewers to be consulted to determine if the application is complete. If "a reasonable person would conclude that the applicant has submitted all of the items required on the local agency's submittal requirement checklist" the application is complete. (Gov. Code § 65589.5(h)(6)(F)(iii).) When the departmental and technical reviews come in, the planning staff can send them to the applicant as advisories on potential compliance issues. Later, after the application is complete and before the compliance period expires, the jurisdiction can send comprehensive compliance comments as required by Gov. Code § 65589.5(j)(2).

The question of What Triggers the Start of the Compliance Review Period? really does not matter in this case:

A. If the jurisdiction's attorneys believe that the Author is right and the compliance review period starts when the **complete** application is ***submitted***, then when the jurisdiction receives an application that ***is*** complete they can take the full 30 days to send the letter of completeness if they want to, but if the Author is right the clock for the compliance period started running on the date the complete application was submitted anyway.

B. If the jurisdiction's attorneys believe that the Author is wrong and the compliance review period does not start until the jurisdiction affirmatively ***determines*** that the application is complete, then the jurisdiction can take the full 30 days to send the letter of completeness (to get some extra time to simultaneously conduct compliance review on the complete application) and then use the full 30- or 60-day Time Period Allowed for Compliance Review.

If the applicant and jurisdiction have a good working relationship, the Author recommends that the parties discuss the completeness and compliance review process, in light of HCD guidance and the suggestions here, and work together to achieve a complete application as quickly as possible. Meanwhile, the parties can hash out the compliance matters and apply state housing laws to determine whether the offended development standards are actually applicable. The applicant may even offer to extend the compliance review period by 30 days as a gesture of good faith in exchange for a smooth completeness review process. Jurisdictions that understand the process required by state law should welcome the extension, because they face a very short deadline to approve or disapprove a project that is exempt from CEQA, before Deemed Approval — New with AB 130. (See How AB 130 Changes the Entitlement Timeline.)

1st Submittal

Creating a complete first submittal is a major undertaking. As explained under Lists of Required Information, a jurisdiction's LORI typically requires dozens of plans, reports, studies, and calculations. Most jurisdictions no longer accept paper submittals; they have various electronic processes from simple email submission to complex online portals. Some jurisdictions require a submittal "appointment" even when submitting electronically. For the first submittal, the application is not considered submitted until the processing **fee is paid**. Usually, the planning department calculates the submittal fee **after** receiving the application, making it impossible to transmit the application and pay the fee on the same date. While HCD has issued guidance to jurisdictions encouraging them to simplify and streamline the submittal process,[84] fee payment remains a significant source of delay, and jurisdictions use the fee to "gate-keep" the submittal process. Remember that there is a 180-Day Deadline for 1st Submittal of the Full Development Permit Application, including payment of the fee, from the date the SB 330 preliminary application was submitted. Applicants should submit early to ensure they do not miss this deadline.

To reduce the number of resubmittals and the duration of the review for completeness, applicants should contact the jurisdiction to ask about the submittal process, obtain the LORI, and have the fee amount calculated well in advance of the planned submittal date. A model email request is provided under How to Ensure You Have the Entire LORI and the Fee Amount for a Complete 1st Submittal.

[84] See for example, this August 2024 HCD letter to the Town of Los Gatos: https://www.hcd.ca.gov/sites/default/files/docs/planning-and-community/HAU/losgatos-hau891-ta-08302024.pdf.

1st Completeness Review

The completeness review process is described across two long paragraphs under Gov. Code § 65943(a) and (b) that anticipate three rounds of completeness review. Jurisdictions typically take the full 30 days to review each submittal of the development permit application. The following quotes take the process step by step:

> 65943. (a) Not later than 30 calendar days after any public agency has received an application for a development project, the agency shall determine in writing whether the application is complete and shall immediately transmit the determination to the applicant for the development project. ...

The 30-day time limit for the completeness review commences when the jurisdiction "has received" the application. The phrase "has received an application for a development project" is a matter of some contention, because each jurisdiction determines its own submittal process and requirements. Applicants should count the 30-day deadline for the first completeness review from **the date on the payment receipt** for the processing fee (assuming payment occurs on or after the date the submittal is transmitted).

1st Letter of Incompleteness (The Real LORI)

The first submittal of the development permit application virtually always results in a "letter of incompleteness." Gov. Code § 65943(a) continues:

> ... If the application is determined to be incomplete, the lead agency shall provide the applicant with an exhaustive list of items that were not complete. That list shall be limited to those items actually required on the lead agency's submittal requirement checklist. ...

This written notice must include "an exhaustive list of items that were not complete," and that list is "limited to those items actually required" by the LORI. Jurisdictions **should** simply use the LORI as a checklist: the items and information are either submitted or not submitted. If all the items are submitted, the application is complete. If items are missing, the letter of incompleteness should list each item that is on the LORI but not in the application. Unfortunately, jurisdictions seldom conduct completeness review as a simple submittal checklist, and instead use each round of review for a full analysis of the project for compliance with all development standards and for CEQA.

Continuing with Gov. Code § 65943(a):

> ... In any subsequent review of the application determined to be incomplete, the local agency shall not request the applicant to provide any new information that was not stated in the initial list of items that were not complete. ...

As explained earlier, many Jurisdictions Fail to Post a Complete List of Required Items, instead having multiple forms, handouts, and websites that the jurisdiction will contend are part of their required items for completeness. Because jurisdictions so often do not provide a clear LORI, the list of items identified as incomplete in the first letter of incompleteness serves as the **real LORI**. The jurisdiction cannot request any new items after providing the exhaustive list in the first incompleteness letter.

Unfortunately, despite the requirement to provide an "exhaustive list" limited to items that were listed on the LORI but missing from the application, incompleteness letters often make it very difficult to determine exactly what is required to achieve completeness. Therefore, applicants should create their ***own*** checklist of incomplete items and send it in an email to the jurisdiction as explained in the text box: Example of Email to Confirm The "Real" LORI.

Example of Email to Confirm The "Real" LORI

Upon receipt of the 1st incompleteness letter, applicants should review it and create their own checklist of items that are listed as "incomplete" in the letter. The applicant should send their checklist of incomplete items to the jurisdiction and ask the jurisdiction to confirm that the application **will be determined complete** upon submittal of the incomplete items. Applicants can send an email to this effect:

> On [date] the applicant received the written notice, pursuant to Gov. Code § 65943(a), that the housing development permit application for [identify the project] ("Project") was not complete. The letter identified the following items as incomplete:
>
> [list of incomplete items]
>
> Gov. Code § 65943(a) requires that:
>
> > *In any subsequent review of the application determined to be incomplete, the local agency shall not request the applicant to provide any new information that was not stated in the initial list of items that were not complete.*
>
> Please confirm that the above list of incomplete items is the entire and accurate list of items necessary to complete the application, and that the application **will** be determined to be complete in accordance with Gov. Code § 65943(a) if all of the items in the above list are provided.

Why the 1st Submittal is Always Determined to be Incomplete

Gov. Code § 65943 reads as if the completeness review is a stand-alone process, limited to confirming that the application contains the required information, but in reality jurisdictions conduct completeness review, compliance review, and the review for CEQA exemption simultaneously, despite HCD guidance that this violates the Permit Streamlining Act (see Jurisdictions Should Not Combine and/or Confuse Completeness and Compliance).

Jurisdictions have a lot to review in a short period of time. When they provide the applicant with a determination that the application is complete, that determination triggers a 30- or 45-day Time Period for the Review for Exemption, and when they provide the determination that the project is exempt, it triggers a Deadline for Initial Approval or Disapproval of the Project. (For the PRC § 21080.66 Statutory Exemption — New with AB 130, the trigger for the approval/disapproval deadline may not require a determination that the project is exempt. See Unclear Deadline for Approval or Disapproval of Projects that are Exempt Pursuant to PRC § 21080.66.) This is one reason jurisdictions almost always send at least one letter of incompleteness: it simply gives the jurisdiction more time to review the application.

Of course, the other reason is that applicants often fail to provide all of the required items. Applicants can avoid inadvertently omitting items by requesting written confirmation of which items will be required (see How to Ensure You Have the Entire LORI) and leaving plenty of time to compile a complete submittal package (see 180-Day Deadline for 1st Submittal of the Full Development Permit Application).

If the Jurisdiction Fails to Provide the Incompleteness Letter, the Application is Deemed Complete

Jurisdictions are usually very careful to send letters of incompleteness within 30 days, because if they miss the 30-day deadline, the application is **deemed complete**. Continuing with Gov. Code § 65943(a):

> ... If the written determination is not made within 30 days after receipt of the application, **and the application includes a statement that it is an application for a development permit**, the application shall be deemed complete for purposes of this chapter. ...

The application should include "a statement that it is an application for a development permit."[85] (See text box: Statement of Application.) If the jurisdiction misses the 30-day deadline for completeness review, the full development permit application is deemed complete, and the compliance review period automatically commences.[86]

Statement of Application

If the jurisdiction misses the 30-day deadline to provide a written determination that the application is **in**complete, the application will be **deemed** complete pursuant to Gov. Code § 65943(a), but only if "the application includes a statement that it is an application for a development permit...."

The Author recommends that applicants place prominently on the application a clear statement to the effect:

> This is an application for a housing development permit, as defined in Gov. Code § 65905.5(b)(3), and the application must be reviewed pursuant to the Permit Streamlining Act (Gov. Code § 65920 et. seq.).

A Late Incompleteness Letter May Constitute the (Non)Compliance Determination

Because Jurisdictions Combine Compliance Review with Completeness Review, their letters of incompleteness typically include compliance comments, along with boilerplate language to the effect that compliance review is not complete and that additional compliance comments will be provided after the application is complete. If the jurisdiction transmits the incompleteness letter to the applicant ***after*** the 30-day deadline, the **late** incompleteness letter may constitute written notice of noncompliance that satisfies Gov. Code § 65589.5(j)(2)(A) and meets the 30- or 60-day Time Period Allowed for Compliance Review.

The Author recommends that applicants carefully track all milestone dates, familiarize themselves with the rules for Computation of Time Periods and Deadlines, and if the jurisdiction fails to provide written notice by the end of the 30-day completeness review period, consult an attorney.

2nd Submittal

To maintain the vesting of the SB 330 preliminary application, the applicant must ***re***submit the development permit application by the 90-Day Deadline for Each Resubmittal of the Full Development Permit Application. Applicants should ensure that their second submittal includes every single item identified as incomplete in the 1st Letter of Incompleteness (The Real LORI). The Author recommends clearly documenting that each incomplete item is included in the resubmittal. If the applicant has sent the email recommended in the text box Example of Email to Confirm The "Real" LORI, the 2nd Submittal should include a copy of that email and mark it up with the filename of items in the resubmittal and with references to exactly where in the plan set missing information is provided. Or, if the incompleteness letter had a clear checklist of missing items, mark up the incompleteness letter to indicate where the jurisdiction can find the LORI items that are provided with the resubmittal.

Note: many jurisdictions require that **every** item be resubmitted with the second submittal, even if it was previously submitted and has not changed. This requirement is not strictly consistent with Gov. Code § 65943(a), which requires that:

> ... the local agency shall not request the applicant to provide any new information that was not stated in the initial list of items that were not complete ... the agency's determination shall specify those parts of the application which are incomplete and shall indicate the manner in which they can be made complete, including a list and thorough

[85] Per Gov. Code § 65940, the LORI, "including the statement of application required by Section 65943, shall be made available to all applicants ..." which indicates the jurisdiction bears some responsibility for ensuring applications include the statement of application.

[86] See What does HCD Say? for discussion of this situation where an application is deemed complete due to the expiration of the deadline.

> description of the specific information needed to complete the application. The applicant shall submit materials to the public agency in response to the list and description.

Nevertheless, the Author generally recommends that applicants comply with the submittal instructions of the jurisdiction.

Should the 2nd Submittal Include Responses to Compliance Comments?

Jurisdictions routinely include **compliance** comments in response to each submittal. There is nothing inherently wrong with this; it helps the applicant by flagging development standards with which the project might be inconsistent, even before the jurisdiction has all of the information necessary to provide a comprehensive compliance review. As long as the jurisdiction clearly differentiates between incomplete LORI items and potential non-compliance with development standards, inclusion of compliance comments is not against HCD guidance.

Oftentimes the compliance comments are quite correct; applicants and their consultants miss things and get things wrong. Other times the project is inconsistent with a jurisdiction's standards, but those standards do not apply to the project because they are preempted by state law. And, of course, jurisdictions include comments that reflect the community's priorities and design guidelines even though subjective standards are inapplicable to housing development projects.

It is certainly reasonable for the applicant to make and submit changes with the 2nd submittal. However, the applicant may wish to wait until the application is complete, and the jurisdiction has provided compliance comments covering **all** of the submitted materials, before responding to **any** of the compliance items. (Since jurisdictions almost never provide the comprehensive compliance determination required by Gov. Code § 65589.5(j)(2)(A), the next best thing is the compliance comments in the ***completeness*** letter.) A non-**compliant** application is still **complete** if it contains the required items, so it is not necessary for the applicant to address compliance comments until the jurisdiction accepts the application as complete.

2nd Completeness Review

Recall that the 1st Letter of Incompleteness (The Real LORI) is the last chance for the jurisdiction to identify exactly what is required for a complete application. For completeness, the jurisdiction is prohibited from requiring anything that wasn't identified in the first incompleteness letter. Gov. Code § 65943(a) continues:

> ... In any subsequent review of the application determined to be incomplete, the local agency shall not request the applicant to provide any new information that was not stated in the initial list of items that were not complete. ...

The second completeness review is described in the latter half of Gov. Code § 65943(a):

> ... Upon receipt of any resubmittal of the application, a new 30-day period shall begin, during which the public agency shall determine the completeness of the application. ...

The phrase "Upon receipt of any resubmittal" indicates that Gov. Code § 65943(a) anticipates at least one resubmittal will be required to achieve a complete application. If the jurisdiction determines that the second submittal is incomplete, it must provide the applicant with a second letter of incompleteness within 30 days of the resubmittal, or the application will be deemed complete.

2nd Letter of Incompleteness

A diligent applicant should be able to provide a complete application on the second submittal, and the jurisdiction should determine the application to be complete if the second submittal contains the items identified as incomplete in the first incompleteness letter. Unfortunately, jurisdictions routinely find the second submittal to be incomplete. If the jurisdiction determines that the second submittal is incomplete, the final sentences of Gov. Code

§ 65943(a) direct the jurisdiction to provide clear communication of exactly ***how*** to achieve a complete application:

> ... If the application is determined not to be complete, the agency's determination shall specify those parts of the application which are incomplete and **shall indicate the manner in which they can be made complete**, including a list and thorough description of the specific information needed to complete the application. The applicant shall submit materials to the public agency in response to the list and description.

When jurisdictions provide this clear and specific communication about **actual LORI items that are missing, and exactly how to make them complete**, the Author considers the jurisdiction's planning department to be professional and acting in good faith. If the jurisdiction provides a second incompleteness letter with clear instructions on how to complete the application, the onus is on the applicant to ensure the third submittal includes the missing information.

If, however, the second letter of incompleteness is vague about what is needed to achieve completeness, adds new items that were not listed in the first letter of incompleteness, or demands **compliance** before the jurisdiction will determine the application to be complete, the jurisdiction is not following state law. The applicant should consult an attorney.

Withholding the Determination of Completeness Constitutes Disapproval of the Project

AB 1413 (2024) and AB 1893 (2024) greatly expanded the definition of "disapprove the housing development project" in the Housing Accountability Act. Improperly determining the application to be incomplete, or withholding the determination of completeness, constitute disapproval of the project, and both are grounds for legal action to enforce the Housing Accountability Act, per Gov. Code § 65589.5(h)(6)(F):

> (6) "Disapprove the housing development project" includes any instance in which a local agency does any of the following:
>
> ...
>
> (F) (i) Determines that an application for a housing development project is incomplete pursuant to subdivision (a) or (b) of Section 65943 and includes in the determination an item that is not required on the local agency's submittal requirement checklist. The local agency shall bear the burden of proof that the required item is listed on the submittal requirement checklist.
>
> (ii) In a subsequent review of an application pursuant to Section 65943, requests the applicant provide new information that was not identified in the initial determination and upholds this determination in the final written determination on an appeal filed pursuant to subdivision (c) of Section 65943. The local agency shall bear the burden of proof that the required item was identified in the initial determination.
>
> (iii) Determines that an application for a housing development project is incomplete pursuant to subdivision (a) or (b) of Section 65943, a reasonable person would conclude that the applicant has submitted all of the items required on the local agency's submittal requirement checklist, and the local agency upholds this determination in the final written determination on an appeal filed pursuant to subdivision (c) of Section 65943.
>
> (iv) If a local agency determines that an application is incomplete under Section 65943 after two resubmittals of the application by the applicant, the local agency shall bear the burden of establishing that the determination is not an effective disapproval of a housing development project under this section.

Before proceeding to legal action, the applicant may need to appeal the incompleteness determination as provided by Gov. Code § 65943(c), which can be done after the third incompleteness determination. However, the third submittal should clearly state that it ***is*** a complete application and that improperly determining it to be incomplete would be a violation of the Housing Accountability Act.

3rd Submittal

After receiving the second incompleteness letter with its clear explanation of how to make the application complete, the applicant should be able to make a ***complete*** third submittal.

Typically, the jurisdiction will have provided compliance comments with each incompleteness letter, so the applicant will be aware of the items that the jurisdiction considers to be inconsistent or noncompliant with development standards. The applicant should ensure that the third submittal is entirely complete and is compliant with the ***applicable*** development standards (considering state laws that preempt local development standards).

After providing the written notice that the application is complete, the jurisdiction has only a 30- or 45-day Time Period for the Review for Exemption. Therefore, the applicant should ensure that the third submittal provides all the information that the jurisdiction needs to determine that the project is exempt from CEQA.

The applicant should treat the third submittal as the ***final*** application, and notify the jurisdiction of its obligation under Gov. Code § 65589.5(j)(2):

> (2) (A) If the local agency considers a proposed housing development project to be inconsistent, not in compliance, or not in conformity with an applicable plan, program, policy, ordinance, standard, requirement, or other similar provision as specified in this subdivision, it shall **provide the applicant with written documentation identifying the provision or provisions, and an explanation of the reason or reasons it considers the housing development to be inconsistent, not in compliance, or not in conformity** as follows:
>
> > (i) Within 30 days of the date that the application for the housing development project is determined to be complete, if the housing development project contains 150 or fewer housing units.
> >
> > (ii) Within 60 days of the date that the application for the housing development project is determined to be complete, if the housing development project contains more than 150 units.
>
> (B) If the local agency fails to provide the required documentation pursuant to subparagraph (A), the housing development project shall be deemed consistent, compliant, and in conformity with the applicable plan, program, policy, ordinance, standard, requirement, or other similar provision.

Obtaining a comprehensive compliance review as early as possible will givo the applicant and jurisdiction time to hash out any compliance issues. The Author's interpretation of the law is that the 30- or 60-day time period for compliance review starts on the date the complete application is **submitted.** (See Overview of the Issue of Ambiguity Regarding the Start of the Compliance Review Period.) However, other practitioners disagree with this interpretation, and the applicant should focus on obtaining **documentation** of exactly ***which*** provisions of the local development standards the jurisdiction considers the project to be non-compliant with, and ***why***.

The text box 3rd Submittal Request for Compliance Comments has the Author's recommendation for how to prompt the jurisdiction to provide the compliance determination required by Gov. Code § 65589.5(j)(2)(A) as early as possible.

3rd Submittal Request for Compliance Comments

When making the third submittal of the development permit application, the Author recommends that applicants explicitly request that the jurisdiction provide comprehensive **compliance** comments ***with*** the **completeness** letter, or to specify the date on which the jurisdiction will provide the comprehensive compliance determination required by Gov. Code § 65589.5(j)(2)(A). The third submittal should also clearly assert that failure to determine the application complete is a violation of the Housing Accountability Act. Email a request for compliance comments, to the effect:

> This final submittal of the application for a housing development permit, as defined in Gov. Code § 65905.5(b)(3), is entirely complete and includes every item identified as incomplete in the incompleteness letter dated [date]. Failing to determine this application complete would constitute disapproval of the project, and a cause for legal action under the Housing Accountability Act. (Gov. Code § 65589.5(h)(6)(F)(i).)
>
> In addition to making the determination required by Gov. Code § 65943 that the application is complete, please either:
>
> 1. Include the comprehensive, itemized list of compliance comments, with references to each provision of an "applicable plan, program, policy, ordinance, standard, requirement, or other similar provision" and provide the reasons why the jurisdiction considers the project to be "inconsistent, not in compliance, or not in conformity." Please include a clear statement that the compliance documentation meets the requirements of Gov. Code § 65589.5(j)(2)(A).
> 2. Or, if the compliance documentation required by Gov. Code § 65589.5(j)(2)(A) is not provided with the completeness letter, please state in the letter the date by which the compliance documentation will be provided. Because the applicant has submitted a complete application on [date], **the deadline to provide the compliance documentation is [deadline]**, in accordance with Gov. Code § 65589.5(h)(10) and Gov. Code § 65589.5(j)(2)(A)(i) [or (ii) if the project is over 150 units].

#2 above asserts the Author's interpretation that, for projects of 150 units or less the compliance comments are due on the same date as the completeness determination, 30 days after **submittal** of the complete application. If the project proposes more than 150 units, the compliance determination deadline is 60 days after submittal of the complete application. See Overview of the Issue of Ambiguity Regarding the Start of the Compliance Review Period. If the jurisdiction disagrees with that interpretation, this statement is intended to elicit the jurisdiction's response with their interpretation of what date is the deadline for them to provide the compliance review.

3rd Completeness Review

It is possible, but unlikely, that the full development permit application will be determined complete after the first or second submittal. It is also possible that the process will take more than three reviews. But if the jurisdiction determines the third submittal to be ***in***complete, the applicant has the right to submit an Appeal of the Staff's Determination that an Application is Incomplete, rather than making another resubmittal. Thus, in most cases, the third submittal should be the **final** submittal.

The first and second completeness reviews are covered by subdivision (a) of Gov. Code § 65943. Moving from subdivision (a) to subdivision (b), Gov. Code § 65943(b) describes the final completeness review:

> (b) Not later than 30 calendar days after receipt of the submitted materials described in subdivision (a), the public agency shall determine in writing whether the application as supplemented or amended by the submitted materials is complete and shall immediately transmit that determination to the applicant. In making this determination, the public agency is limited to determining whether the application as supplemented or amended includes the information

> required by the list and a thorough description of the specific information needed to complete the application required by subdivision (a). If the written determination is not made within that 30-day period, the application together with the submitted materials shall be deemed complete for purposes of this chapter.

The third completeness review "is limited to determining whether the application as supplemented or amended **includes the information** required by the list and a thorough description of the specific information." The application is **complete** if it contains the specific information indicated in the second letter of incompleteness, regardless of whether the project is **compliant**.

The statute anticipates that it **may** take three submittals to achieve completeness. It does not mean it will always take three rounds of review. But with each resubmittal the statute increases the level of documentation and explanation required to justify the determination that the application is incomplete.

Completeness Review Periods Can be Extended by Mutual Agreement

A jurisdiction cannot unilaterally extend deadlines, but an applicant can build good will by granting reasonable time extensions when the jurisdiction requests them. Gov. Code § 65943(d) allows extension of the completeness review deadlines by mutual agreement:

> (d) Nothing in this section precludes an applicant and a public agency from mutually agreeing to an extension of any time limit provided by this section.

When a jurisdiction requests a time extension, it obviously is aware of the impending deadline and is unlikely to miss that deadline and cause the application to be deemed complete. Granting a time extension when the jurisdiction is acting in good faith and both parties are making progress toward a complete application might help avoid another round of review or a lengthy appeal process.

Engage an Attorney if the Jurisdiction is Improperly Withholding Completeness

As explained under Withholding the Determination of Completeness Constitutes Disapproval of the Project, improperly withholding the completeness determination is a violation of the Housing Accountability Act. If the applicant has followed the advice on How to Ensure You Have the Entire LORI and the jurisdiction attempts to require information or documentation that was not included in the LORI, or if the jurisdiction does not determine the application is complete after a third submittal, an attorney should be engaged.

Engaging an attorney early can avoid the cost and delay of an appeal or lawsuit. The attorney will explain that the Housing Accountability Act places the burden of proof for an incompleteness determination on the jurisdiction, and that the application ***is*** complete if a reasonable person would conclude that the application is complete. (Gov. Code § 65589.5(h)(6)(F).) Applicants do not want to fight a lawsuit that would delay their project, nor do jurisdictions want to fight a lawsuit they are almost certain to lose. Engaging an attorney is about avoiding lawsuits. Your attorney will be able to engage directly with the jurisdiction's attorney to discuss the relevant legal matters and work toward a resolution as quickly as possible.

Appeal of the Staff's Determination that an Application is Incomplete

Gov. Code § 65943(b) describes the third completeness review and limits it "to determining whether the application as supplemented or amended **includes the information** required" as described in the second incompleteness letter. An argument can be made that the applicant has the right to appeal the ***second*** incompleteness letter, but it is certainly the case that after three rounds of review, if the jurisdiction still refuses to determine the application complete, subdivision (c) requires the jurisdiction to hear an appeal. Gov. Code § 65943(c) begins:

> (c) If the application together with the submitted materials are determined not to be complete pursuant to subdivision (b), the public agency shall provide a process for the applicant to appeal that decision ...

Incompleteness letters are generated by the jurisdiction's planning department with input from other departments. The ultimate authority for approving or disapproving the project rests with the legislative body of the jurisdiction and/or their designees. Planning staff does not have authority to disapprove a project, and Withholding the Determination of Completeness Constitutes Disapproval of the Project. Therefore, when the applicant disputes the planning department's determination that an application is incomplete, the applicant has the right to appeal. Gov. Code § 65943(c) continues:

> ... in writing to the governing body of the agency or, if there is no governing body, to the director of the agency, as provided by that agency. A city or county shall provide that the right of appeal is to the governing body or, at their option, the planning commission, or both.

Note that the Permit Streamlining Act applies to all sorts of approvals required for projects that are subject to CEQA, some of which are issued by agencies other than a city or county. Therefore, Gov. Code § 65943(c) refers to "the governing body of the agency" and "the director of the agency." In each city and county, there exists a Planning Agency of the Jurisdiction. However, a jurisdiction ***cannot*** require that the appeal of the completeness determination go first to the Director of Planning. For a city or county, Gov. Code § 65943(c) stipulates that the right of appeal is to the legislative body and/or the planning commission.

This means that the jurisdiction **can** require that the appeal of the planning department's incompleteness determination go only to the planning commission (and not be appealable to the legislative body); or go only to the legislative body (and not first to the planning commission). Or the jurisdiction can provide a two-step appeal process, first to the planning commission and then (if the planning commission upholds the incompleteness) to the city council or county board of supervisors. However, even if the jurisdiction chooses to have a two-step appeal process, **the entire appeal of the incompleteness determination is limited to 60 days.** Gov. Code § 65943(c) continues:

> There shall be a final written determination by the agency on the appeal not later than 60 calendar days after receipt of the applicant's written appeal. The fact that an appeal is permitted to both the planning commission and to the governing body **does not extend the 60-day period**. Notwithstanding a decision pursuant to subdivision (b) that the application and submitted materials are not complete, if the final written determination on the appeal is not made within that 60-day period, the application with the submitted materials shall be deemed complete for the purposes of this chapter.

Applicants should note that the 60-day appeal period follows three rounds of review, each of up to 30 days, and in between each review the applicant must obtain the missing LORI items and prepare the resubmittal package. Even if an applicant wastes no time in making responsive resubmittals, the completeness appeal determination will, at best, come more than six months after the first submittal.

CHAPTER 9: COMPLIANCE REVIEW

The third part of the Three-Part Process for Reviewing an Application for a Housing Development Permit is to review the project for **compliance** (which is variously referred to as "consistency review," "conformance review," or "compliance review") with the development standards that are **applicable** to the project. The compliance review process is **not** found in the Permit Streamlining Act, which is applicable to all discretionary projects; it is the Housing Accountability Act that prescribes the rules for compliance review. (Primarily, Gov. Code § 65589.5(j).) When a jurisdiction reviews a development permit application for a discretionary project that is ***not*** a **housing** development project as defined by the Housing Accountability Act, the jurisdiction need not follow the process described in this chapter and has broad discretion to review the project and disapprove it or approve it with conditions. But for housing projects, the jurisdiction's discretion is extremely limited.

Various state laws limit the applicability of local development standards. Chief among them is the Housing Accountability Act, which allows a jurisdiction to apply ***only*** **objective** standards when reviewing a housing development project. (Gov. Code § 65589.5(f) and (j).) Further, for housing development projects that contain specified percentages of affordable units that the jurisdiction needs to meet its state housing goals, the Housing Accountability Act limits the discretion of the jurisdiction to apply even objective standards, and "shall not disapprove" such projects except in extremely rare circumstances. (Gov. Code § 65589.5(d).) The term "disapprove the housing development project" means not only disapproval of the development permit **application** itself, but a long list of other actions and inactions that prevent the housing **project** from being commenced or completed, including "... to harass or to cause unnecessary delay or needless increases in the cost of the proposed housing development project ...." (Gov. Code § 65589.5(h)(6)(D).)

In addition, if the project qualifies for the State Density Bonus Law, it is entitled to waivers or reductions of development standards that would preclude construction of the project **as designed and proposed**. (Gov. Code § 65915(e), *Wollmer v. City of Berkeley*, 122 Cal. Rptr. 3d 781 (Cal. Ct. App. 2011), *Bankers Hill 150 v. City of San Diego*, 74 Cal.App.5th 755, 289 Cal. Rptr. 3d 268 (Cal. Ct. App. 2022).)

Where to Find More Information

As mentioned in the introduction to Chapter 2: Key Concepts for Projects and Permits, the Institute for Local Government provides resources that practitioners on both sides of the planning counter will find useful. The Housing Laws and Policies chapter of *The Planning Commissioner Handbook* has an overview of housing issues that jurisdictions must plan for and laws they must implement, including a short section on the jurisdiction's Limited Authority to Deny Housing Projects. The Legal Issues and Application Review chapters are also good background for understanding to the material in this chapter.

CHAPTER CONTENTS

Jurisdictions Focus on Compliance and Conformity with Local Standards

The staff and officials of a city or county play three roles in controlling the use of land within their jurisdiction:

1. A legislative role, in which they adopt a general plan, zoning ordinances, and development code.
2. A quasi-judicial role, in which they review development proposals for compliance with the adopted development standards.
3. An enforcement role, in which they ensure compliance with the laws, and the conditions of approval that apply to a project.

The role of the jurisdiction's planning department in project review is to **police** the land use regulations. As expressed in *The Planning Commissioner Handbook*:[87]

> The legal basis for all planning and land use regulation is the "police power," which is the government's power to regulate in the name of the public's health, safety and welfare. The Tenth Amendment to the United States Constitution reserves this power to the states and the California Constitution in turn grants the same power to cities and counties to the extent that local regulations do not conflict with state law.

From the local jurisdiction's point of view, compliance with the land-use plan and consistency with the community vision, as expressed in the general plan and as interpreted by staff and decisionmakers, is paramount. A property owner is not entitled to use their land unless and until the jurisdiction grants a development permit. Decisionmakers must provide a fair and impartial hearing (procedural due process), but except when state or federal law preempts local police power, decisionmakers have discretionary power to apply the local development standards, to impose conditions of approval, or to reject projects for virtually any reason.

If Not for State Housing Laws, Projects Would Virtually Never be Approved as Proposed

Even when decisionmakers and citizens broadly support increased housing development, the competing priorities of various interest groups mean that **someone** is likely to vociferously oppose any significant project.

> Land use decision-making is admittedly volatile: developers want entitlements, environmentalists want growth management, and neighborhood organizations want a say in the approval process. Plus, any number of historic preservation groups, cultural groups, unions, taxpayer organizations, and affordable housing advocates may take issue with any given decision.[88]

Decisionmakers want to be responsive to public concerns, so they tend to subject projects to an exhaustive public process and are prone to imposing compromises, usually involving making a project smaller. Land use regulations are so complex and subjective that it is easy for project opponents to find something about the project that is not "consistent" with local ordinances, policies, and standards. Were it not for state housing laws that restrict the discretion of local decisionmakers, housing projects would almost never be approved as proposed.

Even though state housing laws preempt many local standards, jurisdictions will generally try to enforce and impose both objective development standards and subjective community vision. Compliance review begins as soon as a project proposal is submitted and continues through the final approval of the project. After each round of review, the jurisdiction will provide the applicant with comments pointing out standards, goals, and policies with which the project is not in compliance or not in conformity. The reviews often do not consider whether those standards are applicable, given state law, and can legally be imposed on the project. It falls on the **applicant** to assert and enforce the rights of the project under state housing laws.

---

[87] https://www.ilgplanninghandbook.org/legal-issues.

[88] *An Ounce of Prevention: Best Practices for Making Informed Land Use Decisions*, page 1. https://www.ca-ilg.org/sites/main/files/file-attachments/2006_-_an_ounce_of_prevention.pdf?1394063580.

Applicants Should Focus on Completeness and CEQA

This chapter explains the very limited discretion that jurisdictions have to disapprove or impose conditions on housing development projects. Except when the jurisdiction is able to make specified findings (which they are very rarely able to make) the decisionmakers must approve the project and may not apply conditions of approval that would render the project infeasible or, in many cases, that would require any redesign of the project.

Jurisdictions Combine Compliance Review with Completeness Review, providing comments after each round of completeness review, but the applicant is not required to resolve compliance comments to the jurisdiction's satisfaction before the jurisdiction determines that the application is complete.

Therefore, applicants should focus on getting the jurisdiction to accept the application as complete and make the CEQA determination (see "Accepted as Complete" — The Trigger for the Review for Exemption from CEQA), which triggers a Deadline for Initial Approval or Disapproval of the Project. Once the CEQA determination is made, the project is on The Path to Final Approval covered in Chapter 10: Deadlines and Enforcement.

Demand Detailed and Comprehensive Compliance Documentation

The applicant should insist that the jurisdiction provide one clear, comprehensive compliance determination, referencing specific provisions of published, objective development standards. A valid compliance review must meet the requirement at Gov. Code § 65589.5(j)(2)(A):

> (2) (A) If the local agency considers a proposed housing development project to be inconsistent, not in compliance, or not in conformity with an applicable plan, program, policy, ordinance, standard, requirement, or other similar provision as specified in this subdivision, **it shall provide the applicant with written documentation identifying the provision or provisions, and an explanation of the reason or reasons it considers the housing development to be inconsistent, not in compliance, or not in conformity** as follows:
>
> > (i) Within 30 days of the date that the application for the housing development project is determined to be complete, if the housing development project contains 150 or fewer housing units.
> >
> > (ii) Within 60 days of the date that the application for the housing development project is determined to be complete, if the housing development project contains more than 150 units.

The compliance review period begins when the applicant **submits** the housing development permit application that the jurisdiction later determines to be **complete** (see Overview of the Issue of Ambiguity Regarding the Start of the Compliance Review Period).

As explained in Chapter 8: Completeness Review, it typically takes at least three submittals before jurisdictions will determine that the development permit application is complete. It is very common for jurisdictions to send each determination letter with comments covering **both** completeness and compliance matters. Compliance comments included with ***in***completeness letters obviously are not based on the complete application. The reviews provided with ***in***completeness letters do **not** constitute a compliance review in the meaning of the Housing Accountability Act.

In theory, the jurisdiction should determine the application to be complete and **then** wrap up their compliance review and send one comprehensive document citing "the provision or provisions, and an explanation of the reason or reasons it considers the housing development to be inconsistent, not in compliance, or not in conformity" as required by Gov. Code § 65589.5(j)(2)(A).

Unfortunately, it is far more common that jurisdictions include compliance comments in the same letter that determine the application to be complete. That letter will very often include a statement to the effect "the application is still under review and additional compliance comments will be provided." Until the end of the 30- or 60-day Time Period Allowed for Compliance Review, the jurisdiction can continue the review for compliance.

The project is **deemed compliant** with any provision of the development standards not documented in the manner required by Gov. Code § 65589.5(j)(2)(A) by the end of the compliance review period. The problem is that the deadline is difficult to enforce, as explained under What Triggers the Start of the Compliance Review Period?, and in the real world Jurisdictions Almost Never Provide the Required Compliance Documentation until the staff report is published a few days before the hearing. To encourage jurisdictions to provide proper documentation, the Author recommends treating the 3rd Submittal as the final and complete application, and reminding the jurisdiction of its obligation to provide the compliance determination (see text box: 3rd Submittal Request for Compliance Comments). That request asks the jurisdiction to provide a clear statement that the compliance review comments included with the completeness letter meet the requirements of Gov. Code § 65589.5(j)(2)(A), and no further comments are forthcoming; or that further comments will be provided by a stated **deadline**.

Upon receipt of the completeness letter, if it does not clearly indicate that the letter is intended to meet the compliance determination requirements of Gov. Code § 65589.5(j)(2)(A) the applicant should send an email reminding the jurisdiction of the requirement, and again requesting the comprehensive compliance documentation. (See text box: Post-Completeness Demand for Compliance Comments.) Obtaining comprehensive compliance comments, with references to specific provisions of the local development code, allows the applicant to respond appropriately: either correcting the compliance issue, explaining to the jurisdiction why the provision does not apply to the project, or requesting a waiver or reduction of the standard if the project qualifies for the State Density Bonus Law.

The applicant should respond to all the comments to create "a preponderance of the evidence on the record"[89] that the project is compliant with the standards, or that compliance is not required due to state housing laws, and that the jurisdiction **must**, therefore, approve the project.

While the Author recommends prompting the jurisdiction to provide the required compliance review documentation, your attorney may recommend that you **not prompt** the jurisdiction to provide compliance comments and simply rely on the ***deemed*** compliance provided by Gov. Code § 65589.5(j)(2)(B). For example, if the jurisdiction sends the completeness letter on the final day of the 30-day completeness review period and the project is 150 units or less, the 30-day compliance review period will have expired because the completeness review and compliance review run concurrently. (If the Author's interpretation is correct, as explained under What Triggers the Start of the Compliance Review Period?.) It may be strategic to let the deadline expire and then notify the jurisdiction that the project has been deemed compliant with any and all development standards that were not specifically enumerated as compliance issues in the completeness letter. Always follow the advice of your own attorney who understands the particulars of your project and situation.

[89] For all housing development projects, "the local agency shall base its decision regarding the proposed housing development project upon written findings supported by a preponderance of the evidence on the record ...." (Gov. Code § 65589.5(j)(1).)

Post-Completeness Demand for Compliance Comments

If the letter determining that the application is complete does not clearly state that the compliance review has concluded and the compliance comments in the letter meet the requirements of Gov. Code § 65589.5(j)(2)(A), the Author recommends that applicants send an email reminding the jurisdiction of its obligation:

> Thank you for providing the letter dated [date] determining that the application is complete. While the letter provides some compliance comments, it does not comprehensively "provide the applicant with written documentation identifying the provision or provisions, and an explanation of the reason or reasons it considers the housing development to be inconsistent, not in compliance, or not in conformity" with references to each provision of an "applicable plan, program, policy, ordinance, standard, requirement, or other similar provision" as required by Gov. Code § 65589.5(j).
>
> The proposed housing development project contains [number] housing units. Because the applicant has submitted a complete application on [Date], **the deadline to provide the compliance documentation is [deadline]**, in accordance with Gov. Code § 65589.5(h)(10) and Gov. Code § 65589.5(j)(2)(A)(i) [or (ii) if the project is over 150 units]. [OPTIONAL: **The applicant hereby extends that deadline to [extension date]**.]
>
> After the deadline, for any provision not properly documented (i.e., cited with a reference to a specific section of a plan, program, policy, ordinance, standard, requirement, or other similar provision, and with an explanation or the reason or reasons the jurisdiction considers the Project not to be in compliance or conformity to the cited provision) as required by Gov. Code § 65589.5(j)(2)(A), the project "shall be **deemed** consistent, compliant, and in conformity with the applicable plan, program, policy, ordinance, standard, requirement, or other similar provision."

Be aware that the jurisdiction may dispute that the 30- or 60-day deadline for providing the compliance comments starts from the date of **submittal** of the complete application (i.e., from the date of the final resubmittal of the development permit application, which was determined to be complete, as explained in What Triggers the Start of the Compliance Review Period?). The jurisdiction may say that the 30- or 60-day deadline is counted from the date of the **letter of completeness**, which would make the deadline at most 30 days later. Therefore, it may be worthwhile for the applicant to simply "extend" the deadline to the later date that is 30 or 60 days after the date of the completeness letter.

Which Compliance Comments Are Actually *Applicable*?

When responding to compliance comments, the applicant needs some understanding of state housing laws to know which development standards are **applicable**, and therefore which of the many compliance comments the project actually needs to comply with. Subdivision (j) of the Housing Accountability Act sets forth the basic rules for compliance review that apply to all housing development projects. The first paragraph of subdivision (j) **requires** that jurisdictions approve projects that comply with the applicable development standards. Gov. Code 65589.5(j)(1):

> (j) (1) When a proposed housing development project complies with ***applicable*****, objective general plan, zoning, and subdivision standards and criteria, including design review standards, in effect at the time that the application was deemed complete**, but the local agency proposes to disapprove the project or to impose a condition that the project be developed at a lower density, the local agency shall base its decision regarding the proposed housing development project upon written findings **supported by a preponderance of the evidence on the record** that both of the following conditions exist: [see next section, A Project Can be Disapproved with a Finding of Specific Adverse Impact on Public Health or Safety.]

The following sections discuss the various types of development standards that do or do not apply, and the compliance provisions of subdivision (j) and other subdivisions of the Housing Accountability Act that apply to **all** housing development projects. Projects that qualify for the additional protections of subdivision (d) are discussed under Subdivision (d) Projects Must be Approved, even if Not Compliant.

A Project Can be Disapproved with a Finding of Specific Adverse Impact on Public Health or Safety

Other than for CEQA matters, the only legal reason for disapproving a housing project that complies with all applicable development standards is a finding that the project would have an unmitigable specific adverse impact upon public health or safety, as provided in paragraphs (A) and (B) of Gov. Code 65589.5(j)(1):

> (A) The housing development project would have a specific, adverse impact upon the public health or safety unless the project is disapproved or approved upon the condition that the project be developed at a lower density. As used in this paragraph, a "specific, adverse impact" means a significant, quantifiable, direct, and unavoidable impact, based on objective, identified written public health or safety standards, policies, or conditions as they existed on the date the application was deemed complete.
>
> (B) There is no feasible method to satisfactorily mitigate or avoid the adverse impact identified pursuant to paragraph (1), other than the disapproval of the housing development project or the approval of the project upon the condition that it be developed at a lower density.

In the minds of some members of every community, more people living near them constitutes an adverse impact on their health and safety. Some project opponents and decisionmakers invariably believe that housing development has negative impacts. Vocal opponents will raise a litany of minor annoyances and inconveniences to the level of a public safety crisis. For them, there is always too much traffic, noise, and crime; and too little police, fire, and health services; and the cause of all of it is too much density — too many people. None of those vague and unsubstantiated fears, however, constitutes a "specific, adverse impact upon the public health or safety." Again quoting Gov. Code 65589.5(j)(1):

> ... a "specific, adverse impact" means a significant, quantifiable, direct, and unavoidable impact, based on objective, identified written public health or safety standards, policies, or conditions as they existed on the date the application was deemed complete.

The same definition of "specific, adverse impact," applies under both subdivision (j) and subdivision (d) of the Housing Accountability Act, and this book has additional discussion of this potential finding under Finding 2: The Project Would Have an Unmitigable Adverse Impact on Public Health or Safety.

Per Gov. Code § 65589.5(a)(3):

> (3) It is the intent of the Legislature that the conditions that would have a specific, adverse impact upon the public health and safety, as described in paragraph (2) of subdivision (d) and paragraph (1) of subdivision (j), arise infrequently.

Project opponents will bring up all sorts of alleged potential impacts, but to disapprove the project, there must be a "significant, quantifiable, direct, and unavoidable impact, based on objective, identified written public health or safety standards, policies, or conditions." Further, the jurisdiction would have to consider (and find to be infeasible) any means "to satisfactorily mitigate or avoid the adverse impact" other than disapproving the project or reducing its density.

Finally, per Gov. Code 65589.5(j)(1):

> ... the local agency shall base its decision regarding the proposed housing development project upon written findings **supported by a preponderance of the evidence on the record** ...

The record is the project application, the staff review of that application, public comment entered into the record before the hearing, and the presentations, public comments, and questions and answers during the hearing. The decisionmaking body then closes the hearing and takes action based on the evidence in the record.

With respect to the project application, the jurisdiction cannot require the applicant to provide new reports and studies after the application is complete, but can "request the applicant to clarify, amplify, correct, or otherwise supplement the information required for the application." (Gov. Code § 65944(a).) The decisionmakers cannot require the applicant to ***disprove*** impacts purported by project opponents. There must be written findings, those findings must be based on the preponderance of the evidence on the record, and only then may the jurisdiction decide to disapprove the project.

Development Standards That Were Not in Effect on the Vesting Date Do Not Apply

Only development standards published and in effect on the vesting date are applicable. For projects vested by an SB 330 preliminary application, the vesting rights are provided by Gov. Code § 65589.5(o):

> (o) (1) Subject to paragraphs (2), (6), and (7), and subdivision (d) of Section 65941.1, a housing development project shall be subject only to the **ordinances, policies, and standards** adopted and in effect when a preliminary application including all of the information required by subdivision (a) of Section 65941.1 was submitted.
>
> > ...
> >
> > (4) For purposes of this subdivision, **"ordinances, policies, and standards" includes general plan, community plan, specific plan, zoning, design review standards and criteria, subdivision standards and criteria, and any other rules, regulations, requirements, and policies of a local agency**, as defined in Section 66000, including those relating to **development impact fees, capacity or connection fees or charges, permit or processing fees, and other exactions**.

The very broad definition of "ordinances, policies, and standards" at paragraph (4) includes any "policies of a local agency" as defined at Gov. Code § 66000(c):

> (c) "Local agency" means a county, city, whether general law or chartered, city and county, school district, special district, authority, agency, any other municipal public corporation or district, or other political subdivision of the state.

See Which Development Standards are "Vested" by an SB 330 Preliminary Application? for a full discussion of the vested ordinances, policies, and standards.

Subjective Standards Do Not Apply

Only **objective** development standards can be applied to a housing development project. Subjective standards are not applicable. "Objective" is defined at Gov. Code § 65589.5(h)(9):

> "Objective" means involving no personal or subjective judgment by a public official and being uniformly verifiable by reference to an external and uniform benchmark or criterion available and knowable by both the development applicant or proponent and the public official.

This definition is one of the most powerful limits on a jurisdiction's discretion. It does not matter whether the decisionmakers "like" the project or can think of ways to make it "better." The project cannot be disapproved if it meets the published objective criteria.

Sometimes it will be difficult to discern whether a standard is subjective, objective, or a combination of both. For example, a standard might read "The front setback shall be not less than 10 feet, unless the prevailing setback of the properties along the street segment is less than 10 feet, in which case the front setback shall be no less than the prevailing setback." Certainly, "not less than 10 feet" is an objective standard, but if the term "prevailing setback" is not defined in an objective manner, then that part of the standard might not be objective depending on the context. If **all** of the other properties along the street segment had **less** than a 10-foot setback, then clearly the project can have less than a 10-foot setback. The question is "what is the prevailing setback?" What does "prevailing" mean? If four properties had a 5-foot setback, and the fifth property had a 10-foot setback, is the prevailing setback 5 feet (the majority of the setbacks) or is it 6 feet (the average of the setbacks)? If the applicant wants to minimize the project's front setback, they will argue that the prevailing setback is 5 feet. In this example, the "reasonable person" test is important. Per Gov. Code § 65589.5(f)(4):

> (4) For purposes of this section, a housing development project or emergency shelter shall be **deemed** consistent, compliant, and in conformity with an applicable plan, program, policy, ordinance, standard, requirement, or other similar provision if there is substantial evidence that would allow a **reasonable person** to conclude that the housing development project or emergency shelter is consistent, compliant, or in conformity.

A reasonable person could conclude that "prevailing" means the majority of the setbacks (rather than the average) and therefore the project is **deemed** compliant with the standard when it provides a 5-foot front setback. It does not matter that a reasonable person could *also* conclude that "prevailing" means the 6-foot average setback.

The legislature intends for the Housing Accountability Act to be interpreted strongly in **favor** of the housing project. Per Gov. Code § 65589.5(a)(2)(L):

> (L) It is the policy of the state that this section be interpreted and implemented in a manner to afford the fullest possible weight to the interest of, and the approval and provision of, housing.

If the interpretation of a provision of the Housing Accountability Act is ever disputed, the right interpretation is the one that leads to approval of the project as proposed.

Development Standards That are Not Properly Documented Do Not Apply (But Don't Risk It)

The second paragraph of subdivision (j) requires that jurisdictions must provide written documentation of development standards with which the jurisdiction alleges the project not to be compliant, and if the jurisdiction fails to provide that documentation the project is **deemed compliant** with the development standard. Per Gov. Code 65589.5(j)(2):

> (2) (A) If the local agency considers a proposed housing development project to be inconsistent, not in compliance, or not in conformity with an applicable plan, program, policy, ordinance, standard, requirement, or other similar provision as specified in this subdivision, it **shall provide the applicant with written documentation identifying the provision or provisions, and an explanation of the reason or reasons it considers the housing development to be inconsistent, not in compliance, or not in conformity** as follows:
>
> [see 30- or 60-day Time Period Allowed for Compliance Review, below.]
>
> (B) **If the local agency fails to provide the required documentation** pursuant to subparagraph (A), **the housing development project shall be deemed consistent, compliant, and in conformity** with the applicable plan, program, policy, ordinance, standard, requirement, or other similar provision.

In other words, if the jurisdiction does not provide documentation citing the specific provision, and explaining why the jurisdiction alleges the project does not comply with that provision, then the jurisdiction loses the right to enforce that provision on the project, because the project "shall be deemed consistent, compliant, and in conformity" with the provision.

In the real world, this restriction on the applicability of development standards is hard for applicants to enforce. First, the deadline for the compliance review is a matter of confusion and disagreement as explained under What Triggers the Start of the Compliance Review Period?. Second, decisionmakers (especially elected officials) have a hard time accepting that the determination of which standards apply to the project, and whether the project is compliant with those standards, is made by the jurisdiction's staff before the project comes to a hearing.

Relying on deemed compliance rather than actually resolving compliance issues is risky, and the applicant may find themselves in a protracted lawsuit to enforce a poorly understood aspect of the Housing Accountability Act, based on a deadline that practitioners disagree about. The Author strongly recommends that applicants Demand Detailed and Comprehensive Compliance Documentation, but work with the jurisdiction's staff to resolve all compliance issues related to **applicable** development standards, notwithstanding any "deemed compliance."

30- or 60-day Time Period Allowed for Compliance Review

This section repeats and restates the Author's interpretation explained in detail under What Triggers the Start of the Compliance Review Period?. Attorneys for jurisdictions may not agree with this interpretation, and the Author recommends that **in some cases** applicants simply extend the deadline if necessary to conform to the jurisdiction's interpretation, as explained in the text box: Post-Completeness Demand for Compliance Comments. However, this issue is no longer academic for projects that use the PRC § 21080.66 Statutory Exemption — New with AB 130, because if the jurisdiction misses the Unclear Deadline for Approval or Disapproval of Projects that are Exempt Pursuant to PRC § 21080.66 it results in Deemed Approval — New with AB 130.

From the date the applicant submits a ***complete*** application, the jurisdiction has 30 days (for projects with 150 or fewer units) or 60 days (for projects with more than 150 units) to provide the written documentation required by Gov. Code § 65589.5(j)(2)(A). As discussed under Overview of the Issue of Ambiguity Regarding the Start of the Compliance Review Period, the start of the compliance review period is the date of the final ***submittal*** of the full development permit application, which the jurisdiction **later** determines to be complete. This is because the ***definition*** of "determined to be complete" is that the applicant has ***submitted*** a complete application. Gov. Code § 65589.5(h)(10):

> (10) Notwithstanding any other law, "determined to be complete" means that the applicant has ***submitted*** a complete application pursuant to Section 65943.

Therefore, Gov. Code § 65589.5(j)(2)(A)(i) and (ii) should be read in accordance with the definition above:

> (2) (A) If the local agency considers a proposed housing development project to be inconsistent, not in compliance, or not in conformity with an applicable plan, program, policy, ordinance, standard, requirement, or other similar provision as specified in this subdivision, it shall provide the applicant with written documentation identifying the provision or provisions, and an explanation of the reason or reasons it considers the housing development to be inconsistent, not in compliance, or not in conformity as follows:
>
> > (i) Within 30 days of the date [**that the applicant has submitted a complete application** pursuant to Section 65943], if the housing development project contains 150 or fewer housing units.
> >
> > (ii) Within 60 days of the date [**that the applicant has submitted a complete application** pursuant to Section 65943], if the housing development project contains more than 150 units.

Because of the definition of "determined to be complete" the 30- or 60-day compliance review period runs concurrently with the **final** 30-day completeness review period.

However, the jurisdiction's attorney may not accept that the compliance review period runs **concurrently**, and instead interpret Gov. Code § 65589.5(j)(2)(A)(i) and (ii) based on the plain language:

> > (i) Within 30 days of the date that the application for the housing development project is **determined to be complete**, if the housing development project contains 150 or fewer housing units.

> (ii) Within 60 days of the date that the application for the housing development project is **determined to be complete**, if the housing development project contains more than 150 units.

In this case, the compliance review period would start no more than 30 days later and run **sequentially** after the date the jurisdiction makes the affirmative determination that the application is complete and issues the completeness letter.

Applicants can use the model language in the text boxes: 3rd Submittal Request for Compliance Comments or Post-Completeness Demand for Compliance Comments to extend the deadline so that the applicant and jurisdiction agree on the date by which the comprehensive compliance documentation must be provided. However, for projects that use the PRC § 21080.66 Statutory Exemption — New with AB 130, extending the deadline may not be advisable. Please consult your attorney.

Density Bonus Provisions Allow Projects to Waive or Modify Development Standards

The third paragraph of subdivision (j) makes it clear that the State Density Bonus Law (SDBL) can be used to exceed the density otherwise allowed by the applicable development standards, provide incentives/concessions that change or avoid development standards, and waive or reduce otherwise-applicable development standards. Gov. Code 65589.5(j)(3):

> (3) For purposes of this section, the receipt of a density bonus, incentive, concession, waiver, or reduction of development standards pursuant to Section 65915 shall not constitute a valid basis on which to find a proposed housing development project is inconsistent, not in compliance, or not in conformity, with an applicable plan, program, policy, ordinance, standard, requirement, or other similar provision specified in this subdivision.

A full discussion of the SDBL is beyond the scope of this book, but it is a powerful tool. For projects that qualify for the SDBL pursuant to its subdivision (b), which contains the most commonly used density bonus options, local jurisdictions are prohibited from applying development standards that would have the effect of physically precluding construction of a proposed development. Per Gov. § 65915(e)(1):

> (e) (1) **In no case may a city, county, or city and county apply any development standard that will have the effect of physically precluding the construction of a development meeting the criteria of subdivision (b)** at the densities or with the concessions or incentives permitted by this section. Subject to paragraph (3), an applicant may submit to a city, county, or city and county a proposal for the waiver or reduction of development standards that will have the effect of physically precluding the construction of a development meeting the criteria of subdivision (b) at the densities or with the concessions or incentives permitted under this section, and may request a meeting with the city, county, or city and county. If a court finds that the refusal to grant a waiver or reduction of development standards is in violation of this section, the court shall award the plaintiff reasonable attorney's fees and costs of suit. This subdivision shall not be interpreted to require a local government to waive or reduce development standards if the waiver or reduction would have a specific, adverse impact, as defined in paragraph (2) of subdivision (d) of Section 65589.5 upon health or safety, and for which there is no feasible method to satisfactorily mitigate or avoid the specific, adverse impact. This subdivision shall not be interpreted to require a local government to waive or reduce development standards that would have an adverse impact on any real property that is listed in the California Register of Historical Resources, or to grant any waiver or reduction that would be contrary to state or federal law.

The courts have interpreted subdivision (e) of the SDBL rather expansively. In *Wollmer v. City of Berkeley*, 122 Cal. Rptr. 3d 781 (Cal. Ct. App. 2011) the court ruled (emphasis added):

> Standards may be waived that physically preclude construction of a housing development meeting the requirements for a density bonus, **period.** (§ 65915, subd. (e)(1).)

In *Bankers Hill 150 v. City of San Diego*, 74 Cal.App.5th 755, 289 Cal. Rptr. 3d 268 (Cal. Ct. App. 2022), the court applied the Wollmer decision and found (emphasis added):

> When a developer meets the requirements of the Density Bonus Law, a local government is obligated to permit increased building density, grant incentives, and waive any conflicting local development standards unless certain limited exceptions apply.
>
> [T]he City was **obligated to waive those standards if they conflicted with the Project's design** ...

These appeals court decisions make it clear that SDBL waivers and reductions of development standards apply to the project **as designed**. The jurisdiction shall not apply development standards that would physically preclude construction of the project **as proposed**. The jurisdiction cannot require a redesign of the project to make it consistent with the development standard.

Definition of Development Standard for Purposes of the SDBL

The SDBL uses a different definition for "development standard" than the definition of "ordinances, policies, and standards" that defines the development standards vested by an SB 330 preliminary application, discussed under Which Development Standards are "Vested" by an SB 330 Preliminary Application?. For purposes of the SDBL, the definition of "development standard" at Gov. Code § 65915(o)(2) applies:

> (2) "Development standard" includes a site or construction condition, including, but not limited to, a height limitation, a setback requirement, a floor area ratio, an onsite open-space requirement, a minimum lot area per unit requirement, or a parking ratio that applies to a residential development pursuant to any ordinance, general plan element, specific plan, charter, or other local condition, law, policy, resolution, or regulation that is adopted by the local government or that is enacted by the local government's electorate exercising its local initiative or referendum power, whether that power is derived from the California Constitution, statute, or the charter or ordinances of the local government.

The words "or other local condition, law, policy, resolution, or regulation that is adopted by the local government or that is enacted by the local government's electorate" in the above SDBL definition mirror the language "and any other rules, regulations, requirements, and policies of a local agency" in the Housing Accountability Act's definition of "ordinances, policies, and standards." Both definitions are very expansive. The essential difference is that "ordinance, policies, and standards" relates to all "local agencies" (not just the jurisdiction), while "development standards" as defined by the SDBL applies only to the "local government" (i.e., the jurisdiction). (Gov. Code § 65589.5(o)(1) and (4) and Gov. Code § 65915(o)(2).)

Zoning Standards that are Inconsistent with the General Plan Do Not Apply

Gov. Code § 65860 requires that jurisdictions keep their zoning ordinances consistent with the general plan, however for various reasons (primarily the periodic updates to the housing element and land use element of the general plan) the zoning designation of a site and the development standards in the zoning code can become inconsistent with the general plan. For housing projects, the jurisdiction cannot require the applicant to rezone the project's site to bring it into consistency with the general plan and may not apply zoning standards that are inconsistent with the general plan. Continuing with the fourth and final paragraph of subdivision (j), Gov. Code 65589.5(j)(4) reads:

> (4) For purposes of this section, a proposed housing development project is not inconsistent with the applicable zoning standards and criteria, and shall not require a rezoning, if the housing development project is consistent with the objective general plan standards and criteria but the zoning for the project site is inconsistent with the general plan. If the local agency has complied with paragraph (2), the local agency may require the proposed housing development project to comply with the objective standards and criteria of the zoning which is consistent with the general plan, however, the standards and criteria shall be applied to facilitate and accommodate

> development at the density allowed on the site by the general plan and proposed by the proposed housing development project.

In short, any development standard contained in the zoning code that is inconsistent with a provision of the general plan does not apply to a housing development project.

In addition, Gov. Code § 65589.5(f)(5) provides that the zoning and general plan land use designation are vested when the application is deemed complete:

> (5) For purposes of this section, a change to the zoning ordinance or general plan land use designation subsequent to the date the application was deemed complete shall not constitute a valid basis to disapprove or condition approval of the housing development project or emergency shelter.

For this provision, the vesting is provided by either an SB 330 preliminary application, or by the full development permit application, as discussed in Chapter 7: Vesting the Development Standards.

Development Standards Must Be Applied to Facilitate the Allowed Density

Per Gov. Code § 65589.5(f)(1), the jurisdiction can require a project to comply with "objective, quantifiable, written development standards, conditions, and policies" in effect on the vesting date. However, those standards must be applied to facilitate the density allowed for the project site.

> (f) (1) Except as provided in paragraphs (6) and (8) of this subdivision, and subdivision (o), nothing in this section shall be construed to prohibit a local agency from requiring the housing development project to comply with objective, quantifiable, written development standards, conditions, and policies appropriate to, and consistent with, meeting the jurisdiction's share of the regional housing need pursuant to Section 65584. **However, the development standards, conditions, and policies shall be applied to facilitate and accommodate development at the density permitted on the site and proposed by the development.** Nothing in this section shall limit a project's eligibility for a density bonus, incentive, or concession, or waiver or reduction of development standards and parking ratios, pursuant to Section 65915.

In other words, the project must be allowed to achieve the density allowed on the site (however that density is expressed). As an example, if the applicant proposes a project on a site where the applicable density is expressed as a floor area ratio[90] of 3.0 FAR, but the zoning restricts the height of the building to two stories, it is impossible for the project to achieve the density of 3.0 in only two stories.[91] The height limitation would have to be adjusted to facilitate the FAR proposed by the project, up to the density limitation of 3.0 FAR.

The Project is Compliant if a Reasonable Person Would Conclude the Project is Compliant

One of the reasons the Author recommends that applicants Demand Detailed and Comprehensive Compliance Documentation is so that the jurisdiction is forced to "show their cards" and provide the applicant with the jurisdiction's rationale for alleging that the project is not compliant with a specified development standard. If the applicant disputes that rationale, they can provide evidence for an interpretation that the project actually is compliant with the standard. Per Gov. Code § 65589.5(f)(4):

> (4) For purposes of this section, a housing development project or emergency shelter shall be **deemed consistent, compliant, and in conformity** with an applicable plan, program, policy, ordinance, standard, requirement, or other similar provision if there is **substantial evidence that would allow a reasonable person** to conclude that the housing development project or emergency shelter is consistent, compliant, or in conformity.

---

[90] Floor area ratio or "FAR" is the ratio of the total "floor area" (as defined in the local code, which may not count all of the "building area" as defined by the California Building Code) of the building or buildings on the site, to the land area of the project site. I.e., a 10,000 square foot site with an applicable FAR of 3.0 would allow 30,000 square feet of floor area.

[91] This assumes that basement area is not included in the local definition of "floor area," which is typically the case.

By engaging with the jurisdiction's staff to resolve compliance comments, the applicant's goal should be to obtain a staff determination that the project is compliant with the applicable standards, usually in the form of a "staff report." The goal is for the staff report to make findings that the project is consistent with all applicable development standards (taking into account state laws) and recommend approval of the project. Even if the decisionmaking body disagrees with the staff determination as to compliance with a particular development standard, the jurisdiction would have a tough time arguing that its own staff are not "reasonable" people or that the staff report does not constitute substantial evidence of compliance. When the "reasonable" staff concludes that the project is compliant with the development standard, the project is deemed compliant with that standard, and it does not matter if other "reasonable people" (like the planning commissioners) would come to a different determination.

If the dispute over the development standard in question cannot be resolved such that the staff finds the project compliant, the applicant should submit substantial evidence into the record that would allow a reasonable person to find the project in compliance. See Subjective Standards Do Not Apply for an example applying the reasonable person standard. One way to create the substantial evidence for the reasonable person standard is to show a **precedent** — if the jurisdiction approved another project under the applicant's preferred interpretation of the provision it will be difficult to for the jurisdiction to argue that their prior approval was not a "reasonable" interpretation of the development standard.

Subdivision (d) Projects Must be Approved, even if *Not* Compliant

So far, this chapter has focused on the provisions of the of the Housing Accountability Act that apply to **all** housing development projects, starting with subdivision (j) that includes the compliance review process, and discussing various limits on the applicability of local development standards.

Projects that qualify as "housing for very low, low-, or moderate-income households" as defined at Gov. Code § 65589.5(h)(3) are further protected by subdivision (d) of the Housing Accountability Act. The jurisdiction "shall not disapprove" a project that qualifies under subdivision (d) even if the project is **not** compliant with applicable local standards, unless it can make specific, narrow findings enumerated at Gov. Code 65589.5(d)(1) through (6). Subdivision (d) begins:

> (d) For a **housing development project for very low, low-, or moderate-income households**, or an emergency shelter, a local agency **shall not disapprove the housing development project** or emergency shelter, or condition approval in a manner that renders the housing development project or emergency shelter infeasible, including through the use of design review standards, unless it makes written findings, based upon a preponderance of the evidence in the record, as to one of the following: ...

Housing development projects that qualify for subdivision (d) are sometimes referred to as "affordable developments" and those that do not qualify for subdivision (d) are sometimes called "market-rate developments." However, the term "affordable housing" sometimes refers only to 100% affordable projects, and some projects that do not qualify for subdivision (d) will have affordable units. To avoid confusion, the Author will use the term "subdivision (d) project" for a project that qualifies for subdivision (d), and "subdivision (j) project" for those that do not qualify for subdivision (d) and rely solely on the language at Gov. Code § 65589.5(j) for the approval requirements. But remember that subdivision (j) applies to ***all*** housing projects and subdivision (d) provides ***additional*** protection to qualifying projects.

Note that subdivision (d) also applies to emergency shelters, which are not a "housing development project" as defined by Gov. Code § 65589.5(h)(2), but which are also protected by subdivision (d).

There are two ***sub***-types of subdivision (d) projects: Builder's Remedy Projects that are defined at Gov. Code § 65589.5(h)(11), and receive the additional protections of Gov. Code § 65589.5(f)(6), and projects proposed on sites "identified as suitable or available for very low, low-, or moderate-income households in the jurisdiction's housing element" that are covered by the exception at Gov. Code § 65589.5(d)(5)(A) and receive the additional protections of Gov. Code § 65589.5(f)(8), which the Author refers to as Mini Builder's Remedy Projects.

Whereas subdivision (j) protects "a proposed housing development project complies with applicable, objective general plan, zoning, and subdivision standards and criteria, including design review standards, in effect at the time that the application was deemed complete," subdivision (d) projects (including Builder's Remedy Projects and Mini Builder's Remedy Projects) "shall not" be disapproved, even if they are **not** compliant with otherwise applicable, objective development standards, ***unless*** the jurisdiction can make a required finding specified by Gov. Code 65589.5(d)(1) through (6).

Definitions for Various Levels of Affordability that Qualify a Project for Subdivision (d)

In order to qualify for subdivision (d), a housing development project must meet one of the affordability levels that define "housing for very low, low-, or moderate-income households," per Gov. Code § 65589.5(h)(3):

> (3) (A) "Housing for very low, low-, or moderate-income households" means housing for lower income households, mixed-income households, or moderate-income households.
>
> (B) "Housing for lower income households" means a housing development project in which 100 percent of the units, excluding managers' units, are dedicated to lower income households, as defined in Section 50079.5 of the Health and Safety Code, at an affordable cost, as defined by Section 50052.5 of the Health and Safety Code, or an affordable rent set in an amount consistent with the rent limits established by the California Tax Credit Allocation Committee. The units shall be subject to a recorded deed restriction for a period of 55 years for rental units and 45 years for owner-occupied units.
>
> (C) (i) "Housing for mixed-income households" means any of the following:
>
> (I) A housing development project in which at least 7 percent of the total units, as defined in subparagraph (A) of paragraph (8) of subdivision (o) of Section 65915, are dedicated to extremely low income households, as defined in Section 50106 of the Health and Safety Code.
>
> (II) A housing development project in which at least 10 percent of the total units, as defined in subparagraph (A) of paragraph (8) of subdivision (o) of Section 65915, are dedicated to very low income households, as defined in Section 50105 of the Health and Safety Code.
>
> (III) A housing development project in which at least 13 percent of the total units, as defined in subparagraph (A) of paragraph (8) of subdivision (o) of Section 65915, are dedicated to lower income households, as defined in Section 50079.5 of the Health and Safety Code.
>
> (IV) A housing development project in which there are 10 or fewer total units, as defined in subparagraph (A) of paragraph (8) of subdivision (o) of Section 65915, that is on a site that is smaller than one acre, and that is proposed for development at a minimum density of 10 units per acre.
>
> (ii) All units dedicated to extremely low income, very low income, and low-income households pursuant to clause (i) shall meet both of the following:
>
> (I) The units shall have an affordable housing cost, as defined in Section 50052.5 of the Health and Safety Code, or an affordable rent, as defined in Section 50053 of the Health and Safety Code.
>
> (II) The development proponent shall agree to, and the local agency shall ensure, the continued affordability of all affordable rental units included pursuant to this section for 55 years and all affordable ownership units included pursuant to this section for a period of 45 years.
>
> (D) "Housing for moderate-income households" means a housing development project in which 100 percent of the units are sold or rented to moderate-income households, as defined in Section 50093 of the Health and

Safety Code, at an affordable housing cost, as defined in Section 50052.5 of the Health and Safety Code, or an affordable rent, as defined in Section 50053 of the Health and Safety Code. The units shall be subject to a recorded deed restriction for a period of 55 years for rental units and 45 years for owner-occupied units.

In summary, projects meeting any one of these three definitions of affordability qualify for subdivision (d):

1. "Housing for lower income households" (i.e., 100% affordable projects, deed restricted for lower income households).
2. "Housing for mixed-income households" which can qualify at any of these four affordability levels:
    a. 7% of base units restricted to extremely low income,
    b. 10% of base units restricted to very low income,
    c. 13% of base units restricted to lower income, or
    d. No affordability requirement for projects with 10 or fewer base units on a site smaller than one acre, with an overall density including base plus bonus units not less than 10 units per acre.
3. "Housing for moderate-income households" (i.e., 100% of units deed restricted for moderate-income households).

Potential Findings that Would Allow a Jurisdiction to Disapprove a Subdivision (d) Project

The jurisdiction "shall approve" a subdivision (d) project, unless the jurisdiction makes one of the findings listed in paragraphs (1) through (6) of subdivision (d).

Finding 1: The Jurisdiction Has a Certified Housing Element *and* Has Already Met Its RHNA

Before quoting paragraph (1) of subdivision (d), the Author provides some background information necessary to understand why exceedingly few jurisdictions will be able to disapprove a subdivision (d) project by making this first of the six potential findings.

HCD conducts a Regional Housing Needs Allocation (RHNA, pronounced "REE-nuh")[92] that evaluates California's housing needs, and assigns the number of housing units needed to regions (regions are called a "councils of local governments" or "COGs") and by income category. (Figure 20.) Each region then allocates a share of those units to each of the region's constituent jurisdictions. This process is conducted over "cycles" that vary by region from approximately 5 to 10 years and start at different times in different regions. The regions covering most of the state's population are on an approximately 8-year cycle, which started in June of either 2020, 2021, 2022, or 2023, which is the Sixth Cycle RHNA. Across the state, the Sixth Cycle RHNA was roughly double the total number of units allocated for the Fifth Cycle. Many jurisdictions had their allocation of units more than tripled. This substantial increase seeks to address California's housing shortage after decades of under-supply because jurisdictions did not meet the housing goals of prior RHNA Cycles, which previously had no effective enforcement mechanism.

[92] https://www.hcd.ca.gov/rhna

Figure 20: List of COGs/Regions, their Sixth Cycle planning period, and their RHNA allocations.

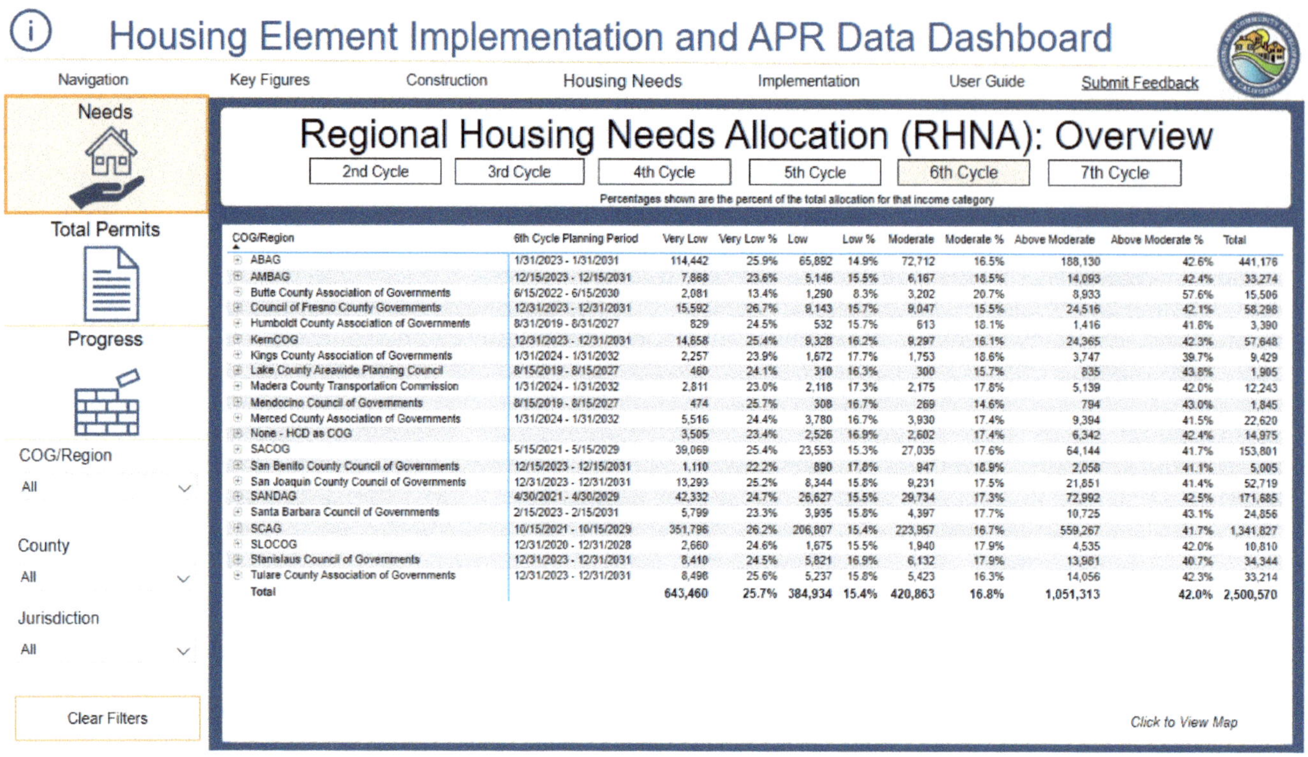

COG/Region	6th Cycle Planning Period	Very Low	Very Low %	Low	Low %	Moderate	Moderate %	Above Moderate	Above Moderate %	Total
ABAG	1/31/2023 - 1/31/2031	114,442	25.9%	65,892	14.9%	72,712	16.5%	188,130	42.6%	441,176
AMBAG	12/15/2023 - 12/15/2031	7,868	23.6%	5,146	15.5%	6,167	18.5%	14,093	42.4%	33,274
Butte County Association of Governments	6/15/2022 - 6/15/2030	2,081	13.4%	1,290	8.3%	3,202	20.7%	8,933	57.6%	15,506
Council of Fresno County Governments	12/31/2023 - 12/31/2031	15,592	26.7%	9,143	15.7%	9,047	15.5%	24,516	42.1%	58,298
Humboldt County Association of Governments	8/31/2019 - 8/31/2027	829	24.5%	532	15.7%	613	18.1%	1,416	41.8%	3,390
KernCOG	12/31/2023 - 12/31/2031	14,858	25.4%	9,328	16.2%	9,297	16.1%	24,365	42.3%	57,648
Kings County Association of Governments	1/31/2024 - 1/31/2032	2,257	23.9%	1,672	17.7%	1,753	18.6%	3,747	39.7%	9,429
Lake County Areawide Planning Council	8/15/2019 - 8/15/2027	460	24.1%	310	16.3%	300	15.7%	835	43.8%	1,905
Madera County Transportation Commission	1/31/2024 - 1/31/2032	2,811	23.0%	2,118	17.3%	2,175	17.8%	5,139	42.0%	12,243
Mendocino Council of Governments	8/15/2019 - 8/15/2027	474	25.7%	308	16.7%	269	14.6%	794	43.0%	1,845
Merced County Association of Governments	1/31/2024 - 1/31/2032	5,516	24.4%	3,780	16.7%	3,930	17.4%	9,394	41.5%	22,620
None - HCD as COG		3,505	23.4%	2,526	16.9%	2,602	17.4%	6,342	42.4%	14,975
SACOG	5/15/2021 - 5/15/2029	39,069	25.4%	23,553	15.3%	27,035	17.6%	64,144	41.7%	153,801
San Benito County Council of Governments	12/15/2023 - 12/15/2031	1,110	22.2%	890	17.8%	947	18.9%	2,058	41.1%	5,005
San Joaquin County Council of Governments	12/31/2023 - 12/31/2031	13,293	25.2%	8,344	15.8%	9,231	17.5%	21,851	41.4%	52,719
SANDAG	4/30/2021 - 4/30/2029	42,332	24.7%	26,627	15.5%	29,734	17.3%	72,992	42.5%	171,685
Santa Barbara Council of Governments	2/15/2023 - 2/15/2031	5,799	23.3%	3,935	15.8%	4,397	17.7%	10,725	43.1%	24,856
SCAG	10/15/2021 - 10/15/2029	351,796	26.2%	206,807	15.4%	223,957	16.7%	559,267	41.7%	1,341,827
SLOCOG	12/31/2020 - 12/31/2028	2,660	24.6%	1,675	15.5%	1,940	17.9%	4,535	42.0%	10,810
Stanislaus Council of Governments	12/31/2023 - 12/31/2031	8,410	24.5%	5,821	16.9%	6,132	17.9%	13,981	40.7%	34,344
Tulare County Association of Governments	12/31/2023 - 12/31/2031	8,498	25.6%	5,237	15.8%	5,423	16.3%	14,056	42.3%	33,214
Total		643,460	25.7%	384,934	15.4%	420,863	16.8%	1,051,313	42.0%	2,500,570

Access this data dashboard here: https://www.hcd.ca.gov/housing-open-data-tools/apr-dashboard. Select **Housing Needs** on the top row, then click **Needs** on the left. For a further breakdown by jurisdiction, select a specific COG, County, or Jurisdiction in the dropdowns.

Figure 21: Only 58 out of 539 California jurisdictions have an "out of compliance" housing element as of 1/1/2026.

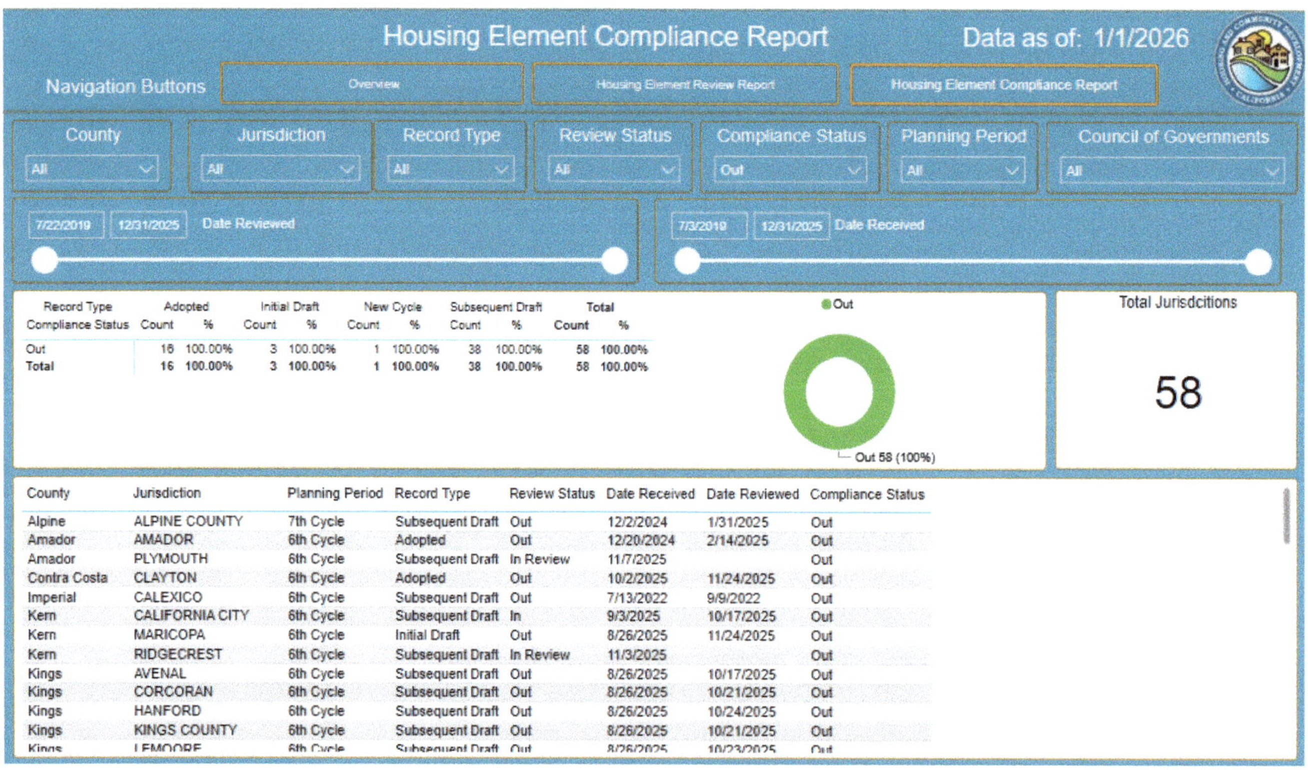

Record Type / Compliance Status	Adopted Count	Adopted %	Initial Draft Count	Initial Draft %	New Cycle Count	New Cycle %	Subsequent Draft Count	Subsequent Draft %	Total Count	Total %
Out	16	100.00%	3	100.00%	1	100.00%	38	100.00%	58	100.00%
Total	16	100.00%	3	100.00%	1	100.00%	38	100.00%	58	100.00%

County	Jurisdiction	Planning Period	Record Type	Review Status	Date Received	Date Reviewed	Compliance Status
Alpine	ALPINE COUNTY	7th Cycle	Subsequent Draft	Out	12/2/2024	1/31/2025	Out
Amador	AMADOR	6th Cycle	Adopted	Out	12/20/2024	2/14/2025	Out
Amador	PLYMOUTH	6th Cycle	Subsequent Draft	In Review	11/7/2025		Out
Contra Costa	CLAYTON	6th Cycle	Adopted	Out	10/2/2025	11/24/2025	Out
Imperial	CALEXICO	6th Cycle	Subsequent Draft	Out	7/13/2022	9/9/2022	Out
Kern	CALIFORNIA CITY	6th Cycle	Subsequent Draft	In	9/3/2025	10/17/2025	Out
Kern	MARICOPA	6th Cycle	Initial Draft	Out	8/26/2025	11/24/2025	Out
Kern	RIDGECREST	6th Cycle	Subsequent Draft	In Review	11/3/2025		Out
Kings	AVENAL	6th Cycle	Subsequent Draft	Out	8/26/2025	10/17/2025	Out
Kings	CORCORAN	6th Cycle	Subsequent Draft	Out	8/26/2025	10/21/2025	Out
Kings	HANFORD	6th Cycle	Subsequent Draft	Out	8/26/2025	10/24/2025	Out
Kings	KINGS COUNTY	6th Cycle	Subsequent Draft	Out	8/26/2025	10/21/2025	Out
Kings	LEMOORE	6th Cycle	Subsequent Draft	Out	8/26/2025	10/23/2025	Out

Access this data dashboard here: https://www.hcd.ca.gov/housing-open-data-tools/housing-element-review-compliance-report. Select the **Housing Element Compliance Report** navigation button and select the **Compliance Status** or search for a specific jurisdiction.

Gov. Code § 65581 requires jurisdictions to "prepare and implement housing elements ... toward the attainment of the state housing goal." The state housing goal is the jurisdiction's share of the RHNA. Each jurisdiction is required to plan for its RHNA in its housing element, designate land at adequate density in its land use element, and zone land in its zoning code sufficient to accommodate the number of units allocated to the jurisdiction in each income category:[93] above moderate income, moderate income, low income, and very low income (including extremely low income units). The housing element must be submitted to and certified by HCD, which maintains a dashboard of Housing Element Compliance[94] data showing whether each jurisdiction is "in compliance," meaning it has a certified housing element. As of the end of 2025, only 58 out of 539 total jurisdictions had not achieved HCD certification of their housing element,[95] as shown in Figure 21.

Each year (between April and June), jurisdictions are required to report progress toward meeting their RHNA for each income category. The data from these "annual progress reports" are compiled by HCD into an online dashboard[96] that the public can use to check RHNA progress by jurisdiction. As an example, Figure 22 is a screen shot of the City of Los Angeles' progress toward meeting its RHNA, as of its 2025 annual progress report. At the halfway point of the 8-year Sixth Cycle, the City of Los Angeles had only issued permits for 25% of its above-moderate RHNA, 1.1% of its moderate RHNA, 8.0% of low income, and 3.2% of very low income.

Figure 22: The Housing Element Implementation and APR Dashboard shows each jurisdiction's RHNA progress.

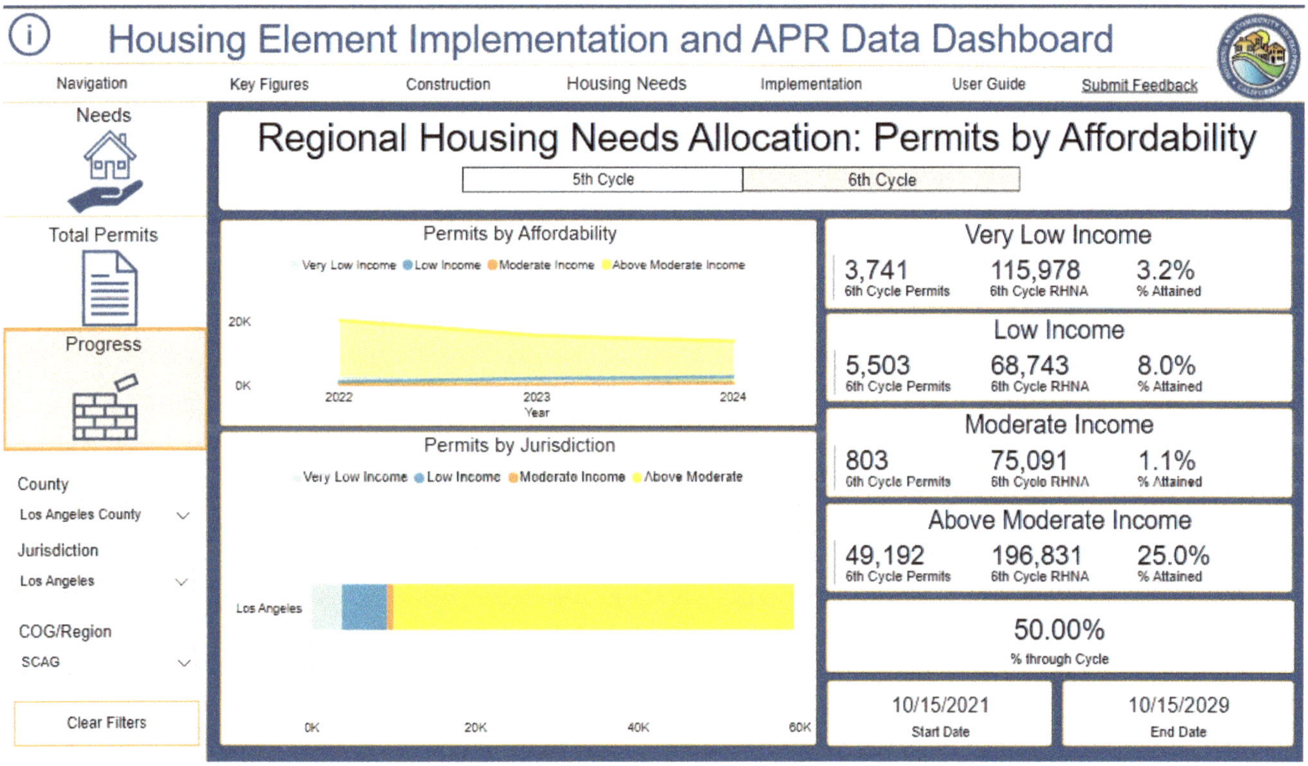

Access this data dashboard here: https://www.hcd.ca.gov/housing-open-data-tools/apr-dashboard. Select **Housing Needs** on the top row, click **Progress** on the left, and use the dropdown menus to select the jurisdiction.

---

[93] https://www.hcd.ca.gov/planning-and-community-development/housing-elements/building-blocks/projected-housing-needs-regional-housing-needs-allocation.

[94] https://www.hcd.ca.gov/housing-open-data-tools/housing-element-review-compliance-report.

[95] One additional jurisdiction, the City of La Puente in Los Angeles County, has lost compliance due to an HCD enforcement action.

[96] https://www.hcd.ca.gov/housing-open-data-tools/apr-dashboard.

With that background in mind, Gov. Code 65589.5(d)(1) is the first potential finding that a jurisdiction can make to disapprove a subdivision (d) project:

> (1) The jurisdiction **has adopted a housing element** pursuant to this article that has been revised in accordance with Section 65588, is **in substantial compliance** with this article, and the jurisdiction has met or exceeded its share of the regional housing need allocation pursuant to Section 65584 for the planning period for the income category proposed for the housing development project, provided that any disapproval or conditional approval shall not be based on any of the reasons prohibited by Section 65008. **If the housing development project includes a mix of income categories, and the jurisdiction has not met or exceeded its share of the regional housing need for one or more of those categories, then this paragraph shall not be used to disapprove or conditionally approve the housing development project.** The share of the regional housing need met by the jurisdiction shall be calculated consistently with the forms and definitions that may be adopted by the Department of Housing and Community Development pursuant to Section 65400. In the case of an emergency shelter, the jurisdiction shall have met or exceeded the need for emergency shelter, as identified pursuant to paragraph (7) of subdivision (a) of Section 65583. Any disapproval or conditional approval pursuant to this paragraph shall be in accordance with applicable law, rule, or standards.

This first potential finding has two tests, both of which must be met to make Finding 1:

1. The jurisdiction must have adopted a housing element that is in "substantial compliance."
2. The jurisdiction must have met or exceeded its RHNA for each of the income categories proposed by the project.

Jurisdictions that do not have a certified housing element, ***or*** that have not already built the units required for the planning period (i.e., the current RHNA Cycle) in **each** of the income categories proposed by the project, cannot use Gov. Code 65589.5(d)(1) to disapprove a subdivision (d) project.

First Test for Finding 1

For the first test, the jurisdiction's housing element must have been certified by HCD prior to the project's vesting date (see Chapter 7: Vesting the Development Standards). In the past, jurisdictions contended that their housing element could be in "substantial compliance" without certification by HCD. This matter was settled by the Legislature when it passed AB 1886 (2024), which added Gov. Code § 65589.55 to clarify "existing law":

> 65589.55. (a) For purposes of a local agency's approval, conditional approval, or disapproval of a housing development project pursuant to subdivision (d) of Section 65589.5, a housing element or amendment shall be considered in substantial compliance with this article **only if the element or amendment was in substantial compliance, as determined by the departmen**t or a court of competent jurisdiction, when a preliminary application, including all of the information required by subdivision (a) of Section 65941.1, was submitted or, if a preliminary application was not submitted, when a complete application pursuant to Section 65943 was submitted.
>
> (b) This section does not constitute a change in, but is **declaratory of, existing law**.

A housing element is **not** in substantial compliance until it is **determined** to be in substantial compliance either by HCD or a court. If HCD certified the jurisdiction's housing element prior to the project's vesting date, the jurisdiction passes the first test for making the finding under Gov. Code 65589.5(d)(1). If the project's vesting date was during a period of time that the jurisdiction's housing element was out of compliance, the jurisdiction cannot make Finding 1.

Second Test for Finding 1

For the second test, the jurisdiction must have met its RHNA for all the income categories proposed by the project. The test is in relation to the RHNA cycle the jurisdiction is currently in ("... for the planning period ..." Gov. Code

65589.5(d)(1)). For example, Figure 22 shows the City of Los Angeles' progress halfway through the Sixth Cycle; since Los Angeles has not met 100% of its RHNA in any income category, subdivision (d) projects proposing units in any income category cannot be disapproved in the City of Los Angeles.

Although it is out of date, HCD's *Housing Accountability Act Technical Assistance Advisory*[97] remains a helpful resource for understanding the findings required to disapprove a subdivision (d) project. It explains (page 14):

> This requirement to meet or exceed its RHNA is in relationship to units **built** in the local government, not zoning. A local government's housing element Annual Progress Report pursuant to Government Code section 65400 can be used to demonstrate progress towards RHNA goals.

And an HCD webpage[98] topic *Jurisdiction RHNA Credit for New Housing Units Since Start Date of RHNA Projection Period* explains:

> The jurisdiction authorized to permit a particular residential development may take RHNA credit for new units approved, permitted, and/or built since the start date of the RHNA projection period. ...
>
> For projects approved, but not yet built, the jurisdiction must demonstrate the units **can be built** within the remaining planning period ...

Although this guidance leaves some ambiguity about approved but not yet built units, in most cases, the applicant can simply use HCD's Housing Element Implementation and APR Dashboard (Figure 22) to confirm that the jurisdiction has **not** issued enough building permits in each of the project's income categories to meet the second test. If the jurisdiction is *close* to meeting its RHNA in all of the income categories proposed by the project, then the applicant should ask the jurisdiction whether it can make the finding required by Gov. Code 65589.5(d)(1) and contact HCD's Housing Accountability Unit to submit a Technical Assistance Request[99] if questions remain.

Very few jurisdictions met their RHNA in the Fifth Cycle, and with the Sixth Cycle significantly increasing the number of units required for most jurisdictions, it is very unlikely that a jurisdiction will pass the second test and be able to make the finding under Gov. Code 65589.5(d)(1) to disapprove a subdivision (d) project. However, if the jurisdiction has met the RHNA for all income categories *proposed* by the project, the applicant might consider *changing* the proposal to include units from an income category that the jurisdiction has **not** met (e.g., propose very low income units if the jurisdiction has met its low income RHNA).

Finding 2: The Project Would Have an Unmitigable Adverse Impact on Public Health or Safety

Whether under subdivision (j) or subdivision (d) of the Housing Accountability Act, a housing project **can** be disapproved with a finding that the project would cause an unmitigable "specific, adverse impact upon the public health or safety." For subdivision (d) the finding is explained at Gov. Code 65589.5(d)(2):

> (2) The housing development project or emergency shelter as proposed would have a specific, adverse impact upon the public health or safety, and there is no feasible method to satisfactorily mitigate or avoid the specific, adverse impact without rendering the development unaffordable to low- and moderate-income households or rendering the development of the emergency shelter financially infeasible. As used in this paragraph, a "specific, adverse impact" means a significant, quantifiable, direct, and unavoidable impact, based on objective, identified written public health or safety standards, policies, or conditions as they existed on the date the application was deemed complete. The following shall not constitute a specific, adverse impact upon the public health or safety:
>
> > (A) Inconsistency with the zoning ordinance or general plan land use designation.

---

[97] https://www.hcd.ca.gov/community-development/housing-element/housing-element-memos/docs/hcd-memo-on-haa-final-sept2020.pdf.
[98] https://www.hcd.ca.gov/planning-and-community-development/housing-elements/building-blocks/projected-housing-needs-regional-housing-needs-allocation.
[99] https://www.hcd.ca.gov/hau.

> (B) The eligibility to claim a welfare exemption under subdivision (g) of Section 214 of the Revenue and Taxation Code.

A potential finding of adverse impact was covered in detail under A Project Can be Disapproved with a Finding of Specific Adverse Impact on Public Health or Safety. That discussion is based on Gov. Code 65589.5(j)(1), but recall that subdivision (j) applies to all housing development projects. The provisions of subdivision (d) apply in addition to the provisions of subdivision (j). The same definition of "specific adverse impact" is used in both subdivision (d) and (j), and in both subdivisions the finding can only be made if "there is no feasible method to satisfactorily mitigate or avoid" the impact. Gov. Code § 65589.5(a)(3) also applies to both subdivisions:

> (3) It is the intent of the Legislature that the conditions that would have a specific, adverse impact upon the public health and safety, as described in paragraph (2) of subdivision (d) and paragraph (1) of subdivision (j), arise infrequently.

While legitimate findings of adverse health or safety impacts are unlikely, and the Legislature intends that they "arise infrequently," project opponents will allege health and safety impacts against most housing projects. Just as for subdivision (j) projects, project opponents latch onto health and safety findings as a last resort and try to convince decisionmakers (particularly elected officials with a political need to be responsive to voters) to disapprove housing projects on the basis of unsubstantiated adverse impacts.

The difference between a subdivision (d) project and a subdivision (j) project is that the jurisdiction must approve a project that meets the requirements of subdivision (d) even if the project is **not** compliant with all applicable development standards. However, the jurisdiction is not required to approve a project that would have a specific adverse impact, with no means to mitigate or avoid the impact. The definition of "specific, adverse impact" makes it clear that even subdivision (d) projects cannot ignore objective development standards related to public health and safety:

> ... a "specific, adverse impact" means a significant, quantifiable, direct, and unavoidable impact, based on objective, identified written public health or safety standards, policies, or conditions as they existed on the date the application was deemed complete.

Distinguishing between "public health or safety standards, policies, or conditions" that could be the basis for a finding of "adverse impact upon the public health and safety," and other "ordinances, policies, and standards" that are not related to public health and safety, but are perceived by the public as "impacts" is a key challenge for subdivision (d) projects (or, for example, a project that uses the State Density Bonus Law to waive or reduce a development standard that opponents perceive as "impacting" them.)

The classic example of this dichotomy is traffic impact. Project opponents perceive increased traffic as a safety impact, but increased traffic is not sufficient grounds for a public safety finding. A project may create enough traffic that it would cause an intersection to operate at a "level of service" (LOS) that the development standards consider to be "unacceptable." But LOS is a measure of traffic ***delay***, not traffic safety. The jurisdiction cannot make a health and safety finding solely on the basis of an "unacceptable" impact on traffic delay (i.e., LOS). A subdivision (d) project (or SDBL project that used a waiver or concession on the jurisdiction's LOS standard) could not be disapproved because of an "unacceptable" LOS. Nor is LOS an adverse impact under CEQA; per the Guidelines § 15064.3(a), "a project's effect on automobile delay shall not constitute a significant environmental impact."

Finding 3: State or Federal Law Requires Disapproval

The third potential finding is at Gov. Code 65589.5(d)(3):

> (3) The denial of the housing development project or imposition of conditions is required in order to comply with specific state or federal law, and there is no feasible method to comply without rendering the development unaffordable to low- and moderate-income households or rendering the development of the emergency shelter financially infeasible.

This one is easy. Both applicants and jurisdictions must comply with state and federal law. If there is no feasible way to comply with state and federal law and still build the project with the affordable units that qualify it for subdivision (d), the jurisdiction can make Finding 3 and disapprove the project.

Finding 4: The Project Site is for Agriculture or Resource Preservation; or Does Not Have Water or Sewer

The fourth potential finding at Gov. Code 65589.5(d)(4) describes two site characteristics that are grounds for disapproval of a subdivision (d) project:

> (4) The housing development project or emergency shelter is proposed on land zoned for agriculture or resource preservation that is surrounded on at least two sides by land being used for agricultural or resource preservation purposes, or which does not have adequate water or wastewater facilities to serve the project.

First, if the site is zoned for agricultural or "resource preservation" ***and*** the site is "surrounded on at least two sides" by land that is actually being used for those purposes, the jurisdiction can make Finding 4. Second, if the site does not have adequate water or sewer to serve the project, the jurisdiction can make Finding 4.

The Author is not aware of any HCD guidance or case law interpreting this provision, but the Author can imagine situations where the proper interpretation of Gov. Code 65589.5(d)(4) could be disputed. Applicants disputing a jurisdiction's interpretation of Finding 4 could seek technical assistance from HCD's Housing Accountability Unit,[100] and should consult an attorney if a jurisdiction attempts to apply this finding.

Finding 5: Housing Element is Certified, *and* Project is Inconsistent with *Both* Zoning and General Plan

The fifth potential finding is the most complex. Gov. Code 65589.5(d)(5) has two tests, subject to two exceptions:

> (5) On the date an application for the housing development project or emergency shelter was deemed complete, the jurisdiction had adopted a revised **housing element that was in substantial compliance** with this article, ***and*** the housing development project or emergency shelter was **inconsistent with *both* the jurisdiction's zoning ordinance and general plan land use designation** as specified in any element of the general plan.
>
>> (A) This paragraph shall not be utilized to disapprove or conditionally approve a housing development project proposed on a site, including a candidate site for rezoning, that is identified as suitable or available for very low, low-, or moderate-income households in the jurisdiction's housing element if the housing development project is consistent with the density specified in the housing element, even though the housing development project was inconsistent with both the jurisdiction's zoning ordinance and general plan land use designation on the date the application was deemed complete.
>>
>> (B) If the local agency has failed to identify a zone or zones where emergency shelters are allowed as a permitted use without a conditional use or other discretionary permit, has failed to demonstrate that the identified zone or zones include sufficient capacity to accommodate the need for emergency shelter identified in paragraph (7) of subdivision (a) of Section 65583, or has failed to demonstrate that the identified zone or zones can accommodate at least one emergency shelter, as required by paragraph (4) of subdivision (a) of Section 65583, then this paragraph shall not be utilized to disapprove or conditionally approve an emergency shelter proposed for a site designated in any element of the general plan for industrial, commercial, or multifamily residential uses. In any action in court, the burden of proof shall be on the local agency to show that its housing element does satisfy the requirements of paragraph (4) of subdivision (a) of Section 65583.

[100] https://www.hcd.ca.gov/hau.

Unfortunately HCD's *Housing Accountability Act Technical Assistance Advisory*[101] has not been updated since September, 2020, and its guidance is no longer current for Gov. Code 65589.5(d)(5) which was substantially amended by AB 1893 (2024). The Author therefore provides his interpretation of this potential finding, based on the out-of-date advisory, the legislative analysis of AB 1893 (2024), and his experience and research.

First Test for Finding 5

The first test for Finding 5 is the same as the First Test for Finding 1: the jurisdiction must have adopted a housing element that had been certified by HCD on or before the project's vesting date.

Second Test for Finding 5

If a subdivision (d) project is consistent with **either** the zoning ordinance **or** the general plan land use designation, then the second test is not met, and the jurisdiction cannot make Finding 5.

To meet the second test, on the vesting date the project must have been inconsistent (i.e., not compliant) with the applicable development standards of the zoning ordinance, ***and in addition*** the project must have been inconsistent (i.e., not compliant) with the "general plan land use designation as specified in ***any*** element of the general plan." Some background is helpful to understand this odd phrasing.

A general plan consists of many different "elements," and the naming and organization of the elements varies somewhat by jurisdiction. In most cases the element that designates the general plan land use of a site is called the "land use element," but it can have other names. Furthermore, some general plans consist of multiple "community plans" that designate general plan land uses, and some include things like "airport land-use compatibility plans" that have special designations near airports. The language "was inconsistent with [the] general plan land use designation as specified in ***any*** element of the general plan" covers all these potential sources of land use designations. Here again is Gov. Code 65589.5(d)(5) with the odd phrasing in bold:

> (5) On the date an application for the housing development project or emergency shelter was deemed complete, the jurisdiction had adopted a revised housing element that was in substantial compliance with this article, and the housing development project or emergency shelter **was inconsistent with both the jurisdiction's zoning ordinance and general plan land use designation as specified in *any* element of the general plan**.

The odd phrasing also may be interpreted to cover a situation where different elements of the general plan assign the project site with **two or more different land use designations**. If the project was inconsistent with the land use designation in ***any*** of the elements (and was also inconsistent with the zoning ordinance), the odd phrasing "was inconsistent with [the] general plan land use designation as specified in ***any*** element of the general plan" could be interpreted to allow disapproval of the project.

It is common for the ***housing*** element of the general plan to assign a new general plan designation to a site, as discussed under Exception A to Finding 5: Housing Element Sites Suitable for Below-Market-Rate Housing. ***Other than*** when the ***housing*** element applies a new land use designation to a site, a situation where two different general plan land use designations are applied to the same housing project site would rarely occur in the real world. If it does, contact HCD's Housing Accountability Unit for technical assistance[102] and engage an attorney.

Exception A to Finding 5: Housing Element Sites Suitable for Below-Market-Rate Housing

Housing elements are typically updated separately from, and on a different schedule than, the rest of the general plan, and to meet the jurisdiction's RHNA obligations and comply with other state housing laws, it is often

[101] https://www.hcd.ca.gov/community-development/housing-element/housing-element-memos/docs/hcd-memo-on-haa-final-sept2020.pdf.
[102] https://www.hcd.ca.gov/hau.

necessary for the housing element to upzone sites with new land use designations. The rest of the general plan and the zoning code are updated later, but until then a site may be identified with a different land use designation in the ***housing*** element than in the ***land use*** element (or other general plan elements).

It doesn't make sense that Gov. Code 65589.5(d)(5) would allow a jurisdiction to disapprove a project that is consistent with the new land use designation applied by the housing element, but inconsistent with an old land use designation in another element of the general plan. And in most cases Gov. Code 65589.5(d)(5) would not allow a jurisdiction to disapprove a site assigned a new land use designation in the housing element.

For sites identified in the housing element as suitable for below-market-rate housing units, Finding 5 has an exception under Gov. Code 65589.5(d)(5)(A).

> (A) This paragraph shall not be utilized to disapprove or conditionally approve a housing development project proposed on a site, including a candidate site for rezoning, that is identified as suitable or available for very low, low-, or moderate-income households in the jurisdiction's housing element if the housing development project is consistent with the density specified in the housing element, even though the housing development project was inconsistent with both the jurisdiction's zoning ordinance and general plan land use designation on the date the application was deemed complete.

However, this exception does **not** cover sites that the housing element lists as suitable for market-rate housing but does not identify as suitable for moderate income or lower income housing units.

This exception is covered in detail under the heading Mini Builder's Remedy Projects, after first explaining Builder's Remedy Projects.

Exception B to Finding 5: Emergency Shelters

The second exception to Finding 5 under Gov. Code 65589.5(d)(5)(B) relates to emergency shelters:

> (B) If the local agency has failed to identify a zone or zones where emergency shelters are allowed as a permitted use without a conditional use or other discretionary permit, has failed to demonstrate that the identified zone or zones include sufficient capacity to accommodate the need for emergency shelter identified in paragraph (7) of subdivision (a) of Section 65583, or has failed to demonstrate that the identified zone or zones can accommodate at least one emergency shelter, as required by paragraph (4) of subdivision (a) of Section 65583, then this paragraph shall not be utilized to disapprove or conditionally approve an emergency shelter proposed for a site designated in any element of the general plan for industrial, commercial, or multifamily residential uses. In any action in court, the burden of proof shall be on the local agency to show that its housing element does satisfy the requirements of paragraph (4) of subdivision (a) of Section 65583.

For an emergency shelter, even if the jurisdiction passes the First Test for Finding 5 (it has a certified housing element) and the Second Test for Finding 5 (the emergency shelter is inconsistent with both the zoning ordinance and the general plan land use designation), the jurisdiction **still** cannot disapprove the emergency shelter if the exception under Gov. Code 65589.5(d)(5)(B) applies.

Exception B should be read together with Gov. Code § 65589.5(f)(2):

> (2) Except as provided in subdivision (o), nothing in this section shall be construed to prohibit a local agency from requiring an emergency shelter project to comply with objective, quantifiable, written development standards, conditions, and policies that are consistent with paragraph (4) of subdivision (a) of Section 65583 and appropriate to, and consistent with, meeting the jurisdiction's need for emergency shelter, as identified pursuant to paragraph (7) of subdivision (a) of Section 65583. However, the development standards, conditions, and policies shall be applied by the local agency to facilitate and accommodate the development of the emergency shelter project.

Emergency shelters are such a special case, and so often highly contentious, that applicants proposing emergency shelters should engage an attorney to assist in applying and enforcing the Housing Accountability Act.

Finding 6: The Project is Not a Builder's Remedy Project

The last of the six potential findings is at Gov. Code 65589.5(d)(6):

> (6) On the date an application for the housing development project or emergency shelter was deemed complete, the jurisdiction did not have an adopted revised housing element that was in substantial compliance with this article and the housing development project is not a builder's remedy project.

The two tests that must be met for the jurisdiction to make Finding 6 are both expressed in the negative:

1. The jurisdiction had ***not*** adopted a housing element that was in "substantial compliance" on the project's vesting date.
2. The housing development project is ***not*** a builder's remedy project.

This provision is a lot easier to understand if we deal with the second test first. If the project ***is*** a builder's remedy project, then the jurisdiction cannot make Finding 6.

The first element of the definition of a builder's remedy project (Gov. Code § 65589.5(h)(11)(A)) is that the project meets one of the Definitions for Various Levels of Affordability that Qualify a Project for Subdivision (d), so all subdivision (d) projects meet that first element of the definition. The second element of the definition of a builder's remedy project (Gov. Code § 65589.5(h)(11)(B)) is that the jurisdiction's housing element was ***out of compliance*** on the project's vesting date. Therefore, the first test for Finding 6 is **always** satisfied for a builder's remedy project. Builder's Remedy Projects are covered in detail under the next heading.

In most cases, the project will meet the rest of the requirements to be defined as a builder's remedy project, and the jurisdiction will not be able to make Finding 6. But if the project does ***not*** meet the Definition of Builder's Remedy Project and the jurisdiction did ***not*** have a certified housing element on the vesting date, then the jurisdiction can make Finding 6 and disapprove the project. One reason a project might not meet the definition of a builder's remedy project is when the project site abuts certain industrial sites. (Gov. Code § 65589.5(h)(11)(E).) Should the applicant find themselves in this unlikely situation, they could submit a new SB 330 preliminary application **after** the jurisdiction achieves housing element certification, to prevent the jurisdiction from making Finding 6.

Builder's Remedy Projects

With the passage of SB 330 (2019), housing projects could ***vest*** the out-of-compliance status of a jurisdiction's housing element and use the then-current version of subdivision (d), paragraph (5) of the Housing Accountability Act (now known as builder's remedy 1.0) to obtain approval of a project that was compliant with neither the zoning code nor the general plan.[103] Builder's remedy 1.0 allowed virtually any project that met the definition of a "housing development project" to be built anywhere in a jurisdiction that did not have a compliant housing element on the project's vesting date, with unlimited density, and without regard to any local development standards. There were, however, many challenges to using builder's remedy 1.0, the two most significant being the inability to obtain a CEQA exemption in most cases, and the requirement that the project provide 20% of ***all*** of the units at lower-income rents (with unlimited density, there could be no "bonus units"). Despite these challenges, a number of builder's remedy projects were approved, and even more projects applied under builder's remedy

---

[103] For a brief primer on builder's remedy 1.0, see this now-out-of-date overview from the Association of Bay Area Governments: https://abag.ca.gov/sites/default/files/documents/2022-10/Builders-Remedy-and-Housing-Elements.pdf.

1.0 but eventually were approved (usually under a "development agreement") after negotiations between the jurisdiction and developer.

AB 1893 (2024) substantially amended the Housing Accountability Act to create builder's remedy 2.0, using and defining the term "builder's remedy" for the first time, and reducing the amount of affordable housing necessary to qualify not only for builder's remedy but for the entirety of subdivision (d). The amendments passed as AB 1893 (2024) made builder's remedy 2.0 projects explicitly compatible with other housing laws like the State Density Bonus Law and laws that provide for ministerial processing of qualifying housing projects. Builder's remedy 2.0 projects are not allowed *unlimited* density, but can select a base density up to a limit that is much higher than the density limit of the site's general plan designation, zoning, or other density standard. Builder's remedy 2.0 projects are required to comply with certain local development standards (explained further, below) but those standards are applied to facilitate the higher density of the builder's remedy project. Builder's remedy 2.0 projects are *deemed* compliant with the general plan and zoning code, so they qualify for any CEQA exemption that the project would otherwise qualify for, if it was not a builder's remedy project.

Definition of Builder's Remedy Project

With the passage of AB 1893 (2024), the term "builder's remedy project" is now defined at Gov. Code § 65589.5(h)(11). Taking each subparagraph of the definition in turn, and providing some tips and insights for each provision, the components of the definition of "builder's remedy project" are:

> (11) "Builder's remedy project" means a project that meets all of the following criteria:

A Builder's Remedy Projects is a Sub-Type of Subdivision (d) Project

Subparagraph (A) provides the first element of the definition of a builder's remedy project: that it meets the requirements to be a subdivision (d) project. See Definitions for Various Levels of Affordability that Qualify a Project for Subdivision (d).

> (A) The project is a housing development project that provides housing for very low, low , or moderate-income households.

The term "housing for very low, low-, or moderate-income households" is defined by Gov. Code § 65589.5(h)(3) and is the same term used in Gov. Code § 65589.5(d).

A Builder's Remedy Project Must be Vested at a time When the Housing Element is Out of Compliance

Subparagraph (B) is the second element of the definition: the project's vesting date must be a date when the jurisdiction did not have a compliant housing element.

> (B) On or after the date an application for the housing development project or emergency shelter was deemed complete, the jurisdiction did not have a housing element that was in substantial compliance with this article.

See Figure 21 for a screen shot of HCD's Housing Element Compliance[104] data where applicants can check whether the jurisdiction's housing element is "in compliance."

Calculating the Maximum Base Density for a Builder's Remedy Project

Subparagraph (C) is a lengthy provision that sets the maximum base residential density for a builder's remedy project.

[104] https://www.hcd.ca.gov/housing-open-data-tools/housing-element-review-compliance-report.

(C) The project has a density such that the number of units, as calculated before the application of a density bonus pursuant to Section 65915, complies with all of the following conditions:

(i) The density **does not *exceed*** the **greatest** of the following densities:

(I) Fifty percent greater than the minimum density deemed appropriate to accommodate housing for that jurisdiction as specified in subparagraph (B) of paragraph (3) of subdivision (c) of Section 65583.2.

The "density deemed appropriate to accommodate housing" is known as the "Mullin density"[105] or "default density." It varies by jurisdiction from 10 to 30 dwelling units per acre. Unfortunately there is no single authoritative list or map of Mullin density by jurisdiction, and the statute at Gov. Code § 65583.2(c)(3)(B) is a bit difficult to parse. After reviewing the statute, contact the jurisdiction's planning department to confirm the Mullin density. Multiply the Mullin density by 1.5.

(II) Three times the density allowed by the general plan, zoning ordinance, or state law, whichever is greater.

This is often the "greatest of the following densities." Check the general plan and zoning ordinance, and if using one of the special state housing laws like AB 2011 (2022) the density allowed by the state law, and multiply the highest of those densities by 3.

(III) The density that is consistent with the density specified in the housing element.

Remember that to meet the definition of a builder's remedy project, on the date the project is vested, the jurisdiction's housing element is not in compliance, and not yet effective. During the time it takes to process the housing development permit application for the builder's remedy project, the jurisdiction will likely achieve HCD certification of its housing element. The Author has seen no HCD guidance or case law on this, but he believes the intent of Gov. Code § 65589.5(h)(11)(C)(i)(III) is that ***if*** the newly certified housing element assigns a density to the project site that is **higher** than the density calculated under (I) or (II), the builder's remedy project can use the density in the housing element. Usually the density calculated under (I) or (II) will be greater than the housing element density, because the Mullin density under (I) is multiplied by 1.5 and the density under (II) is multiplied by 3, but the housing element density under (III) doesn't have a multiplier. But if the housing element density ***is*** higher than the density calculated under (I) or (II), the applicant should consult with an attorney to confirm the proper interpretation of Gov. Code § 65589.5(h)(11)(C)(i)(III). The question is whether the vesting of the application precludes the use of the development standards in the ***new*** housing element (which was not in effect on the vesting date), or whether (as the Author interprets this provision) the builder's remedy project is allowed to use the density in the new housing element irrespective of the application's vesting date.

Add 35 Units per Acre of Base Density for Qualifying Sites

Once the greatest of the densities calculated under (I), (II), or (III) is determined, Gov. Code § 65589.5(h)(11)(C)(ii) adds an additional 35 dwelling units per acre of density if the project site meets any one of three qualifications:

(ii) Notwithstanding clause (i), the greatest allowable density shall be **35 units per acre more** than the amount allowable pursuant to clause (i), if **any portion of the site** is located within any of the following:

(I) One-half mile of a major transit stop, as defined in Section 21064.3 of the Public Resources Code.

[105] Mullin density is named after then-Assemblymember Gene Mullin, the lead author of AB 2348 (2004), which added Gov. Code § 65583.2 that created the "default densities" under Gov. Code § 65583.2(c)(3)(B). It was not named after the mathematician Ronald C. Mullin, whatever Google AI might say!

Please be aware that there are several different definitions of a "major transit stop" that apply to different sections of state law; and there are different ways to calculate the distance from the major transit stop. Always check the cited section of law. In this case, the major transit stop must be existing on the date the builder's remedy project is approved. It cannot be a "future" major transit stop as some other law sections allow. If any portion of the project site is within a half-mile radius (as the crow flies, not a half-mile "walk shed") the builder's remedy project adds 35 to the number of dwelling units per acre calculated under Gov. Code § 65589.5(h)(11)(C)(i).

> (II) A very low vehicle travel area, as defined in subdivision (b) of Section 65589.5.1.

The definition of "very low vehicle travel area" at Gov. Code § 5589.5.1(b)(6) is quite complex. Ask the jurisdiction's public works / engineering department to confirm whether the site is located in a very low vehicle travel area and confirm their determination with a competent traffic engineer.

> (III) A high or highest resource census tract, as identified by the latest edition of the "CTCAC/HCD Opportunity Map" published by the California Tax Credit Allocation Committee and the Department of Housing and Community Development.

The CTCAC/HCD Opportunity Map is updated each year.[106] An application's vesting applies only to local development standards, not to the maps created by a state agency. The Author has seen no HCD guidance or case law to indicate that the CTCAC/HCD Opportunity Map is "locked in" on a builder's remedy project's vesting date. Check the map that was effective/adopted on the vesting date, and if the map changes such that the project site is no longer in a "high or highest resource census tract" as the project approaches its hearing date (and the project relies on the site being in a high or highest resource census tract for the additional 35 units per acre of density), contact HCD's Housing Accountability Unit to submit a Technical Assistance Request[107] and consult an attorney.

Situations Where a Minimum Density is Specified

Subparagraph (D) provides the rules for builder's remedy projects that are required to meet a *minimum* density threshold.

> (D) (i) On sites that have a minimum density requirement and are located within one-half mile of a commuter rail station or a heavy rail station, the density of the project shall not be less than the minimum density required on the site.
>
> (I) For purposes of this subparagraph, "commuter rail" means a railway that is not a light rail, streetcar, trolley, or tramway and that is for urban passenger train service consisting of local short distance travel operating between a central city and adjacent suburb with service operated on a regular basis by or under contract with a transit operator for the purpose of transporting passengers within urbanized areas, or between urbanized areas and outlying areas, using either locomotive-hauled or self-propelled railroad passenger cars, with multitrip tickets and specific station-to-station fares.
>
> (II) For purposes of this subparagraph, "heavy rail" means an electric railway with the capacity for a heavy volume of traffic using high speed and rapid acceleration passenger rail cars operating singly or in multicar trains on fixed rails, separate rights-of-way from which all other vehicular and foot traffic are excluded, and high platform loading.
>
> (ii) On all other sites with a minimum density requirement, the density of the project shall not be less than the local agency's minimum density or one-half of the minimum density deemed appropriate to

[106] https://www.treasurer.ca.gov/ctcac/opportunity.asp.
[107] https://www.hcd.ca.gov/hau.

> accommodate housing for that jurisdiction as specified in subparagraph (B) of paragraph (3) of subdivision (c) of Section 65583.2, whichever is lower.

If the project site is within a half mile of a "commuter rail" or "heavy rail" station as defined, ***and*** the project site has a minimum density requirement, the density of the builder's remedy project cannot be less than the minimum density requirement. If the project site has a minimum density requirement, but is **not** within a half mile of a "commuter rail" or "heavy rail" station, then Gov. Code § 65589.5(h)(11)(D)(ii) applies, and the minimum (overall) density is the **lower** of the minimum density required by the development standards of the jurisdiction for the project site, or one-half the Mullin density.

Unless the minimum density of the project site is expressed as a minimum ***base*** density, the minimum density requirement would consider the ***overall*** density of the project including base plus bonus density. Builder's remedy projects can use State or local density bonus laws, and builder's remedy projects do **not** have to use the entire base density before adding bonus units. (See A Builder's Remedy Project May Use the SDBL With a Base Density Less Than the Maximum.)

Sites Abutting Certain Industrial Uses Are Not Eligible for Builder's Remedy

Subparagraph (E) excludes from the definition of builder's remedy projects that are located on sites that abut adjacent sites that have recently been used for certain heavy industrial purposes.

> (E) The project site does not abut a site where more than one-third of the square footage on the site has been used, within the past three years, by a heavy industrial use, or a Title V industrial use, as those terms are defined in Section 65913.16.

A builder's remedy project **can** be proposed and approved on an industrial site. However, a builder's remedy project is prohibited from occurring on a project site that ***abuts*** sites that have been used for certain industrial uses. The prohibition is very narrow: the industrial use must be "more than one-third of the square footage on the site" abutting the project site, the use must have occurred within the past three years, and the use must be defined as a "heavy" or "Title V" industrial use, per Gov. Code § 65913.16.

A project that is disqualified by the above subparagraph (E), does ***not*** meet the definition of "builder's remedy project."

"Builder's Remedy Project" is Newly Defined, and Interpretations May Vary

The definition of "builder's remedy project" has only been in effect since January 1, 2025, when AB 1893 (2024) became effective. Portions of the definition leave room for interpretation and HCD and the courts have not yet provided much guidance for those interpretations. Builder's remedy projects are among the most contentious housing projects. The Author strongly advises applicants proposing builder's remedy projects to engage an attorney with experience in builder's remedy projects and a deep understanding of housing laws. The applicant's attorney should confirm each component of the definition.

Additional Protections and Provisions for Builder's Remedy Projects

Gov. Code § 65589.5(f) contains a long list of provisions that qualify and modify the protections provided by other sections of the Housing Accountability Act. Paragraphs (1) through (5) of subdivision (f) have been covered elsewhere in this book. Paragraphs (6) and (7) apply to builder's remedy projects. Paragraph (8) applies to Mini Builder's Remedy Projects. The final paragraph (9) defines, for the purposes of subdivision (f), the term "objective, quantifiable, written development standards, conditions, and policies."

To understand the provisions of subdivision (f) that apply to builder's remedy projects, we need to review the entirety of the subdivision.

Recap of Paragraphs (1) through (5) of Subdivision (f)

Here is a quote of paragraphs (1) through (5) of subdivision (f), with links to the above discussions in brackets:

> (f) (1) Except as provided in paragraphs (6) [applicable to Builder's Remedy Projects] and (8) [applicable to Mini Builder's Remedy Projects] of this subdivision, and subdivision (o) [relating to Which Development Standards are "Vested" by an SB 330 Preliminary Application?], nothing in this section shall be construed to prohibit a local agency from requiring the housing development project to comply with objective, quantifiable, written development standards, conditions, and policies [Paragraph (9) Defines "Objective, Quantifiable, Written Development Standards, Conditions, and Policies"] appropriate to, and consistent with, meeting the jurisdiction's share of the regional housing need pursuant to Section 65584. However, the development standards, conditions, and policies shall be applied to facilitate and accommodate development at the density permitted on the site and proposed by the development. Nothing in this section shall limit a project's eligibility for a density bonus, incentive, or concession, or waiver or reduction of development standards and parking ratios, pursuant to Section 65915. [See also Density Bonus Provisions Allow Projects to Waive or Modify Development Standards.]
>
> (2) Except as provided in subdivision (o), nothing in this section shall be construed to prohibit a local agency from requiring an emergency shelter project to comply with objective, quantifiable, written development standards, conditions, and policies that are consistent with paragraph (4) of subdivision (a) of Section 65583 and appropriate to, and consistent with, meeting the jurisdiction's need for emergency shelter, as identified pursuant to paragraph (7) of subdivision (a) of Section 65583. However, the development standards, conditions, and policies shall be applied by the local agency to facilitate and accommodate the development of the emergency shelter project. [See also Exception B to Finding 5: Emergency Shelters.]
>
> (3) Except as provided in subdivision (o), nothing in this section shall be construed to prohibit a local agency from imposing fees and other exactions otherwise authorized by law that are essential to provide necessary public services and facilities to the housing development project or emergency shelter. [See also The Vesting of the SB 330 Preliminary Application Applies to New Fees.]
>
> (4) For purposes of this section, a housing development project or emergency shelter shall be deemed consistent, compliant, and in conformity with an applicable plan, program, policy, ordinance, standard, requirement, or other similar provision if there is substantial evidence that would allow a reasonable person to conclude that the housing development project or emergency shelter is consistent, compliant, or in conformity. [See also The Project is Compliant if a Reasonable Person Would Conclude the Project is Compliant.]
>
> (5) For purposes of this section, a change to the zoning ordinance or general plan land use designation subsequent to the date the application was deemed complete shall not constitute a valid basis to disapprove or condition approval of the housing development project or emergency shelter. [See also Zoning Standards that are Inconsistent with the General Plan Do Not Apply.]

Paragraph (6) of Subdivision (f) Applies to Builder's Remedy Projects

For a builder's remedy project, paragraph (6) applies notwithstanding paragraphs (1) through (5) of subdivision (f). Gov. Code § 65589.5(f)(6):

> **(6) *Notwithstanding paragraphs (1) to (5)***, inclusive, all of the following apply to a housing development project that is a **builder's remedy project**:

All of the subparagraphs (A) through (G) of paragraph (6) apply to builder's remedy projects.

Subparagraph (A) Changes the Applicable General Plan and Zoning

Subparagraph (A) of paragraph (6) means that a builder's remedy project need not comply with the development standards of the general plan designation and zoning that would otherwise apply to the project site.

> (A) A local agency may only require the project to comply with the objective, quantifiable, written development standards, conditions, and policies that would have applied to the project **had it been proposed on a site with a general plan designation and zoning classification that allow the density and unit type proposed by the applicant**. ...

Instead, the applicant will identify some other general plan designation and zoning classification that would allow the "density and unit type proposed by the applicant." As an example, assume the applicant proposes a builder's remedy project on a site that the general plan and zoning have designated only for single-family dwelling units at a density of 5 units per acre, with a height limit of 28 feet, lot coverage ratio of 25%, and setback requirements of 20 feet on all sides; call the zoning "R-1." The applicant proposes a multifamily project at a base density of 20 units per acre. The applicant identifies a different general plan designation and zoning classification in the same jurisdiction that allows multifamily dwelling units and allows the proposed base density of 20 units per acre; call this zoning "RM-2" and say it allows a height of 35 feet, lot coverage of 50%, and setbacks of 10 feet on all sides. The "local agency may only require the project to comply with the objective, quantifiable, written development standards, conditions, and policies that would have applied" if the project site was designated RM-2. The applicable height limit for the project is 35 feet, lot coverage ratio is 50%, and setback requirements are 10 feet.

Now, say the builder's remedy project is proposed at 50 units per acre base density, but none of the general plan designations or zoning classifications in the jurisdiction allow that density. Subparagraph (A) continues:

> (A) ... **If the local agency has no general plan designation or zoning classification that would have allowed the density and unit type proposed by the applicant**, the development proponent may **identify any** objective, quantifiable, written **development standards**, conditions, and policies associated with a different general plan designation or zoning classification within that jurisdiction, **that facilitate the project's density and unit type**, and those shall apply.

The applicant would identify development standards from various different general plan designations and zoning classifications that would ***facilitate*** the project. Those standards would not "allow" the 50 units of base density, because none of the development standards in any of the jurisdiction's general plan designations or zoning classifications allow 50 units per acre. But the applicant would identify, for example, a zone that allows more lot coverage and another zone that allows a taller building, so that the 50 unit-per-acre density is facilitated.

Subparagraph (B) Requires Approval of the Builder's Remedy Project *as Proposed*

Continuing with the hypothetical builder's remedy project proposed at a base density of 50 units per acre, even if ***none*** of the development standards in ***any*** general plan designation or zoning classification would allow the builder's remedy project, development standards cannot be applied that would render the project infeasible. Per Gov. Code § 65589.5(f)(6)(B)(i):

> (B) (i) Except as authorized by paragraphs (1) to (4), inclusive, of subdivision (d) [i.e., Potential Findings that Would Allow a Jurisdiction to Disapprove a Subdivision (d) Project], a local agency shall not apply any individual or combination of objective, quantifiable, written development standards, conditions, and policies to the project that do any of the following:
>
> > (I) Render the project infeasible.
> >
> > (II) Preclude a project that meets the requirements allowed to be imposed by subparagraph (A), as modified by any density bonus, incentive, or concession, or waiver or reduction of development

> standards and parking ratios, pursuant to Section 65915, from being constructed **as proposed by the applicant**.
>
> (ii) The local agency shall bear the burden of proof of complying with clause (i).

Furthermore, if there ***is*** a general plan designation or zoning classification that would allow a project at 50 units per acre, the development standards specified in that designation or classification can only be applied to the project to the extent that they do ***not preclude*** construction of the project ***as proposed*** by the applicant (Gov. Code § 65589.5(f)(6)(B)(i)(II), above).

Subparagraph (C) Provides Two Additional SDBL Incentives/Concessions

Subparagraph (C) grants additional State Density Bonus Law benefits to builder's remedy projects.

> (C) (i) A project applicant that qualifies for a density bonus pursuant to Section 65915 shall receive two incentives or concessions in addition to those granted pursuant to paragraph (2) of subdivision (d) of Section 65915.

Builder's remedy projects that qualify for the State Density Bonus Law receive two **extra** incentives/concessions in addition to the number of incentives/concessions calculated in accordance with the SDBL.

A Builder's Remedy Project May Use the SDBL With a Base Density Less Than the Maximum

For purposes of the State Density Bonus Law, builder's remedy projects are allowed to **choose a base density** that "does not exceed the greatest" density calculated in accordance with Gov. Code § 65589.5(h)(11)(C). This is a very important benefit for a builder's remedy project, that is provided by Gov. Code § 65589.5(f)(6)(C)(ii) and (iii):

> (ii) For a project seeking density bonuses, incentives, concessions, or any other benefits pursuant to Section 65915, and notwithstanding paragraph (6) of subdivision (o) of Section 65915, for purposes of this paragraph, maximum allowable residential density or base density means the density permitted for a builder's remedy project pursuant to subparagraph (C) of paragraph (11) of subdivision (h).
>
> (iii) A local agency shall grant any density bonus pursuant to Section 65915 based on the number of units proposed and allowable pursuant to subparagraph (C) of paragraph (11) of subdivision (h).

For an SDBL project that is **not** a builder's remedy project, the definition at Gov. Code § 65915(o)(6) is:

> "Maximum allowable residential density" or "base density" means the greatest number of units allowed under the zoning ordinance, specific plan, or land use element of the general plan ...

That is, the SDBL project must use the **entire** base density before benefitting from bonus units. But a builder's remedy project can **select** a base density up to the maximum calculated under Gov. Code § 65589.5(h)(11)(C). The builder's remedy project that qualifies for the SDBL is **not** required to use the entire base density before benefitting from bonus units.

As an example, assume the builder's remedy project has a maximum base density calculated by Gov. Code § 65589.5(h)(11)(C) of 50 units per acre, and assume the project site is two gross acres. The maximum allowable residential density for the project is 100 units. Assume the project selects the "housing for mixed-income households" with 10% very low income units from the Definitions for Various Levels of Affordability that Qualify a Project for Subdivision (d), and provides 10 units at very low income rents. Referring to the table in the SDLB under Gov. Code § 65915(f)(2), with 10% of base units reserved for very low income households, the project would qualify for a density bonus of 32.5%. With 100 units of base density, the project would qualify for 33 bonus units,[108] for 133 units in total.

[108] Gov. Code § 65915(f)(5): "All density calculations resulting in fractional units shall be rounded up to the next whole number."

But suppose the developer ***only*** wants to build 100 units in total. If the project had a base density of 100 units, but was **not** a builder's remedy project, the Housing Accountability Act would require the project to provide 10 very low income units (10% of the 100 units of base density) to qualify for subdivision (d). The project would qualify for 33 bonus units under SDLB, but those bonus units would go to waste, because the developer only wants to build 100 units. The project would provide 10 very low income units, but receive no bonus units.

However, since the project **is** a builder's remedy project, its base density is the density selected by the applicant **up to** the maximum calculated by Gov. Code § 65589.5(h)(11)(C). The applicant could select a base density of 38 units per acre, which is 76 units for the two-acre site. The project would provide 8 (10% of 76 rounded up) very low income units. 8 divided by 76 is over 10% but less than 11%, so the table under Gov. Code § 65915(f)(2) would qualify the project for a density bonus of 32.5%. 76 base units times a density bonus of 32.5%, rounded up, is 25 bonus units. The project could build up to 101 units in total, with 8 units provided at very low income rents. Because it is a builder's remedy project, the project would provide 2 **fewer** very low income units than a non-builder's remedy project would be required to provide, under the assumptions in the previous paragraph.

A Builder's Remedy Project Receives Additional SDBL Benefits by Providing Extremely Low Income Units

A project can qualify as "housing for mixed-income households" (and therefore qualify for builder's remedy) with 7% **extremely** low income units (see Definitions for Various Levels of Affordability that Qualify a Project for Subdivision (d)). The State Density Bonus Law does not have a table specific to extremely low income units, but extremely low income units qualify as very low income units, and very low income units qualify as low income units. (Health and Safety Code § 50105(b), Health and Safety Code § 50079.5(b), Health and Safety Code § 50053(b).) A project (including a subdivision (d) project) that is **not** a builder's remedy project receives no additional benefit under the SDBL for providing the units at extremely low income instead of very low income. A **non**-builder's remedy project providing 7% extremely low income units would consult the table under Gov. Code § 65915(f)(2) and receive a density bonus of 25%, and would consult Gov. Code § 65915(d)(2)(A) and receive only one incentive/concession.

Read in context, Gov. Code § 65589.5(f)(6)(C)(iv):

> (6) Notwithstanding paragraphs (1) to (5), inclusive, all of the following apply to a housing development project that **is a builder's remedy project:**
>
> > (C) ...
> >
> > > (iv) A project that dedicates units to extremely low-income households pursuant to subclause (I) of clause (i) of subparagraph (C) of paragraph (3) of subdivision (h) shall be eligible for the same density bonus, incentives or concessions, and waivers or reductions of development standards as provided to a housing development project that dedicates **three percentage points more** units to very low income households pursuant to paragraph (2) of subdivision (f) of Section 65915.

A builder's remedy project providing 7% extremely low income units is treated as if it provided 10% very low income units and receives a 32.5% density bonus and receives two incentives/concessions under Gov. Code § 65915(d)(2)(A), plus an additional two incentives/concessions in accordance with Gov. Code § 65589.5(f)(6)(C)(i).

The same hypothetical builder's remedy project with the 76 units of base density would provide 6 (7% of 76 rounded up) **extremely** low income units to obtain the same 32.5% density bonus as 8 very low income units. The project would provide ***4* fewer** affordable units than the **non**-builder's remedy project with 100 units of base density described previously.

All Affordable Units Are Counted for Both the HAA and the SDBL

This provision Gov. Code § 65589.5(f)(6)(C)(v) simply confirms that same affordable units that qualify the project for subdivision (d) and builder's remedy also qualify the project for the SDBL.

> (v) All units dedicated to extremely low-income, very low income, low-income, and moderate-income households pursuant to paragraph (11) of subdivision (h) shall be counted as affordable units in determining whether the applicant qualifies for a density bonus pursuant to Section 65915.

Subparagraph (D) Deems a Builder's Remedy Project Compliant for All Purposes

Moving to subparagraph (D), Gov. Code § 65589.5(f)(6)(D) reads:

> (D) (i) The project shall not be required to apply for, or receive approval of, a general plan amendment, specific plan amendment, rezoning, or other legislative approval.
>
> (ii) The project shall not be required to apply for, or receive, any approval or permit not generally required of a project of the same type and density proposed by the applicant.
>
> (iii) Any project that complies with this paragraph shall be deemed consistent, compliant, and in conformity with an applicable plan, program, policy, ordinance, standard, requirement, redevelopment plan and implementing instruments, or other similar provision **for all purposes**, and shall not be considered or treated as a nonconforming lot, use, or structure **for any purpose**.

These provisions under subparagraph (D) ensure that:

1. No general plan amendment, rezoning, or other legislative approval can be required for a builder's remedy project.
2. The builder's remedy project cannot be required to obtain any special approval that would not be required if the project was not a builder's remedy project.
3. Builder's remedy projects that are compliant with Gov. Code § 65589.5(f)(6) are deemed compliant with all development standards for all purposes (and therefore the jurisdiction "shall approve" them, and they can use any of the CEQA exemptions or other provisions of state law that would apply if the project was not a builder's remedy project).
4. A builder's remedy project is **not** considered a nonconforming use after it is built.

Subparagraph (E) Prohibits Special Requirements or Other Obstacles to a Builder's Remedy Project

Per Gov. Code § 65589.5(f)(6)(E):

> (E) A local agency shall not adopt or impose any requirement, process, practice, or procedure or undertake any course of conduct, including, but not limited to, increased fees or inclusionary housing requirements, that applies to a project solely or partially on the basis that the project is a builder's remedy project.

The jurisdiction cannot impose any special requirements, or other obstacles, on a project "on the basis that" it is a builder's remedy project.

Subparagraph (F) Makes Builder's Remedy Density Consistent with AB 2011 and SMAP Projects

Projects that qualify for ministerial processing under special housing laws can also be builder's remedy projects. Per Gov. Code § 65589.5(f)(6)(E):

> (F) (i) A builder's remedy project shall be deemed to be in compliance with the residential density standards for the purposes of complying with subdivision (b) of Section 65912.123.

For a builder's remedy project that also qualifies for the Affordable Housing and High Road Jobs Act of 2022, created by AB 2011 (2022), the density allowed for a builder's remedy project is deemed compliant with the requirements of Gov. Code § 65912.123(b).

> (ii) A builder's remedy project shall be deemed to be in compliance with the objective zoning standards, objective subdivision standards, and objective design review standards for the purposes of complying with paragraph (5) of subdivision (a) of Section 65913.4.

For a builder's remedy project that also qualifies for Streamlined Ministerial Approval Processing (SMAP, formerly known as SB 35 / SB 423), the builder's remedy project is deemed compliant with the development standards for purposes of Gov. Code § 65913.4(a)(5).

Subparagraph (G) Limits Local Affordable Housing Requirement for Builder's Remedy Projects

A jurisdiction's inclusionary ordinance is significantly curtailed for builder's remedy projects. Starting with Gov. Code § 65589.5(f)(6)(G)(i):

> (G) (i) (I) If the local agency had a local affordable housing requirement, as defined in Section 65912.101, that on January 1, 2024, required a greater percentage of affordable units than required under subparagraph (A) of paragraph (11) of subdivision (h), or required an affordability level deeper than what is required under subparagraph (A) of paragraph (11) of subdivision (h), then, except as provided in subclauses (II) and (III), the local agency may require a housing development for mixed-income households to comply with an otherwise lawfully applicable local affordability percentage or affordability level. The local agency **shall not require** housing for mixed-income households to comply with **any other aspect** of the local affordable housing requirement.

The **percentage** of affordable units, and the **level** of affordability of those units, specified in an "otherwise lawfully applicable" local affordable housing requirement (called "inclusionary housing" or "inclusionary zoning" ordinances) **can** be imposed on builder's remedy project (subject to the limitations, below). **No other aspect** of the local affordable housing requirement can be imposed (e.g., a requirement that units be deed-restricted as affordable in *perpetuity*, rather than the period of years specified in state law, cannot be imposed).

Continuing with Gov. Code § 65589.5(f)(6)(G)(i)(II) through (IV):

> (II) Notwithstanding subclause (I), the local affordable housing requirements shall not be applied to require housing for mixed-income households to dedicate more than 20 percent of the units to affordable units of any kind.
>
> (III) Housing for mixed-income households that is required to dedicate 20 percent of the units to affordable units shall not be required to dedicate any of the affordable units at an income level deeper than lower income households, as defined in Section 50079.5 of the Health and Safety Code.
>
> (IV) A local agency may only require housing for mixed-income households to comply with the local percentage requirement or affordability level described in subclause (I) if it first makes written findings, supported by a preponderance of evidence, that compliance with the local percentage requirement or the affordability level, or both, would not render the housing development project infeasible. If a reasonable person could find compliance with either requirement, either alone or in combination, would render the project infeasible, the project shall not be required to comply with that requirement.

These subclauses limit the applicability of the local affordable housing requirement. The local affordable housing requirement cannot exceed 20% of the base units, and if it requires the full 20%, it cannot require an affordability level deeper than low income. To apply ***any*** local affordable housing requirement at all (i.e., the requirements of

(I), meaning the percentage and/or level of affordability prescribed by the local affordable housing requirement), the jurisdiction **must** make the written findings required by (IV).

Moving to Gov. Code § 65589.5(f)(6)(G)(ii) and (iii):

> (ii) Affordable units in the development project shall have a comparable bedroom and bathroom count as the market rate units.
>
> (iii) Each affordable unit dedicated pursuant to this subparagraph shall count toward satisfying a local affordable housing requirement. Each affordable unit dedicated pursuant to a local affordable housing requirement that meets the criteria established in this subparagraph shall count towards satisfying the requirements of this subparagraph. This is declaratory of existing law.

The provision at (iii) is declaratory of existing law, and simply reiterates that affordable units used to qualify for various state laws also qualify for local affordable housing requirements, and vice versa.

The provision at (ii) is an interesting change given that state laws had not previously required bedroom/bathroom comparability, other than for "replacement units." (Gov. Code § 65915(c)(3)(D) and Gov. Code § 66300.6(b)(4)(C).) HCD has pointed out that **not** requiring comparability can be **beneficial** to providing affordable housing. For example, in a letter *RE: 145 W Renette Avenue, City of El Cajon – Letter of Technical Assistance* dated February 16, 2023,[109] HCD addressed these questions (page 3 and 4):

> **Does SDBL contain comparability requirements for affordable units?**
>
> No, the SDBL does not contain an across-the-board requirement that the design quality or attributes of the affordable units match those of the market-rate units (i.e., a comparability requirement pertaining to floor area, bedroom count, interior finishes, etc.), nor does it require that the affordable units be physically dispersed among the market-rate units (i.e., a dispersal requirement) for new and existing units.[omitted footnote] In fact, the SDBL suggests the opposite – that "[t]he density bonus shall be permitted in geographic areas of the housing development other than the areas where the units for the lower income households are located." (Gov. Code, § 65915, subd. (i).)
>
> …
>
> **Does SDBL allow for a development to "float" a deed restriction among units?**
>
> Yes. The SDBL does not prohibit a development to "float" a deed restriction among units. Floating refers to the concept of using a deed restriction that does not identify which specific unit(s) are to be affordable (and at what affordability level), but rather allows any of the units in the development to serve as the affordable units on an evolving basis. This approach provides a number of benefits in the context of infill development on sites with existing units that are to be retained.
>
> First, it provides flexibility that can reduce displacement of tenants. For example, if a tenant of an affordable unit's income increases such that they no longer qualify for their current unit, floating could be utilized to move the deed restriction to another unit while allowing the tenant to stay in their unit.
>
> Second, to avoid displacement, the new units could accommodate the affordable units at the time of initial lease up, and then be dispersed to the existing units once the older, existing units are vacated through the typical turnover of rental units.
>
> Third, HCD understands deed restrictions do not typically specify which individual units (e.g., Units 204, 208, and 210 in Building B) are affordable. Instead, they indicate the number of units by bedroom count and affordability level. Property managers must be able to demonstrate that tenants of the specific income level are occupying the appropriate affordable units somewhere within the development. Some local agencies' inclusionary zoning ordinances require specific units to be identified on the project site plan or floor plans, typically to verify that affordable units are dispersed among the market-rate units. As discussed above, the City should consider how its policies will impact the ongoing management of

[109] https://www.hcd.ca.gov/sites/default/files/docs/planning-and-community/HAU/el-cajon-hau484-ta-02162024.pdf.

the development and consider how a more flexible "floating" approach might benefit the City's efforts to create and preserve affordable housing.

As a matter of law and good affordable housing policy, the jurisdiction should **not** require identification of specific units as the units qualifying the project for builder's remedy. Tracking the comparability requirement without identifying specific units that remain the affordable units, and continuing to allow affordable units to "float," will require some reasonable methodology for averaging the bedroom/bathroom counts.

In a letter *RE: City of Saratoga – Vineyard One – Letter of Technical Assistance*, dated August 12, 2025,[110] HCD recommended one way that the comparability requirement could be satisfied. The letter explains:

> [O]ne methodology HCD recommends to both ensure compatibility provisions are met and provide flexibility to the bedroom distribution within a project is to ensure that the average number of bedrooms and bathrooms be similar between the proposed market rate and affordable units.
>
> 1. Calculate the average number of bedrooms. Add up all the bedrooms in the market rate units and divide by the total number of market rate units. Add up all the bedrooms in the affordable units and divide by the total number of affordable units.
> 2. Calculate the average number of bathrooms. Add up all the market rate bathrooms and divide by the total number of market rate units. Add up all the bathrooms in the affordable units and divide by the total number of affordable units.
> 3. Ensure the average number of bedrooms and bathrooms are comparable in the affordable units as the market rate units.

The guidance in the HCD letter for a methodology to meet the comparability requirement is helpful. However, two caveats about the interpretations in the letter:

1. The letter misstates the scope of Gov. Code § 65589.5(f)(6)(G)(ii), which applies ***only*** to builder's remedy projects (Gov. Code § 65589.5(f)(6) "... all of the following apply to a housing development project **that is a builder's remedy project** ..."). Comparability is ***not*** required "for a housing development to qualify as 'housing for mixed-income households'" as misstated in the HCD letter.
2. The Vinyard One project is a builder's remedy project,[111] and the City of Saratoga has an inclusionary housing ordinance that would apply to the Vinyard One project.[112] Therefore, the HCD letter does not address whether Gov. Code § 65589.5(f)(6)(G)(ii) should be interpreted in context with Gov. Code § 65589.5(f)(6)(G)(i) and (iii) to apply **only** when there is a local affordable housing requirement, or be read independently to apply to **any** builder's remedy project.

The provision at Gov. Code § 65589.5(f)(6)(G)(ii) requiring that the affordable units in a builder's remedy project be comparable in bedroom/bathroom count with the other units in the project **could** be interpreted in context, between Gov. Code § 65589.5(f)(6)(G)(i) and (iii) (which both deal with local affordable housing requirements), to apply **only** when there is a local affordable housing requirement that is otherwise lawfully applicable.

Paragraph (7) Facilitates Transition from Builder's Remedy 1.0 to 2.0

The provisions of Gov. Code § 65589.5(f)(7) facilitate the transition from builder's remedy 1.0 to 2.0:

> (7) (A) For a housing development project application that is deemed complete before January 1, 2025, the development proponent for the project may choose to be subject to the provisions of this section that were in place

---

[110] https://www.hcd.ca.gov/sites/default/files/docs/planning-and-community/HAU/saratoga-hau-2105-ta-081225.pdf.
[111] https://www.saratoga.ca.us/611/4-ChesterAllendale-Vineyard-One.
[112] https://library.municode.com/ca/saratoga/codes/code_of_ordinances?nodeId=CH15ZORE_ART15-82INHOOR.

> on the date the preliminary application was submitted, or, if the project meets the definition of a builder's remedy project, it may choose to be subject to ***any or all of*** the provisions of this section applicable as of January 1, 2025.
>
> (B) Notwithstanding subdivision (c) of Section 65941.1, for a housing development project deemed complete before January 1, 2025, the development proponent may choose to revise their application so that the project is a builder's remedy project, without being required to resubmit a preliminary application, even if the revision results in the number of residential units or square footage of construction changing by 20 percent or more.

Paragraph (7)(A) and (B) allow builder's remedy projects vested prior to the January 1, 2025 effective date of AB 1893 (2024) to:

(A) Use builder's remedy 1.0 or "choose to be subject to ***any or all of*** the provisions" of builder's remedy 2.0.

(B) Maintain the project's SB 330 vesting, **without** respect to the amount of base density shown in the preliminary application (see Only "Base Density" Matters for the SB 330 Preliminary Application), and revise the application to use the base density chosen by the applicant up to the maximum calculated in accordance with Gov. Code § 65589.5(f)(6)(C)(ii).

The Author interprets the phrase "choose to be subject to ***any or all of*** the provisions" of builder's remedy 2.0 to mean that applicants that switch to a builder's remedy 2.0 project can choose **which** of the builder's remedy provisions that became effective on January 1, 2025, the project will be subject to and choose ***not*** to be subject to some of those new provisions. The Author's interpretation is based on the fact that the words "any or all of" were not in the version of the bill that passed the Assembly, and were deliberately added to AB 1893 (2024) by a Senate amendment between the June 20 and the June 26, 2024 versions of the bill.[113] The June 20, 2024, version read:

> (7) (A) For a housing development project application that is deemed complete before January 1, 2025, the development proponent for the project may choose to be subject to the provisions of this section that were in place on the date the preliminary application was submitted, or, if the project meets the definition of a builder's remedy project, it may **choose to be subject to the provisions** of this section applicable as of January 1, 2025.

The June 26, 2024, version read:

> (7) (A) For a housing development project application that is deemed complete before January 1, 2025, the development proponent for the project may choose to be subject to the provisions of this section that were in place on the date the preliminary application was submitted, or, if the project meets the definition of a builder's remedy project, it may **choose to be subject to *any or all of* the provisions** of this section applicable as of January 1, 2025.

The June 26 version of Gov. Code § 65589.5(f)(7)(A) survived two more Senate amendments on August 21 and August 23, 2024, to become law. The clear intent is that the applicant may choose ***not*** to be subject to the provisions of builder's remedy in total, but may choose to be subject to any of the provisions the applicant chooses. This necessarily means that **the applicant can choose *not* to be subject to *certain* provisions** of the Housing Accountability Act related to builder's remedy, that were added or amended by AB 1893 (2024).

Paragraph (8) is for Mini Builder's Remedy Projects

Paragraph (8) applies to Mini Builder's Remedy Projects and will be covered in that section.

Paragraph (9) Defines "Objective, Quantifiable, Written Development Standards, Conditions, and Policies"

Paragraph (9) applies to all of subdivision (f) including (f)(1) through (5), which apply to projects that are not builder's remedy projects.

---

[113] Use the Compare Versions tab on the Legislative Information website to see the evolution of AB 1893 (2024) into the current "Chaptered" version.

> (9) For purposes of this subdivision, "objective, quantifiable, written development standards, conditions, and policies" means criteria that involve no personal or subjective judgment by a public official and are uniformly verifiable by reference to an external and uniform benchmark or criterion available and knowable by both the development applicant or proponent and the public official before submittal, including, but not limited to, any standard, ordinance, or policy described in paragraph (4) of subdivision (o). Nothing herein shall affect the obligation of the housing development project to comply with the minimum building standards approved by the California Building Standards Commission as provided in Part 2.5 (commencing with Section 18901) of Division 13 of the Health and Safety Code. In the event that applicable objective, quantifiable, written development standards, conditions, and policies are mutually inconsistent, a development shall be deemed consistent with the criteria that permits the density and unit type closest to that of the proposed project.

Paragraph (9) provides a definition of the term "objective, quantifiable, written development standards, conditions, and policies" that is used in paragraphs (f)(1), (f)(2) and (f)(6). The definition includes ordinances, policies, and standards as defined by Gov. Code § 65589.5(o)(4), even if the project was vested by a full development permit application rather than by an SB 330 preliminary application (see Chapter 7: Vesting the Development Standards).

If the "applicable objective, quantifiable, written development standards, conditions, and policies are mutually inconsistent" the project is deemed consistent with the criteria that allows the density and unit type "closest to that of the proposed project."

Nothing in the definition limits the California Building Standards.

Mini Builder's Remedy Projects

The Author uses the term "mini builder's remedy project" for projects that meet the requirements for Exception A to Finding 5: Housing Element Sites Suitable for Below-Market-Rate Housing. Recapping the relevant information presented earlier under Subdivision (d) Projects Must be Approved, even if Not Compliant:

Subdivision (d) projects are those that qualify as "housing for very low, low-, or moderate-income households" as defined at Gov. Code § 65589.5(h)(3). Even if the project is **not** compliant with applicable local development standards, the jurisdiction "shall not disapprove" a project that qualifies under subdivision (d), unless it can make one of the six findings at Gov. Code 65589.5(d)(1) through (6).

Finding 5: Housing Element is Certified, and Project is Inconsistent with Both Zoning and General Plan allows the jurisdiction to disapprove a subdivision (d) project if the jurisdiction's housing element was in compliance (i.e., had been certified by HCD) prior to the project's vesting date, **and** the project is inconsistent with ***both*** the zoning and the general plan. Gov. Code 65589.5(d)(5):

> (5) On the date an application for the housing development project or emergency shelter was deemed complete, the jurisdiction had adopted a revised **housing element that was in substantial compliance** with this article, ***and*** the housing development project or emergency shelter was **inconsistent with *both* the jurisdiction's zoning ordinance and general plan land use designation** as specified in any element of the general plan.

Gov. Code 65589.5(d)(5)(A) is an **exception** that negates the above paragraph (5) if the project site was identified in the housing element "as suitable or available for very low, low-, or moderate-income households," so long as the project does not exceed the base density specified in the housing element for the project site:

> > (A) This paragraph shall not be utilized to disapprove or conditionally approve a housing development **project proposed on a site**, including a candidate site for rezoning, that is **identified as suitable or available for very low, low-, or moderate-income households in the jurisdiction's housing element** if the housing development project is ***consistent with the density specified in the housing element***, even though the

> housing development project was inconsistent with both the jurisdiction's zoning ordinance and general plan land use designation on the date the application was deemed complete.

Projects proposed on housing element sites that are suitable for moderate income or lower income households cannot be disapproved, if they are consistent with the density specified in the housing element, "even though the housing development project was inconsistent with both the jurisdiction's zoning ordinance and general plan land use designation."

Two Tests for Applying the Mini Builder's Remedy Exception

If the jurisdiction had a certified housing element on the project's vesting date, and the project is inconsistent with both the zoning code and the general plan land use designation, the jurisdiction can make Finding 5: Housing Element is Certified, and Project is Inconsistent with Both Zoning and General Plan and disapprove the subdivision (d) project, ***unless*** the subdivision (d) project meets one the exceptions at Gov. Code 65589.5(d)(5)(A) or (B). Quoting the first exception again:

> (A) This paragraph shall not be utilized to disapprove or conditionally approve a housing development **project proposed on a site**, including a candidate site for rezoning, that is **identified as suitable or available for very low, low-, or moderate-income households in the jurisdiction's housing element** if the housing development project is ***consistent with the density specified in the housing element***, even though the housing development project was inconsistent with both the jurisdiction's zoning ordinance and general plan land use designation on the date the application was deemed complete.

This exception has two tests:

1. The project site is identified in the housing element as "suitable or available for very low, low-, or moderate-income households."
2. The project complies with the density specified for that site in the housing element.

If the project passes both tests, it cannot be disapproved, and the jurisdiction cannot place conditions on its approval.[114] A project that meets Exception A to Finding 5: Housing Element Sites Suitable for Below-Market-Rate Housing is essentially the same as a builder's remedy project, except that the project must comply with the density limitation applied to the site in the housing element. That's why the Author refers to projects proposed on housing element sites as "mini builder's remedy" projects. A mini builder's remedy project cannot be disapproved unless the jurisdiction can make one of the *other* findings in subdivision (d) (e.g., an unmitigable adverse impact on human health or safety).

First Test for Exception A to Finding 5

To be a mini builder's remedy project, the project site must be identified in the housing element, which must indicate that the site is **"suitable or available for very low, low-, or moderate-income households."**

Continuing to build on the background information in this chapter, Gov. Code § 65583 requires that:

> 65583. The housing element shall consist of an identification and analysis of existing and projected housing needs and a statement of goals, policies, quantified objectives, financial resources, and scheduled programs for the preservation, improvement, and development of housing. **The housing element shall identify adequate sites for housing**, including rental housing, factory-built housing, mobilehomes, and emergency shelters, and shall make adequate provision for the existing and projected needs of all economic segments of the community. The housing element shall contain all of the following: ...

[114] Builder's remedy and mini builder's remedy projects **can** be disapproved or conditioned if the jurisdiction can make one of the **other** findings at Gov. Code 65589.5(d)(1) through (6).

For an example of a housing element following the process required by Gov. Code § 65583, see the *City of Los Angeles 2021 - 2029 Housing Element, Chapter 4, Adequate Sites for Housing*.[115] The introduction to that chapter explains (emphasis added):

> Under Housing Element law, the City must demonstrate that it has adequate land zoned to accommodate the entirety of its 2021-2029 Regional Housing Needs Assessment (RHNA) **allocation of 456,643 housing units**. This Chapter identifies the City's inventory of land suitable for residential development without the need for any legislative action by the City (in accordance with CA Government Code §65583.2), identifies additional alternative methods of satisfying the RHNA (pursuant to CA Government Code §65583.1), provides an analysis of the inventory's compliance with Affirmatively Furthering Fair Housing (AFFH) requirements, and identifies the need for rezoning programs to accommodate the RHNA allocation. The methodology used to identify these sites and conduct the AFFH analysis is also described here. This Chapter also includes information on the availability and suitability of infrastructure to support the development of housing.
>
> The analysis demonstrates that, during the 6th cycle, the City has an anticipated unit **potential of 230,947 units**, of which 72,640 units are lower-income. As a result of the gap between the 6th cycle RHNA Allocation and the City's anticipated unit potential, the City's Housing Element identifies a need to create a Rezoning Program to meet the **255,432-unit shortfall**. To accommodate this shortfall, **the City proposes a Rezoning Program** that prioritizes additional housing capacity, particularly lower-income capacity, in Higher Opportunity Areas, promotes housing near transit, and protects environmentally sensitive areas. The Rezoning Program also proposes to integrate value capture strategies and utilize affordable housing overlays to maximize affordable housing production, promote mixed-income communities, and provide advantages to majority affordable projects. A detailed description of the proposed Rezoning Program, including the methodology used to develop the Inventory of Candidate Sites for Rezoning, is also provided in this Chapter.

Each jurisdiction's housing element is required to identify an inventory of suitable sites within the jurisdiction that will accommodate the RHNA for each income category. HCD provides jurisdictions with standard spreadsheet forms to compile this data. The two primary lists of housing element sites are the Inventory of Adequate Sites for Housing (Table A), and the Candidate Sites to be Rezoned (Table B).

The California Department of General Services maintains a statewide database and mapping tool[116] that includes housing element sites as well as an inventory of excess state-owned property and surplus land owned by local jurisdictions. See Figure 25 and Figure 26 for screen shots from this tool. Searching the data and map is a great first step in determining if a site is a housing element site, but the applicant should thoroughly review the jurisdiction's housing element to understand the status of the project site and the programs that may apply to it. Housing element site data may be updated periodically, so always confirm with the jurisdiction whether the subject site is or is not a housing element site, and what income category or categories it is suitable for.

Inventory of Adequate Sites for Housing (Table A)

First, the jurisdiction compiles a list of sites that are already zoned and suitable for housing, and lists each site's capacity for lower income, moderate income, and above moderate income housing units. This is Table A in the standard HCD forms. As an example, Figure 23 (left half of the spreadsheet table) and Figure 24 (right half) show a small portion of the spreadsheet that is Los Angeles' Inventory of Suitable Sites (Table A). The total capacity calculated by that spreadsheet is the "potential of 230,947 units" mentioned in the introduction to Chapter 4 of Los Angeles' housing element that is quoted above.

Los Angeles' Table A spreadsheet spans almost 200,000 rows, each of them identifying a site suitable for housing. However, the vast majority of the sites are already developed with other uses, or for other reasons are unlikely to

[115] https://planning.lacity.gov/odocument/f5ac3c70-3f89-44c4-a05c-58f93d32c426/Chapter_4_-Adequate_Sites_for_Housing_(Adopted).pdf.
[116] https://www.dgs.ca.gov/RESD/Projects/Page-Content/Projects-List-Folder/Housing-and-Local-Land-Development-Opportunities.

be developed during the Sixth RHNA Cycle. The City and its consultants applied a formula that takes into consideration the *likelihood* of redevelopment, and reasonable capacity of each site for housing units, and applied a *reduction factor* to the calculation of Density x Site Area. For example, the third site in Figure 23, 11667 N Glenoaks Blvd, has a Max Density Allowed of 108 units/acre, and is 0.68 acres, but Table A only counts that site for 0.034 units (third row of Figure 24).

The final column in Figure 24 shows the Income Category the site has been counted as suitable for. The sites listed as "Above Moderate" do **not** meet the first test, because they are not "identified as suitable or available for very low, low-, or moderate-income households." The sites listed as "Moderate" or "Lower" **do** meet the first test. For example, 11667 N Glenoaks Blvd is suitable for lower income households, and therefore is a mini builder's remedy site. A subdivision (d) project cannot be disapproved on this site if its density (before any density bonus) is 108 units per acre or less.

Figure 23: Left half of City of Los Angeles Table A (small sample of City's spreadsheet).

Appendix 4.1. Inventory of Adequate Sites for Housing (Table A)

Jurisdiction Name	Site Address/Intersection	5 Digit ZIP Code	Assessor Parcel Number	Consolidated Sites	General Plan Designation (Current)	Zoning Designation (Current)	Minimum Density Allowed (units/acre)	Max Density Allowed (units/acre)	Parcel Size (Acres)	Existing Use/Vacancy	Infrastructure
LOS ANGELES	12708 W FOOTHILL BLVD	91342	2514005033		Highway Oriented Commercial	[Q]C2-1VL-CUGU	0	21	0.343000905	Commercial - Office Building - One Story	YES - Current
LOS ANGELES	13650 W BROWNELL ST	91340	2523006013		Low Residential	(T)(Q)R1-1-CUGU	0	1 unit per lot	0.560827275	Residential - Single Family Residence - Vacant Land	YES - Current
LOS ANGELES	11667 N GLENOAKS BLVD	91331	2524022010		Community Commercial	C2-1-CUGU	0	108	0.679947653	Commercial - Shopping Center (Neighborhood, Community) - One Story	YES - Current
LOS ANGELES	11655 N GLENOAKS BLVD	91331	2524022011		Community Commercial	C2-1-CUGU	0	108	0.616423767	Commercial - Shopping Center (Neighborhood, Community) - One Story	YES - Current
LOS ANGELES	11555 N GLENOAKS BLVD	91331	2524023022		Highway Oriented Commercial	[Q]C2-1VL-CUGU	0	21	0.819959966	Commercial - Shopping Center (Neighborhood, Community) - One Story	YES - Current
LOS ANGELES	13219 W PAXTON ST	91331	2524030027		Highway Oriented Commercial	[Q]C2-1VL-CUGU	0	21	0.355228687	Industrial - Warehousing, Distribution, Storage - Warehousing, Distribution, Under 10,000 SF - One Story	YES - Current
LOS ANGELES	12928 W VAUGHN ST	91340	2527008039		Low Residential	R1-1-CUGU	0	1 unit per lot	0.929096485	Institutional - Church - One Story	YES - Current
LOS ANGELES	12843 W HEMINGWAY DR	91340	2527011BRK		Low Medium II Residential	[T][Q]RD2-1-CUGU	0	14	1.640106656	Residential - Single Family Residence - Detached - Condominium	YES - Current
LOS ANGELES	11808 1/2 N BROMONT AVE	91331	2527022BRK		Low Medium II Residential	(Q)RD1.5-1-CUGU	0	29	1.292327427	Residential - Single Family Residence - Detached - Condominium	YES - Current
LOS ANGELES	12529 W FILMORE ST	91331	2527022BRK		Low Medium II Residential	(Q)RD1.5-1-CUGU	0	29	1.283147301	Residential - Single Family Residence - Detached - Condominium	YES - Current
LOS ANGELES	10228 N GLENOAKS BLVD	91331	2528007015		Light Manufacturing	[Q]C2-1VL	0	108	1.724330836	Commercial - Parking Lot (Commercial Use Property) - Lots - Patron or Employee - One Story	YES - Current
LOS ANGELES	12500 W FILMORE ST	91331	2532001027		Medium Residential	R3-1-CUGU	0	54	6.400958259	Residential - Five or More Units or Apartments (Any Combination) - 4 Stories or Less	YES - Current
LOS ANGELES	11449 N SPROULE AVE	91331	2532006006		Low Medium II Residential	(Q)RD6-1-CUGU	0	7	0.876663299	Residential - Double, Duplex, or Two Units - 4 Stories or Less	YES - Current

Figure 24: Right half of City of Los Angeles Table A (small sample of City's spreadsheet).

Publicly-Owned	Site Status	Identified in Last/Last Two Planning Cycle(s)	Lower Income Capacity	Moderate Income Capacity	Above Moderate Income Capacity	Total Capacity	Existing Units	Maximum Units Allowed - Base Zoning	Maximum Units Allowed - Bonus Zoning	PIN	Community Plan Area	Rent Stabilization Ordinance	Income Category
NO - Privately-Owned	Available	Not Used in Prior Housing Element	0	0.109982029	0	0.109982029	0	0	0	216B161 68	Arleta - Pacoima		Moderate
NO - Privately-Owned	Available	Not Used in Prior Housing Element	0	0	0.03377561	0.03377561	0	0	0	213B157 385	Arleta - Pacoima		Above Moderate
NO - Privately-Owned	Available	Used in Prior Housing Element - Non-Vacant	0.033965664	0	0	0.033965664	5	0	0	213B157 277	Arleta - Pacoima		Lower
NO - Privately-Owned	Available	Used in Prior Housing Element - Non-Vacant	0.040134754	0	0	0.040134754	6	0	0	213B157 303	Arleta - Pacoima		Lower
NO - Privately-Owned	Available	Not Used in Prior Housing Element	0	0.056430344	0	0.056430344	10	0	0	213B161 602	Arleta - Pacoima		Moderate
NO - Privately-Owned	Available	Not Used in Prior Housing Element	0	0.058786697	0	0.058786697	0	0	0	213B157 638	Arleta - Pacoima		Moderate
NO - Privately-Owned	Available	Used in Prior Housing Element - Non-	0	0	0.000305657	0.000305657	0	0	0	216B161 297	Arleta - Pacoima		Above Moderate
NO - Privately-Owned	Available	Not Used in Prior Housing Element	0	0.033719037	0	0.033719037	24	0	0	216B161 752	Arleta - Pacoima		Moderate
NO - Privately-Owned	Available	Not Used in Prior Housing Element	0	0.15268309	0	0.15268309	32	0	0	213B161 79	Arleta - Pacoima		Moderate
NO - Privately-Owned	Available	Not Used in Prior Housing Element	0	0.15268309	0	0.15268309	32	0	0	213B161 91	Arleta - Pacoima		Moderate
NO - Privately-Owned	Available	Not Used in Prior Housing Element	0.721274096	0	0	0.721274096	1	0	0	204B165 142	Arleta - Pacoima		Lower
NO - Privately-Owned	Available	Not Used in Prior Housing Element	0	0	3.577911907	3.577911907	128	0	0	213B165 143	Arleta - Pacoima	Yes	Above Moderate
NO - Privately-Owned	Available	Not Used in Prior Housing Element	0	0.383771759	0	0.383771759	2	0	0	213B161 799	Arleta - Pacoima		Moderate

Figure 23 and Figure 24 were excerpted from https://planning.lacity.gov/odocument/f8e2050f-2b3b-4ca3-b793-d9ffcd2fc8d4/Appendix_4.1_-_Housing_Element_Sites_Inventory_(Table_A).xlsx.

Figure 25: Searchable map of housing element sites. Screenshot shows Los Angeles Housing Table A sites.

Figure 26: Searchable map of housing element sites. Screenshot shows Los Angeles Housing Table B sites.

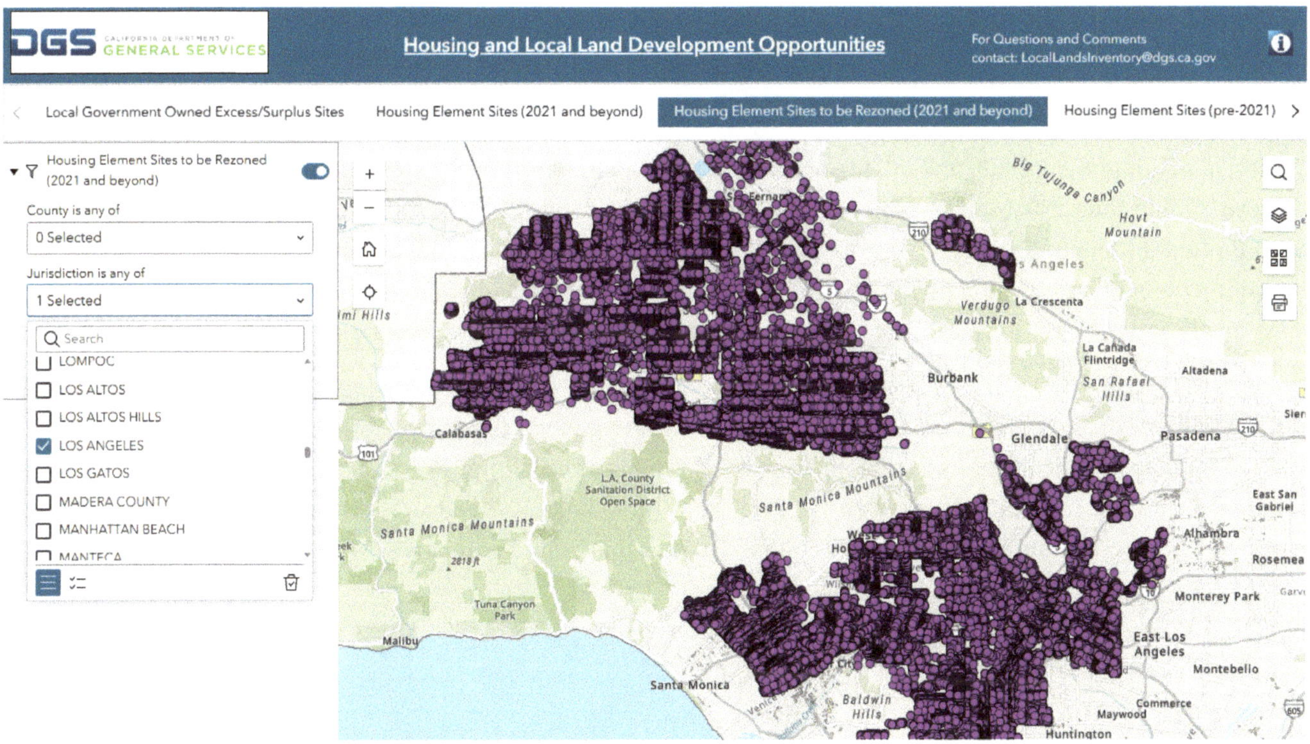

For a statewide map of housing element sites (updated periodically) see https://www.dgs.ca.gov/RESD/Projects/Page-Content/Projects-List-Folder/Housing-and-Local-Land-Development-Opportunities. The above screen shots have City of **Los Angeles** selected in the drop down. Figure 25 has **Housing Element Sites** selected, which are the Table A sites. Figure 26 has **Housing Element Sites to be Rezoned** selected, which are the Table B sites. The map contains data for "2021 and beyond" which is approximately the earliest start of the Sixth RHNA Cycle for the various regions/COGs (see Figure 20).

Candidate Sites to be Rezoned (Table B)

If there are not enough sites already zoned and suitable to meet the housing needs for all income categories, the municipality has a "shortfall" of sites. If the jurisdiction has a shortfall of sites zoned and suitable for housing, its housing element must include "rezoning programs" to up-zone enough sites to accommodate the shortfall. Sites that are candidates for one or more of the rezoning programs proposed by the housing element are compiled in a list that shows the capacity of the sites after rezoning. This list is Table B.

The City of Los Angeles had a RHNA "allocation of 456,643 housing units" but applied a "target buffer" to arrive at a "target capacity" of 486,379 units.[117] Per the introduction to Chapter 4 of the City of Los Angeles housing element, quoted earlier, subtracting the "potential of 230,947 units" from the target capacity, Los Angeles had a "255,432-unit shortfall."

A small portion of the spreadsheet that is Los Angeles' Candidate Sites Identified to be Rezoned to Accommodate Housing Shortfall Need (Table B)[118] is shown in Figure 27 (left half of table) and Figure 28 (right half).

For example, the tenth site in Figure 27, 235 S Figueroa St, has a Current General Plan Designation of Regional Center Commercial and Current Zoning of C4-4D; and Proposed General Plan Designation of Transit Core and Proposed Zoning of [HB3-G1-5] [CX2-FA] [CPIO] (in Los Angeles' entirely new "hybrid, or modular, zoning" zoning code[119]).

The final column in Figure 28 for 235 S Figueroa St shows the Income Category that the site is suitable for includes "VLI, LI, and ABMI" so the site is identified as suitable for housing for low income, very low income, and above moderate income (i.e., market-rate) households. Because the site is "identified as suitable or available for very low, low-, or moderate-income households" 235 S Figueroa St is a mini builder's remedy site.

Second Test for Exception A to Finding 5

To be a mini builder's remedy project, the project must be "**consistent with the density specified in the housing element**." Mini builder's remedy projects do **not** follow the process for Calculating the Maximum Base Density for a Builder's Remedy Project at Gov. Code § 65589.5(h)(11)(C). To be a mini builder's remedy project (with all the protections of subdivision (d) and the Additional Protections and Provisions for Mini Builder's Remedy Projects discussed below) a project must comply with the density limitations specified in the housing element.

Using the 235 S Figueroa St example from the previous section, as shown in Figure 27, a mini builder's remedy project will follow the density standards of the Transit Core general plan designation and [HB3-G1-5] [CX2-FA] [CPIO] zoning classification. As shown in Figure 28, the new zoning for 235 S Figueroa St (the tenth row) will require a Minimum Density Allowed of 20 units/acre (first column), and a Max Density Allowed of 492.557 units/acre (second column). However, the column Base Density Per Acre shows "No Max."

---

[117] https://planning.lacity.gov/odocument/f5ac3c70-3f89-44c4-a05c-58f93d32c426/Chapter_4_-Adequate_Sites_for_Housing_(Adopted).pdf pages 149 and 150.
[118] https://planning.lacity.gov/odocument/fae1614c-59f5-4294-b9d1-e00e491999dc/Appendix_4.7_Candidate_Sites_Identified_to_be_Rezoned_(Table_B).xlsx.
[119] https://planning.lacity.gov/blog/what-new-zoning-code-0.

Figure 27: Left half of City of Los Angeles Table B (small sample of City's spreadsheet).

Table B: Candidate Sites Identified to be Rezoned to Accommodate Shortfall Housing Need, Table Starts in Cell A2

Jurisdiction Name	Site Address/Intersection	5 Digit ZIP Code	Assessor Parcel Number	Very Low-Income	Low-Income	Moderate-Income	Above Moderate-Income	Type of Shortfall	Parcel Size (Acres)	Current General Plan Designation	Current Zoning	Proposed General Plan (GP) Designation	Proposed Zoning
Los Angeles	1601 E OLYMPIC BLVD	90021	5146009006	0.000	0.000	0.000	3529.600	Shortfall of Sites	19.412	Heavy Manufacturing	M2-2D, M3-2D	Hybrid Industrial	[MB4-SH1-5] [IX4-FA]
Los Angeles	777 S ALAMEDA ST	90021	5146009008	0.000	0.000	0.000	3293.600	Shortfall of Sites	18.114	Light Manufacturing	M2-2D	Hybrid Industrial	[MB4-SH1-5] [IX4-FA]
Los Angeles	17941 CHATSWORTH ST	91344	2715025055	0.000	0.000	0.000	2920.810	Shortfall of Sites	18.641	Community Commercial	(Q)C2-1L	0	0
Los Angeles	0	0	5133029905	0.000	0.000	0.000	2619.200	Shortfall of Sites	10.804	Light Manufacturing	M2-2D	Markets	[DM1-SH1-5] [IX3-FA] [CPIO]
Los Angeles	18000 CHATSWORTH ST	91344	2731008023	0.000	0.000	0.000	2568.096	Shortfall of Sites	16.391	Community Commercial	C2-1VL	0	0
Los Angeles	9725 LAUREL CANYON BLVD	91331	2626003014	0.000	0.000	0.000	2112.552	Shortfall of Sites	16.180	Neighborhood Office Commercial	(Q)C2-1VLD	0	0
Los Angeles	800 N WESTERN AVE	90029	7445011015	0.000	0.000	0.000	2089.642	Shortfall of Sites	13.336	Neighborhood Commercial	[Q]C2-1XL	0	0
Los Angeles	1312 E 7TH ST	90021	5146009003	0.000	0.000	0.000	2013.600	Shortfall of Sites	11.071	Light Manufacturing	M2-2D	Hybrid Industrial	[MB4-SH1-5] [IX4-FA]
Los Angeles	6433 FALLBROOK AVE	91307	2038040031	0.000	0.000	0.000	1983.878	Shortfall of Sites	12.678	Community Commercial	QC2-1VL	Community Center	[MB3-CDF1-5] [IX4-FA] [CPIO]
Los Angeles	235 S FIGUEROA ST	90012	5151001024	90.440	90.440	0.000	1627.920	Shortfall of Sites	4.590	Regional Center Commercial	C4-4D	Transit Core	[HB3-G1-5] [CX2-FA] [CPIO]
Los Angeles	10216 MASON AVE	91311	2741005008	0.000	0.000	0.000	1734.797	Shortfall of Sites	11.073	Neighborhood Office Commercial	(Q)C2-1L	0	0
Los Angeles	12755 BURBANK BLVD	91607	2341018001	0.000	0.000	0.000	1732.787	Shortfall of Sites	19.061	Low Medium I Residential	R1-1, RD3-1	0	0
Los Angeles	15600 MIDWOOD DR	91344	2605002011	0.000	0.000	0.000	1710.288	Shortfall of Sites	10.914	Community Commercial	(Q)C2-1VL	0	0
Los Angeles	22816 VICTORY BLVD	91367	2039007030	0.000	0.000	0.000	1704.960	Shortfall of Sites	10.882	Community Commercial	P-1VL, C2-1VL, C2-1	Community Center	0
Los Angeles	3200 MOTOR AVE	90034	4316033002	0.000	0.000	0.000	1688.367	Shortfall of Sites	17.765	Low Residential	R1-1	0	0
Los Angeles	1625 E 8TH ST	90021	5146009001	82.080	82.080	0.000	1477.440	Shortfall of Sites	9.025	Heavy Manufacturing	M2-2D	Hybrid Industrial	[MB4-SH1-5] [IX4-FA]
Los Angeles	12639 GLENOAKS BLVD	91342	2508027013	0.000	0.000	0.000	1538.016	Shortfall of Sites	11.781	Community Commercial	C2-1VL-CPIO	0	0
Los Angeles	0	0	2148032902	714.800	714.800	0.000	0.000	Shortfall of Sites	8.208	Public Facilities	PF-1XL-RIO	Regional Center	0
Los Angeles	11051 VICTORY BLVD	91406	2336001020	0.000	0.000	0.000	1406.592	Shortfall of Sites	10.768	Neighborhood Office Commercial	(T)(Q)C1.5-1VL	Neighborhood Center	0
Los Angeles	404 S FIGUEROA ST	90071	5151020009	69.320	69.320	0.000	1247.760	Shortfall of Sites	3.519	Regional Center Commercial	C4-4D	Transit Core	[HB5-G1-5] [CX3-FA] [CPIO]

Figure 28: Right half of City of Los Angeles Table A (small sample of City's spreadsheet).

Minimum Density Allowed	Maximum Density Allowed	Total Capacity	Vacant/ Nonvacant	Description of Existing Uses	PIN	Base Density Per Acre	Community Plan Area	Rent Stabalization Ordinance	Income Category	Applicable Rezoning Program (Program informing values in Column Q listed first)
0	227.282	3529.600		Industrial - Warehousing, Distribution, Storage - Warehousing, Distribution, Under 10,000 SF - One Story, 0	123A213 10	No Max	Central City	No	ABMI	DT CPU
0	227.289	3293.600		Commercial - Store Combination - Store and Office Combination - One Story, 0	124-5A215 30	No Max	Central City	No	ABMI	DT CPU
0	163.215	2920.810		Commercial - Restaurant, Cocktail Lounge - Fast Food - Walk Up - One Story, 0	207B125 100		Granada Hills - Knollwood	No	ABMI	DB50
0	303.046	2619.200		Miscellaneous - Government Owned Property, 0	123A209 2	No Max	Central City	No	ABMI	DT CPU
0	163.209	2568.096		Commercial - Office Building - One Story, 0	207B125 637		Granada Hills - Knollwood	No	ABMI	DB50 , ARO
0	163.205	2112.552		Commercial - Department Store - Discount Department Store (Target, etc.) - One Story, 0	201B161 692		Arleta - Pacoima	No	ABMI	DB50
0	163.223	2089.642		Commercial - Shopping Center (Neighborhood, Community) - One Story, 0	021B193 193		San Pedro	No	ABMI	DB50
0	227.349	2013.600		Commercial - Store Combination - Store and Office Combination - One Story, 0	124-5A213 138	No Max	Central City	No	ABMI	DT CPU
0	145.136	1983.878		Commercial - Shopping Center (Regional) - One Story, 2	180B097 434	54	Canoga Park - Winnetka - Woodland Hills - West Hills	No	ABMI	DB50 , CPK CPU, AHO
20	492.557	1808.800		Commercial - Office Building - Five Stories, 0	132A209 92	No Max	Central City	No	VLI, LI, ABMI	DT CPU , ARO, AHO
0	163.200	1734.797		Commercial - Shopping Center (Regional) - One Story, 0	204B109 191		Chatsworth - Porter Ranch	No	ABMI	DB50
0	113.635	1732.787		Industrial - Motion Picture, Radio and Television Industry - Transmission Facility - One Story, 0	174B161 182		North Hollywood - Valley Village	No	ABMI	OPP RC , R2RD
0	163.236	1710.288		Commercial - Restaurant, Cocktail Lounge - Restaurant, Cocktail Lounge, Tavern - One Story, 0	213B145 23		Granada Hills - Knollwood	No	ABMI	DB50
0	28.395	1704.960		Commercial - Shopping Center (Regional) - One Story, 0	180B097 629	54	Canoga Park - Winnetka - Woodland Hills - West Hills	No	ABMI	DB50 , CPK CPU, P
0	99.000	1688.367		Institutional - Homes for Aged and Others - One Story, 0	123B161 610		West Los Angeles	No	ABMI	TOC EXP , OPP RC2
20	227.379	1641.600		Industrial - Industrial - Lift, 0	123A215 2	No Max	Central City	No	VLI, LI, ABMI	DT CPU
0	163.192	1538.016		Commercial - Shopping Center (Regional) - Lift, 0	219B153 17		Sylmar	No	ABMI	DB50
20	217.718	1429.600		Industrial - Heavy Manufacturing - One Story, 0	180B105 19	108	Canoga Park - Winnetka - Woodland Hills - West Hills	No	LI	CPK CPU , PF, MURC
0	72.531	1406.592		Commercial - Department Store - Discount Department Store (Target, etc.) - One Story, 0	180B173 615	108	North Hollywood - Valley Village	No	ABMI	DB50 , NH CPU
20	492.525	1386.400		Commercial - Hotel and Motel - Hotel - 50 Rooms and Over, 0	130-5A209 238	No Max	Central City	No	VLI, LI, ABMI	DT CPU , ARO

Figure 27 and Figure 28 were excerpted from https://planning.lacity.gov/odocument/fae1614c-59f5-4294-b9d1-e00e491999dc/Appendix_4.7_Candidate_Sites_Identified_to_be_Rezoned_(Table_B).xlsx.

Table B provides only limited data on minimum, maximum, and base density; the applicant will need to review the text of the housing element for any other information on density standards associated with the rezoning programs or proposed general plan designation and zoning classification. For the 235 S Figueroa St example, the applicant will need to review the Applicable Rezoning Programs (final column) DT CPU, ARO, and AHO (which will be explained in the housing element) as well as any information included in the housing element for the proposed new Transit Core general plan designation and [HB3-G1-5] [CX2-FA] [CPIO] zoning classification.

At the time the housing element is certified the new general plan designations and zoning classifications may not exist in written form (jurisdictions generally have up to three years after certification of the housing element to complete the rezoning programs, including general plan amendment). The mini builder's remedy project only needs to be "consistent with the density specified in the housing element," so the applicant need only review and apply the density standards **contained** in the housing element, not the subsequent updates to the zoning code and general plan.

Differences Between Builder's Remedy and Mini Builder's Remedy Projects

Both builder's remedy projects and mini builder's remedy projects are subdivision (d) projects and must meet one of the Definitions for Various Levels of Affordability that Qualify a Project for Subdivision (d). Builder's remedy projects arise from the inability of a jurisdiction to make Finding 6: The Project is Not a Builder's Remedy Project. Mini builder's remedy projects arise from Exception A to Finding 5: Housing Element Sites Suitable for Below-Market-Rate Housing.

The essential differences between a builder's remedy project and a mini builder's remedy project are:

1. A builder's remedy project cannot be disapproved **or conditioned in a manner that renders the project infeasible** (Gov. Code 65589.5(d)(1)) if:[120]
    a. It is proposed anywhere, except Sites Abutting Certain Industrial Uses Are Not Eligible for Builder's Remedy, in a jurisdiction that did not have a compliant housing element on the project's vesting date.
    b. It is consistent with the density for a builder's remedy project calculated pursuant to Gov. Code § 65589.5(h)(11)(C).
2. A mini builder's remedy project cannot be disapproved **or conditionally approved** (Gov. Code 65589.5 (d)(5)(A)) if:[121]
    a. It is proposed on a site identified in the certified housing element "as suitable or available for very low, low-, or moderate-income households."
    b. It is consistent with the density specified in the housing element for that site.

Additional Protections and Provisions for Mini Builder's Remedy Projects

The same language that describes the mini builder's remedy exception at Gov. Code 65589.5(d)(5)(A) is used in Gov. Code § 65589.5(f)(8) to identify "subparagraphs (A), (B), and (D) of paragraph (6) and paragraph (9)" as provisions that provide additional protections to mini builder's remedy projects:

> (8) A housing development project **proposed on a site** that is identified as **suitable or available for very low, low-, or moderate-income households** in the jurisdiction's housing element, that is ***consistent with the density specified*** in the most recently updated and adopted housing element, and that is inconsistent with both the jurisdiction's zoning ordinance and general plan land use designation on the date the application was deemed

[120] Builder's remedy and mini builder's remedy projects **can** be disapproved or conditioned if the jurisdiction can make one of the **other** findings at Gov. Code 65589.5(d)(1) through (6).
[121] Ibid.

complete, **shall be subject to the provisions of subparagraphs (A), (B), and (D) of paragraph (6) and paragraph (9)**.

As explained under Additional Protections and Provisions for Builder's Remedy Projects, all of the subparagraphs (A) through (G) under Gov. Code § 65589.5(f)(6), plus paragraphs (7) and (9) apply to builder's remedy projects. A sub-set of those provisions — subparagraphs (A), (B), and (D) of paragraph (6) and paragraph (9) — provide additional protections for mini builder's remedy projects.

Subparagraph (A) Changes the Applicable General Plan and Zoning for a mini builder's remedy project in the same manner as previously explained for builder's remedy projects. Either:

1. The applicant identifies a general plan designation and zoning classification that has been adopted within that jurisdiction, and that would **allow** the "density and unit type proposed by the applicant;" or
2. If the general plan and zoning do not contain designations that **allow** the proposed density and unit type, the applicant identifies development standards from various different general plan designations and zoning classifications that would ***facilitate*** the project.

As explained previously, Subparagraph (B) Requires Approval of the Builder's Remedy Project as Proposed. Subparagraph (B) applies to a mini builder's remedy project in the same way:

1. Even if ***none*** of the development standards in ***any*** general plan designation or zoning classification would allow the mini builder's remedy project, development standards cannot be applied that would render the project infeasible (Gov. Code § 65589.5(f)(6)(B)(i)(I)).
2. If there ***is*** a general plan designation or zoning classification that would allow a project at the density specified for the site in the housing element and proposed for the mini builder's remedy project, the development standards specified in that general plan designation or zoning classification can only be applied to the extent that they do ***not preclude*** construction of the project ***as proposed*** by the applicant.

Subparagraph (C), which provides additional benefits to a builder's remedy project that uses the State Density Bonus Law, does ***not*** apply to a mini builder's remedy project, so a mini builder's remedy project:

1. Does **not** receive two additional SDBL incentives/concessions.
2. **Cannot** select a base density, for SDBL purposes, that is lower than the maximum density specified for the site in the housing element.
3. Does **not** receive additional benefits if it provides extremely low income units.

Subparagraph (D) Deems a Builder's Remedy Project Compliant for All Purposes, and the same applies to a mini builder's remedy project. The provisions of subparagraph (D) ensure that:

1. No general plan amendment, rezoning, or other legislative approval can be required for a mini builder's remedy project.
2. The mini builder's remedy project cannot be required to obtain any special approval that would not be required if the project was not a mini builder's remedy project.
3. Mini builder's remedy projects that are compliant with Gov. Code § 65589.5(f)(6) are deemed compliant with all development standards for all purposes (and therefore the jurisdiction "shall approve" them, and they can use any of the CEQA exemptions or other provisions of state law that would apply if the project was not a mini builder's remedy project).
4. A mini builder's remedy project is **not** considered a nonconforming use after it is built.

Subparagraphs (E), (F), and (G) of paragraph (6) and paragraph (7) of subdivision (f) do **not** apply to a mini builder's remedy project, but paragraph (7) (facilitating the transition from builder's remedy 1.0 to 2.0) is irrelevant, and provisions of subparagraphs (E), (F), and (G) that apply to builder's remedy projects are unlikely to be material to the approval of a mini builder's remedy project.

Paragraph 8 is quoted at the beginning of this section and provides the Additional Protections and Provisions for Mini Builder's Remedy Projects explained above.

Paragraph (9) Defines "Objective, Quantifiable, Written Development Standards, Conditions, and Policies" and applies equally to builder's remedy projects and mini builder's remedy projects.

CHAPTER 10: DEADLINES AND ENFORCEMENT

This chapter starts with a detailed explanation of how deadlines are calculated under state law and covers the critical deadlines and milestones in the path to final approval of a housing project. It includes general advice on critical milestones, hearings by lesser decisionmakers, obtaining final approval, and post-approval considerations. The chapter concludes with a review of the enforcement provisions in the Housing Accountability Act, and in the new Gov. Code § 65914.2 that was added by AB 712 (2025). To an even greater extent than in the previous chapters, this chapter involves critical interpretations upon which the approval of a project may rest. The Author's interpretations should not be relied upon as legal advice. Please ***consult a qualified attorney***.

Where to Find More Information

Jurisdictions can obtain assistance in understanding and applying state housing laws from the Department of Housing and Community Development (HCD) and can seek recognition as a pro-housing community through the Prohousing Designation Program (PDP), which allows them to apply for the Prohousing Incentive Program (PIP). HCD has published a series of HCD Memos that explain various laws and programs, and has provided over 1,000 Accountability and Enforcement Letters to jurisdictions that are archived and available for download via a Microsoft Excel file that can be searched and sorted by topic and jurisdiction. HCD's Housing Accountability Unit (HAU) provides assistance to jurisdictions when they have questions about the proper interpretation and application of housing laws. The larger regional associations of governments (known as Councils of Governments or "COGs") produce many resources for their constituent jurisdictions; they make most of those resources available to anyone via their websites. For example, the Association of Bay Area Governments (ABAG) has a landing page dedicated to housing, and provides Technical Assistance documents on various housing laws and topics. Ignorance of the laws is not a defense, and jurisdictions that are dedicated to following state housing laws and meeting their housing needs will avail themselves of all the information necessary to ensure their compliance.

Applicants have many resources available to assist them if it becomes necessary to enforce state housing laws. The same tools available to jurisdictions are available to applicants, including access to all of the HCD letters, and the ability to request assistance from the HAU. Support is also available from the various "Yes In My Backyard" (YIMBY) organizations. YIMBY Action is an organization that advocates for housing reform both nationally and regionally. California YIMBY provides resources and information in support of housing, and sponsors, endorses, and tracks legislation. The network of *local* YIMBY organizations write support letters and turn out to support projects at hearings. YIMBY Law is one of the housing organizations that sues local governments when they violate the Housing Accountability Act (see Who Can Bring an Action to Enforce the Housing Accountability Act?). The California Housing Defense Fund (CalHDF) is another of those housing organizations, and you can submit a case on their website to have CalHDF consider bringing an action in court. CalHDF also provides an explainer on the Housing Accountability Act, that is a good introduction to this chapter.

CHAPTER CONTENTS

Computation of Time Periods and Deadlines

State housing laws prescribe time limits for various actions of both jurisdictions and applicants. The consequences of missing a deadline can be severe, from an application being deemed approved because a jurisdiction failed to approve or disapprove the project by Deadline for Initial Approval or Disapproval of the Project (see Deemed Approval — New with AB 130), to a builder's remedy project losing its SB 330 vesting and becoming entirely infeasible (see Deadlines to Maintain SB 330 Vesting).

The Government Code prescribes the rules for the "Computation of Time" under Gov. Code § 6800 through 6808 for purposes of processing development permits and other actions of the government. The Code of Civil Procedure (CCP), which governs civil court actions, uses the same basic rules, but provides additional details in its "Preliminary Provisions" under CCP § 2 through 34, which applies to ***all*** codes and regulations both state and local. The rules in the CCP for calculating deadlines will be followed in the event of a lawsuit, for example, to enforce the Housing Accountability Act, and applied by the courts to determine whether a deadline was missed. The discussion below includes relevant citations to both the Government Code and the Code of Civil Procedure.

Basic Rule for Time Periods and Deadlines

Every time period prescribed within the Government Code excludes the first day and includes the last day, unless the last day is a holiday, which is also excluded. Per Gov. Code § 6800:

> 6800. The time in which any act provided by law is to be done is computed by excluding the first day, and including the last, unless the last day is a holiday, and then it is also excluded.

This simple statement belies a great deal of complexity. The text box below provides a simplification of the rules explained under the following sub-headings.

Time Periods and Deadlines Simplified

With respect to ***all*** "provisions of law providing or requiring an act to be performed on a particular day or within a specified period of time, [in any] code or statute, ordinance, rule, or regulation" (CCP § 12a(b)), the time period for the act to be performed:

1. Starts on the day **after** the triggering event (i.e., at midnight).
2. Expires at the end of (i.e., at midnight) the **last** day of the time period, ***but*** if the last day is a **holiday** the time period is extended to the end of the first subsequent day that is not a holiday.
3. If the time period is stated as "business days" all holidays are excluded.

Holidays include Saturday and Sunday, **judicial holidays** (CCP § 12a), and (for purposes of the business of a public agency) any day that the office of the "city, county, state, or public office, other than a branch office" is **closed** for the entire day (CCP § 12b).

The Superior Court of Los Angeles County maintains a website that lists the judicial holidays for the next six years: https://www.lacourt.ca.gov/pages/cp/gi-court-holidays.

City, county, state, and other public offices may be closed on other holidays as designated by the public agency, or due to labor agreements, emergencies, etc. Check the agency's website, ordinances, or (for charter cities and counties) the charter to see what dates their office is closed. An individual's day off, or a department or branch office being closed, does not constitute the city, county, state, or public office being closed.

Practitioners should confirm deadlines by **consulting with a qualified attorney**.

Days, Calendar Days and Business Days

Most time periods in the various state housing laws are expressed in "days." The statute may use the term "calendar days," "business days," or simply "days." Som examples:

Gov. Code § 65943:

> 65943. (a) Not later than **30 calendar days** after any public agency has received an application for a development project, the agency shall determine in writing whether the application is complete and shall immediately transmit the determination to the applicant for the development project. ...

Gov. Code § 65941.1(b):

> (b) (1) A development proponent that submits a preliminary application providing the information required by subdivision (a) may include in its preliminary application a request for a preliminary fee and exaction estimate, which the city, county, or city and county shall provide within **30 business days** of the submission of the preliminary application. ...

PRC § 21080.2:

> 21080.2. In the case of a project described in subdivision (c) of Section 21065 [i.e., when a jurisdiction will issue a development permit to a nongovernmental entity], the determination required by Section 21080.1 shall be made within **30 days** from the date on which an application for a project has been received and accepted as complete by the lead agency. This period may be extended **15 days** upon the consent of the lead agency and the project applicant.

The terms "days" or "calendar days" have the same meaning. Per Gov. Code § 6806:

> 6806. A day is the period of time between any midnight and the midnight following.

Gov. Code § 6808 defines California's time zone and daylight savings time. Midnight is the end of one day and the beginning of the next, regardless of changing the clock.

The term "business days" excludes holidays and days when the jurisdiction's office is closed, as explained under Which Days are Holidays?.

Weeks Months, Years, and Fractions of Years

"Week" means 7 consecutive days. (Gov. Code § 6805.)

"Month" means a calendar month, unless the statute specifies otherwise. (Gov. Code § 6806 and CCP § 17(b)(4).)

"Year" is a trickier definition. January 1st is the first day of the year (Gov. Code § 6801), and Gov. Code § 6802 legally defines a "leap year." However, a "year" is **always** 365 days, and February 29th is "reckoned together" with February 28th, per Gov Code § 6803:

> 6803. "Year" means a period of 365 days; "half year," 182 days; "quarter of a year," 91 days. The added day of a leap year, and the day immediately preceding, if they occur in any such period, shall be reckoned together as one day.

The Author's interpretation of the phrase "shall be reckoned together as one day" is that if a time period spans across February 29th, February 29th does not count as one of the days in the time period. February 28th/29th is a single "day" that spans from midnight at the **beginning** of February 28th through midnight at the **end** of February 29th. And, for example, if the 60th day of a 60-day time period falls on February 29th, that is actually the 59th day of the time period because February 28th and 29th are the same day; the deadline is March 1st (unless that is a holiday). Essentially, ***do not count February 29th***; it is not a day and cannot be the deadline.

Regardless of any leap year, a time period of 2 years that, for example, starts on January 1, 2026, will always exclude the first day and end at the end of January 2, 2028, because again, February 28 and 29 are "reckoned together as one day."

Some time periods are expressed as fractional or decimal years. For example, as explained under Duration of Vesting When an SB 330 Preliminary Application Applies, the SB 330 vesting continues after final approval of the project, but expires if construction is not commenced within 2.5- or 3.5-years after final approval of the project. Per Gov. Code § 65589.5(o)(2)(D):

> (D) The housing development project has not commenced construction **within two and one-half years, or three and one-half years** for an affordable housing project, following the date that the project received **final approval**. For purposes of this subparagraph: ...

2.5 years or two and one-half years is (365 x 2 + 182 =) 912 days, and 3.5 years or three and one-half years is (365 x 3 + 182 =) 1,277 days.

Which Days are Holidays?

The legal definition of which days are "holidays" is complex. It includes judicial holidays as specified in CCP § 135, and in addition (for the purposes of the business of "any city, county, state, or public office") any day that a jurisdiction is closed for the whole day. The defining statutes contain a series of cross-references. The basic definition of "holiday," for purposes of time periods and deadlines, is found at CCP § 12a:

> 12a. (a) If the last day for the performance of any act provided or required by law to be performed within a specified period of time is a holiday, then that period is hereby extended to and including the next day that is not a holiday. For purposes of this section, **"holiday" means all day on Saturdays, all holidays specified in Section** 135 and, to the extent provided in Section 12b,[[122]] **all days that by terms of Section** 12b **are required to be considered as holidays**.
>
> (b) **This section applies to** Sections 659, 659a, and 921, and to all other provisions of law providing or requiring an act to be performed on a particular day or within a specified period of time, whether expressed in this or **any other code or statute, ordinance, rule, or regulation**.

Sections 659, 659a, and 921 of the Code of Civil Procedure prescribe time limits related to law suits. However, subdivision (b) makes CCP § 12a universally applicable to all time periods prescribed by "any other code or statute, ordinance, rule, or regulation" in California (e.g., the Government Code, CEQA Statutes and Guidelines, and local codes).

The phrase "all day on Saturdays" makes it clear that the entirety of a Saturday is a holiday for purposes of calculating a deadline, even though certain laws do not include all of Saturday as a holiday.[123] Sundays are judicial holidays included in this definition by the cross-reference to Section 135.

The cross-reference to Section 135 means that For Purposes of Calculating Time Limits, all Judicial Holidays are "Holidays", and the cross-reference to Section 12b means that In Addition, any Full Day on which the Jurisdiction is Closed is a Holiday for That Jurisdiction.

For Purposes of Calculating Time Limits, all *Judicial Holidays* are "Holidays"

The phrase in CCP § 12a, "For purposes of this section, "holiday" means ... all holidays specified in Section 135," refers to the **judicial holidays** as defined by CCP § 135:[124]

> 135. **Every full day designated as a holiday by Section** 6700 **of the Government Code**, including that Thursday of November declared by the President to be **Thanksgiving Day**, is a judicial holiday, except the date corresponding with the second new moon following the winter solstice, or the third new moon following the winter solstice should an intercalary month intervene, known as "Lunar New Year," the 15th day of the month of Kartik in the Hindu lunar calendar

[122] The reference "Section 12b" is to CCP § 12b **not** to subparagraph (b) of Section 12a. CCP § 12b applies to the business of a jurisdiction; "business days" for a jurisdiction's business do not include days when the jurisdiction is closed for the whole day.

[123] See for example Gov. Code § 6702, which provides that "Saturday from noon to midnight is a holiday ...."

[124] AB 268 (2025) designated Diwali as a holiday on the list at Gov Code § 6700, but amended CCP § 135 to exclude it from judicial holidays.

of each year, known as "Diwali," April 24, known as "Genocide Remembrance Day," September 9, known as "Admission Day," the second Monday in October, known as "Columbus Day," and any other day appointed by the President, but not by the Governor, for a public fast, thanksgiving, or holiday. **If a judicial holiday falls on a Saturday or a Sunday, the Judicial Council may designate an alternative day** for observance of the holiday. **Every Saturday and the day after Thanksgiving Day** are judicial holidays. Officers and employees of the courts shall observe only the judicial holidays established pursuant to this section.

The cross-reference from CCP § 12a to CCP § 135 means that all **judicial holidays** are holidays for purposes of Calculating the First and Last Day of a Time Period. CCP § 135 explicitly designates as judicial holidays: Saturdays, Thanksgiving Day, and the day after Thanksgiving. It adds the list of state holidays at Gov Code § 6700, but excludes the following state holidays listed at Gov Code § 6700 from the definition of judicial holiday. These state holidays are **not** "holidays," as defined by CCP § 12a, for the purposes of calculating time periods:

1. Lunar New Year
2. Diwali
3. Genocide Remembrance Day
4. Admission Day
5. Columbus Day
6. "[A]ny other day appointed by the President, but not by the Governor, for a public fast, thanksgiving, or holiday"

Note that "If a judicial holiday falls on a Saturday or a Sunday, the Judicial Council may designate an alternative day for observance of the holiday." (CCP § 135.) Rather than looking at the list of state holidays at Gov Code § 6700 and trying to figure out the exceptions, and which days are holidays if a judicial holiday falls on a weekend, the applicant should simply refer to the list of judicial holidays posted on the California Judicial Branch's website.[125] For example, below are the judicial holidays for 2026.

JUDICIAL HOLIDAYS IN 2026

Thursday	January 1, 2026	New Year's Day (2026)
Monday	January 19, 2026	Martin Luther King, Jr. Birthday
Thursday	February 12, 2026	Lincoln Day
Monday	February 16, 2026	Presidents' Day
Tuesday	March 31, 2026	Cesar Chavez Day
Monday	May 25, 2026	Memorial Day
Friday	June 19, 2026	Juneteenth
Friday	July 3, 2026	Independence Day
Monday	September 7, 2026	Labor Day
Friday	September 25, 2026	Native American Day

[125] For whatever reason, the main Judicial Branch website at https://courts.ca.gov/about/court-holidays only has the **current** year's list of holidays. The webpages of some lower courts have posted judicial holidays for the next several years. For example, https://www.lacourt.ca.gov/holiday/ui/index.aspx has judicial holidays through 2030 as of the publication of this book.

Wednesday	November 11, 2026	Veterans Day
Thursday	November 26, 2026	Thanksgiving Day
Friday	November 27, 2026	Day after Thanksgiving
Friday	December 25, 2026	Christmas Day

In Addition, any *Full* Day on which the Jurisdiction is *Closed* is a Holiday for *That* Jurisdiction

The phrase in CCP § 12a, "For purposes of this section, "holiday" means ... all days that by terms of Section 12b are required to be considered as holidays," refers to CCP § 12b:

> 12b. If any city, county, state, or public office, other than a branch office, is **closed for the whole of any day**, insofar as the **business of that office** is concerned, **that day shall be considered as a holiday** for the purposes of computing time under Sections 12 and 12a.

This means that, ***in addition to*** all of the judicial holidays, days when the public agency is **closed** are holidays for purposes of calculating deadlines for the business of that public agency. The whole city, county, state, or public office must be closed for the whole day for it to be considered a holiday. An individual's day off, or a department or branch office being closed, does not constitute the city, county, state, or public office being closed. Nor would, for example, an evacuation of the jurisdiction's office building for a period less than a whole day be a holiday.

Because jurisdictions may be closed on days that are not judicial holidays, always check the jurisdiction's website for a holiday calendar. If the website does not have a list of holidays, check the jurisdiction's code or charter (for a charter city or county) to see if there are any locally designated holidays.

For example, the City and County of San Francisco has a holiday calendar[126] that lists Indigenous Peoples Day and Italian American Heritage Day, both occurring on October 12, 2026. For purposes of the business of San Francisco, October 12, 2026, is a holiday **in addition to the judicial holidays** listed in the above table and must be excluded from the computation of time periods and deadlines for San Francisco to comply with state housing laws. The judicial holidays Lincoln Day, Cesar Chavez Day, and Native American Day are **not** on San Francisco's holiday calendar, but February 12, March 31, and September 25, 2026, must **also** be excluded from time periods and deadlines for the conduct of the business of San Francisco, because CCP § 12a includes **both** judicial holidays and days when the jurisdiction is closed.

Calculating the First and Last Day of a Time Period

The calculation of the start and end of a statutory time period is prescribed by a complex interaction of California laws. The text box: Time Periods and Deadlines Simplified has a summary. The rules for calculating deadlines are found in CCP § 2 through 34. Time periods **start the day after** the trigger for the time limit occurs and **expire at midnight on the last day** of the time period. If the last day of a time period is a holiday, **the time period is extended to the next day that is not a holiday**. Per CCP § 12:

> 12. The time in which any act provided by law is to be done is computed by excluding the first day, and including the last, unless the last day is a holiday, and then it is also excluded.

That language is identical to the language quoted under Basic Rule for Time Periods, found at Gov. Code § 6800:

> 6800. The time in which any act provided by law is to be done is computed by excluding the first day, and including the last, unless the last day is a holiday, and then it is also excluded.

[126] https://www.sf.gov/information--city-and-county-san-francisco-holiday-schedule.

If the time period is expressed as "business days," holidays do not count toward the days in the time period. The definition of a holiday is explained under Which Days are Holidays?

Counting Backward

Some time periods are triggered by an action or event in the future, and the time period must be calculated by counting backward from the date of that future action or event. This is most common when there is a **notice period** associated with a **hearing.**

CCP § 12c provides direction specific to counting backward from a ***hearing date***:

> 12c. (a) Where any law requires an act to be performed no later than a specified number of days before a hearing date, the last day to perform that act shall be determined by **counting backward from the hearing date**, excluding the day of the hearing as provided by Section 12.
>
> (b) Any additional days added to the specified number of days because of a particular method of service shall be computed by counting backward from the day determined in accordance with subdivision (a).

So, when counting backward from a hearing date, the "first day" of the computation under CCP § 12 is the hearing date, which is excluded from the time period, and the "last day" is the latest date on which the act may be done (e.g., notice may be made). The act may be done on the "last day" or earlier than the last day.

Notwithstanding CCP § 12a or CCP § 13, the Author's interpretation[127] of CCP § 12c is that if the "last day" counting backward is a holiday, then the act **must** be done no later than the first business day **before** that holiday. The Author's interpretation is conservative: if the act is done on a business day **before** the "last day"/holiday it will meet the deadline. Another interpretation is that the act **could** be done on the "last day" even if that day is a holiday, but it is not clear to the Author whether an act done on a holiday is legally counted as done on that day, especially when counting backward.

Example: Public Hearing for a Zoning Ordinance or Amendment

Gov. Code § 65854 as amended by AB 2094 (2024) specifies the notice period prior to a planning commission hearing on a proposed zoning ordinance or amendment:

> 65854. (a) The planning commission shall hold a public hearing on the proposed zoning ordinance or amendment to a zoning ordinance.
>
> (b) (1) Except as provided in paragraph (2), notice of the hearing shall be given pursuant to Section 65090.
>
> (2) If a proposed ordinance or amendment to a zoning ordinance affects the ***permitted uses*** of real property, notice of the hearing shall be given pursuant to Sections 65090 and 65091, except that the notice shall be published, posted, mailed, and delivered, or advertised, as applicable, at least **20 days before the hearing**.

Paragraph (b)(2) requires a 20-day notice period when the ordinance or amendment will affect the permitted uses of a real property, rather than the normal 10-day notice period required by paragraph (b)(1), which cross references to Gov. Code § 65090:

> 65090. (a) When a provision of this title requires notice of a public hearing to be given pursuant to this section, notice shall be published pursuant to Section 6061 in at least one newspaper of general circulation within the jurisdiction of the local agency which is conducting the proceeding at least **10 days prior to the hearing**, or if there is no such newspaper

[127] The Author has reviewed the Legislative Counsel's Digest and the Senate Floor, Senate Judiciary, and Assembly Judiciary analyses of AB 2119 (2010) that added CCP § 12c, available at https://leginfo.legislature.ca.gov/faces/billAnalysisClient.xhtml?bill_id=200920100AB2119. He bases his interpretation on the Senate Judiciary analysis (page 3, emphasis added): "The filing and service deadline then will need to be verified by counting backward from the potential hearing date, excluding from the count the date of the hearing, to make certain the filing and service **deadlines do not fall on a holiday** and conforms to Code of Civil Procedure Section 12."

of general circulation, the notice shall be posted at least **10 days prior to the hearing** in at least three public places within the jurisdiction of the local agency. ...

In this example, it is clear that the triggering event is a hearing, and the notice period runs 10 or 20 days prior to the hearing date. Therefore, the notice period would be counted backward from the hearing date in accordance with CCP § 12c.

If the hearing date is a Tuesday and the notice period is 10 days, the Tuesday is excluded and counting backward 10 days makes the "last day" a Saturday. The Author's interpretation[128] is that the notice must be provided no later than the Friday before the Saturday holiday (assuming that the Friday is not also a holiday). Under the Author's interpretation the party receiving the notice will receive it on a business day and have the full 10 days for their response to the notice.

Missing a Deadline (Usually) Has Consequences

State housing laws have increasingly imposed consequences for missing deadlines and strengthened enforcement of time limits for jurisdictions to act. HCD has enforcement authority over most state housing laws and maintains an archive of Technical Assistance and Enforcement Letters.[129] Many of those letters discuss deadlines. Both applicants and jurisdictions can request technical assistance from HCD to interpret housing laws generally, and to solicit interpretations and guidance for specific projects.

For the applicant, the Deadlines to Maintain SB 330 Vesting are critical, especially for Builder's Remedy Projects. The section on Deadlines to Maintain SB 330 Vesting contains examples of how the Town of Los Gatos tried to stop builder's remedy projects. While those projects did not, despite what Los Gatos claimed in court, lose their vesting rights, it should be clear that applicants must strictly comply with time periods and deadlines.

Likewise, applicants should carefully track the deadlines applicable to jurisdictions. Some real-life examples will demonstrate how important it is to correctly calculate time periods and deadlines, and how serious the consequences of a missed deadline can be.

Example 1: Richards Ranch Project — 30 Day Completeness Review

Gov. Code § 65943 sets the 30-day time period for completeness review, after which an application for a development permit is **deemed** complete. Deemed completeness, in turn, triggers the start of the 30- or 45-day Time Period for the Review for Exemption, and if the project is determined to be exempt from CEQA that determination triggers a Deadline for Initial Approval or Disapproval of the Project.

The "Richards Ranch" project in the Orcutt area of unincorporated Santa Barbara County proposed 750 units. The developer submitted a full development permit application on May 31, 2024, and the County issued letters of incompleteness three times as the developer struggled to get the jurisdiction to determine the application complete[130] so that other deadlines would be triggered and the project eventually would get a hearing. (See The Real World of Development Permit Review for the Author's similar experiences.) However, the applicant and the County disagreed on whether the *third* letter of incompleteness was issued within the statutory time limit of 30 days. As reported in an HCD letter *RE: County of Santa Barbara – Richards Ranch – Letter of Technical Assistance*, dated August 25, 2025:[131]

---

[128] Ibid.

[129] Select "Technical Assistance and Enforcement Letters" at this website: https://www.hcd.ca.gov/hau. After downloading the Microsoft Excel file, search or sort by the jurisdiction and the area of law.

[130] For example, the county attempted to stop the project over a typographical error, as reported in a different HCD letter dated April 7, 2025: https://www.hcd.ca.gov/sites/default/files/docs/planning-and-community/HAU/santabarbara-co-hau-1423-ta-04072025.pdf.

[131] https://www.hcd.ca.gov/sites/default/files/docs/planning-and-community/HAU/santa-barbara-county-hau-1423-ta-082525.pdf.

> HCD understands there is a disagreement between the County and the applicant regarding when the 30-day period began for the second resubmittal due to the Martin Luthur King, Jr., holiday on January 20, 2025. HCD understands that the County's web based application submittal system was open and received the application on January 20, 2025. The applicant operated under the assumption that the date of submittal was recorded on that date and did not receive notification to the contrary from the County during the assumed 30-day period. Moreover, the County's website contains an applicant-facing interface that stated the date of application receipt as January 20, 2025.
>
> State law provides that the time in which any act provided by law is to be done is computed by excluding the first day, and including the last, unless the last day is a holiday, and then it is also excluded.[footnote omitted] This would mean that the holiday is only excluded if it falls on the final day of the 30-day period. However, in this case, the holiday fell on the day of submission, January 20, meaning the first calendar day of the 30-day period fell on January 21, not on January 22 as the County asserts. As a result, the 30-day period ended on February 19, but the County issued an incompleteness determination on February 20, a day late. Therefore, a determination was not issued by the County within the 30-day period and the application must be deemed complete.

In this example, the time period is counted forward from the submittal date. The first day is always excluded, so January 20, 2025, would have been excluded regardless of it being a holiday. The time period under Gov. Code § 65943 is **not** expressed as "business days" so intervening holidays count toward the 30-day deadline. The County did not get an "extra" day because the application was submitted on a holiday. If instead the ***last*** day of the time period had fallen on a holiday, the time period would have been extended to the next business day.

The consequence of the jurisdiction missing the deadline to send an incompleteness letter was that the application was deemed complete, triggering the CEQA review and compliance review periods.

Example 2: *Latinos Unidos de Napa v. City of Napa* (2011) — 30 Day NOD Posting Requirement

In a 2011 court case,[132] that the California Planning & Development Report called[133] "a feat of chronological gymnastics," the Court of Appeal found that the Clerk of Napa County did not post a CEQA Notice of Determination (NOD) for the required posting period of 30 full days, and therefore a CEQA lawsuit was **not** barred by a shorter Statute of Limitations for CEQA Lawsuits that applies when CEQA determinations are properly posted. The Clerk posted the NOD at approximately 10:00 am on June 17, 2009, and it remained posted until approximately 10:00 am on July 17. That period spans thirty-one (31) twenty-four-hour periods. Latinos Unidos (an affordable housing advocacy group) came to the Clerk's office at approximately 11:00 am on July 17 and saw no NOD posted.

On September 17, 2009, Latinos Unidos sued to overturn the subject CEQA determination. The City of Napa won the case at the trial court, arguing that 10:00 am on June 17 to 10:00 am on July 17 is 31 days, and that even though time periods begin the day **after** the trigger for the time period, the posting had continued for the required 30 days. The trial court granted Napa's motion to dismiss.

Latinos Unidad appealed. The Court of Appeal reversed the trial court, finding a **partial** day does not count toward a time period.[134] In other words, not only did the first day not count, but the last day did not count, because the NOD was not posted for the entire 30th day. Therefore, the NOD was not properly posted, and the shorter 30-day statute of limitations provided by Guidelines § 15112(c)(1) did not apply. The full 180-day statute of limitations had not expired on September 17, 2009, when Latinos Unidos filed their court action.

---

[132] *Latinos Unidos de Napa v. City of Napa* (2011) 196 Cal. App. 4th 1154, No. A129584.

[133] https://www.cp-dr.com/articles/node-3046.

[134] The Court of Appeal based its finding on *Scoville v. Anderson* (1901) 131 Cal. 590 and other case law.

The consequence of the county clerk not keeping the posting up for the full 30th day was that the lawsuit, which would otherwise have been barred by the shorter statute of limitations, was allowed to proceed. See Filing and Posting CEQA Notices for more information on CEQA filings and postings.

The Path to Final Approval

As explained in Chapter 9: Compliance Review, subject to narrow exceptions involving specified written findings, the jurisdiction **must approve** the housing development project (in many cases requiring the project to be approved **as proposed**), and cannot impose conditions that would render the project infeasible. Jurisdictions Focus on Compliance and Conformity with Local Standards, but Applicants Should Focus on Completeness and CEQA, because they control the **critical path** of the project schedule.

Critical Path Milestones

The "critical path" is the chain of activities/tasks that control the end date of a schedule. Each task on the critical path has a duration, and the sequence of those durations determines the duration of the entire schedule. Tasks that are not on the critical path are not "driving" the schedule. For a typical housing development project, the milestones on the critical path leading to final, unappealable approval of the project, without the possibility of a CEQA lawsuit, are:

1. SB 330 preliminary application submittal. (See Chapter 6: SB 330 Preliminary Application.)
1. Full development permit application submittal. (See Chapter 5: Overall Development Permit Review Process & How AB 130 Changes It.)
2. Application "accepted as complete," or deemed complete due to the jurisdiction missing a 30 day deadline for written notice of incompleteness in accordance with Gov. Code § 65943(a) or (b). (See Chapter 8: Completeness Review.)
3. Preliminary CEQA determination. (See Deadline for Initial Approval or Disapproval of the Project.)
4. Initial approval / disapproval by the planning commission or a lesser decisionmaker (see Decisionmakers and Decisionmaking Bodies), or Deemed Approval — New with AB 130.
5. Appeal(s) of the decision(s) of lesser decisionmakers.
6. Final approval / disapproval of the project.
7. Expiration of the Statute of Limitations for CEQA Lawsuits.

Applicants should focus on achieving these milestones because they drive the schedule.

Always Submit an SB 330 Preliminary Application

As explained in the introduction to Chapter 6: SB 330 Preliminary Application, the Author cannot think of any situation where a preliminary application should not be submitted. Submitting an SB 330 preliminary application does not extend the timeline for the project, because the preliminary application requires only a small subset of the information that the applicant must submit for a full development permit application, and the preliminary application is deemed complete upon submittal.

Not submitting an SB 330 preliminary application can cause delays, especially for projects using the PRC § 21080.66 Statutory Exemption — New with AB 130. The SB 330 preliminary application will Trigger the Tribal Process for the PRC 21080.66 CEQA Exemption, which can take up to 148 days. In addition, as explained in Chapter 7: Vesting the Development Standards, an SB 330 preliminary application vests more development standards, earlier, and for a longer period of time than if the project had only the vesting rights provided by the full development permit application. ***Not*** having those SB 330 vesting rights could cause project delays if development standards change.

Make the 1st Submittal of the Full Development Permit Application as Complete as Practicable

After submitting the SB 330 preliminary application, the applicant must meet the 180-Day Deadline for 1st Submittal of the Full Development Permit Application. As explained in The Real World of Development Permit Review and in Chapter 8: Completeness Review it is very difficult to submit a *complete* full development permit application on the first try, and even if the 1st submittal *is* complete, the jurisdiction is still likely to take three rounds of review before determining the application to be complete.

However, the key milestone that drives the entitlement schedule is the CEQA determination, and the jurisdiction will review each submittal for CEQA, so applicants should strive to make the 1st submittal of the development permit application as nearly complete as they can, with all the information that the jurisdiction needs to determine that the project qualifies for the requested CEQA exemption.

Achieve a Complete Application

It typically takes at least three submittals before the jurisdiction will accept the application as complete. Each resubmittal must meet the 90-Day Deadline for Each Resubmittal of the Full Development Permit Application. After each submittal, the jurisdiction has 30 days to review the application for completeness, and if they fail to send written notice within 30 days, the application will be **deemed complete** in accordance with Gov. Code § 65943. For a detailed explanation, with tips for achieving application completeness without unnecessary delay, see Chapter 8: Completeness Review.

Focus on Obtaining the Determination that the Project is Exempt from CEQA

The date on which the jurisdiction accepts the application as complete (or the application is deemed complete because the jurisdiction misses the 30-day deadline to deliver an incompleteness letter) triggers a 30- or 45-day Time Period for the Review for Exemption. However, there are no automatic consequences if the jurisdiction does not make a CEQA determination within that time period; the project is **not** deemed exempt.

Most housing projects are exempt from CEQA. If the applicant does not request otherwise, the jurisdiction should apply the PRC § 21080.66 Statutory Exemption — New with AB 130 automatically, but the applicant should decide which CEQA exemption(s) they want applied to the project. Use a Pre-App Review to Begin CEQA Consultation with the jurisdiction and determine the required documentation necessary for the jurisdiction to apply the desired exemption; this is especially important for exemptions other than PRC § 21080.66. Provide the necessary documentation to establish that the site and project qualify for the desired CEQA exemption, with the 1st Submittal. Otherwise, the process of reviewing the project to determine whether it qualifies for a CEQA exemption could significantly delay the project.

If the project does not qualify for a CEQA exemption, the Initial Study and Environmental Determinations Other Than Exemptions will extend the project schedule for many months.

Know the Deadline for the First Approval / Disapproval of the Project

With the passage of AB 130 (2025), once the jurisdiction makes the determination that a project is exempt from CEQA (or adopts a Negative Declaration or Mitigated Negative Declaration), the jurisdiction is on a strict, self-enforcing deadline to approve or disapprove the project. The deadline depends on the type of CEQA exemption, as explained under Deadline for Initial Approval or Disapproval of the Project. Know the deadline. If the jurisdiction misses the deadline the consequence is Deemed Approval — New with AB 130.

Expect the Decision(s) of Lesser Decisionmakers to be Appealed

Appeals are very common. The appeal process is prescribed by the jurisdiction in its local code, so it is unique to every jurisdiction. If the Know the Deadline for the First Approval / Disapproval of the Project is by a decisionmaker lesser than the planning commission there will likely be two levels of appeal: for example, first appealing the zoning administrator or planning director's decision to the planning commission, and then appealing the planning commission decision to the legislative body. (See Decisionmakers and Decisionmaking Bodies.) In addition, hearings can be "continued" to a later date. Community meetings, hearings before advisory bodies, multiple levels of decisionmakers, and continuances of hearings are a major driver of project delays, but jurisdictions cannot subject a project to more than five total meetings / hearings, after the ***submittal*** of the **complete** full development permit application.

The Final Approval / Disapproval of the Project is Often by the Elected Legislative Body

Approvals by lesser decisionmakers are appealable to the legislative body of the jurisdiction (i.e., the city council or county board of supervisors). The decision of the legislative body is final. Applicants should anticipate that one or more appeals will be filed and the ultimate decision to approve or disapprove the project will be made by the elected legislative body of the jurisdiction. The City Councilmembers or County Supervisors are politicians, and depending on the political climate around housing and the controversy about the specific project it is possible that they will make decisions based on politics rather than on an objective review of the project in keeping with state laws.

For applicants, one purpose of the project documentation leading up to the final hearing is to **ensure that it would be a *violation* of the Housing Accountability Act** if the decisionmakers do not approve the project as proposed. But applicants should also engage with neighbors, community leaders, pro-housing advocates, and elected officials to build political support for the project. Give the politicians strong political reasons to say "yes."

Don't Celebrate Until the CEQA Statute of Limitations Expires

As explained under Statute of Limitations for CEQA Lawsuits, the statute of limitations is **not** an "appeal period" and the applicant can proceed with the development process without waiting for the statute of limitations to expire. However, until the expiration of the statute of limitations, there is a risk that project opponents will bring an action in court to challenge the project's CEQA determination. Once the statute of limitations has expired, a lawsuit seeking to overturn the CEQA determination cannot succeed. Take a moment to celebrate, the project is well and truly entitled.

Five Hearing Rule

SB 330 (2019) added the "five hearing rule" at Gov. Code § 65905.5. Put simply, the jurisdiction "shall not conduct more than five hearings" (as "hearing" is defined by Gov. Code § 65905.5(b)(2)), and is required to "either approve or disapprove the application at any of the five hearings." The five hearing limit includes "continued" hearings and appeal hearings. If the jurisdiction does not "either approve or disapprove the application at any of the five hearings," the project is not automatically deemed approved, but the applicant can bring an action to enforce the rule, as explained under Enforcing the Five Hearing Rule.

Taking each of the subdivisions and paragraphs of Gov. Code § 65905.5 in turn:

> 65905.5. (a) Notwithstanding any other law, if a proposed housing development project complies with the applicable, objective general plan and zoning standards in effect at the time an application is deemed complete, after the application is deemed complete, a city, county, or city and county **shall not conduct more than five hearings** pursuant to Section 65905, or any other law, ordinance, or regulation requiring a public hearing in connection with the approval of that

housing development project. If the city, county, or city and county continues a hearing subject to this section to another date, the **continued hearing shall count as one of the five hearings** allowed under this section. The city, county, or city and county shall consider and **either approve or disapprove the application at any of the five hearings** allowed under this section consistent with the applicable timelines under the Permit Streamlining Act (Chapter 4.5 (commencing with Section 65920)).

The definitions applicable to this Section are in subdivision (b), starting with the term "deemed complete," which is not the same definition as "deemed complete" in the Housing Accountability:

(b) For purposes of this section:

(1) "Deemed complete" means that the application has met all of the requirements specified in the relevant list compiled pursuant to Section 65940 that was available at the time when the application was submitted.

This definition of "deemed complete" does ***not*** mean the date the SB 330 preliminary application was submitted, like it does in the Housing Accountability Act. The cross-reference to Gov. Code § 65940 means that "deemed complete" is in reference to the list of required items for a ***full*** development permit application, so "the application has met all of the requirements ... pursuant to Section 65940 ... at the time when the application was submitted" means the date that the final application, which the jurisdiction later determined to be complete, was **submitted**; or the date the full development permit application is **deemed complete** because the jurisdiction failed to meet the 30-day time limit for completeness review prescribed by Gov. Code § 65943(a) or (b).

Because "deemed complete" in this Section is ***not*** in reference to the SB 330 preliminary application, meetings and hearings that occur ***before*** the complete full application is submitted do not count toward the five hearings.

Next, "hearing" is broadly defined, but it does not include hearings/meetings that are not "conducted by" the jurisdiction, and it does not include hearings/meetings related to a "legislative approval":

(2) "Hearing" includes any public hearing, workshop, or similar meeting, including any appeal, **conducted by the city or county** with respect to the housing development project, including any meeting relating to Section 65915, whether by the legislative body of the city or county, the planning agency established pursuant to Section 65100, or any other agency, department, board, commission, or any other designated hearing officer or body of the city or county, or any committee or subcommittee thereof. "Hearing" **does not include a hearing to review a legislative approval**, including any appeal, required for a proposed housing development project, including, but not limited to, a general plan amendment, a specific plan adoption or amendment, or a zoning amendment, or any hearing arising from a timely appeal of the approval or disapproval of a legislative approval.

HCD provided guidance on the interpretation of the phrase "conducted by the city or county" in a letter *RE: City of Oceanside – 503 Vista Bella – Letter of Support and Technical Assistance,*[135] dated May 14, 2025 (page 4, emphasis in original):

Five Hearing Rule

Do community outreach meetings count towards the five hearing limit when the local agency requires them to be conducted as part of the project entitlement process?

Yes, community meetings count towards the five hearing limit when they are required to be conducted by law, ordinance, or regulation. HCD understands that the Project has already been heard at two community meetings (December 13, 2023 and May 15, 2024), one Planning Commission hearing (October 28, 2024), and one City Council hearing (January 22, 2025) after the application was deemed complete on September 25, 2023. Therefore, to require any hearing beyond the City Council hearing scheduled for May 21, 2025 would violate the five hearing rule.

---

[135] https://www.hcd.ca.gov/sites/default/files/docs/planning-and-community/HAU/oceanside-hau-1922-los-ta-051425.pdf.

> The statute is clear that after the application is deemed complete, the City "shall not conduct more than five hearings pursuant to Section 65905, or any other law, ordinance, regulation requiring a public hearing in connection with the approval of that housing development project."[footnote omitted] The City's Enhanced Notification Program[footnote omitted] requires applicants proposing housing development projects containing five or more units to draft and implement a Community Outreach Plan as part of the entitlement process, whereby the City establishes the number of hearings and the manner in which the community meetings are noticed and conducted. Since the City requires the meetings to be held and dictates the process that the applicant must follow, the community meetings are, in effect, conducted by the City for the purposes of this statute and count towards the five hearing limit.

Based on this HCD guidance, any meeting or hearing that the jurisdiction ***requires to be conducted*** should count towards the five hearing limit, even if the applicant "conducts" the meeting, as is often the case for community meetings. A meeting or hearing that is not required or conducted by the jurisdiction (e.g., impromptu meetings between the developer and neighbors, or voluntary community meetings held by the developer that were not required by the jurisdiction, and where the employees or officials of the jurisdiction did not conduct the meeting) does not count toward the five hearing limit.

A "hearing to review a legislative approval" is one in which a new or amended ordinance, regulation, or other legislation is considered or adopted. Paragraph (2) gives the examples of amendments to or adoption of a general plan, specific plan, or zoning code. A hearing to review a project for consistency with ***existing*** ordinances, policies, and standards is ***not*** a "hearing to review a legislative approval."

The definition of "housing development project" is the same as in the Housing Accountability Act, except it includes a project to develop one single family home.

> (3) (A) "Housing development project" has the same meaning as defined in paragraph (2) of subdivision (h) of Section 65589.5.
>
> (B) "Housing development project" includes, but is not limited to, projects that involve no discretionary approvals and projects that involve both discretionary and nondiscretionary approvals.
>
> (C) "Housing development project" includes a proposal to construct a single dwelling unit. This subparagraph shall not affect the interpretation of the scope of paragraph (2) of subdivision (h) of Section 65589.5.

In subdivision (c), the five hearing rule provides "reasonable person" and "receipt of a density bonus" provisions in paragraph (1); and a "zoning for the project site is inconsistent with the general plan" provision in paragraph (2) that mirror similar provisions in the Housing Accountability Act.

> (c) (1) For purposes of this section, a housing development project shall be deemed consistent, compliant, and in conformity with an applicable plan, program, policy, ordinance, standard, requirement, or other similar provision if there is substantial evidence that would allow a reasonable person to conclude that the housing development project is consistent, compliant, or in conformity. The receipt of a density bonus including any incentives, concessions, or waivers pursuant to Section 65915 shall not constitute a valid basis on which to find that a proposed housing development project is inconsistent, not in compliance, or not in conformity, with an applicable plan, program, policy, ordinance, standard, requirement, or other similar provision.
>
> (2) A proposed housing development project is not inconsistent with the applicable zoning standards and criteria, and shall not require a rezoning, if the housing development project is consistent with the objective general plan standards and criteria, but the zoning for the project site is inconsistent with the general plan. If the local agency complies with the written documentation requirements of paragraph (2) of subdivision (j) of Section 65589.5, the local agency may require the proposed housing development project to comply with the objective standards and criteria of the zoning that is consistent with the general plan; however, the standards and criteria shall be applied

> to facilitate and accommodate development at the density allowed on the site by the general plan and proposed by the proposed housing development project.

Per subdivision (a), the five hearing rule only applies "if a proposed housing development project complies with the applicable, objective general plan and zoning standards in effect at the time an application is deemed complete," and per subdivision (b) "deemed complete" for purposes of the five hearing rule is with respect to the **full** development permit application rather than the SB 330 preliminary application. Yet paragraph (2) of subdivision (c) references Gov. Code § 65589.5(j)(2) in the Housing Accountability Act where "deemed complete" means the submittal date of the SB 330 preliminary application. Applicants should be aware of this odd inconsistency in the vesting of development standards, and hopefully the Legislature will clean up the inconsistency between Gov. Code § 65905.5 and Gov. Code § 65589.5.

Subdivision (d) relates to CEQA review. For Environmental Determinations Other Than Exemptions public and hearings are required to review, adopt, and/or certify the environmental documents and determinations. The five hearing limit **may be exceeded** if necessary for CEQA purposes.

> (d) Nothing in this section supersedes, limits, or otherwise modifies the requirements of, or the standards of review pursuant to, Division 13 (commencing with Section 21000) of the Public Resources Code.

Subdivision (e) is only relevant to projects submitted before 2022. Gov. Code § 65905.5 has been amended several times since it was added in 2019. AB 130 (2025) removed provisions in this and many other housing laws that would have caused them to "sunset" on a certain date. Before that, SB 8 (2021) cleaned up the language in subdivisions (b) and (c) and extended the sunset date for this Section. Subdivision (e) states that the changes made by SB 8, which became effective on January 1, 2022, were "declaratory of existing law," but that if a project had submitted a ministerial project application before January 1, 2022, that application was not affected by SB 8's changes to Gov. Code § 65905.5(b)(3)(B).

> (e) The amendments to subdivisions (b) and (c) made by the act adding this subdivision do not constitute a change in, but are declaratory of, existing law. However, the amendments to this section in subparagraph (B) of paragraph (3) of subdivision (b) shall not affect a project for which an application was submitted to the city, county, or city and county before January 1, 2022.

Enforcing the Five Hearing Rule

Gov. Code § 65905.5 prescribes no consequences if the jurisdiction violates the five hearing rule, but with the passage of AB 1893 (2024), failure to comply with Gov. Code § 65905.5 is included in the definition of "disapprove the housing development project." (Gov. Code § 65589.5(h)(6)(F).) Thus, failure to "either approve or disapprove the application at any of the five hearings" is grounds for Enforcing the Housing Accountability Act. In addition, Gov. Code § 65905.5 is a "housing reform law" and failure to comply with it is grounds for Enforcing Other Housing Reform Laws.

Strategy Note — Hearings by Lesser Decisionmakers

The following is general guidance, based on the Author's experience, and applies only to **discretionary** housing development permits. It **does *not* apply to *ministerial*** permits, since state law prohibits public hearings for ministerial applications, ministerial approvals cannot be appealed, and CEQA does not apply to ministerial projects. It ***does*** apply to **administrative decisions** on **discretionary** development permits, such as when a Zoning Administrator (ZA) or Development Director has the authority to approve certain types of discretionary projects, subject to appeal. See Planning Agency of the Jurisdiction and Decisionmakers and Decisionmaking Bodies for background information relevant to this section.

Why Do Jurisdictions Appoint Lesser Decisionmakers

Without a planning commission, the city council or county board of supervisors would be too busy reviewing development permits to do other work, so all but the smallest jurisdictions appoint a planning commission. Larger jurisdictions often adopt development codes that assign authority for review and approval of some types of projects to an administrator (a Zoning Administrator, Development Director, or the Director's designee) so that the planning commission can work on long-range planning and more complex projects. As state laws have increasingly limited the discretion of local agencies to disapprove, modify, or demand revisions and concessions from housing development projects, jurisdictions have increasingly considered assigning authority for approval of various types of housing projects to administrators. Under the development code of some jurisdictions, if there is no *written* opposition to a housing project, the project can be approved by an administrator without a public hearing.

Project Appeals are Time-Consuming and Costly

Despite all the state laws prohibiting disapproval of housing projects that meet objective standards, housing development project approvals are routinely and frequently appealed. Appeals add months to the approval process, as each hearing requires a public notice period, decision makers only meet a couple times per month (and take time off over summer and winter holiday periods), and considerable time is spent negotiating with appellants and modifying project plans in response to the demands of the opposition and the jurisdiction's elected officials. These months of delay are very costly.

Project opponents, who don't understand the complex interaction between state and local laws, may appeal the project based on perceived flaws in the decisionmaker's approval. Appellants simply write a letter of appeal and pay a fee of a few hundred dollars. Those appeals then delay the project and cost the developer potentially hundreds of thousands of dollars. The appeals process gives project opponents time to organize, search the plans for purported inconsistencies with the local code or state laws, pitch their arguments and grievances to elected officials, and drum up controversy on local news websites and social media.

The Developer May Need to Appeal Their Own Project

Not all appeals are by opponents; the **applicant** may need to appeal. Applicants appeal for three main reasons:

1. The project was improperly or ***illegally* disapproved**. In this case, the applicant would appeal the disapproval of the project and (together with their attorney) provide legal arguments for why the project as proposed must be approved in compliance with the state housing laws. They would also educate the jurisdiction on the potential consequences of violating those laws.
2. The project was ***legally* disapproved**, and by making the proper findings. In this case, the applicant would appeal the disapproval and revise the project to bring it into compliance, if possible.
3. The project was **approved, but *not* as proposed** (i.e., conditions of approval were imposed on the project that are not acceptable to the applicant). If the jurisdiction violated state law, the appeal would provide legal arguments as in #1. If the applicant simply wants a second chance to convince the jurisdiction to approve the project as proposed, or with different changes or conditions than those that were imposed, the appeal would make the case for the original or a revised proposal.
    a. Note that it is often less risky to "take the win" of a less-than-perfect approval, than to appeal that approval and risk a disapproval at the appeal hearing. Always read and understand the appeal process in the local development code. Appeals are often "de novo," meaning that the appeal is a new hearing and the entire project is reconsidered, not just the specific matters that were appealed.

b. Most jurisdictions have a type of application called a "major modification" that allows the applicant to go back and make substantive changes to the project after final approval. If the modification application is disapproved, the original approval stands. That is much less risky than a "de novo" hearing.

Applicants will generally want to avoid appeals, but as explained below, they should take projects first to the planning commission and not go directly to the city council or board of supervisors (given the option).

Projects Can be Moved Up to a Higher Decisionmaker

In most cases, the local development code will provide that the jurisdiction **can**, on a case-by-case basis, have the planning commission conduct hearings that normally would be heard by an administrator, and have the city council or county board of supervisors take jurisdiction of projects before they are heard by the planning commission. Often the characteristics of the project determine whether an administrator has authority to review and approve the project. For example, a jurisdiction's development code may provide that projects conforming to all development standards will be heard by an administrator, but projects that request a variance must be heard before the planning commission.

The Planning Commission is Usually Best for the First Hearing

Given the option, the Author would generally prefer to take any housing project that relies on state laws to the planning commission, even if the project **could** be approved by a lesser decisionmaker. Unlike a planning commission hearing, a representative from the City Attorney or County Counsel is typically **not** present at an administrative hearing, so the administrator cannot seek legal advice during the hearing. Furthermore, the administrator is one individual, so they do not have the benefit of commentary and discussion amongst peers that is part of a planning commission hearing. Administrators are employees of the planning department and generally see their role as policing the local development code, but most housing projects use state laws that preempt local development standards. The administrator may not feel they have the authority to go against the development code or general plan policies, even if state law preempts those standards.

Planning Commissioners, who are volunteers appointed by the city council or county board of supervisors, care very much about the way their community is developed and are often strong advocates of housing and economic development. They are typically familiar with state laws that apply to housing projects. They have often read *The Planning Commissioner Handbook*[136] and may be architects or other building-industry professionals. In most cases, the staff report recommends approval of the project. Planning Commissioners tend to show deference to the professional planning staff and the jurisdiction's attorneys, who write the staff report and represent the jurisdiction during the hearing. Planning Commissioners generally follow state housing laws and the local development code to the best of their ability. They are the decision-making body most likely to "get it right."

If the planning commission **approves** the project, and then the project is appealed to the city council or county board of supervisors, the Councilmembers or Supervisors (who appointed the Planning Commissioners because of their interest and expertise in development matters) are not inclined to undermine the planning commission. The council or board is likely to **reject an appeal** of a project that the planning commission has approved.

If the planning commission **disapproves** the project, or does not approve the project the way the applicant wants, the applicant can appeal the decision to the council or board. This gives the developer one final chance to work through political channels to get the project approved as proposed, without resorting to a lawsuit to enforce state housing laws.

---

[136] https://www.ilgplanninghandbook.org/.

The Planning Commissioners are Reasonable People

Several state housing laws stipulate a "reasonable person standard" that is very pro-housing. In the Housing Accountability Act, the reasonable person standard is at Gov. Code § 65589.5(f)(4):

> (4) For purposes of this section, a housing development project or emergency shelter shall be deemed consistent, compliant, and in conformity with an applicable plan, program, policy, ordinance, standard, requirement, or other similar provision if there is substantial evidence that would allow a **reasonable person** to conclude that the housing development project or emergency shelter is consistent, compliant, or in conformity.

If the planning commission approves a project, and their decision is appealed to the city council or board of supervisor, the applicant should advise the jurisdiction that the approval of the planning commission is clear evidence that the project is "deemed consistent, compliant, and in conformity" because the planning commissioners are reasonable people who concluded that the project is compliant when they approved the project. Even if the appellant's arguments are also reasonable, the council/board should approve the project, because the reasonable person standard was met when the planning commissioners concluded that the project was compliant.

If the council/board disapproves the project, the applicant has a strong case for Enforcing the Housing Accountability Act in court. The court should find that the substantial evidence in the record allowed the reasonable people of the planning commission to conclude that the project was compliant. State laws require that housing development permits ***shall be approved*** if they are consistent with the applicable objective standards. Under the reasonable person standard, the project ***is* consistent** with the standard in question if a reasonable person could conclude that the project is consistent with that standard.

Avoid Going Directly to the City Council / Board of Supervisors

In certain cases, it may be possible, or required, to have the project's first approval/disapproval hearing before the city council or board of supervisors. For example, in small jurisdictions that do not have a planning commission, or when a Councilmember or Supervisor "calls up" the project in accordance with a provision of local code. The applicant may think that a one-and-done hearing before the city council or board of supervisors is preferable to a hearing before the planning commission with the high likelihood of an expensive and time-consuming appeal.

But skipping the planning commission and going directly to the city council or board of supervisors for the first hearing on a project is risky. Councilmembers and Supervisors are **politicians** that are prone to siding with angry neighbors. They are often resentful of the state's interference in their conduct of local development affairs. They do not always defer to the recommendations of their own planning staff and attorneys. If possible, applicants should avoid going directly to the council or board, and have the project heard before the planning commission.

When the council/board of the jurisdiction approves or denies the development permit application, that decision **cannot be appealed**. Some jurisdictions do have a process for "reconsideration" of a final decision, but reconsiderations are unusual, and unlikely to overturn a denial of the development permit. When a project has been disapproved or approved with unacceptable conditions by the council/board, the applicant should confirm that the project has **exhausted its administrative remedies**.[137] Then, in cases where the council/board has violated state housing laws, the developer (and other persons with "standing") can file a lawsuit for a "writ of mandate." See Enforcing the Housing Accountability Act.

[137] Consult an attorney. Courts typically will not hear a case until all administrative remedies (i.e., appeals) have been exhausted.

The Housing Accountability Act Requires that Projects *Shall be Approved* Unless ...

As explained in Chapter 9: Compliance Review, jurisdictions are required to approve a housing development project, unless they make specific "written findings" supported by / based upon "a preponderance of the evidence on the record." Further, the jurisdiction cannot impose conditions that would render a subdivision (d) project infeasible (see Subdivision (d) Projects Must be Approved, even if Not Compliant) or that would require a subdivision (j) project to be developed at a lower density. (Gov. Code § 65589.5(d) and (j)(1).) The Housing Accountability Act and other housing reform laws impose many other limits on a jurisdiction's discretion to disapprove or impose conditions on housing projects.

Congratulations, Your Project is Approved! Now What?

Track the date of final approval of the project. If construction is not commenced by the deadlines at Gov. Code § 65589.5(o)(2)(D) (for projects that are 100% affordable, 3.5 years after final approval, and for other projects 2.5 years) the project's **SB 330 vesting rights expire**, as explained under Duration of Vesting When an SB 330 Preliminary Application Applies. The definition of "final approval" for purposes of this provision is at Gov. Code § 65589.5(o)(2)(D)(ii):

> (ii) "Final approval" means that the housing development project has received all necessary approvals to be eligible to apply for, and obtain, a building permit or permits and either of the following is met:
>
> > (I) The expiration of all applicable appeal periods, petition periods, reconsideration periods, or statute of limitations for challenging that final approval without an appeal, petition, request for reconsideration, or legal challenge having been filed.
> >
> > (II) If a challenge is filed, that challenge is fully resolved or settled in favor of the housing development project.

In addition, the local development code, or the conditions of approval of the project, will specify a time period after which the **entitlement will expire**, if not extended (by a local-code mechanism, or state law). Usually, this time period is also tied to a definition of "final approval." Generally, pulling any type of building, grading, or demolition permit "vests" the entitlement, and construction can continue as long as needed without the entitlement expiring. Check the local code and conditions of approval and consult your attorney.

The plan check and permitting process are now subject to state laws regarding "postentitlement phase permits," which are beyond the scope of this book. Note however that although postentitlement phase permits (e.g., a building permit) are not development permits, failure to meet the deadlines for review and approval of postentitlement phase permits ***also*** constitutes disapproval of a housing development project. (Gov. Code § 65589.5(h)(6)(C).)

Things that Constitute Disapproval of a Housing Development Project

A jurisdiction violates the Housing Accountability Act if it disapproves a housing development project without making the required findings specified in subdivision (d) or (j) as appropriate. But there are many other things that constitute a disapproval of the project, and are grounds for bringing an action to enforce the Housing Accountability Act. Gov. Code § 65589.5(h)(6) gives the definition of "disapprove the housing development project" as a list of prohibited conduct:

> (6) "Disapprove the housing development project" includes any instance in which a local agency does any of the following:
>
> > (A) Votes or takes final administrative action on a proposed housing development project application and the application is disapproved, including any required land use approvals or entitlements necessary for the issuance of a building permit.

(B) Fails to comply with the time periods specified in subdivision (a) of Section 65950. An extension of time pursuant to Article 5 (commencing with Section 65950) shall be deemed to be an extension of time pursuant to this paragraph.

(C) Fails to meet the time limits specified in Section 65913.3.

(D) Fails to meet the time limit specified in Section 17970.3 of the Health and Safety Code.

(E) Fails to cease a course of conduct undertaken for an improper purpose, such as to harass or to cause unnecessary delay or needless increases in the cost of the proposed housing development project, that effectively disapproves the proposed housing development without taking final administrative action if all of the following conditions are met:

(i) The project applicant provides written notice detailing the challenged conduct and why it constitutes disapproval to the local agency established under Section 65100.

(ii) Within five working days of receiving the applicant's written notice described in clause (i), the local agency shall post the notice on the local agency's internet website, provide a copy of the notice to any person who has made a written request for notices pursuant to subdivision (f) of Section 21167 of the Public Resources Code, and file the notice with the county clerk of each county in which the project will be located. The county clerk shall post the notice and make it available for public inspection in the manner set forth in subdivision (c) of Section 21152 of the Public Resources Code.

(iii) The local agency shall consider all objections, comments, evidence, and concerns about the project or the applicant's written notice and shall not make a determination until at least 60 days after the applicant has given written notice to the local agency pursuant to clause (i).

(iv) Within 90 days of receipt of the applicant's written notice described in clause (i), the local agency shall issue a written statement that it will immediately cease the challenged conduct or issue written findings that comply with both of the following requirements:

(I) The findings articulate an objective basis for why the challenged course of conduct is necessary.

(II) The findings provide clear instructions on what the applicant must submit or supplement so that the local agency can make a final determination regarding the next necessary approval or set the date and time of the next hearing.

(v) (I) If a local agency continues the challenged course of conduct described in the applicant's written notice and fails to issue the written findings described in clause (iv), the local agency shall bear the burden of establishing that its course of conduct does not constitute a disapproval of the housing development project under this subparagraph in an action taken by the applicant.

(II) If an applicant challenges a local agency's course of conduct as a disapproval under this subparagraph, the local agency's written findings described in clause (iv) shall be incorporated into the administrative record and be deemed to be the final administrative action for purposes of adjudicating whether the local agency's course of conduct constitutes a disapproval of the housing development project under this subparagraph.

(vi) A local agency's action in furtherance of complying with the California Environmental Quality Act (Division 13 (commencing with Section 21000) of the Public Resources Code), including, but not limited to, imposing mitigating measures, shall not constitute project disapproval under this subparagraph.

(F) Fails to comply with Section 65905.5. For purposes of this subparagraph, a builder's remedy project shall be deemed to comply with the applicable, objective general plan and zoning standards in effect at the time an application is deemed complete.

(G) (i) Determines that an application for a housing development project is incomplete pursuant to subdivision (a) or (b) of Section 65943 and includes in the determination an item that is not required on the local agency's submittal requirement checklist. The local agency shall bear the burden of proof that the required item is listed on the submittal requirement checklist.

(ii) In a subsequent review of an application pursuant to Section 65943, requests the applicant provide new information that was not identified in the initial determination and upholds this determination in the final written determination on an appeal filed pursuant to subdivision (c) of Section 65943. The local agency shall bear the burden of proof that the required item was identified in the initial determination.

(iii) Determines that an application for a housing development project is incomplete pursuant to subdivision (a) or (b) of Section 65943, a reasonable person would conclude that the applicant has submitted all of the items required on the local agency's submittal requirement checklist, and the local agency upholds this determination in the final written determination on an appeal filed pursuant to subdivision (c) of Section 65943.

(iv) If a local agency determines that an application is incomplete under Section 65943 after two resubmittals of the application by the applicant, the local agency shall bear the burden of establishing that the determination is not an effective disapproval of a housing development project under this section.

(H) Violates subparagraph (D) or (E) of paragraph (6) of subdivision (f).

(I) Makes a written determination that a preliminary application described in subdivision (a) of Section 65941.1 has expired or that the applicant has otherwise lost its vested rights under the preliminary application for any reason other than those described in subdivisions(d) and (e) of Section 65941.1.

(J) (i) Fails to make a determination of whether the project is exempt from the California Environmental Quality Act (Division 13 (commencing with Section 21000) of the Public Resources Code), or commits an abuse of discretion, as defined in subdivision (b) of Section 65589.5.1 if all of the conditions in Section 65589.5.1 are satisfied.

(ii) This subparagraph shall become inoperative on January 1, 2031.

(K) (i) Fails to adopt a negative declaration or addendum for the project, to certify an environmental impact report for the project, or to approve another comparable environmental document, such as a sustainable communities environmental assessment pursuant to Section 21155.2 of the Public Resources Code, as required pursuant to the California Environmental Quality Act (Division 13 (commencing with Section 21000) of the Public Resources Code), if all of the conditions in Section 65589.5.2 are satisfied.

(ii) This subparagraph shall become inoperative on January 1, 2031.

Thus, "disapprove the housing development project" means not only the act of a decisionmaker or decisionmaking body to disapprove rather than approve the project, but a long list of improper conduct by the jurisdiction prior to action by a decisionmaker.

Enforcing the Housing Accountability Act

If a jurisdiction acts to "disapprove the housing development project" as that term is defined (see Things that Constitute Disapproval of a Housing Development Project), including imposing conditions on the approval of a housing project in violation of the Housing Accountability Act, the remedy is to file an action in court, as provided in Gov. Code § 65589.5(k) through (p).

Who Can Bring an Action to Enforce the Housing Accountability Act?

The applicant is not the only person that can bring an action to enforce the Housing Accountability Act. Gov. Code § 65589.5(k)(1)(A)(i) gives ***many*** people and organizations standing to sue:

> (k) (1) (A) (i) The applicant, a person who would be eligible to apply for residency in the housing development project or emergency shelter, or a housing organization may bring an action to enforce this section. ...

A housing organization may bring an action if the project is **outright disapproved**, but not if the project is approved, but with HAA-violating conditions of approval. (Gov. Code § 65589.5(k)(2).) All others may file a petition if the project is disapproved ***or*** approved with **conditions** that violate the Housing Accountability Act.

If a Jurisdiction Violates the Housing Accountability Act, a Court *Shall Issue* an Order ...

When an action is brought to enforce the Housing Accountability Act, and the court finds that the Act was violated, the Act provides very clear direction to the court. First, the court "shall issue an order or judgment compelling compliance." Gov. Code § 65589.5(k)(1)(A) continues:

> (k) (1) (A) (i) ... If, in any action brought to enforce this section, a court finds that any of the following are met, the court shall issue an order pursuant to clause (ii):
>
> (I) The local agency, in violation of subdivision (d), disapproved a housing development project or conditioned its approval in a manner rendering it infeasible for the development of an emergency shelter, or housing for very low, low-, or moderate-income households, including farmworker housing, without making the findings required by this section.
>
> (II) The local agency, in violation of subdivision (j), disapproved a housing development project complying with applicable, objective general plan and zoning standards and criteria, or imposed a condition that the project be developed at a lower density, without making the findings required by this section.
>
> (III) The local agency, in violation of subdivision (o), required or attempted to require a housing development project to comply with an ordinance, policy, or standard not adopted and in effect when a preliminary application was submitted.
>
> (IV) The local agency violated a provision of this section applicable to a builder's remedy project.
>
> (ii) If the court finds that one of the conditions in clause (i) is met, the court shall issue an order or judgment compelling compliance with this section within a time period not to exceed 60 days, including, but not limited to, an order that the local agency take action on the housing development project or emergency shelter. ...

In other words, if the court finds that the Housing Accountability Act was violated, the court shall issue an order or judgement compelling compliance with the Act and order the jurisdiction to take action (i.e., hold a new hearing, or administratively approve or modify the approval) in accordance with the court's order. The jurisdiction, in this case, could again disapprove the project or impose conditions, so long as the disapproval or condition of approval does not violate the Housing Accountability Act or the court's order.

However, the court may go beyond this minimum order or judgement.

If the Jurisdiction Acted in Bad Faith, the Court *May* Direct *Approval* of the Project

The Housing Accountability Act directs the court to take additional actions if the jurisdiction acted in bad faith, which is defined at Gov. Code § 65589.5(l):

> (l) ... For purposes of this section, "bad faith" includes, but is not limited to, an action or inaction that is frivolous, pretextual, intended to cause unnecessary delay, or entirely without merit.

Gov. Code § 65589.5(k)(1)(A)(ii) continues:

> (ii) ... The court may issue an order or judgment directing the local agency to approve the housing development project or emergency shelter if the court finds that the local agency acted in bad faith when

> it disapproved or conditionally approved the housing development or emergency shelter in violation of this section. ...

In other words, if the court finds that the jurisdiction acted in bad faith, the court *may* order the jurisdiction to ***approve*** the project (instead of just ordering the jurisdiction to take action that is compliant with the HAA).

Example 1: *District Square, LLC v. City of Los Angeles*

In *District Square, LLC v. City of Los Angeles*, Case No. 20STCP00654 (Los Angeles Superior Court, filed 2020) the court found that "The City's Bad Faith Actions Compel a Decision That the City Must Approve the Project" because (page 20):[138]

> The APC [South Los Angeles Area Planning Commission] clearly acted in bad faith and acted on its own frolic and detour, egged on by a political liaison and the testifying residents to impose its own view of appropriate public policy — i.e., to take a stand against gentrification. It matters not that the APC believed it was acting in the community's best interest. The APC does not set policy and it does not create law; its obligation is to apply existing law to evaluation of a project. The Legislature concluded in the HAA that local governments are impeding housing development by imposing subjective policies that limit the approval of housing, increase the cost of land for housing, and require that high fees and exactions be paid by producers of housing. §65589.5(a)(1)(B). That is exactly what the APC did by imposing its own views that gentrification is bad, displacement (even indirect displacement) must be accounted for, and the need for affordable housing trumps all. That is not the law, and there can be no legitimate dispute that the APC acted knowingly and deliberately to violate the law.
>
> Compounding this deliberate violation, District Square notes that -- after it filed suit in February 2020 and knowing that the APC had violated the law -- the City attempted to mask the APC's intentional violation by issuing the LOD six months after-the-fact, which made false representations intended to bolster the APC's decision. [reference omitted] The City's mandamus opposition is based entirely on the false LOD findings, in particular seizing upon the LOD's "phony CEQA finding" to make a specious argument that CEQA somehow compels the denial of the Project. [reference omitted] The City's bad faith justifies an "order or judgment directing the local agency to approve the housing development project" and District Square's entitlement to an award of reasonable attorney's fees and costs of suit. §65589.5(k)(1)(A)(ii). [reference omitted]

This case demonstrates that sometimes decisionmakers will utterly disregard the advice and findings of their own staff and attorneys. However, the Housing Accountability Act is enforceable, and applicants have effective redress to the courts.

Example 2: *Cesar Chavez 888, LLC v. City of Los Angeles et. al.*

Apparently, the City of Los Angeles did not learn its lesson from the judgement in *District Square, LLC v. City of Los Angeles*, because it lost a similar case in 2025: *Cesar Chavez 888, LLC v. City of Los Angeles et. al.*, Case No. 24STCP01880 (Los Angeles Superior Court, filed 2024). Per the Ruling on Petition for Writ of Mandate:[139]

> **The Court finds that the City acted in bad faith** when it denied approval of the Project. ...
>
> Significantly, the Commissioners who denied the Project acknowledged it was not possible to come up with a health and safety impact from the Project that would warrant denial under the HAA. (AR 2720 [Commissioner Avila-Hernandez: "I don't think I could develop a written, factual public health and safety impact response"], 2768 [Commissioner Gutierrez: "[F]rom my understanding, the findings that I shared earlier were not sufficient enough for it be like taken into account for the motion; is that correct in my understanding? ... Commissioner Avila-Hernandez: "That's also my understanding that the findings that we've tried to link to it are not sufficient. Based on the standard from the statewide law"].

---

[138] https://planning.lacity.gov/odocument/669b0bdd-a267-4756-9d4d-56234c1a149c/DIR-2018-3204_(2).pdf.

[139] Case number 24STCP01880, downloadable for a fee from https://www.lacourt.ca.gov/pages/lp/access-a-case/tp/find-case-information/cp/os-civil-case-access.

> Even though the Commissioners who formed the majority in granting the Appeal and denying the Project were aware of the HAA's requirements, they voted against the Project anyway. While their concerns about potential displacement and gentrification may have been well-intentioned, the State has made abundantly clear that the production of new housing must be prioritized.[footnote omitted] Accordingly, the Court finds that respondents acted in bad faith when they disapproved the Project, as the disapproval was entirely without merit. **Because the APC acted in bad faith, the Court will issue a judgment directing respondents to approve the Project.**

The court gave the City of Los Angeles 60 days to comply with its order, and the City reported back to the court after complying with the order and approving the project. The East Los Angeles Area Planning Commission reversed its illegal disapproval of the subject project at a hearing on May 28, 2025.[140] The court awarded the plaintiff/applicant attorney's fees in the amount of $170,260.50.[141]

The Court *Shall Retain Jurisdiction* to Ensure that its Order or Judgment is Carried Out

Regardless of whether a jurisdiction acted in bad faith or not, after rendering judgement, the court retains jurisdiction over the case to ensure its order is complied with. Gov. Code § 65589.5(k)(1)(A)(ii) continues:

> (ii) … The court shall retain jurisdiction to ensure that its order or judgment is carried out …

If the jurisdiction does not comply with the court's order or judgement, the provisions of Gov. Code § 65589.5(k)(1)(B) and (C) would apply.

The Court *Shall Award Attorney's Fees* to the Plaintiff, Unless…

Even if the jurisdiction did not act in bad faith, if the court finds that the jurisdiction violated the Housing Accountability Act (i.e., "one of the conditions in clause (i) is met," see If a Jurisdiction Violates the Housing Accountability Act, a Court Shall Issue an Order …) the court **shall award attorney's fees** to the plaintiff, except under extraordinary circumstances, or when the disapproval was CEQA-related and in good faith. Gov. Code § 65589.5(k)(1)(A)(ii) continues:

> (ii) … and shall award reasonable attorney's fees and costs of suit to the plaintiff or petitioner, provided, however, that the court shall not award attorney's fees in either of the following instances:
>
> > (I) The court finds, under extraordinary circumstances, that awarding fees would not further the purposes of this section.
> >
> > (II) (ia) In a case concerning a disapproval within the meaning of subparagraph (J) or (K) of paragraph (6) of subdivision (h), the court finds that the local agency acted in good faith and had reasonable cause to disapprove the housing development project due to the existence of a controlling question of law about the application of the California Environmental Quality Act (Division 13 (commencing with Section 21000) of the Public Resources Code) or implementing guidelines as to which there was a substantial ground for difference of opinion at the time of the disapproval.
> >
> > > (ib) This subclause shall become inoperative on January 1, 2031.

The award of attorney's fees happens after the jurisdiction **complies** with the court's order(s), so it includes the costs through the full resolution of the case.

[140] Ibid, Return to Writ of Mandate.
[141] Ibid, Minute Order.

The Court *May Issue Further/Other Orders*

Whether or not the jurisdiction acted in bad faith, the jurisdiction must comply with the court's order within 60 days, or the court may issue further orders to compel compliance, and **may order the jurisdiction to approve the project**, per Gov. Code § 65589.5(k)(1)(C):

> (C) If the court determines that its order or judgment has not been carried out within 60 days, the court may issue further orders as provided by law to ensure that the purposes and policies of this section are fulfilled, **including, but not limited to, an order to vacate the decision of the local agency and to approve the housing development project**, in which case the application for the housing development project, as proposed by the applicant at the time the local agency took the initial action determined to be in violation of this section, along with any standard conditions determined by the court to be generally imposed by the local agency on similar projects, shall be deemed to be approved unless the applicant consents to a different decision or action by the local agency.

But regardless of whether the jurisdiction acted in bad faith, at any time, the court has the power to go beyond the minimum orders **required** by the Housing Accountability Act and impose other orders, including "to compel immediate enforcement of any writ ..." per Gov. Code § 65589.5(k)(1)(D):

> (D) Nothing in this section shall limit the court's inherent authority to make any other orders to compel the immediate enforcement of any writ brought under this section, including the imposition of fees and other sanctions set forth under Section 1097 of the Code of Civil Procedure.

When someone brings "an action to enforce" the Housing Accountability Act pursuant to Gov. Code § 65589.5(k)(1), the "action" is a "petition for writ of mandate" (see The Action is a Writ of Mandate and the Jurisdiction Shall File the Record of Proceedings) and in addition to the **requirements** of the Housing Accountability Act the court has all of the options that apply to a writ of mandate as prescribed by Chapter 2 of Title 1 of Part 3 of the Code of Civil Procedure.

The Court *Shall Impose Fines* if the Jurisdiction Does not Comply with the Order or Judgment

If the jurisdiction does not comply with the court's order, the court must impose fines. Unless the jurisdiction is found to have acted in bad faith, the fine is a minimum of $10,000 per unit, per Gov. Code § 65589.5(k)(1)(B):

> (B) **Upon a determination that the local agency has failed to comply with the order or judgment compelling compliance** with this section within the time period prescribed by the court, **the court shall impose fines** on a local agency that has violated this section and require the local agency to deposit any fine levied pursuant to this subdivision into a local housing trust fund. The local agency may elect to instead deposit the fine into the Building Homes and Jobs Trust Fund. The fine shall be in a minimum amount of ten thousand dollars ($10,000) per housing unit in the housing development project on the date the application was deemed complete pursuant to Section 65943. In determining the amount of the fine to impose, the court shall consider the local agency's progress in attaining its target allocation of the regional housing need pursuant to Section 65584 and any prior violations of this section. Fines shall not be paid out of funds already dedicated to affordable housing, including, but not limited to, Low and Moderate Income Housing Asset Funds, funds dedicated to housing for very low, low-, and moderate-income households, and federal HOME Investment Partnerships Program and Community Development Block Grant Program funds. The local agency shall commit and expend the money in the local housing trust fund within five years for the sole purpose of financing newly constructed housing units affordable to extremely low, very low, or low-income households. After five years, if the funds have not been expended, the money shall revert to the state and be deposited in the Building Homes and Jobs Trust Fund for the sole purpose of financing newly constructed housing units affordable to extremely low, very low, or low-income households.

If the jurisdiction failed to comply with the court's order, ***and*** acted in **bad faith**, the fine is at least **5 times higher**, per Gov. Code § 65589.5(l):

> (l) If the court finds that the local agency (1) acted in bad faith when it violated this section and (2) failed to carry out the court's order or judgment within the time period prescribed by the court, the court, in addition to any other remedies provided by this section, shall multiply the fine determined pursuant to subparagraph (B) of paragraph (1) of subdivision (k) by a factor of five. If a court has previously found that the local agency violated this section within the same planning period, the court shall multiply the fines by an additional factor for each previous violation. For purposes of this section, "bad faith" includes, but is not limited to, an action or inaction that is frivolous, pretextual, intended to cause unnecessary delay, or entirely without merit.

Between fines and attorney's fees, jurisdictions that defy the Housing Accountability Act risk potentially millions of dollars of taxpayer money.

The Action is a Writ of Mandate and the Jurisdiction Shall File the Record of Proceedings

Subdivisions (m) and (n) provide (by cross-referencing CCP § 1094.5) that the "action to enforce" the Housing Accountability Act shall be a writ of mandate and those subdivisions prescribe certain details for the processing of the writ. These matters can best be explained by an attorney with experience in enforcing housing laws, and the Author provides the text of Gov. Code § 65589.5(m) and (n) without comment:

> (m) (1) Any action brought to enforce the provisions of this section shall be brought pursuant to Section 1094.5 of the Code of Civil Procedure, and the local agency shall prepare and certify the record of proceedings in accordance with subdivision (c) of Section 1094.6 of the Code of Civil Procedure no later than 30 days after the petition is served, provided that the cost of preparation of the record shall be borne by the local agency, unless the petitioner elects to prepare the record as provided in subdivision (n) of this section. A petition to enforce the provisions of this section shall be filed and served no later than 90 days from the later of (1) the effective date of a decision of the local agency imposing conditions on, disapproving, or any other final action on a housing development project or (2) the expiration of the time periods specified in subparagraph (B) of paragraph (5) of subdivision (h). Upon entry of the trial court's order, a party may, in order to obtain appellate review of the order, file a petition within 20 days after service upon it of a written notice of the entry of the order, or within such further time not exceeding an additional 20 days as the trial court may for good cause allow, or may appeal the judgment or order of the trial court under Section 904.1 of the Code of Civil Procedure. If the local agency appeals the judgment of the trial court, the local agency shall post a bond, in an amount to be determined by the court, to the benefit of the plaintiff if the plaintiff is the project applicant.
>
>> (2) (A) A disapproval within the meaning of subparagraph (J) of paragraph (6) of subdivision (h) shall be final for purposes of this subdivision, if the local agency did not make a lawful determination within the time period set forth in paragraph (5) of subdivision (a) of Section 65589.5.1 after the applicant's timely written notice.
>>
>>> (B) This paragraph shall become inoperative on January 1, 2031.
>>
>> (3) (A) A disapproval within the meaning of subparagraph (K) of paragraph (6) of subdivision (h) shall be final for purposes of this subdivision, if the local agency did not make a lawful determination within 90 days of the applicant's timely written notice.
>>
>>> (B) This paragraph shall become inoperative on January 1, 2031.
>
> (n) In any action, the record of the proceedings before the local agency shall be filed as expeditiously as possible and, notwithstanding Section 1094.6 of the Code of Civil Procedure or subdivision (m) of this section, all or part of the record may be prepared (1) by the petitioner with the petition or petitioner's points and authorities, (2) by the respondent with respondent's points and authorities, (3) after payment of costs by the petitioner, or (4) as otherwise directed by the court. If the expense of preparing the record has been borne by the petitioner and the petitioner is the prevailing party, the expense shall be taxable as costs.

Cases Challenging a Housing *Approval* — Award of Attorney's Fees

When a plaintiff challenges the ***approval*** of a housing development project, there are two provisions of state law related to the award of attorney's fees that jurisdictions should be aware of.

Jurisdictions that *Approve* a Project in Good Faith "Rarely if Ever" Pay the Plaintiff's Attorney's Fees

Subdivision (p) of the Housing Accountability Act is a provision that protects jurisdictions that approve projects in good faith. If a plaintiff challenges a jurisdiction's ***approval*** of a housing development project, courts should "rarely if ever" award attorney's fees to the plaintiff "if a local agency, acting in good faith, approved a housing development project ..." per Gov. Code § 65589.5(p):

> (p) (1) Upon any motion for an award of attorney's fees pursuant to Section 1021.5 of the Code of Civil Procedure, in a case challenging a local agency's approval of a housing development project, a court, in weighing whether a significant benefit has been conferred on the general public or a large class of persons and whether the necessity of private enforcement makes the award appropriate, shall give due weight to the degree to which the local agency's approval furthers policies of this section, including, but not limited to, subdivisions (a), (b), and (c), the suitability of the site for a housing development, and the reasonableness of the decision of the local agency. **It is the intent of the Legislature that attorney's fees and costs shall rarely, if ever, be awarded if a local agency, acting in good faith, approved a housing development project** that satisfies conditions established in paragraph (1), (2), or (3) of subdivision (a) of Section 65589.5.1 or paragraph (1), (2), or (3) of subdivision (a) of Section 65589.5.2.
>
> (2) This subdivision shall become inoperative on January 1, 2031.

Again, subdivision (p) regards cases that challenge ***approval*** of a project. In cases challenging a ***disapproval*** of a housing development project in violation of the Housing Accountability Act, The Court Shall Award Attorney's Fees to the Plaintiff, Unless... there were "extraordinary circumstances," or the disapproval was due to a good-faith application of CEQA.

When Jurisdictions Prevail in Defending an Approval the Court May Award Them Attorney's Fees

When a civil action is brought against a jurisdiction that approved a housing development project, and the jurisdiction is the prevailing party, the court may require the plaintiff to pay the jurisdiction's reasonable cost of defending the approval, per Gov. Code § 65914:

> 65914. (a) In any civil action or proceeding, including, but not limited to, an action brought pursuant to Section 21167 of the Public Resources Code, against a public entity that has issued planning, subdivision, or other approvals for a housing development, to enjoin the carrying out or approval of a housing development or to secure a writ of mandate relative to the approval of, or a decision to carry out the housing development, the court, after entry of final judgment and the time to appeal has elapsed, and after notice to the plaintiff or plaintiffs, **may award all reasonably incurred costs of suit, including attorney's fees, to the prevailing public entity or nonprofit housing corporation** that is the real party in interest and the permit applicant of the low- and moderate-income housing if it finds all of the following:
>
> (1) The housing development meets or exceeds the requirements for low- and moderate-income housing as set forth in Section 65915.
>
> (2) The action was frivolous and undertaken with the primary purpose of delaying or thwarting the low- or moderate-income nature of the housing development or portions thereof.
>
> (3) The public entity or nonprofit housing corporation that is the real party in interest and the permit applicant of the low- and moderate-income housing making application for costs under this section has prevailed on all issues presented by the pleadings and the public entity or nonprofit housing corporation that is the real party in interest and the permit applicant of the low- and moderate-income housing actively, through counsel or otherwise, took part on a continuing basis in the defense of the lawsuit.

(4) A demand for a preliminary injunction was made by the plaintiff and denied by a court of competent jurisdiction, or the action or proceeding was dismissed as a result of a motion for summary judgment by any defendant, and the denial or dismissal was not reversed on appeal.

(b) In any appeal of any action described in subdivision (a), the reviewing court may award all reasonably incurred costs of suit, including attorney's fees, to the prevailing public entity or nonprofit housing corporation that is the real party in interest and the permit applicant of the low- and moderate-income housing if the court reviews and upholds the trial court's findings with respect to paragraphs (1) to (4), inclusive, of subdivision (a).

(c) Nothing in this section shall be construed to limit the application of any other remedies or rights provided under law.

Jurisdictions should take threats of lawsuits from disgruntled neighbors with a grain of salt. State laws are strongly weighted in favor of approval of housing. Plaintiffs challenging housing projects are unlikely to prevail. If the jurisdiction that approved the project prevails, the plaintiff will likely pay the jurisdiction's costs of defending the housing approval. If the plaintiff prevails, the jurisdiction is unlikely to pay the plaintiff's cost of suit.

Enforcing Other Housing Reform Laws — New with AB 712

Many different housing bills have been passed over the last decade, but enforcement of the laws has been lacking. The Housing Accountability Act has had a clear and effective enforcement mechanism, with rules of evidence and presumptions that strongly favor approval of housing, and with the requirement that courts award to plaintiffs the reasonable cost of suit to enforce the HAA. In addition, heavy fines are imposed if the jurisdiction defies the court's order or judgement. But that enforcement mechanism applied only to the Housing Accountability Act.

AB 712 (2025) added Gov. Code § 65914.2, which allows applicants to enforce ***any*** "housing reform law" with the same right to collect attorney fees, and imposing essentially the same fines, as apply to actions in court to enforce the Housing Accountability Act. In addition, Gov. Code § 65914.2 prevents jurisdictions from requiring that applicants indemnify them against legal actions to enforce housing laws. Taking the new law in steps:

65914.2. (a) It is the intent of the Legislature in enacting this section to do both of the following:

(1) Establish minimum uniform, transparent, fair, and effective remedies against public agencies that are found by a court of law to have violated housing reform laws.

(2) Prevent public agencies from undermining these minimum uniform, transparent, fair, and effective remedies through the imposition of reimbursement and indemnification agreements on applicants for housing development approvals with respect to legal challenges involving the agency's own alleged violation of housing reform laws.

Subdivision (a) provides the statement of legislative intent. It makes clear that the purpose of the law is to provide for the effective enforcement of all "housing reform laws," which Gov. Code § 65914.2(d)(2) defines very broadly:

(2) "Housing reform law" means any law or regulation, or provision of any law or regulation, that establishes or facilitates rights, safeguards, streamlining benefits, time limitations, or other protections for the benefit of applicants for housing development projects, or restricts, proscribes, prohibits, or otherwise imposes any procedural or substantive limitation on a public agency for the benefit of a housing development project.

Thus, the remedies in Gov. Code § 65914.2 are universal to all housing reform laws and regulations.

Note that, unlike the Housing Accountability Act that gives standing to "the applicant, a person who would be eligible to apply for residency in the housing development project or emergency shelter, or a housing organization" (see Who Can Bring an Action to Enforce the Housing Accountability Act?), **only the applicant** has standing to bring an action under this new law. (Gov. Code § 65914.2(b) "in any action brought by the applicant .. where the applicant is the prevailing party…".)

Note that by this definition, the Housing Accountability Act is a housing reform law, and the provisions of Gov. Code § 65914.2 should also apply to violations of the HAA, when an action is brought by an applicant.

Subdivision (b) prescribes the remedies that shall be imposed on jurisdictions when the applicant is the prevailing party.

> (b) Notwithstanding any other law, and in addition to any other available remedies, in any action brought by the applicant for a housing development project against a public agency to enforce the public agency's compliance with a housing reform law as applied to the applicant's housing development project, **where the applicant is the prevailing party, the following shall apply:**
>
> (1) The applicant shall be entitled to **reasonable attorney's fees and costs**.
>
> (2) (A) In the case of an action against a public agency that is a local agency:
>
> (i) (I) **If the local agency was advised in writing prior to the commencement of the action** by either the Attorney General or the Department of Housing and Community Development that the local agency's decision, action, or inaction **would represent a violation of a specific housing reform law in substantially the same manner as alleged by the applicant** in its lawsuit, **the court *shall***, consistent with subclause (II), **impose a fine** in an amount not less than the minimum fines described in subparagraph (B) of paragraph (1) of subdivision (k) of Section 65589.5, unless the housing development projects consists of four or fewer units, in which case, the court shall impose a fine in an amount not less than fifty thousand dollars ($50,000) per violation.
>
> (II) The court shall not impose the fine described in subclause (I) unless, after the Attorney General or Department of Housing and Community Development sends the written communication to the local agency, **the applicant provides written notice to the local agency of its intent to commence an action**. The notice shall identify the factual elements of the dispute and the legal theory forming the basis for the allegation that the local agency's decision, action, or inaction violated the housing reform law. The notice shall be provided to the local agency **at least 60 days before commencement of the action**.
>
> (III) For any action commenced or intended to be commenced under this section, any period of limitation for actions under any California law shall be extended for a period of 60 days beginning on the date the applicant provides written notice, pursuant to subclause (II), to the local agency indicating its intent to commence an action.
>
> (ii) (I) **If a court has previously found that the local agency violated the same housing reform law** on which an applicant prevailed in its lawsuit, **within the same planning period**, the court shall impose a fine in an amount not less than the minimum fines described in clause (i) **multiplied by a factor of five**.
>
> (II) For the purpose of imposing a fine under subclause (I), any subsequent violation of the same housing reform law shall be considered to have occurred within the same planning period if the local agency does not have a housing element considered to be in substantial compliance, as described in Section 65585.03.
>
> (B) Notwithstanding Chapter 2 (commencing with Section 910) of Part 3 of Division 3.6 of Title 1, the applicant shall not be required to present a claim to seek the fine described in subparagraph (A).
>
> (C) Nothing in this subdivision limits the application of Section 1021.5 of the Code of Civil Procedure or limits the availability of fees to a successful party under that section.

Although it mirrors the enforcement provisions of subdivision (k) of the Housing Accountability Act, the provision regarding the imposition of fines under Gov. Code § 65914.2(b)(2) is different from that under Gov. Code § 65589.5(k)(1)(B). In the Housing Accountability Act, fines are imposed when the jurisdiction "has failed to comply with the order or judgement." In this new law, fines are imposed when the jurisdiction has been advised in writing by the Attorney General or HCD "that the local agency's decision, action, or inaction would represent a violation of a specific housing reform law in substantially the same manner as alleged by the applicant in its lawsuit."

The sequence of events leading to the imposition of the fine under Gov. Code § 65914.2(b)(2)(A) is:

1. The Attorney General or HCD advises the jurisdiction in writing, before or after the alleged violation of the housing reform law occurs, that "that the local agency's decision, action, or inaction would represent a violation of a specific housing reform law in substantially the same manner as alleged by the applicant."
2. The applicant provides the jurisdiction with 60 days written notice of the applicant's intent to commence legal action. The notice must provide the facts and legal theory of the allegation.
3. The legal action is commenced, and the court finds that the jurisdiction violated the housing reform law.
4. The court shall impose a fine not less than the amount specified in Gov. Code § 65589.5(k)(1)(B) (i.e., a minimum of $10,000 per unit), with a minimum of $50,000 for projects with four or fewer units.
5. If a court has previously found that the jurisdiction violated the same housing reform law, within the same RHNA cycle, the fine shall be **five times** the amount otherwise applicable.

Again, the definition of "housing reform law" is broad and includes the Housing Accountability Act. Thus, when the **applicant** is the prevailing party in an action brought pursuant to the Housing Accountability Act, the fines described above shall be imposed on the jurisdiction if the conditions described above are met, **even if the jurisdiction complies with the court's order and judgement**. (See The Court Shall Impose Fines if the Jurisdiction Does not Comply with the Order or Judgment, and compare Gov. Code § 65589.5(k)(1)(B) to Gov. Code § 65914.2(b)(2)(A).)

To avoid the potential loss in court and the imposition of fines and reimbursement of attorney's fees, the jurisdiction would need to resolve its violation of the housing reform law within the 60 day notice period.

Subdivision (c) prevents jurisdictions from requiring applicants to indemnify them against court actions to enforce housing reform laws:

> (c) (1) A public agency shall not require an applicant for a housing development project to indemnify, defend, or hold harmless the public agency in any manner with respect to an action brought by the applicant, or any other person, alleging that the public agency violated the applicant's rights or deprived the applicant of the benefits or protections provided by a housing reform law.
>
> > (2) A requirement, condition of approval, or agreement in violation of paragraph (1) is against public policy and void and unenforceable.
> >
> > (3) This subdivision shall not be construed to derogate any claim that a requirement as described in paragraph (1) is or was unlawful under previously existing law.

Subdivision (d) provides definitions. Other than the definition of "housing reform law" discussed above, the other definitions are existing standard definitions made by reference to other sections of the Government Code.

> (d) For purposes of this section:
>
> > (1) "Housing development project" has the same meaning as provided in paragraph (3) of subdivision (b) of Section 65905.5.
> >
> > (2) "Housing reform law" means any law or regulation, or provision of any law or regulation, that establishes or facilitates rights, safeguards, streamlining benefits, time limitations, or other protections for the benefit of applicants for housing development projects, or restricts, proscribes, prohibits, or otherwise imposes any procedural or substantive limitation on a public agency for the benefit of a housing development project.

(3) "Local agency" has the same meaning as used in Section 65930.

(4) "Planning period" means the time period between the due date for one housing element and the due date for the next housing element for each revision according to the applicable schedule described in paragraphs (2) and (3) of subdivision (e) of Section 65588.

(5) "Public agency" has the same meaning as in Section 65932.

As always, this book uses the term "jurisdiction" to mean city or county, which are included in the above definition of "local agency" and "public agency." This new law, as with most others, applies more broadly than just to cities and counties, but this book is focused on the process of obtaining housing development permits from cities and counties. (See The Term "Jurisdiction" and Other Public Entities and Agencies.)

Setting Your Attorney Up to Win

Enforcement of state housing laws starts when the SB 330 preliminary application is submitted and continues through every submittal and interaction with the jurisdiction. Understanding state housing laws will help the applicant ensure that the project "shall be approved" as proposed. Many housing projects face strong opposition from various interest groups, neighbors, staff, appointed decisionmakers, and/or elected officials. State housing law is firmly on the side of the project, but unfortunately some politicians have chosen to defy state law and improperly disapprove or condition projects. As they work through the process and face opposition, applicants should be thinking, "how can we avoid disapproval of the project, how can we avoid a lawsuit challenging approval of the project or its CEQA determination, and if it comes to a lawsuit, will our attorney win?"

Go Get 'Em

The Author hopes this book gives applicants more knowledge and more confidence when pursuing housing development permits in California. The Author cannot anticipate what challenges your project may face, and this book is not a substitute for the advice of your attorney, but it does provide a framework and foundation for discussing ***your*** project with ***your*** attorney.

And for other practitioners (the staff of jurisdictions, attorneys, legislators, housing advocates, and even those who might be on the side of the opposition) the Author hopes this book was informative and provided an insight into the way an applicant/development manager strives to put complex state housing laws into practice. You won't like every project, but remember only **projects that *pencil* produce housing.**

www.ingramcontent.com/pod-product-compliance
Lightning Source LLC
LaVergne TN
LVHW070909210926
848482LV00017B/1027
* 9 7 9 8 9 9 4 8 9 4 4 0 8 *